TRANSPACIFIC FEMININITIES

TRANSPACIFIC FEMININITIES

THE MAKING OF THE MODERN FILIPINA

Denise Cruz

Duke University Press Durham & London 2012

Designed by Amy Ruth Buchanan
Typeset in Quadraat by Keystone Typesetting, Inc.
Library of Congress Cataloging-in-Publication
Data appear on the last printed page of
this book.

An earlier version of chapter 5 appeared in
American Quarterly, Volume 63, Issue 1, March
2011, pages 1–32. Copyright © 2011 The American
Studies Association.

For JEB and NWB

CONTENTS

ACKNOWLEDGMENTS

I have often thought of this book as being grounded in and inspired by women who, in their lives, imaginations, and representations, were variable, boundless, and transformative. And similarly, as I reflect now upon both process and product, I am reminded of those whose varied and extensive efforts have transformed this project.

Ken Wissoker has been an ideal editor and collaborator. Through multiple years and in many locations he had the foresight to see my book not for what it was but always for what it could be, and I am truly grateful for his guidance, dedication, and friendship. I also thank Leigh Barnwell; Christine Dahlin; the board and staff of Duke University Press; the copyeditor Lawrence Kenney, who provided meticulous suggestions on my prose; and Marilyn Bliss for a thoughtful index.

Martin Manalansan and Allan Punzalan Isaac offered pivotal advice that had dramatic effects on the shape of this book, from the overall contours of its argument to its minute details. Without question, their generosity and insight have been critical. An initial group of readers helped me envision this project even in its earliest stages. I thank King-Kok Cheung for her unflagging optimism and enthusiasm, and Richard Yarborough for his wisdom, honesty, and care. Both have taught me much about what it means to be a mentor and teacher. As I navigated through many transitions, their support, along with that of Jinqi Ling and Michael Salman, has been both unequivocal and incredible.

The research for and writing of this book were made possible by generous funding from the Ford Foundation Predoctoral, Dissertation, and Postdoctoral Fellowships, administered by the National Academy of Sciences, and by the camaraderie of an amazing community of Ford scholars, staff, and advisors, especially Chris O'Brien, Pamela Tyler, Randy Higgins, and Joan Rosenthal. At various points in its development, this project was also funded by grants from the Graduate Division at UCLA, the UCLA Institute for American Cultures, the UCLA Global Fellows Program, the Foreign Language Area Studies Awards, and the College Arts and Humanities Institute at Indiana University. The book's final stages were partially supported by an Indiana University New Frontiers grant. A program of the Office of the Vice President for Research, New Frontiers in the Arts and Humanities is funded by the Office of the President and administered by the Office of the Vice Provost for Research. I acknowledge the staff of the American Historical Collection at Ateneo de Manila University, especially Waldette Cueto; the Microform and Media Services at the University of the Philippines at Diliman and Ateneo University; the Ateneo Library of Women's Writings; the National Library in Manila; UCLA Special Collections; the Bentley Library at the University of Michigan, especially Malgosia Myc; and Joel Salud of the *Philippines Graphic* and Enrique Locsin of the *Philippines Free Press*.

In Bloomington and Los Angeles my work has been fostered by many mentors, colleagues, and friends. At Indiana University and in Bloomington I am especially grateful to Judith Brown, Deb Cohn, Ed Comentale, Jonathan Elmer, Jennifer Fleissner, Ross Gay, Shannon Gayk, Donald Gray, Rae Greiner and Zak Symanski, Susan Gubar, Paul Gutjahr, Vivian Halloran, George Hutchinson, Patricia Ingham, Christoph Irmscher, Josh Kates, Sandra Latcha, Joan Pong Linton, Ellen McKay, Laura Patterson, Micol Seigel and Sarah Zanti, Erin Thomas, Steve Watt, and Ellen Wu. Alita Hornick, Lisa LaPlante, and Alex Teschmacher managed many details, and my students Candice Williams, Molly Hamer, Kaitlin Riley, and Tina Bartelome deserve special mention. My early career at the University of California, Los Angeles, was supported by A. R. Braunmuller, Liz DeLoughrey, Helen Deutsch, Jeanette Gilkinson, Yogita Goyal, N. Katherine Hayles, Rachel Lee, Françoise Lionnet, Marissa López, Chris Mott, Felicity Nussbaum, Rafael Perez-Torres, and La Tonya Rease-Miles. Emily Russell, Sam See, and John Alba Cutler offered key suggestions that influenced an initial draft of this book.

At home and abroad, a *barkada* of Filipina and Filipino academics and a community of Asian American and Ethnic Studies scholars have been continuous sources of inspiration. I am especially grateful to Celine Parreñas

Shimizu, Rhacel Salazar Parreñas, Dylan Rodríguez, and Augusto Espiritu, who took an early interest in this project and in my career. I cite many others in my notes, but I also want to recognize Nerissa Balce, Rick Baldoz, Victor Bascara, Francisco Benitez, Jan Christian Bernabe, Jody Blanco, Rick Bonus, Lucy Mae San Pablo Burns, Oscar Campomanes, Ernesto Chavez, Kandice Chuh, Vince Diaz, Linda España-Maram, Kale Bantigue Fajardo, Vernadette Gonzales, Theodore S. Gonzalves, Josephine Lee, Anita Mannur, Victor Mendoza, Koritha Mitchell, Vicente Rafael, Robyn Rodriguez, Jeff Santa Ana, Sarita See, David Delgado Shorter, and Neferti Tadiar. For their assistance during periods of archival research in the Philippines and Tagalog-language study, I thank Joi Barrios, Milagros Laurel, Cristina Pantoja Hidalgo, the UP College of Arts and letters, Soledad Reyes, Donald Goertzen, Barbara Gaerlan, Inno Sotto, Pacita Gavino, Manita Manolo, Nenita Pambid Domingo, Tina and Monchito Mossesgeld, the Narcisos, the Garilaos, Lourdes Luis, and Ida Siason.

Purnima Bose, Kathryn Lofton, Derek Pacheco, Matthew Guterl, Jennifer Lee, Karen Inouye, and Martin Joseph Ponce offered words of encouragement, time, and careful readings on many occasions. Cruzes, Sottos, Blackmans, Shepards, Schiros, family, and close friends have wished me well along the way, especially Courtney Cruz, Anthony Schiro, Mandy Gillin, Cassidy Brown, Julie Seo, Kristin Searcy, Lisa Ainsworth, and Matea Gold. Sherry Blackman, Samantha Schalk, and the incomparable J Ashley Calkins helped me find time and space at critical moments.

For as long as I can remember I have relied upon Crissy Cruz Schiro's laughter, love, confidence, and patience, and I have looked to Kevin Cruz for wry humor and honesty. As the years have slipped into a decade, Samantha Pinto and Nush Powell have been, in a word and in countless ways, phenomenal. Throughout the writing of this book I have spoken nearly every day with Scott Herring and Shane Vogel. As writers, they reminded me of the joy that can be found in crafting a sentence. As colleagues, they have helped me navigate many twists and turns. And as family, they have made Bloomington feel like home. I have also thought often of Paz Ilano Cruz and Lily Pascual Sotto, who lived as transpacific Filipinas during my period of study.

No words of gratitude do justice to the love, generosity, and tremendous efforts of my parents. While I tend to search continuously for the right phrase, Nilo Cruz has always had the talent for expressing kindness in sentences without subjects and in wordlessly just doing the perfect thing.

And my imagination truly fails when it comes to Muni Cruz, who was the first to know that I would, someday, write a book. Let me say, then, just this: you were and will always be an inspiration. Thank you.

In choosing one of this book's central metaphors, I turned to the language of untraveled roads and intersections, of byways and midways. I return to this vocabulary now to dedicate this book to the two people who have walked with me and will continue to do so through all bends and curves, foreseen and unplanned, in moments of triumph, difficulty, and everything in between. Every day they remind me that wonder exists and can be found in many places and forms—from a downtown square in the Bay Area to a winding Parisian street to a quiet sunroom in an Indiana college town; from the first purple blooms on a spot of frozen ground to marks of pink chalk on a door to the amazing fact that a moon can exist—it's true—both in a book and "up the sky." To Jeb and Nate Blackman, these pages, and all my love, are for you.

TRANSPACIFIC FILIPINAS, MADE AND REMADE

The women who grace the cover and center spread of the July–December 2006 issue of *Wedding Essentials*, a magazine designed for Manila's most fashionable brides-to-be, initially seem like any other cover girls (figures 1 and 2). Four beautiful Filipinas dressed in gauzy white stand with their arms entwined. They model dresses made of delicate piña fiber and luminous satin, hybrid haute-couture creations inspired by traditional Filipina formal dresses, Western wedding gowns, and Japanese kimonos. Yet these bodies on display are charged with a weighty nationalist task. Titled "The Four Faces of Maria Clara," the spread—advertised on the cover as a calling for Filipina brides to "embrace your heritage, celebrate your culture"—publicizes Philippine wedding gowns that incorporate "native" materials to enhance the Filipina bride's unique beauty.[1] The models, the magazine tells us, represent different types of Filipina femininity: *mestiza, morena, chinita,* and dusky. Accompanying captions divide and categorize their essential characteristics, with observations about each model's presumed ancestral origin, class position, and defining personal qualities. Culled from the sleek pages that document Manila high fashion, "The Four Faces of Maria Clara" makes the contemporary Filipina, distilled into four containable and ostensibly replicable versions.

The cover and center spread are even more remarkable because of the text that accompanies the women's photos. The title alludes to the lead female character in José Rizal's Spanish-language novel *Noli Me Tangere* (1887), a beloved work of literature that has long been read as one of the foundational texts of Philippine nationalism. Rizal's character Maria Clara was a tragic

1. "The Four Faces of Maria Clara," center spread of *Wedding Essentials* 2, no. 2 (July–December 2006). From left to right: *mestiza, morena, chinita,* and *dusky.*

and beautiful mestiza, the illegitimate, fair-skinned daughter of a Spanish friar and an *india*, a woman native to the Philippines.[2] As the love interest of the male hero, Crisóstomo Ibarra, she remains steadfastly and sacrificially loyal, even through grave illness, accusations of betrayal by her lover, and relentless pursuit by a lecherous friar. In the book's closing pages, she is rejected by Ibarra and confined to a convent, where she faces unspeakable violations.

Why would this nineteenth-century literary figure have pop-cultural saliency for the contemporary Filipina bride over a century after Rizal's work was published? Why choose this tragic, violated woman as the face of a twenty-first-century bridal publication? Although Maria Clara's horrific fate makes her a dubious symbol for a magazine that celebrates the blush and bloom of wedded bliss, *Wedding Essentials* nevertheless continues a long-standing tradition that casts her as the epitome of virtuous Filipina femininity. The magazine offers an explanation that draws on her enduring importance in the Philippines as "the image of the ideal Filipina for decades."

2. *Wedding Essentials* 2, no. 2 (July–December 2006), cover.

"She may have succumbed to depression and death in Rizal's novel," the writer of the article, Evangeline Lazam, acknowledges, "but the heroine Maria Clara was reborn in every Filipina woman who is both delicate and strong, graceful and able, compassionate and courageous. The present-day Maria Clara is a woman of substance who treasures the heritage left by her ancestors, heroes, and heroines. Proud of the color of her skin, she has confidence in her identity and is certain of her role in the family as well as in the larger areas of society" (163). This recent version of Maria Clara elides the novel's obsession with the original character's skin, which is "blanca, demasiado blanca tal vez" (white, perhaps too white), her sighs and trembles, and her sacrificial devotion, even as traces of the nineteenth-century original linger.[3] The new Maria Clara's strength and confidence are still circumscribed by what is not so new: her awareness and acceptance of her place in the family and in the nation.

Although the intent of the spread may be to celebrate diverse iterations of

Filipina beauty, the captions, photos, and layout reinforce troubling constructions of race and class difference in the Philippines. Each caption divides the contemporary Maria Claras along hierarchical lines. Mestizas, the "daughters of Spanish and Filipino parents . . . belong to the more powerful upper classes" (164). Despite their position at the pinnacle of Philippine class hierarchy, the text also acknowledges the mestiza's instability; although "confident and adventurous," "sophisticated and stylish," these women are also "thought to be egotistical and snobbish" (164). Next to the mestiza is the morena, described as having "pure Filipino blood" and thus "often equated with *Inang Bayan* [Mother of the Nation], or the Philippines as a Mother. A true Filipina, the *morena* is passionate yet sensible. The bronze-skinned *morena* is the kind of woman who is strong enough to take care of herself, yet she remains honest and down-to-earth" (164). On the other side of the fold are two women characterized as outliers. The chinita, a term that, according to the caption, stems from "the characteristic small eyes of the Chinese," is a woman who hails from "old and wealthy families," an "imperial beauty," "conservative, calm, and stately, yet wrapped in mystery" (165). The final woman is the only one whose name does not stem from a Spanish-language derivative. Hailing "from the very first ethnic group that set foot on Philippine shores," the "dusky" or "dark-skinned Filipina lives a simple and quiet life in the mountains. A gentle and innocent being, she always wears a smile on her face. Even without superfluous adornments, she can stand out by just being natural. Unpretentious and friendly, she can win the hearts of many with her charm and warmth. The likes of her is not a usual sight in an urban setting, and that is what makes her even more interesting" (165).

The *Wedding Essentials* spread locates the four women within a site shaped by intimate connections among continents—the eddies and flows of multiple migrations, trade relations, and imperial conquests.[4] But while naming the Spanish and Chinese influence in the Philippines, the editors also suppress the importance of two other imperial forces and their regimes, the United States (1898–1946) and Japan (1942–45).[5] The layout nevertheless reproduces a racial hierarchy shaped by the Philippines' contact with Spain, China, the United States, and Japan. Proceeding from left to right, the order of photographs privileges Spanish aristocracy and lighter types of native Filipinas, while Chinese and darker women appear on the other side (see figure 1). Both of the women who are of mixed race are identified as such by names that underscore their racial ancestry (mestiza and chinita), while the women who are supposedly more indigenous to the Philippines or of pure blood are identified primarily by color (morena and dusky). Descriptions of physical attributes such as skin color and eye shape bleed into character assessments. The article pits the morena's honesty against the mestiza's selfishness. It also contrasts the chinita's Oriental mystery with the primitive innocence of the dusky woman, whose description identifies her as similar to the people once called *negritos* during the Spanish and American regimes. The magazine's writers and editors, certainly aware of the lasting negative connotations of the term *negrita*, contain this darker woman within the status of happy primitive, far from the urban centers.

The center spread of a contemporary magazine may be different from the texts that make up the rest of my archive, but this image of elite, cosmopolitan, modern Filipina brides nonetheless illustrates some of the central interests of this book. Representations of "the Filipina" remain shifting, uncertain, and fraught even today, and the ontological underpinnings of such contemporary versions have long, tangled roots in debates recurring throughout the twentieth century over who and what made a Filipina. The women found in the sleek layout of *Wedding Essentials* originate in the now-yellowing newspaper articles, periodicals, literary magazines, novels, memoirs, essays, and studies that make up my archive. These four women are preceded by the representations of romantic heroines, uncaring coeds and fellowship students, fearless guerrillas, and feminist academics who are my subjects. Moving backward over the course of a century, *Transpacific Femininities* unravels such connections.

Tying English literary production to the imagining of new Philippine identities and communities, I argue that Filipina and Filipino writers rearticulated transpacific femininities throughout the first half of the twentieth century, in dialogue with models of Spanish, American, Japanese, and indigenous (india) femininities. Filipina and Filipino elites used the venue of English literature to contest, question, and imagine the modern Filipina. In so doing, they took care to delineate the differences between the bourgeois, transpacific Filipina and others. I document this process primarily in Philippine literature in English produced by Filipina and Filipino writers from the early to the mid-twentieth century, when defining the Filipina woman became a cultural obsession.[6] The rapid development of English literature in the Philippines is itself a phenomenon worthy of study (authors were publishing in English only two decades after the U.S. occupation began), but the creation of a national literary tradition was seriously entwined with elites' attempts to define the Filipina—as a writer and reader of English, as a representative model for other women, and as a citizen whose actions and behaviors determined the future of the Philippine republic and the Filipino and Filipina community in the United States. The figure of the Filipina crops up repeatedly in multiple forms and in wide circles: romance novels, memoirs, and short stories; essays, newspaper articles, and letters to the editor; heated debates on the floor of the Philippine Constitutional Convention; conduct manuals for young girls; and studies devoted to the feminist movement. She appears and reappears again and again in sources as diverse as Philippine literary periodicals, magazines in the United States, small publishing operations in both countries, and a major publisher in the United States, Macmillan. While these appearances coalesce in the form of some key cultural icons, they are also incredibly divergent. The transpacific Filipina is notable precisely because, unlike the women of the *Wedding Essentials* spread, she cannot be contained in singular types.

The making and remaking of the modern Filipina is a process that, while a consistent feature of the first half of the twentieth century, is also a complicated cycle. Making the Filipina centers on debates over what I call transpacific femininities, that is, women who are influenced by the contact between the Philippines and the United States, Spain, and Japan. While some of these women are mestizas, they also exhibit a different form of *mestizaje* in that they draw from a long history of colonial contact in the Philippines. They speak multiple languages, travel, and receive advanced degrees from American and Philippine universities. They are cosmopolitan tourists, college coeds, writers, nurses, teachers, doctors, and lawyers. They are inspired by Hollywood starlets, global modern girls and new women, and American university undergraduates. They are defined against or via other versions of the feminine—the girls and maidens of the barrios outside of Manila, the Malay high priestess, and notions of Oriental and indigenous femininity— the same influences that reappeared in the *Wedding Essentials* spread. They are created by men and women who critique government regimes, question normative constraints on women's lives, and become politically active. They are imagined as the mouthpieces of conflict and resolution, the agents of resistance, the means of rethinking the Philippines as a modern, independent nation. But at times they also reinforce dominant versions of normativity, unquestioningly embrace the supposed modernizing benevolence of the United States, and relegate indigenous and rural peoples to the margins.

While I compare how the transpacific Filipina was produced between the United States and the Philippines, I pay close attention to protean dynamics that connect these two countries to Spain and Japan. The chapters that follow analyze these shifts and examine how questions about the modern Filipina responded to the circulation of Orientalist, indigenous, Americanized, and Spanish models. Makings and remakings of the Filipina coincided with and were linked to developing definitions of what it meant to be Filipina and Filipino during three imbricated regimes; to the emergence of middle-class, heterosexual identities and the elite's attempt to control these definitions; and to the marginalization of indigenous peoples and rural or working-class Filipinas and Filipinos. I trace multiple moments of both colonization and decolonization: the transition between Spanish and U.S. regimes in the 1890s, the independence movements and the granting of commonwealth status in the 1920s and 1930s, the Japanese occupation of the 1940s, and the renegotiation of the relations between the new Philippine republic and the United States as well as other Asian nations during the Cold War. With each changeover, elites had to reconstruct their relationship to one empire and project their future with another.

Throughout these imperial and national transitions, the dialogue surrounding transpacific women intersected with international suffrage movements and women's rights campaigns, as Filipinas and Filipinos participated in these larger global debates. Transpacific Filipinas, as figures of representation and as bodies who crossed and transgressed social boundaries, became focal points of tension in elite communities. As a response to persistent anxieties over transpacific women who represented the destabilization of class, gendered, and sexed hierarchies, elites solidified masculinist and nationalist narratives and reinforced idealizations of women as representative of the nation. Working against the presumed stability of these icons, my close readings track the construction of these iconic women and compare them with alternative versions imagined and enacted by Filipina authors. Although not all of the texts advocate or further women's equality or destabilize normative femininity, they all recognize, even in sometimes complex ways, the transpacific Filipina as crucial to national definition, to identities and communities at home and abroad, and to the reformation of the Philippines' changing interactions with other nations.

Transpacific Femininities does more than recover this untapped archive of Philippine literature in English and the previously undiscussed history of transpacific Filipinas. My version of the transpacific builds on previous scholarship on the migration and movement of individuals, communities, and cultures across oceans. Transpacific is a formation that acknowledges the role of the nation-state (and relations among different countries) but also underscores complex relations that are not necessarily bounded by the nation. Inspired by scholars in Pacific and American studies and by critics who have examined the importance of the Atlantic to the African and African American diaspora, I view the Pacific as a region that was crucial to how the United States, and other Western nations, perceived Asia during a moment of tumultuous geopolitical transition.[7] Indeed, if during the sixteenth to nineteenth centuries the Atlantic was central to the spread of European empire in the Americas, from the late nineteenth century to the twentieth century, the Pacific was both a new site of and thoroughfare for global expansion, as the United States and other countries vied for control of Asia and the Pacific Islands.

While the phrase *transpacific femininities* certainly indexes the shuttling of bodies and texts from the Philippines to the United States, ultimately, I rethink the transpacific—a framework that, as I discuss in more detail below, has a complex history in Asian American and Pacific studies—such that the term encompasses more than a geographic location on the map or oceanic crossings. Indeed, the prefix *trans*-, contends Aihwa Ong in *Flexible Citizenship: The Cultural Logics of Transnationality*, "denotes both moving through space or across lines, as well as changing the nature of something" (4). Building on this capacity of *trans*- to describe not only movement across borders, but also states of transition and change, the concept of transpacific femininities is a critical cartography that energizes the book's analysis of the imbrications of class and gendered hierarchies, changing imperial and national dynamics, cultural representations, and authorial strategies. Merging archival recovery with feminist analysis, the conceptual map of *Transpacific Femininities* charts what chapter 1 details as the byways and midways of Philippine literature in English, the untraveled routes and uncrossed intersections that reveal the cyclic importance of transpacific Filipinas. In this book, these unexplored byways—primarily unstudied texts by Filipinas and Filipinos—are examined through their midways, a critical reading practice that combines literary history, cultural critique, and feminist analysis.

Transpacific femininities refers to representations of women and actual Filipina authors, but the term's multiplicity also encompasses three entwined aspects of my methodology. First, I identify the Philippines as a unique site in the Pacific for exploring the overlap of the Spanish, U.S., and Japanese empires, all of which vied for imperial control of the Pacific region and used the Philippines as a strategic location. Second, I counter notions of a passive, feminized Asia (and Asians) by exploring how elites used the venue of Philippine literature in English and constructions of the transpacific Filipina to redefine the terms of national identities, communities, and transpacific relations. Third, and most important, I underscore the previously unacknowledged importance of femininity in the elites' responses to imperial transfers of power and to transformations in the Philippine nation-state. Highlighting these multiple and overlapping layers, the plurality of transpacific femininities emphasizes instabilities and contradictions in these texts (not all of which advocate feminist practices), marks my recovery of an archive created by Filipina authors, and indexes my analysis of representational and political strategies through a feminist lens.

This book has some limits, again illustrated aptly by the *Wedding Essentials* layout. The magazine's audience is similar to the writers and readers of Philippine literature in English in the first half of the twentieth century. The magazine is marketed to those who have or fancy having a connection with the fashion-forward and the cosmopolitan, the wealthy women who lunch regularly in Makati's posh restaurants, the coiffed and well-heeled attendees at Fashion Watch. The writers examined here were also part of a privileged group, those who lived in Manila, who had access to a university education and travel abroad, who spoke and read English. "The single most important demographic fact about Filipino women writers in English," notes Edna Zapanta Manlapaz, "is that they belong to the elite class."[8] I do not aim to recover the lost voice of the indigenous, working-class, or rural woman. Neither can I account for all of the many vibrant literary traditions in the Philippines. Instead, I emphasize fluctuations in representing the Filipina during the early twentieth century to reveal how elites used the English-language essay, the short story, the novel, and the literary article to construct lines of difference that would separate the elite from indigenous and working-class citizens and to reveal how the elite was problematically complicit in the marginalization of these others. While this approach is feminist in its inception, the politics behind these versions of the Filipina are not always so clearly defined. They are not all resistant or subversive. Indeed, as a process that normalized the elite, cosmopolitan, and heterosexual Filipina, the making of the modern Filipina depended on vilifying, romanticizing, and, most often, eliding those who did not fit the model. I thus pay close attention to constructions of rural, working-class, and indigenous women to stress how literary representation and cultural production were linked to the crystallization of an ethnic, racial, and class hierarchy that unfortunately still continues in the Philippines today.

....

Philippine literature in English presents a unique and previously unaccessed print archive that documents the history of transpacific relations. Since the publication of Amy Kaplan and Donald Pease's *Cultures of United States Imperialism* (1993) there has been much U.S.-based critical interest in the intersections between literary endeavors and U.S. empire.[9] Yet these scholarly attempts have remained strikingly bound by the borders of publication within the United States.[10] Even though U.S. scholars of empire might include the Philippines as a site or literature in English as an object of critical analysis, works produced in the Philippines have remained unstudied. Until recently, these trends have been influenced by a lack of attention to elites, in part because of their uneasy ties to the U.S. imperial regime and their questionable affiliation with evolutions of Filipina and Filipino American communities.[11] Building upon and extending these archival parameters, I draw attention to the literary production of the elite precisely because these texts uncover a new plot, one that centers on the transpacific Filipina as its main protagonist.

In the early to mid-twentieth century the roots of Philippine literature in English were grounded in transpacific geopolitical shifts, as Spain, the United States, and Japan fought to establish control over the Pacific region. The story of Philippine literature in English begins with the importance of education to both the U.S. and Japanese imperial regimes. Although each administration adopted oppositional stances toward English—the Japanese, for example, attempted to diminish the importance of American influence by encouraging the use of Nippongo or Nihongo and Tagalog instead of English—fundamentally each administration's interest in language acquisition, retention, and education was quite similar.[12] As a result, the emergence of Philippine literature in English and its conflicted history are tied to how changing imperial and national dynamics affected the creation of a new class of elite men and women. As the Philippines experienced one wave of colonization after another, these elites would consistently turn to making and remaking the transpacific Filipina as a means of defining the boundaries of race, nation, class, gender, and sex.

That a Filipino or Filipina author of English literature was a product of the U.S. educational system is without question. "Our writer," blithely observed A. B. Rotor forty years into the occupation, "is only as old as the public school system."[13] The rise of literature in English was heavily influenced by the U.S. regime's rigorous implementation of a multitiered strategy of colonial tutelage, which included instruction in English, the establishing of English as the national language, and the large-scale creation of a new public school and university system. After the United States acquired the Philippines in 1898 as part of the treaty terms that ended the Spanish–American War (and in exchange for $20 million), English became the islands' official language in 1901. English-language instruction was crucial to American policy in the Philippines and one of the marked differences between the Spanish and U.S. administrations.[14] The use of language itself as a strategy for rule was closely tied with the rhetorical packaging of the American presence in the Philippines as a magnanimous civilizing enterprise. From the early days of the occupation the United States espoused a mission of colonial tutelage, what President William McKinley famously called benevolent assimilation. With the objective of properly educating the archipelago's inhabitants, who were supposedly not fit for self-government, the expansion of educational opportunities in the Philippines was meant to churn out a new generation of Filipinas and Filipinos indoctrinated in the ideologies of well-meaning American democracy.[15]

American imperial education depended on transpacific interchange, not only through the importing of teachers and textbooks, but also through the implementation of exchange programs. Passed almost immediately after the annexation, Act 74 (1901) launched the public education system and was immediately followed by the massive recruitment of American teachers.[16] The Philippines had a private university, the University of Santo Tomás, founded in 1611, long before Harvard University was established, but the American regime extended public education at the collegiate level and inaugurated the first coeducational institutions. In 1908 the U.S. Philippine Commission established the University of the Philippines (UP), modeled after public state universities in the United States.[17] The UP English department and its creative writing program would eventually train many of the nation's authors. The colonial administration encouraged the best and brightest students to travel to the United States to undertake graduate work. In 1903 the Pensionado Act funded students from the Philippines for educational opportunities at universities in the United States. Initially, the first *pensionados* were those who had already matriculated through private schooling in the Philippines, an advantage that was limited to the rich because of educational restrictions imposed by Spain. Even after the program formally ended in the 1920s, those who had the financial means or who were recognized by American institutions as being exceptional were still able to take part in special opportunities that included graduate degree and creative writing programs.[18]

Fueled in part by these developments in U.S. government policy and education, a generation of English-literate Filipinas and Filipinos came of age in the 1920s and 1930s, and the capital, Manila, became the epicenter of literary production in English.[19] Filipina and Filipino writers published furiously in literary periodicals, university journals, pamphlets, and newspapers.[20] Weekly sections of newspapers and magazines such as the *Graphic* soon had substantial readerships in Manila, and the first books of fiction and poetry written by Filipinos followed.[21] But who was reading this literature? The projected audience for English material was undoubtedly an elite population—those who worked in government, politics, or education; who lived in urban centers like Manila; or who studied at universities in the Philippines and the United States. Many publications were edited by expatriates and geared in part toward the American community. Literary critics and historians have previously examined the circulation of English works and the question of readership in the Philippines via census report data, anecdotal evidence, and increased subscription rates in English-language periodicals. Not surprisingly, the areas with the highest rate of English literacy coincided with spaces of transpacific interactions. "English," observed Joseph Hayden in his 1942 study of national development in the Philippines, "is widely employed in transactions between Filipinos and Americans or foreigners, between Filipinos of different language groups, and in polylingual centers such as Manila or Baguio. It is the chief language of national conventions, such as those of the National Federation of Women's Clubs. . . . Highly important, too, is the use of the English in the periodical press and the contemporary literature of the Islands, a subject which leads to a discussion of the degree and character of the literacy which has been achieved in the Philippines."[22]

Although writers in the Philippines enjoyed the relative luxury of developing close associations and affiliations, the American market for Filipina- and Filipino-authored literature was quite different. Publishing opportunities in the United States were scattered and variable. Articles, essays, and pamphlets written by Filipinas and Filipinos first began circulating in the early years of the twentieth century, when the U.S. Anti-Imperialist League disseminated pleas for Philippine independence crafted by activists such as Sixto Lopez, who wrote in Spanish but whose work was translated into English. Newspapers and magazines in the United States featured work devoted to the debate, including articles republished from Philippine periodicals, letters to the editor or opinion pieces by students in the United States, and first-person accounts of life there. Not all of the material published for an American audience, however, advocated independence (indeed, some of these texts, especially those published in the first decade of the occupation, favored U.S. sovereignty), but many authors addressed what they saw as misconceptions about themselves or the islands. As the numbers of Filipinas and Filipinos in the United States increased in the 1910s and 1920s, the growing critical mass of authors soon started circulating their work via independent presses and smaller periodicals targeted specifically at migrants and expatriates. Venues included the *Filipino Students' Magazine*, a student-produced serial at the University of California, Berkeley; the newsletter-like *The Filipino People*, a bilingual publication produced in Washington, D.C., by the office of Manuel Quezon, the future president of the Philippines; and the smaller, community-based, often short-lived papers that cropped up in California, Washington, and other sites on the West Coast.[23] Only a few writers were recognized by mainstream publishing venues like *Story* and *The New Yorker* and publishers like Charles Scribner's Sons and Doubleday and Doran.[24]

The circumstances of Philippine literature in English would soon be dramatically altered. From the 1930s to the 1950s tremendous turmoil gripped the Philippines, as nationalist movements for independence reached their peak and were interrupted by the outbreak of the Pacific War and competing attempts by the United States and Japan to control the islands. Once again language was crucial to geopolitical transitions. As I detail in chapter 1, after decades of struggle for independence, the Philippines finally gained commonwealth status in 1935, with a ten-year transitional period to full independence. English was soon after contested and then reclaimed as one of the commonwealth's national languages, in part because of controversies over which of the more than 170 indigenous Philippine languages and dialects should be prioritized. In 1941 the Japanese bombing of Manila and the resulting occupation interrupted the commonwealth period, completely altering the literary scene in the Philippines and in the United States. As I discuss in chapter 4, the Japanese regime severely restricted and supervised the production of English materials and attempted to institutionalize Nippongo and promote literary production in Philippine languages in order to encourage Filipinos and Filipinas to break ties with the United States. After the Pacific War and after formal independence from the United States was finally recognized in 1946, English continued as the medium of instruction in Philippine schools and in government and official documentation. Even today, especially in city centers like Manila, Philippine English is still spoken, a practice that represents both the continuing neocolonial influence of the United States and how citizens have interwoven English into the fabric of life and culture in the Philippines.[25]

Although English is still spoken, written, read, and taught in the Philippines, its presence in the islands has been freighted with political and ideological complexities. English literary texts present the material traces of contact and conflict in the Philippines, negotiated through imaginings of transpacific femininities. As each chapter details, this body of literature is important not just because of the crucial and contested status of English in the Philippines throughout much of the twentieth century, but also because the complicated status of both English literary production and the transpacific Filipina is a marker of fluctuations in class hierarchy, and symptomatic of the Spanish, U.S., and Japanese empires and their lasting vestiges. As these texts document again and again, the transpacific Filipina was consistently at the center of these controversies.

....

In drawing attention to how and why elites turned to the figure of the transpacific Filipina and the venue of print culture to respond to overlapping empires, *Transpacific Femininities* also imagines new intersections among U.S. and Philippine studies, Asian American studies, and transnational American studies. Scholars in Asian American studies have been especially prescient in questioning the exclusivity of such terms as *nation* and in encouraging transnational models that might account for the movement of Asian Americans across U.S. borders.[26] For while in the American academy transnational turns have become increasingly popular, and the recognition of the United States as an empire has now become a regular feature of academic discourse,[27] in the case of U.S.–Philippine relations, the predominant critical impetus remains one that examines the two in terms of a binational relationship.[28] Recent works by Allan Punzalan Isaac, Julian Go, and others have furthered alternate methods of examining the Philippines itself along different longitudinal and latitudinal lines: such modes of analysis map the larger geographic connections of the tropics or chart connections between the Philippines and Hawai'i, Puerto Rico, and Cuba.[29] These broader linkages offer an analysis attuned to the ebbs and flows of multiple empires.

Although analytically the rubric of the transpacific presents great potential, ideologically it presents deep challenges. By employing the transpacific, this book also navigates still-unresolved tensions between Asian American and Pacific studies. This long-standing debate reached greater institutional visibility in 2004, when the Association for Asian American Studies (AAAS) considered renaming the organization to include the term *Pacific Islander*. As Vicente Diaz, J. Kēhaulani Kauanui, and Amy Ku'uleialoha Stillman have suggested, the solution to longtime conflicts between the two disciplines requires more than the simple, categorical addition to an organization.[30] Some rightly feared that the inclusion of Pacific Islanders would be in name only, or that while a coalition might exist between them, the tendency would be for Asian American studies to eclipse Pacific Islander studies. While AAAS eventually kept its original formation, what presumably resulted from these conversations was a greater awareness of Pacific cultures, histories, and peoples and greater attention to the continued marginalization of indigeneity.

In the field of Pacific studies, critics have long contended that studies of Asian America must acknowledge the Pacific and its peoples. And why not? Historically, the routes of travel to the United States would necessarily and literally have gone by way of the Pacific Islands. Hawai'i was not only a stopover and the first point of entry to the United States from Japan, China, Korea, and the Philippines; the Hawaiian islands also served as the first recruitment site for Asian migrant laborers.[31] Pacific studies scholarship also questions the dominant categorization of the Pacific Islands and of indigenous peoples as not only marginalized but also landlocked, bound in stasis—a characterization of indigeneity and the Pacific that undoubtedly has its roots in imperial and martial history. By contrast, scholars of the Pacific champion alternate ways of viewing this region and, more importantly, indigeneity as dynamic, mobile, active, and engaged.[32]

In using the term *transpacific*, I do not mean to claim that the experiences of Filipinos and Filipinas are interchangeable with those of native peoples of the Pacific Islands and Oceania. Pacific Islands peoples experienced imperialism and militarization quite differently, still live in islands claimed as military zones and territories by other nations, and remain marginalized within academic and mainstream discourse, policy, and memory. My model of transpacific scholarship, however, does attend to representations of the indigenous and to issues of indigeneity, which are often lost in the sweep of the transnational. Making visible some of the earlier, historic origins of the divide between Asian American and Pacific studies scholarship, I also underscore how representational structures both created and dismantled the myths, constructs, and symbols of indigeneity and femininity.

Even applying the terms *indio* and *indigenous* to this period must be done with great care, for variable historical definitions of these terms illustrate the nuances and ruptures in how Filipinas and Filipinos constructed national identity. The early twentieth century saw the careful restructuring of race, class, and religious distinctions and terminology in the Philippines. In that period, as Benedict Anderson, Vicente Rafael, Michael Salman, and Paul Kramer have documented, the term *filipino* itself had shifting meaning.[33] Filipinos and Filipinas struggled with their prior connections to indigenous peoples, as Hispanicized Filipinos and elites attempted to distinguish themselves from non-Christian peoples. In the Spanish colonial context *filipino* had referred to Spanish creoles, those of Spanish ancestry born in the colony. *Indio* and *mestizo* represented larger, more complex categories. From an American perspective in the early twentieth century, the word *indigenous* might have been used to categorize people from the Philippines writ large. The Bureau of Indian Affairs, for example, had a hand in the organization and administration of Philippine policy. In the Philippines most lowlanders were identified as indios; these people, many of whom were considered to be successfully evangelized by Hispanic Catholicism, were thought to be different from the *infieles*, that is, animists who lived in the Luzon Highlands and Muslim peoples in the South (grouped under the category Moros).[34] Filipinos also distinguished between highland peoples and those they identified as Malay. The term *mestizo* could refer to someone of Spanish and indio birth but more often meant Chinese-indio ancestry, and, later, in the American period, could also apply to someone with an American and Chinese racial mixture. The early twentieth century was a period in which these racial categories underwent reorganization, as Filipinas and Filipinos helped reinforce or create a new hierarchy, one that separated their national identity from that of indigenous peoples.

In Philippine literature in English, this nationalist redefinition was dramatized through the bodies of women and their iconic identification with the land. I use the Philippines as a case study to examine how and why such versions of women became important. Scholars of postcolonial studies, American studies, ethnic American studies, and diaspora studies have analyzed the dominant cast of the feminine, one that, especially in the early twentieth century, continues to be that of a woman who is bound to the home and the homeland, who functions as the signifier of nationalist foundation in soil or earth. In postcolonial literature, women become the symbols of the violated land, or *patria*, both the impetus and the inspiration for the male nationalist's need to reclaim normative masculinity as central to the formation of nationalist consciousness. Such narratives—what Doris Sommer calls "foundational fictions"—represent consistent patterns that extend across multiple disciplinary trajectories and cross geographies that range from the Philippines to Aztlán, Latin America, India, and the African diaspora.[35] Normative versions of cultural nationalism also depend upon such tensions between a male-coded cultural nationalism and the unruly actors—be they feminists or queer women of color—who do not fit within its bounds. Feminist scholarship in postcolonial studies, Chicana and Chicano studies, African diaspora studies, Asian American studies, and indigenous studies has worked hard to reveal these dynamics and their repercussions and to move beyond them.[36]

The pivotal literary figures Carlos Bulosan and Jessica Hagedorn illustrate some of the above critical ossifications and their manifestation in Filipina and Filipino American and Asian American studies. These two iconic authors are the pillars of the canon, and what they have come to represent has troubling ramifications, especially for Filipina femininity: Bulosan is now a stand-in for the male cultural nationalist narrative that dominates Asian America in the first half of the twentieth century; Hagedorn is viewed as the voice of the late twentieth-century's feminist, queer, and transnational liberation from these earlier constraints. While Bulosan and Hagedorn are not central to this book, they do signify both the cementing and polarization of how Filipino and Filipina American experience has been defined and ultimately limited by intersecting boundaries of chronology, gender, and geography.[37]

Best known for his autobiographical novel *America Is in the Heart* (1946), Bulosan today stands as the representative figure of Filipino migrant labor history and of the Filipino exile's difficulties in the United States. The first-person narrator of the novel, Allos, leaves his mother and family behind in the Philippines to work in the United States. The novel tracks his growing disillusion with his new home, as he encounters racism and injustice, and his pivot to nostalgic memories of the Philippines, represented by his hardworking and suffering mother. Because *America Is in the Heart* follows Allos's involvement with socialist labor and antiracism movements and the formation of his own brand of Filipino cultural nationalism, Bulosan's text has become the Filipino American (and, to a larger extent, Asian American) nationalist narrative par excellence, one that is easily packaged, distilled, and taught. The influence of the novel is widespread; it appears on syllabuses in disciplines ranging from literary studies to sociology, Asian American studies to history.[38] The popularity of the novel and Bulosan's valorization of his mother have had long-standing gendered and sexed implications for how literature from the Philippines has been read in the United States. Studies of the early twentieth century have thereby been predominantly concerned with the figure of the male migrant laborer, while women remain within the homeland.

If *America Is in the Heart* has become representative not only of early American experiences of Filipinos and Filipinas but also of a certain kind of male cultural nationalism, allegorized as a coming-of-age narrative, Hagedorn's *Dogeaters* (1990) is the exemplary text of the late twentieth century. Hagedorn's novel, with its multiple narratives, postmodern structure, and transnational geographies, symbolizes everything Bulosan's does not. Set entirely in the Philippines, *Dogeaters* centers on the long history of U.S. colonial and neocolonial influence and its damaging repercussions. Whereas *America Is in the Heart* focuses on the developing nationalist consciousness of a single man, *Dogeaters* moves back and forth between multiple points of view; this back and forth itself works to destabilize the trajectory of Filipino patriarchy and American hegemony. In comparison to Bulosan's work, *Dogeaters* is often read as a quintessentially resistant text, one that puts forth a model of transnational queer feminism as part of its incisive critique of U.S. imperial historiography and American neocolonialism.[39]

This treatment of Bulosan and Hagedorn is emblematic of some general tendencies in the broader characterization of Filipino and Filipina literature within Asian American studies.[40] Just as Bulosan's text is "about" narrating the life of a Filipino migrant, so the early twentieth century is read primarily through the lens of Filipino migration and labor and cast as a period ultimately "about" the development of male cultural nationalists. In part, this characterization has stemmed from archival limitations, since material about the lives of Filipina women has only recently become much more accessible.[41] With *Dogeaters* as a prime example, scholarship on later or contemporary Philippine–U.S. dynamics turns to feminist, diaspora, and queer studies as primary rubrics. Bulosan and Hagedorn represent a split between the first and second halves of the twentieth century and the critical narratives that have shaped their contours. The limitations of the bounds of geography (meaning that works produced in the United States remain the primary focus) and chronology (meaning that the early twentieth century has been characterized as the realm of male literary cultural nationalism) have had troubling results: Filipinas have had only a marginal role in discussions of early twentieth-century U.S.–Asian relations. They are relegated to the status of a statistic, a blip on the larger screen either of male migration to the United States or of male-dominated independence debates and nationalist movements.

But what if such foundational patterns in nationalist literatures were, at least for a site like the Philippines, not quite so edified? What if one could track and witness these fluctuations? In the English-language press, in developing literature, and in the venues frequented by elites the dominant representation of the Filipina was not that of a woman bound to the land, but that of a transgressive woman who flouted norms, spoke multiple languages, traveled, and was both the product and producer of a nation and culture in flux. The book's chapters investigate the fuzzy overlap, the blurred messiness of writers' construction of transpacific women—representations that were sometimes contentious, often troubling, at times laudatory, and at still other times deeply critical. Demonstrating that it is possible to trace the continuous development of icons of femininity as well as their solidification and their contestation, the Filipinas in this study exemplify movement over stasis and instability over reification.

Moreover, because of the geographical, chronological, and gendered boundaries that separate the treatment of a novel like Bulosan's from a work like Hagedorn's, it has become difficult to imagine intersections between the interests of nationalism and transnational feminism during the early to mid-twentieth century. Narrating the story of the making and remaking of the modern Filipina calls attention to earlier forms of transpacific feminism, such that this critical practice becomes more than a Western import, more than a politics and scholarly approach that exists solely within the Western academy or other circles of privilege.[42] How does Philippine literature in English attempt to promote an entwined version of both nationalism and transnational feminism? And what might the treatment of this literature tell us about our own critical desires to separate the two? The following pages seek to both illuminate and disrupt these separations and to examine their eventual calcification in the years immediately after the Pacific War, when

Cold War relations that triangulated the Philippines between Asia and the United States led to their reconfiguration. Ultimately, the figure of the transpacific Filipina becomes the site through which these differences might be held up and contained.

....

That Filipina and Filipino writers would return to the transpacific Filipina is no surprise, especially since this period coincided with the emergence of the women's suffrage movement in the Philippines, increased support for Filipina rights in the 1920s and 1930s, and assessments of its effects in the 1950s. In 1905 Concepcion Felix and other elite women founded the Asociación Feminista Filipina, which was dedicated primarily not to suffrage but to issues like regulating women's and children's labor and to lobbying for the inclusion of women in municipal and provincial boards of education.[43] The initial years of the occupation saw the expansion of educational and professional opportunities for Filipinas, as they began graduating from universities, formed women's associations, and entered the workforce. Women soon began campaigning for the vote. Momentum for suffrage propelled the cause forward, and Filipina and Filipino independence activists and politicians began questioning whether or not Filipina suffrage should be included as part of independence efforts. As Mina Roces has documented, the nationalist movement presented a complicated problem for Filipina suffragists, for they were asked to support (and even vote in favor of) a government that would not validate their enfranchisement. Suffragists struggled with the knowledge that their affiliation with American women activists meant they were aligned with a cause that was preventing their nation from gaining independence.[44] Filipino nationalists also worried that the attachment of women's suffrage to their calls for independence might prolong the debate. The issue was not fully resolved at the time the Philippines achieved commonwealth status, and, after a plebiscite determining whether or not women were interested in suffrage, Filipinas were finally granted the vote in 1937.

The women's suffrage movement in the Philippines had definite connections to corresponding initiatives in the United States and around the globe. Indeed, many Filipina feminists increasingly saw themselves as part of a worldwide call for attention to women's rights. In this period, women's clubs formalized links across the nation and between countries. Events and developments for women in the United States paralleled similar happenings across the Pacific. In 1890 the General Federation of Women's Clubs was founded in the United States, followed by the National Association of Colored Women in 1896. In the Philippines the first two decades of the twentieth century saw the creation of more women's organizations, and the National Federation of Women's Clubs embraced the cause of suffrage in the Philippines in 1921.[45] And just as rising numbers of women began attending universities in the Philippines, the same period saw a dramatic increase in university attendance by middle-class white women in the United States.

Even though similar developments for women were occurring on both sides of the Pacific, as Kristin Hoganson has argued, the white, middle-class women's suffrage movement in the United States had an uneasy relationship with the Philippines. Alliance and coalition between Filipinas and white American women were, for the most part, confounded by the contradictory pull of the goals of the anti-imperialism movement in the United States, Philippine independence activists, and U.S. women's suffrage. Notable suffragists like Elizabeth Cady Stanton and Susan B. Anthony did not reject the principles of U.S. imperialist expansion. The debate in the United States was already complicated by tensions between white women and women of color. During the late nineteenth and early twentieth centuries, white, middle-class women who campaigned for suffrage "increasingly cast their lot with those who wielded political power—the men of their race and class."[46] At their worst, women's rights activists in the United States who voiced objections to Philippine independence based these contentions on racist premises. Some suffragists angrily resented the notion that brown men could have more rights than white women. Some championed the cause of suffrage for Filipinas but not Filipinos, arguing that the women were more intelligent and more capable of the political responsibilities attached to enfranchisement. And while Carrie Chapman Catt visited the Philippines to encourage Filipinas to mobilize for women's rights, Hoganson notes the overwhelming failure of white American women to capitalize on the potential for transnational coalition with women in the Philippines.[47]

Filipina and Filipino authors also engaged in the wider, global spread of the new woman and her later counterpart, the modern girl, as pop icons. Although it is difficult to pinpoint exactly when and where the new woman originated, scholars have recently traced her rise to the years immediately preceding the Spanish–American War, which coincided with the rising momentum of the suffrage movement.[48] The Modern Girl Around the World Research Group has analyzed the ways in which the flow of global capitalism resulted in the circulation of images that were strikingly similar in locales ranging from Shanghai to Bombay, London to New York, Okinawa to Sydney. These scholars document how a global interest in representations of a certain kind of woman, made visible by repetitive and iconic visual characteristics ("bobbed hair, painted lips, provocative clothing, elongated body, and open, easy smile"), and her reappearance in diverse sites across the globe during the period between the First and Second World Wars were influenced by increased economic interdependence, the rapid spread of global capitalism, and the resurgence of nationalist movements as colonized nations across the world increased their efforts to gain independence.[49] At the same time, the flows of global capital, the consumption of American and British commodities, and the marketing of the Hollywood film industry in other nations—linked to corporate advertising that banked on the image of the twentieth-century woman conceptualized as modern—contributed to the almost simultaneous worldwide arrival of modern girls.[50]

But these women, as this scholarship demonstrates, were not always merely influenced by a dominant West. Indeed, the same studies that focus on the concurrent creation and circulation of modern women and their connection to developments in global capitalism and commodity advertising also rightly caution against characterizations of these women and their reputation as Westernized or, perhaps more explicitly, Americanized, a move that overestimates the reach of Western imperialism and capitalism. More important, though, these scholars draw attention to how across the globe modern women and their representations incorporated local elements—what the Modern Girl Around the World Research Group has called "multidirectional citation" or "the mutual, though asymmetrical influences and circuits of exchange that produce common figurations and practices in multiple locations."[51] While certain elements of modern girls and women might be mapped in various sites, representational practices also drew from local cultural context; the meaning and use of the modern girl did not always imply an acceptance of the West.

Similarly, the modern Filipina was not just an offshoot of these developments. Rather, her emergence was both product and project, both representational result and method. The new Filipina had her own heyday in the Philippines, as Filipinas and Filipinos responded to circulating constructs of femininity and incorporated their own manifestations. Like many other new women across the globe, the new Filipina incorporated some aspects of the West while retaining some of her own Philippine-specific traits. But these versions were more than new women and modern girls with a Filipina face. As this book details, even though transpacific Filipinas may have had their hair fashionably bobbed, modeled themselves after Hollywood starlets, and worn Chanel No. 5, they also were drawn carefully from other types of femininity in the Philippines.

Although neither explicitly studied nor linked to these other modern women, the transpacific Filipina offers productive opportunities for teasing out these intricate connections between colonial and nationalist contexts. For the transpacific Filipinas of this period are not just negotiations of the West (the United States and Spain), but also a means of processing how those in the Philippines attempted to sort out their relation to (and in some cases to break connections with) other Asians, other peoples in the Philippines, and people of color in the United States. The new Filipinas, uncaring nurses, heartless coeds, and Maria Claras of this book have ties to the Chinese *nuxing*, the Japanese *moga*, and the British suffragette. They have their parallels in Hollywood, Indian, and Australian screen stars. They are connected to the development of the new Negro and new Indian women in the United States. Like these women, the transpacific Filipina becomes "an object of national scrutiny . . . a contested figure and image, either an object of celebration or of attempted control," a means of producing, imagining, responding to, and, in some cases, reinforcing problematic ties not just to the West but also to other Asian nations.[52]

....

The Filipina as new, modern, global, and transpacific was a key cultural figure in the Philippines well before the editors of a twenty-first-century bridal magazine decided to choose four types of women to capture representative aspects of Filipina femininity. The threads that link transpacific femininities of the early to mid-twentieth century to the contemporary Maria Claras featured in *Wedding Essentials*, however, also fray and unravel. Although the image I began with points to transpacific Filipinas' continued importance, the magazine spread illustrates some crucial departures. For while the *Wedding Essentials* layout contains and divides these women into distilled types, easily defined and stabilized, and glosses over the complex imperial interactions that produced them, this study zeroes in on important instabilities and dwells on the uncomfortable and uncertain, the questionable and puzzling. At the same time, I also examine repeated attempts to manage and monitor the Filipina. While some authors celebrated transpacific femininities and their unstable potential, many others were invested in containing this instability as a means of sharpening the borders of elite, heteronormative identities.

The chapters that follow demonstrate how Filipina and Filipino writers made and remade the modern Filipina to respond to fluctuating national identities, communities, and hierarchies and to the layered influences of multiple empires. In each chapter, the transpacific Filipina emerges as a central figure in national, transpacific, and even global relations. In the Philippines she becomes the cornerstone of English-literate elites' definition of what it meant to be Filipina and Filipino during the U.S. and Japanese periods and immediately after the Pacific War. For these writers, making the modern Filipina in turn made the nation and its citizens modern. In some cases, they drew on narratives of the West as a modernizing force, but they also turned toward versions of precolonial women to argue that the Philippines itself carried aspects of modern, liberated femininity well before the arrival of European, American, and Japanese imperial forces.

Undoubtedly, authors also wrestled with the question of how Filipina femininity was constructed by the Spanish, U.S., and Japanese regimes. But representations of Filipinas in imperial discourse—as an exotic other, a fascinating yet frightening spectacle, or a colonial subject who eagerly desired the benefits of empire—form only part of the story. Each chapter argues that imperial changeovers destabilized elite communities and that resulting class tensions coalesced in heated debates over transpacific Filipinas and their place in the Philippines. Filipina and Filipino authors turned to different representational and authorial strategies to reassert the terms of raced, classed, gendered, and sexed hierarchies. With some exceptions, such as Maximo Kalaw, whose work I discuss in chapter 3, Filipinos responded to the threat posed by transpacific women by attempting to reinforce male nationalist narratives, which depended on idealized Filipina icons.[53] Yet, as I argue in chapter 2, even the female icons of male nationalism are consistently marked by unresolved tensions. While the representational projects of imperialist discourse and elite Filipino nationalists attempted to contain transpacific Filipinas, Filipina authors constructed and enacted alternatives both on and off the printed page. In making and remaking the transpacific Filipina, these women crafted representations of Filipinas as central to the Philippines' past, present, and future. They also imagine forms of political coalition and transpacific networks that, although often complicated and unstable, depart from romanticized notions of sisterhood between Filipinas or between Filipinas and white American women.

The first half of the book demonstrates the methods of archival recovery and feminist critique that ground *Transpacific Femininities*. Chapter 1 explores the unmapped routes and intersections—what I call byways and midways—of Filipina and Filipino literary history, its connections to elite constructions of transpacific femininity, and feminist alternatives to imperial and national narratives. In an analysis of two recovered archives of Filipina-authored literature, I chart how women countered dominant representations of Filipinas circulated by the U.S. colonial regime and elite male nationalists in the Philippines. Writing for an American audience during the first decades of the occupation, Filipinas contested racist constructions of women in the Philippines as either savage others or desiring colonial subjects eager for tutelage. In texts that reveal the lingering traces of Spanish influence on the elite, Hispanicized Filipinas carefully distanced themselves from indigenous peoples in the Philippines and other Asian and white, working-class women in the United States, and they imagine problematic alliances with white American women. The second half of the chapter moves across the Pacific to track the responses of Filipina authors to debates in the 1930s over the Philippines' official languages during the transition from occupied territory to commonwealth. To reinforce their place as elite literati, Filipino writers positioned themselves as architects of a national literature in English. To combat these intersections of male nationalism and the publishing world, Filipinas critiqued the dismissal of women's literary contributions and fostered a sisterhood of women writers.

Extending this discussion of the gendered dynamics of nationalist literature, chapter 2 analyzes four recurring icons of Filipina femininity that haunted the literary, cultural, and political landscape of Manila in the 1930s: the Spanish mestiza Maria Clara, the Westernized Filipina coed, the romanticized barrio girl, and the precolonial india. Weaving together an examination of Rizal's *Noli Me Tangere*, debates over Filipina suffrage, newspaper and periodical coverage, and conduct manuals for Filipinas, I track the dominance of each of these icons and the elite's recurring fascination with and anxiety over the specters of shifts in Filipina femininity, as a new generation of women graduated from the coeducational university system and destabilized former social and professional divisions and bourgeois definitions of normative Filipina femininity. Although they were frequently employed by elites as iconic figures, Maria Clara, coed, barrio girl, and india are nevertheless deeply vexed representations that belie the icon's presumed stability, and each recurs throughout the period under study. These unstable constructions are ghostly reminders of imperial and national transformations in the Philippines and their effects on the elite, and they continued to reappear in literary and cultural representations throughout the twentieth century.

The remaining chapters move from these larger cultural debates over transpacific Filipinas to their fraught manifestation in literature produced during three transitional moments: the 1930s, which was the height of the Philippine movements for independence and suffrage, the Second World War and the Japanese occupation, and the postwar period. Drawing on the earlier analysis of the elites' fascination with the coed and the barrio girl, chapter 3 compares two romances, Kalaw's *Filipino Rebel* (Philippines, ca. 1930) and Felicidad Ocampo's *The Brown Maiden* (United States, 1932), and their projection of the exceptional and elite transpacific Filipina's destiny. Kalaw and Ocampo were both connected to the U.S. regime, Ocampo as a nurse and later an employee for the Bureau of Indian Affairs, and Kalaw as an independence activist, academic, and, later, dean of the University of the Philippines. Both novels maintain class divisions among the elite, indigenous, and working-class peoples of the United States and the Philippines. Yet they also present complicated interventions that counter an imperial narrative that idealized U.S. empire as benevolent and valorized the education of exceptional elites as evidence of the occupation's success. Rewriting this plot, *Filipino Rebel* and *The Brown Maiden* contend that the transpacific Filipina's future ability to entwine nationalism and feminism depends on her reeducation. For Kalaw and Ocampo, reeducation is linked not to the educational initiatives formally sponsored by the United States (although their heroines do participate in these ventures), but to the heroines' eventual awareness of the dangers of naïve idealization and their rejection of the drama that would cast the Filipina as eagerly accepting colonial subjectivity. The novels suggest further that coalitions between Filipinas and white American women are confounded not only by national and racial differences but also by divisions that separate the elite from the working class.

Chapter 4 examines the Second World War as a turning point in Philippine, U.S., and Japanese relations, in the status of Philippine literature in English, and in the corresponding constructions of gendered national identity. Focusing on material composed by Filipinas during and immediately after the Pacific War, the chapter analyzes the complex representational and authorial practices of women who reimagine domesticity and sisterhood to claim the transpacific Filipina's importance to the Philippines' future and to critique the gendered divisions that persisted amid imperial and national transitions. The Japanese regime severely restricted publication in English, and some writers began producing Japanese-monitored propaganda pieces under considerable duress. The Japanese occupation created a new set of challenges for the elite, as those who were formerly enfranchised found themselves in the difficult position of choosing between various loyalties and allegiances. In a series of essays written during the occupation, elite Filipina authors reframe transpacific femininity in response to Japan's push for inter-Asian coalition against Western oppression. Rejecting the elite Filipina's prewar frivolity, they offer what one writer calls "practical patriotism" as a new model of domestic femininity, reconstruct a woman's return to the home and the hearth as a nationalist venture, and idealize precolonial indigenous femininity and pan-Asian sisterhood. They depart from the articles and essays written in the late nineteenth and early twentieth centuries, which distance Filipina women from Japanese, Chinese, and Indian women. These constructions, however, are careful maneuvers in a climate of imperial supervision and censorship, and practical patriotism suggests a mode of critique that reads the charged politics of these pieces as a strategy of survival during the war.

The Second World War allowed for a reimagining of relations between the Philippines and the United States, now seen as being allied against the Japanese. The bombings of Pearl Harbor and Manila, which occurred within a few days of each other, as well as Filipinos' service in the U.S. military during the war and the joint experience of the soldiers of both nations during the deadly march of 1942 to the Japanese camp in Bataan, created a series of national traumas that advanced the reimagining of transpacific relations.[54] The people who were once "little brown brothers" in need of tutelage or decried as an immigration nuisance suddenly became crucial allies in the war against Japan. Popular constructions in mainstream media, from films to newspaper articles, overwhelmingly celebrated brotherly relations between U.S. and Filipino men. While men were valorized as united in a transpacific war effort, women were cast as the war's victims. This interest in the Philippines and the change in perceptions about Filipinas and Filipinos led to new opportunities for publication, and a greater number of books by authors from the Philippines circulated in the years after the war.[55] I end the chapter with a response to these rhetorical constructs in Yay Panlilio's memoir *The Crucible: An Autobiography of "Colonel Yay"* (1950), the first Filipina text to be published by a major American press. In her account of her experience as a guerrilla resisting the Japanese, Panlilio presents a complicated politics that seeks to gain recognition for Filipina and guerrilla involvement during the Pacific War. To do so, she rejects pan-Asian sisterhood, grounds her ability to speak to an American audience in her mixed Irish American and Filipina ancestry, and validates a transpacific community between a Filipina author and her white American sisters.

Chapter 5 moves from the rapidly changing dynamic between the Philippines and the United States during the Second World War to revisions of transpacific Filipinas during the Cold War. Nineteen fifty-five was a landmark year for Cold War relations and feminism in the Philippines: it was the year of the Bandung conference in Indonesia, at which representatives of African and Asian nations met to declare themselves either aligned or non-aligned with the United States and the Soviet Union; and the year that marked the fiftieth anniversary of the formal beginnings of the Filipina feminist movement. In keeping with a larger turn toward sentiment that dominated U.S. relations with Asia, the question of the Filipina's heart became ever more important in the years after the Second World War. This chapter considers Cold War sentiment in postwar makings of the elite transpacific Filipina, from the iconic nurse and uncaring coed in Bienvenido Santos's short stories to studies about the development of the Filipina woman written by Filipina feminists, which marshal the sentimental rhetoric of the Cold War to champion women's rights, even as they manipulate an idealized indigenous past. These elite women strategically employ a discourse of the heart to assert the Filipina's importance not only to the Philippines but also to global relations.

The epilogue transitions from the printed pages of the early to mid-twentieth century to multimedia archives of the contemporary moment. I pair David Byrne's recent album *Here Lies Love* (2010) with the work of Filipina bloggers and website administrators who ask and answer the question, What makes a modern Filipina? I gesture toward links between earlier formations of transpacific femininities and the global circulation and consumption of their late twentieth- and twenty-first-century versions. These examples point to a lasting fascination with contemporary icons of transpacific femininity, such as the overseas Filipina worker, recently praised by the former president of the Philippines Gloria Macapagal Arroyo as the nation's most valuable economic export; the mail order bride, advertised as an idealized version of the dutiful wife; and even the frightening yet captivating spectacle of Imelda Marcos. While Byrne's *Here Lies Love* capitalizes on the global circulation of transpacific Filipina icons, Filipina feminist bloggers critique this persistent cycle of commodification. These women build upon and extend the work of previous Filipina authors, and they also offer new versions of online, global feminist networks that call for offline empowerment and cross-class coalitions. Rooted in the complex processes that I follow over the course of the twentieth century, these contemporary multimedia archives attest to the lingering and pressing importance of making and remaking the modern Filipina.

Chapter One

CARTOGRAPHIES OF THE TRANSPACIFIC FILIPINA

In 1915, when the author Emma Sarepta Yule needed a metaphor to describe the early twentieth-century Filipina, she turned to a map. In "The Woman Question in the Philippines," an article that identifies potential comparisons and contrasts between Filipinas and other Asian women, Yule locates Filipina femininity "midway geographically between the dainty kimono maiden of Japan and the veiled lady of India and alongside the 'lily-footed' dame of China." The "woman of the Philippines," she observes, is "unique in the orient. A woman in whose development there has been neither seclusion, nor oppression, nor servitude. A woman who is not and has never been in the category of 'oriental woman' as popularly and fairly correctly conceived."[1] Although she first situates the Filipina at the midpoint of a transpacific cartography that sweeps over Japan, India, and China, for Yule the similarities between the Filipina and other "Oriental" women stop at this intersection of longitudinal and latitudinal lines. She does not question the popular conception of Asian women as being servile, oppressed, secluded, and delicate. Instead, she contends that the Filipina has been wrongfully included in this categorization. The rest of Yule's article transfers her symbolic mapping of the Filipina in transpacific space to a theoretical imagining of transpacific femininity as drawn from and as a response to the lingering traces of Spanish influence, the results of new contact with the United States, and perceptions about other Asian femininities.

"The Woman Question in the Philippines" circulated in two venues: the *Philippines Monthly,* a magazine produced in Manila for English-speaking Filipinas and Filipinos and U.S. expatriates, and, a year later, in Manuel

Quezon's *The Filipino People*, a circular produced in the United States. The essay was reprinted in *Scribner's* in 1920 under the title "Filipino Feminism." Yule, a white American woman who moved to the Philippines during the first years of the U.S. occupation and was on the faculty of the University of the Philippines, intended her observations on feminism to reach a transpacific audience. Her careful construction of the Filipina is a springboard for this chapter's exploration of the entwined development of Philippine literature in English and the emergence of transpacific femininities. I trace a route that originates in the American metropole and travels to the occupied Philippines, a path that illuminates the absolute importance of Filipina femininity to how Filipina and Filipino elites responded to changes in a geopolitical web that stretched from the Philippines to the United States, Japan, China, and other nations in Asia. The resulting tensions and conflicts emerged in documentation of the Philippines and its peoples produced in the United States during the early twentieth century, figures of transpacific women imagined by Filipina and white female authors, early conversations over the state of English literature carried on in print in the Philippines during the 1930s, and the uncertain status of women writers in Manila's predominantly male publishing climate.

My decision to use mapping as a metaphor complicates the relationship between imperial cartography as a method for producing knowledge about and control of colonial subjects. During the occupation of the Philippines, maps were part of the widespread visual circulation of materials consumed by an American public. "Maps," contends David Brody, "facilitate the course of empire. By creating imagined landscapes, which, readers believe, arise out of a desire to represent the truth, maps epitomize an imperial logic."[2] As Amy Ku'leialoha Stillman reminds us, however, although cartography uses visual representation to imagine a landscape for imperial consumption and discipline, one might rethink the meaning of a map and the kind of knowledge it charts, for "the conceptual power of maps is useful for plotting not only locations, but directions of movements and relationships across space as well. These resources allow us to consider interactions of people spatially, and to track how such relationships then continue to move and circulate. Nor are the movements unidirectional, or even simply bidirectional."[3]

Mapping the complex interactions and relationships that informed transpacific femininities during the initial decades of the occupation, my cartography crisscrosses the Pacific to investigate byways and midways, the terms I use to encapsulate the methodology developed in this chapter and employed in the book as a whole. I examine untraveled byways—primarily works written by Filipinas and Filipinos in English that are little known and unstudied—and situate these texts amid their intersecting midways, a combination of transpacific literary history and feminist analysis.[4] Indeed, Yule's choice of the term midway in the early twentieth century speaks to the historical and cultural specificities of how Filipinas were represented in multiple forms of media, from the independent and popular press to the public and private circulation of photographs to well-attended exhibitions and fairs. While a midway refers to the middle, the halfway point that bisects a geographical distance, in North America in the 1890s and 1900s midway became associated specifically with the exhibits that were becoming increasingly popular as large public entertainments, such as the St. Louis World's Fair in 1904. A midway, often carrying proper noun significance (as in the Midway), was "a central avenue along which the chief exhibits or amusements are placed; any area of sideshows or amusements; (slang) a hall." Referring to the middle, too, in terms of state or course, a midway also signifies the inbetweens of space, time, or process and encapsulates the geopolitical shifts that are crucial to transpacific femininities.[5] The term has limitations in that truly exact middles are impossible and even undesirable. Yet through these midways in the territories of literary production, practices of representation, and authorial strategies, I underscore how the making of transpacific femininities was entwined with attempts by an elite fluent in English to reinforce their importance amid the transition from Spanish to U.S. empires in the early years of the twentieth century and again from the U.S. occupation to the Philippine commonwealth in the 1930s.

Celebrations of transpacific femininity like Yule's and the complicated development of Filipina and Filipino authorship in English are both vexed by their connections to long-standing tensions in the creation and maintenance of an English-speaking bourgeoisie. As the terms Filipina and Filipino shifted and coalesced into identities different from their nineteenth-century Spanish meaning of "creoles," elites in both the Philippines and the United States wanted to represent themselves in a way that would circumvent their association with those seen as uncivilized, especially the non-Christian, animist Igorots and Negritos of Luzon, the island on which Manila is located; the Muslim Moros of the southern Philippines; the non-English-speaking masses of Manila; Chinese populations in the Philippines; and rural peoples living in the provinces.[6] Similarly, those Filipina authors who, along with Yule, wrote against the popularized and Orientalist representation of Japanese and Chinese women as veiled and exotic, or weak and oppressed, also questioned not only the characterization of other Asian women in this vein but also their own inclusion in such assessments.

Soon after the United States annexed the Philippines, newspapers, periodicals, and American publishers began circulating a large volume of material debating the validity and morality of the occupation and documenting the islands and its peoples for an American public. English texts written by elites who were involved in the anti-imperialist movement or participants in study-abroad programs in the United States appeared in the early 1900s: some works were written originally in English while others were produced in translation. These authors had to contend with the shifting perceptions in the United States of both Japan and China, as the American public responded to the perceived rise of Japan as an imperial power, the threat this expansion posed, and the influx of Chinese and Japanese laborers. Such developments fueled widespread fears of yellow peril and invading hordes of Asian bodies. These anxieties existed alongside a lingering Orientalist fascination with Asian women as the romantic geisha girl or butterfly figure, popularized by romances, plays, opera, and film.[7]

While a feminist observer like Yule noticed these shifts, elite Filipinas similarly mapped this crossroads in early twentieth-century articles and essays published in American newspapers and periodicals, and their work too strikes an unsteady balance between fears of savage, uncontrollable Asian bodies and the fascination with exotic Orientals. Their texts counter the modes of exhibition and display that persistently held up the islands and its people as objects of consumption for a curious American viewing and reading public, and they call into question the characterization of Philippine peoples as uncivilized and unprepared for the benefits of democracy.[8] They also maneuver in and around competing representations of Filipina women and their connections to exotic yet oppressed Japanese and Chinese women. They contest the benevolent narratives of empire associated with education in the United States and the promotion of white, liberated American femininity as a model. Instead, the authors emphasize that elite Filipinas embody a unique form of transpacific femininity, a combination of the conservative and the modern, and the best elements of Philippine culture with the benefits brought by educational opportunities imported from the West. While they resist notions of Filipinas as unquestioning, desiring colonial subjects, they form fragile and fraught alliances with the West. Ultimately, the women define transpacific Filipinas as resisting discrete and containable identities.

This emphasis on malleability, as we will see, informs later reactions to transpacific Filipinas from the early to the mid-twentieth century, as such instability fuels attempts to manage and control uncontainable women.

Moving from the first decade of the occupation to the late 1930s, when the Philippines went from unincorporated territory to transitional common-wealth, the second half of the chapter turns to yet another literary byway. Across the Pacific a rapidly increasing number of Filipina and Filipino authors would choose English literature as a venue for the imagination of new national identities. Intersections between the production of Philippine literature in English and the elite's tenuous connections to notions of Philippine nationalism would be crucial to this moment. Once the Tydings-McDuffie Act paved the road for the establishment of a Philippine commonwealth, authors found themselves in an especially difficult position, as the status of English as an official language was called into question. Male authors responded by vehemently defending their role as architects of a nationalist literary tradition in English and fiercely debating the purposes and end results of literary production. A series of articles published in Manila during the late 1930s and early 1940s illustrates the contours of this debate. In these essays, Filipino authors uniformly defend the importance of English literature to the Philippines' past and future. These discussions about the continued relevance of a nationalist literary tradition in English reveal elite male writers' desire to insulate themselves and perceptions of their work from competing Tagalog authors and their appeal to the masses.

But this debate, which has long been read in terms of a conversation that pitted aesthetics over politics, was entwined with a concurrent conflict between men and women.[9] While male authors argued about the purposes of English literature, women writers used the occasion to reflect on the challenges of the publishing world in Manila. Periodicals featured sniping back-and-forth between men who dismissed Filipina literary production, and women who defended their merits and criticized the difficulties faced by female authors. Moving to the gendered borders that defined the capital's literary world, the final section charts this friction and explores Filipina authors' strategic responses as they sought alternative formations to counter fraternities of elite male nationalism.

In the early years of the twentieth century Filipina authors contended with various methods of colonial display that circulated in the United States. The policing of Filipina bodies was crucial to these endeavors, and constructions of Filipina and Asian women in the United States were especially important to Filipina writers during the early decades of the occupation. On one hand, cultural productions of people in the Philippines centered on racist taxonomies that classed the islands' inhabitants as savage and uncivilized. In the space of a single sentence, Nerissa Balce astutely sums up the preoccupation with naked brown bodies: "In colonial documents, savage breasts were signs of conquest." The Filipina woman was a key figure in the raced, sexed, and classed hierarchies that justified the U.S. occupation. At first she emerged in visual and print discourse as emblematic of native inscrutability, a sexualized other who flouted imperial control and discipline. The figure of the "Filipina savage" was central to what Balce calls the "erotics of empire," which depended on "the play of earlier racialized and gendered discourses that constructed the Filipina as a new nonwhite other whose alterity incorporated the ideas, images, and vocabularies of the conquests of the New World, the frontier, and the legacies of slavery."[10]

Despite the dominance of the Filipina savage, not all Filipinas were represented in the same way. While erotically charged representations of Filipina *indias* were crucial to the circulation of an imperial archive, elite Filipinas were praised for their remarkable potential to benefit from U.S. involvement in the islands, ostensibly because of their eager imitation of American femininity. Elite women were frequently imagined as desiring subjects who were not only able to mimic the teachings of their colonizers but who were also eager to acquire the symbolic trappings of benevolence. This desire was manifested in their participation in U.S. educational programs, their consumption of Western goods, and their supposedly Western behavior, often identified in opposition to Orientalist notions of femininity.[11] On one hand, the bodies of Filipina *indias* were circulated in the pages of newspapers, in reprinted photographs in books, and in large exhibitions as desirable objects to be consumed by the curious reader or viewer. On the other hand, these media forms represented elite Filipinas as desiring consumers of imperial ideology and Western capital.

The print, photographic, and staged productions that cast Filipinas as either the inscrutable or threatening native or the willing, desiring imperial subject were widespread and varied. Almost immediately after the acquisition of the Philippines, the U.S. public was bombarded with the large-scale representational production of the islands as the country's newest territorial possessions, including book-length studies devoted to the islands and its peoples, flora, fauna, resources, customs, and folk tales; correspondence from eyewitness observers published in newspapers and periodicals; the results of the first Philippine census; and memoirs by soldiers, wives, U.S. officials, educators, and others who had journeyed to the Philippines and written of their experience.[12] By far the largest of the efforts to introduce the American people to their new island possessions was the Philippine exhibit at the St. Louis World's Fair, which included a replica of a village inhabited by representatives of various ethnic groups and examples of model citizens such as the Philippine Scouts, who, because of their involvement with the U.S. regime, were presumably marching steadfastly forward on the road to civilization.

As the rich scholarship on the importance of modes of reportage and display to the U.S. imperial project has demonstrated, these projects were also driven by an interest in colonial containment, in managing racial fear.[13] The language used to describe the Philippines drew upon American and Spanish racist taxonomies that hierarchically constructed other races, Muslims, and animist peoples of the Philippines as uncivilized. The islands' indigenous inhabitants were consistently compared to Native Americans. American policy reflected this racial analogy. U.S. officials initially described people in the Philippines as a group of unorganized tribes, a view reflected in the make-up of the members of the colonial administration and military who first traveled to the Philippines (many had had previous experience with the Native American population). In addition to turn-of-the-century American racist ideologies, these assessments drew on the preexisting classifications inherited from Spanish colonials, which categorized non-Christian peoples like the Negritos, Igorots, and Moros as lesser than indios of Malay ancestry, and on a narrative of racial migration in which Negritos and other darker races were succeeded by more civilized, physically superior Malays.[14]

At first the characterization of people in the Philippines as an assortment of uncivilized and disorganized groups or tribes with no concept or desire for nationhood was a strong premise for rationalizing the imperial presence of the United States. But as the occupation progressed and opposition to the continued holding of the islands increased, it became clear that the American public needed to be further convinced of the worthiness of the project.

The opposition between casting the Philippines and its inhabitants as being in need of civilizing tutelage and the need to not go too far, that is, to emphasize that the colonial subject was recuperable, was a dominant feature not only of the educational initiatives meant to produce model Filipina and Filipino subjects, but also of state-legitimating efforts like the census of the islands, conducted from 1903 to 1905, and the World's Fair. Paul Kramer and Vicente Rafael, for example, point to these two events as endeavors aimed at mending the fissures and cracks in reasoning behind the continued occupation of the islands.[15] The large-scale production of materials about the Philippines was connected to an interest in what Rafael calls "continuous and discrete observation," methods through which "the targets of benevolent assimilation could be identified, apprehended, and delivered for democratic tutelage" to an American public.[16] Yet Kramer argues that in many cases Americans were much more interested in Filipina and Filipino savagery than in their potential for colonial progress. To many who attended the fair in St. Louis, *Filipina* and *Filipino* were synonymous with the fascinating spectacle of Igorots or Negritos rather than with the smartly dressed officers of the Philippine Scouts.[17] These methods of visual display, colonial management, and the encyclopedic cataloguing of information served as a way of racializing Filipina and Filipino subjects.[18]

Amid the widely circulated constructions of the Philippines as needing sponsorship and tutelage, the Filipina figured as an especially intriguing puzzle. In 1900, for example, Will Levington Comfort informed the readers of the *Washington Post* that the "Filipino woman of the Tagal tribe" was "like no one else in the world." "From the white man's standpoint," he notes, the Tagal woman "is least like a woman of any feminine creature." Comfort stresses that the native woman is incomprehensible and illegible; she is "as inscrutable as a bolted door" with a "nature . . . as hard to fathom as a sheet of Chinese correspondence." He makes it clear that he is discussing an india, not "Chinese, Japanese, Eurasians, Mestizos, or half-castes, and pure Castilians" in Luzon, for "reference is not made to any of these." While women in Puerto Rico or Cuba may "thrill" a man with their "great lustrous dark eyes," in contrast, "The glance of the Filipino woman will never thrill you. Her eyes are not large, but they are black and beady and unreadable." Although the woman's native inscrutability is unnerving, Comfort's Tagal woman is especially remarkable because she returns his gaze: "Very often hunger looks out at you, often hatred, but it is not passionate hatred. It is a stare which neither revolts nor appeals. It seems to be the result of instinct rather than an action of the brain. Vaguely the thought sinks into your mind as you peer into her dull, unsmiling eyes—the thought that her gaze has been fixed so long upon the tragedy of living that she regards it stolidly now."[19]

A comparison of Comfort's description of this animal-like, incomprehensible india with another written by Marshall P. Wilder in 1905 underscores the extent to which the circulation of material about Filipinas served to repackage notions of the unreadable and unknowable native woman. Wilder's "Raising of Children Is Chief Philippine Industry," published in the *Chicago Daily Tribune*, capitalizes on the tendency to represent the Philippines as curiosity object and new, exciting possession. In its focus on motherhood, though, the article genders both the Philippines and its industry as feminine. Published shortly after the World's Fair, the article uses the terms of exhibition in a description that employs modes of intrigued observation and careful scrutiny as optical methods of control. With wonder and awe, Wilder depicts the islands and its peoples as a place of fantasy and spectacle for the male viewer:

> Yet here the life appears more unreal and fantastic than any I ever saw elsewhere. Everything looks as if arranged for exhibition, instead of being a cluster of permanent homes. The little nipa houses, almost smothered by the surrounding banana trees, seem temporary and in miniature, as if mere ornaments of the scenery. Every woman leaning from a window, cigaret [sic] in mouth, looks as if she were posing for a picture and were able to remain in her position for an hour at a time. All the sights and sounds suggest the theater and its stage settings; no one would be surprised to come upon a sign reading "For this occasion only."[20]

Wilder holds up the Philippines in its entirety for the captivated American reader, and domestic structures, the people who live in them, and nature itself collapse in a totalizing gaze that encompasses "everything" and "all the sights and sounds." This exhibition of the Philippines renders the islands both "temporary and in miniature," an array of "mere ornaments." The natural world and native peoples serve as the backdrop for a staged event, and though they threaten to overcome the scene this event is also one that might be easily swept away, as indigenous elements become fleeting and impermanent and women are merely props for portraiture, models for the viewer's entertainment.

Wilder's article is also about Filipinas as domestics, involved in the "chief industry" of child rearing. He fills his miniaturization of the Philippines with Filipinas ready to be posed and molded, an endless parade of mothers with hair "as black as the heart of a stage villain" who walk about carrying loads on their backs, so that the entire population of women appears to be, in Wilder's eyes, "like a race of hunchbacks."[21] A muddled fascination with and fear of differently raced and abled bodies slip into Wilder's language, even as he attempts to mediate these tensions through a controlling observer's gaze. Wilder's assessment, however, differs dramatically from Comfort's. The awareness of racial diversity in the Philippines—the difference between the "Native Tagal" woman and the "Chinese, Japanese, Eurasians, mestizos, or half-castes, and pure Castilians" in Luzon—has disappeared, and Wilder can categorize an entire race of women as domestic caregivers.[22]

Encapsulated by eyewitness accounts like those of Comfort and Wilder, colonial observations and displays of Filipina bodies were complemented by the production of photographic material that marveled in exceptional Filipinas who represented the possibilities of progress as administered by the United States and contrasted them with the savagery of indigenous women. These images, which often illustrated book-length volumes devoted to the Philippines and its peoples, reinforced the dividing lines between civilized and uncivilized women of the islands. Along with descriptions of life and people of the islands, Dean Worcester's well-circulated works *The Philippine Islands and Its People: A Record of Personal Observation and Experience, With a Short Summary of the More Important Facts in the History of the Archipelago* (1898, 1899) and *The Philippines Past and Present* (1914, 1921, 1930) included photographs that ostensibly captured for Americans' consumption exemplary and allegedly typical Filipina and Filipino subjects and the differences between a civilized elite and indigenous groups.[23] The images contrast refined Spanish mestizas in the Spanish-inspired *traje de mestiza* (mestiza dress) (figure 3) with Igorot and Mangyan women of the southern islands in "banana-leaf costumes" or "typical dress" (figure 4). One photograph of Bontoc Igorot women makes manifest the possibility of the indigenous woman's never-ending, uncontrollable proliferation. It features a smaller gathering in the foreground, with five women in full view and a partial view of another (see figure 4). A second group stands at an angle, extending behind and beyond those in the foreground and fading into the background. The photograph's perspective, the placement of the women, and the partially visible body presents an optical illusion in which women multiply in seemingly infinite directions. Worcester's photographs oppose the controlled, sparse domestic spaces of the elite with the living situations of those who are pre-

A TYPICAL SPANISH MESTIZA.

3. From Worcester, *The Philippines Past and Present* (1914), 939.

sumably less civilized. He marks one photograph, "A Negrito Family and Their 'House,'" with quotations to anticipate the reader's surprised reaction (figure 5). The images of elite Filipinas, by contrast, are grounded by carpeted floors and careful staging in interiors, while in the images of Igorots, Negritos, and Mangyans the natural world often becomes more than mere background.[24]

The circulation of such visuals in the United States tells a story that documents the successful end products of the civilizing process, as they feature Filipina graduates who will soon shed the confining restrictions of

BONTOC IGOROT WOMEN IN BANANA-LEAF COSTUME.

A NEGRITO FAMILY AND THEIR "HOUSE."

4. From Worcester, *The Philippines Past and Present* (1914), 570.

5. From Worcester, *The Philippines Past and Present* (1921), 192.

traditional Philippine formal wear to don the gleaming white nurse's uniform (figure 6) or, in another photo, taken by George E. Carrothers in 1910, the athletic gear of a women's Methodist hospital basketball team (figure 7). These photographs document the ready processing of transpacific Filipinas as U.S.-produced exports, and they are the representational antecedents for enduring constructions of Filipina women as ideal caregivers, a globally circulated dynamic. Like Wilder's posed and consumed women presented as a race of domestic caregivers, the women in these photographs are the visual models of imperial potential, Filipinas who have capitalized on the combination of their native capacity for care with the benefits of American educational initiatives.

Transpacific Filipina elites found themselves caught between two popular models of Filipina femininity as produced by the United States: the indigenous Filipina, inscrutable and potentially frightening yet ultimately disciplined and controlled; and an elite Filipina who might achieve her true potential through benevolent influence. Accounts of the Philippines accorded elite women this special capacity: Filipinas were thought to be more amenable to the civilizing influence of the United States than the men. In 1899 the *Chicago Daily Tribune* published "Mrs. Aguinaldo's Wardrobe" after U.S. forces captured clothing that belonged to the wife of Emilio Aguinaldo, the president of the first Philippine republic and a general in the war against the United States. "Mrs. Aguinaldo's Wardrobe" speaks to a fascination with elite Filipinas and their ability to be more civilized than the islands' men, for "whatever may be said of the Filipino men," the writer is confident that this is evidence that "the Filipino women are fully up-to-date and abreast of the times." The story bemusedly recounts the confiscation of the "twelve-barrel wardrobe," surely evidence of a woman who was "highly civilized and entirely capable of self-government."[25] The article is short and snappy, laced with the writer's mockery of the necessity of this surrender of clothing and yet also advancing an interest in possible empathy for women like Mrs. Aguinaldo. Indeed, the praise of Mrs. Aguinaldo is notable especially in light of contemporaneous representations of her husband, which drew upon racial stereotypes of African Americans—such as the character Topsy from Harriet Beecher Stowe's novel *Uncle Tom's Cabin*—to frame the Filipino leader as a feminized savage (figure 8).[26]

The remarkable prospect of a Filipina owning a "twelve-barrel wardrobe" becomes symbolic of similarities between Filipinas and American women, who might mutually long for the pleasures of "fashion bazaars,"

FILIPINA TRAINED NURSES.

This photograph shows the members of the first class to graduate from the
government training school.

6. From Worcester, *The Philippines Past and Present* (1921), 442.

7. The 1910 women's basketball team of the Mary J. Johnson Methodist
Hospital (Photo by George E. Carrothers. The Bentley Historical Library,
University of Michigan, Ann Arbor, BL003763, Box 1).

8. "Our New Topsy," a cartoon representation of Emilio Aguinaldo, *Judge*, February 11, 1899 (Picture Collection, The New York Public Library, Astor, Lenox, and Tilden Foundations).

"dainty confections," and "ravishing gowns." Mrs. Aguinaldo's "tragedy" is truly understood by "only the women" in the United States, who "will be able to sympathize fully with their stricken sister in her irreparable loss." "Each of them," the writer muses, "will hope, in her heart of hearts, that poor Mrs. Aguinaldo may have at least saved from the wreck a fall bonnet or two and a Scotch plaid walking skirt."[27]

The reasoning behind this piece ultimately presents an analogy that belittles the cause of Philippine independence and the violence and death that characterized the war. The comparison reduces these grave matters to the desire for the latest fashion trends, a pretty bonnet and a trendy skirt, even as the article satirizes the need to confiscate these items in the first place. Illuminating the flows of global capital and its consumption, "Mrs. Aguinaldo's Wardrobe" imagines an empathetic connection between elite Filipinas and white American women and stitches together the possibility of coalition woven out of the threads of fine silks and satins, fashion-forward lace and trim. This account of glamorous excess contrasts with constructions of women from the Philippines as beady-eyed, inscrutable, malformed natives or ever-working domestic laborers and recognizes the elite Filipina's difference from these other women, a distinction the Filipina might proudly display and wear just as she would European and American dress styles.[28]

The article advances more than a frivolous interest in the latest fashions: the Filipina's characterization as civilized and the potential for transpacific coalition depend not only on her capacity to imitate Western forms of femininity but also on her eager desire to imitate. Similarly, in "Tells of the Busy Filipino Woman," published in the Chicago Tribune in 1901, Laura W. Schwichtenberg reports that women of the Philippines are "anxious to be American in every way. They try to get American cloth for their dresses, wear many diamonds, import ginghams through the Chinese merchants for working costumes, and hoard American gold pieces."[29] Within a few years' time, the marvels of Filipinas' and Filipinos' capacity to learn and imitate, their "quick bright minds and retentive memories" would become "very well known," and newspapers in the United States would soon document the achievements of the remarkable students recruited to study at American institutions.[30]

The emphasis on desire fits in well with the need to showcase such assimilating educational maneuvers as evidence of American philanthropic magnanimity. The elite Filipina's desire—to emulate and become a model of femininity for others—becomes a comforting rationale that reaffirms the continued involvement of the United States in the Philippines as a project of benevolence. Presumptions about women's need to imitate and to accept the tutelage of white women would be critical to the emergence of suffrage movements across the globe, with complex results.[31] The rhetoric of the desiring colonial energizes Filipina authors' responses to the transpacific femininities constructed by articles like "Mrs. Aguinaldo's Wardrobe," as these women make new versions of the transpacific Filipina that specifically distance her from representations that would construct Filipinas as eagerly accepting and consuming Western models.

The conflicting representations of Filipinas as either uncivilized savage or willing colonial subject would be especially unsettling for elite Filipinas and for feminists like Yule, who were sympathetic to the cause of Philippine independence. Although firsthand accounts by Filipinas from the early years of the occupation were rare, a sampling of articles in American periodicals by Maria Guadalupe Quintero de Joseph and M. P. de Veyra underscores a critique of U.S.-produced constructs of Filipina femininity. In these articles, women redefined what made a Filipina. As they navigated the transition from the Spanish regime to their new place in the occupied Philippines, these Filipinas were strategic in their alignments. Although they were certainly invested in accentuating elite Filipinas' achievements, they were careful with their constructions of white American femininity and transpacific sisterhood, and they departed from a wholehearted acceptance of American influence, a narrative of benevolent assimilation, and the Filipina's ostensible role as the willing, desiring imitator. Instead, the essayists make it quite clear that Filipinas are not willing to travel a road mapped and paved for them by the West. Quintero de Joseph's and de Veyra's work, read alongside Yule's observations, complicate representations of networks between Filipinas and white women. As an alternative, these Filipina and white American authors promote a version of elite transpacific femininity that draws from what they posit as the best of multiple worlds. They reject a range of other possible models of the feminine: from the American suffragette and working woman, to representations of Asian women as exotic, mysterious, and powerless, to the popularization of native women in the Philippines as savage primitives, incapable of becoming civilized.

In addition to the dominant characterizations of women of the Philippines, Quintero de Joseph, de Veyra, and Yule contended with prevailing constructions of other women from the East, especially Orientalist notions of Japanese and Chinese women. As the United States began turning its attention further westward to Asia, the turn of the century was marked by an increased popular interest in Japan and China. Before the Russo–Japanese War (1907), which would shift attitudes toward Japan as a rising imperial power and threat to U.S. geopolitics, Americans admired that country's centuries-old culture, history of civilization, and interest in Western modernity. Curious American travelers voyaged to Japan and brought back romantic visions of Asia. The rise of Japonisme was fueled by the import of Japanese art, furniture, and objects, which graced fashionable drawing rooms of the early twentieth century, and the circulation and production of widely popular romances that capitalized on America's fascination with all things Japanese, such as John Luther Long's novella *Madame Butterfly* (1898) and the Chinese-Canadian author Onoto Watanna's (the pseudonym of Winnifred Eaton) *A Japanese Nightingale* (1901). The notion of a Japanese woman as butterfly figure—demure, fragile, naïve, swathed in exotic mystery, and easily controlled by men of the East and the West—became increasingly popular and was manifested in print and on stage.[32]

In contrast, contemporaneous attitudes toward China were dramatically different. While Americans thought of Japanese culture as being refined and civilized, China figured as savage and barbarian and was associated with teeming, uncontrollable masses. Such perceptions were fueled and exacerbated by the large numbers of Chinese laborers arriving in the United States from the mid- to late nineteenth century and the characterization of Chinatowns as sites of disease, degeneracy, and perversion.[33] Constructions of the Chinese as barbarous often emphasized their oppressive behavior toward women, embodied by the figure of the Chinese woman with bound feet.

In "The Woman Question in the Philippines" Yule diagnoses these trends, and she criticizes the ease with which Filipina women have served as figures easily manipulated by a discourse of benevolent American women's liberation of other women. "It is an impressionistic vision that the phrase 'Oriental woman' conjures up in the Westerner's mind," she observes:

> Vague figures appear in the haze, some wrapped in mysterious veils through which gleam lustrous eyes, others with pitiful "lily-feet" showing below mannish silken trouser legs, while kneeling or standing with modest mien is "Japan's most esthetic product," quaint, flower-like. Back in the deeper shadows are the half-clad barbarous creatures of Java, Borneo, the Philippines, and other out-of-the-way regions, the inhabitants of which the world has become familiar with through the "highly educative" exhibits at international expositions. These are the types that have served as an emergency magazine of rhetorical ammunition for the woman's rights platform speaker for half a century or more.[34]

Writing at the peak of American women's suffrage efforts and the corresponding international women's movement, Yule incisively highlights the encompassing "rhetorical ammunition" that relies on recurring references to Asian and Southeast Asian women as symbols of oppressed women in need of rescue, from the veiled and bound "Oriental woman" to "barbarous" peoples from Java, Borneo, and the Philippines in need of enlightenment. These women serve as metaphoric distillations of women's oppression. On exhibition as "impressionistic visions," they have become "familiar," "types" reproduced over and over again, so much so that the phrase "Oriental woman" alone is enough to evoke these images. Yule's observations critique a troubling rhetorical trend that recurs in elite Filipina feminist discourse throughout the first half of the twentieth century, one that still exists in twenty-first-century permutations that invoke a Western mandate to liberate, for example, veiled and oppressed Muslim women.[35]

As their written reflections illustrate, transpacific Filipinas traveling to or studying in the United States during the first two decades of the occupation were quite cognizant of these constructs of Asia and Asian women, and the importance of the Philippines to efforts by the United States to exert influence in Asia and the Pacific. Filipina authors were also well aware of how Asian women were employed by white suffragists in the United States. To address the push and pull of these competing representations, commentators took great care to distinguish their fellow countrywomen from Orientalized notions of Asian women as either mysterious and exotic or inhibited by savage, uncivilized cultures and in need of saving by the West.

Filipinas' responses to their comparison to disempowered Asian women were mixed. While Yule points to this phenomenon as having been produced and circulated by the West, in the early years of the twentieth century some Filipina authors, especially those who were part of the Spanish elite, participated in the valorization of the delicate Filipina as a means of differentiating themselves from white American women. In the essay "American and Filipino Women" (1905), originally published in the Philippine periodical El Renacimiento but recirculated in the American-produced The Independent, Maria Guadalupe Gutierrez Quintero de Joseph, a woman "connected with the Philippine exhibit at St. Louis," refuses to accept that American influence was beneficial.[36] If women suffragists in the United States used the figure of Filipinas and other Asian women as a metaphor for oppression, Quintero de Joseph responds with an oppositional move. Resisting notions of benevolence, she paints a frightening picture of what working women's motherhood has become in the United States, where "children take care of themselves and grow up without affection or die most frequently in their tender years, burned, asphyxiated and even poisoned, while the mother goes to the shop, the factory or the office, or, merely impelled by her adventure-seeking character, sallies forth into the street to enjoy, under one pretext or another, the rights which have been conceded to her equally with man."[37] Rather than complying with a version that would cast her as the willing and desiring imitator of American women and the grateful beneficiary of American tutelage, she emphasizes that these potential changes are "ill befitting and violent as well as unjust."[38] This frightening construction of white femininity accents Quintero de Joseph's desire to solidify the borders that separate white working-class femininity from elite Filipina formations.

The audience for El Renacimiento was the Spanish aristocracy in the Philippines, and Quintero de Joseph distinctly addresses these readers when she valorizes a Hispanophile's version of traditional Filipina modesty and dedication to their homes and families over the dangerous threat of American working women. She praises her countrywomen's "delicate qualities" (a trait she refers to multiple times), their tendency to be "timid . . . dreamer[s]" and "tender . . . being[s] of submission." For Quintero de Joseph these are the factors that set Spanish elite Filipinas apart. Objecting to Western influence because it threatens to fundamentally change and alter a woman's home life, she cautions other elite Filipinas to remain vigilant of the American desire "to make of our women faithful likenesses of its daughters, hybrid beings with all the defects and weaknesses of woman."[39]

While white working-class women pose dangerous threats to their homes and families, to women like Quintero de Joseph transpacific Filipinas can maintain an ideal balance of the modern and the traditional, the West and the East, and the American, Filipino, and Spanish. Her version of transpacific femininity promotes the evolution of a new type of Filipina, "made up from an advantageous mixture of Latinism and Saxonism."[40] Similarly, de Veyra's "The Filipino Woman" (1906) praises her subject's ability to extract the advantages of the East and the West and to purge the traits that are unnatural and too foreign.[41] Quoting from text read by a Filipino speaker "before a ladies' society in Maine," the article notes that even though "a thorough modern education" has been undoubtedly crucial to the development of new opportunities for women of the Philippines, the benefits of such an education are cultivated by women's judicious interest in retaining "the old manners of their mothers."[42] The class tensions in this passage are important, for these descriptions highlight the vexed overlap of Spanish and U.S. empires and the competing alliances between the former, old and traditional Spanish or Latin influence and the influx of new American or Saxon qualities and values.

Writing only a few years after the St. Louis World's Fair, these Filipinas were deeply conscious of comparisons between Filipina and American women and of the Western path to progress that outlined the successful imitation of femininity in the United States as a desirable destination. They were acutely aware of a reading public that was more familiar with the portrayal of the Philippines as uncivilized and ill-prepared for democratic independence. They presented a complicated, even somewhat unwieldy, version of the Filipina as transpacific for consumption in the United States. Without explicitly taking up the question of independence efforts or the continued presence of the United States in the islands, Quintero de Joseph and de Veyra responded to these issues by circulating knowledge about a different type of Filipina, a woman who is educated and refined, a woman capable of preserving qualities that are unique to Filipina femininity while at the same time carefully incorporating the benefits of new educational opportunities. Their work gave depth and complexity to the early twentieth-century Filipina and challenged the one-dimensionality of the inscrutable women remembered in periodicals, captured in black-and-white photographs, and modeled in exhibits that were crucial to the colonial regime. They sought to question the Orientalizing and totalizing gaze of U.S. empire and its reification of Filipinas even as they contested their inclusion within categorical descriptions of Asian women as oppressed and weak, irrelevant and obscure. They resisted the terms of benevolence, the plot that would write them as eager and willing subjects of assimilation to American notions of femininity, and of their manipulation and appropriation by American women.

The Rise of English Literary Nationalism in the Philippines

In manipulating fluctuating transpacific shifts and their resulting effects on the racializing of Filipina elite and indigenous bodies, Filipina essayists in the early twentieth century anticipated some of the concerns faced by women writers twenty years later, during another moment of transition for the Philippines—this time from occupied territory to commonwealth. Again, the archival byways of Philippine literature in English illustrate how print culture in the Philippines became a staging ground for debates about the future of the English-literate bourgeoisie. And again evolving imperial and national intersections prompted anxieties in the elite writer. Faced with competition from Tagalog authors and the prospect of Tagalog becoming one of the commonwealth's new national languages, Filipino authors began fiercely championing the importance of English literature and claiming their place as architects of literary nationalism, often at the expense of Filipina writers, who were excluded from these debates.

The crossing of literary nationalism, imperial changeovers, and the gendered publishing climate would have front-page currency in a leading periodical that was itself a form of midway, the *Herald Mid-Week Magazine*. In an issue from January 1941, Leopoldo Yabes, a scholar of Philippine literature in English, found himself under attack. On the front page of the magazine Yabes was labeled a woman-hater for his dismissal of Filipina authors' failed productivity. The article, entitled "What Is Wrong with Our Women Writers?" did not mince words: "One can hardly expect anything worthwhile, anything vital and significant from the pens of women writers who are at the same time social climbers, sophisticates, pedants, and prudes."[43] Yabes defended himself in print, and the resulting back-and-forth rejoinders between Filipina and Filipino authors were splashed on the magazine's front pages and featured responses made by the leading periodical contributors of the day.

To be sure, the print conversation was evocative of similar debates in other national literary traditions, those that pitted the rise of female authorship against an entrenched faction of men. But the situation in the Philippines was markedly different. It represented the existence of a critical mass of English writers in the Philippines, a group that had grown from the first contributors trying their hand at literature in a new language in the 1920s to the steady rise of vibrant literary production, propelled by men and women who formed their own literary associations and coalesced into diverse camps. It intersected with the political climate at large, since the Philippine commonwealth was only about five years into its transition from U.S.-occupied territory to republic, and authors were using this occasion to meditate on the past, present, and future of English literature in the nation. It spoke to recent developments in the political climate for women (Filipinas had gained suffrage only a few years earlier in 1937) and to accompanying anxieties over the role of women in the commonwealth. And even though it represented the culmination of several decades of development in English literature, in the end the controversy was a moment that would soon be swept away, upstaged by more pressing concerns. In December 1941 the Pacific War arrived in the Philippines. The Japanese occupation began shortly thereafter, bringing with it the destruction and closure of many of the English-language periodicals and the restriction of literary production in English because of its ties to the West.

The Yabes controversy is a useful touchstone, for it charts several unrecognized connections between English literary production, transpacific relations, and the codification of an English-literate Filipina and Filipino elite. Faced with the prospect that the importance of English would wane after the end of the commonwealth period, male authors clung to their position as the builders of a national literature. Their efforts only exacerbated the gendered divide in the publishing world of Manila, as the contributions of women writers were eclipsed by debates over which male school of writing should claim the title of nationalist literature. These fissures emerge in what became an increasingly contentious debate among the English literati of the city, one that was ostensibly about aesthetics over politics. Yet these conversations were also informed by significant shifts in class hierarchy and by male elite nationalists' attempts to reinforce their position in a climate in which the very production of English literature was itself in question. Filipina authors responded to this intersection of politics and publishing through the construction of transpacific femininities, not only in the active defense of their craft in the periodical press, but also through the formation of communities of writers beyond the circle of men.

As the United States and the Philippines moved toward a formal recognition of independence, the 1930s and 1940s were especially difficult for the country's authors. Politicians and scholars vehemently debated the role English would play in an independent Philippines. One of the first tasks faced by the commonwealth administration was to settle the question of the new government's official languages, a debate that is unresolved even today. "The Philippines does not have a national language," observes Rafael. "Instead, it has a history of state and elite *attempts* to institute a national language based on Tagalog in the face of the persistence of a linguistic hierarchy, where the last colonial language, English, continues to be hegemonic."[44] In the 1930s the task at hand was challenging and complicated not only by the use of different colonial languages (Spanish and English), but also by the many other languages and dialects regularly used by the Philippine population. Many upper-class people, even in the first few decades of the twentieth century, still spoke Spanish, and government proceedings were often conducted in both Spanish and English. Yet it soon became evident that the new commonwealth government needed to recognize the importance of one of the indigenous languages.

In 1936 the administration, complying with a constitutional mandate, created the Institute of National Language, which was charged with the task of selecting and justifying which of the Philippine languages should become the basis for an official language.[45] The next year the institute recommended Tagalog. The choice of Tagalog over the other Philippine languages in part stemmed from a long history of privileging Filipinas and Filipinos from the Tagalog-speaking regions, a practice that began in the days of Spanish rule and continued into the American regime. Tagalog was the most commonly used Philippine language in Manila, which functioned as the government's center. After President Quezon approved the decision, a dictionary was printed, and in 1940 public and private schools began teaching Tagalog. In June 1940 legislation was passed to declare Tagalog one of the country's official languages, to take effect on July 4, 1946.[46]

With the government's recognition of Tagalog, Filipino authors became increasingly invested in defending the continued relevance of literary production in English. At first the debate over national language in the Philippines galvanized authors of English literature. They navigated a slippery slope, for justifying the importance of Philippine literature in English was dangerously close to accepting the legitimacy of U.S. rule. Filipino politicians immediately questioned the prospect that English might continue as the primary medium of instruction and government. Some nationalists during the commonwealth period returned consistently to the argument that Philippine literature in English was merely imitative of its European and American forebears. In response, authors quickly rallied to claim the crucial place of English literature in Philippine culture. The 1930s saw the beginnings of concerted efforts to anthologize notable works of Philippine literature in English and, for the first time, to narrate its literary history.[47] The construction of the English literary tradition coincided with the establishment of literary societies, lists of notable fiction, and awards so writers might promote one another's work and legitimize the field.[48]

But the issue was greater than the question of readership, and the ensuing debate in print reinforced the lines that divided an intelligentsia from what they saw as uninformed, uncaring masses. Between 1939 and 1940 the *Herald Mid-Week Magazine* published a series of articles that illustrates the dilemma of the Filipino English author. In the defense of their craft, Filipinos had to begrudgingly acknowledge that, compared to the popularity of Tagalog publications, the market for literature in English was relatively small. Articles with titles such as "Writers without Readers" (1939) and "Filipinos Do Not

Buy Books" (1940) bemoan the lack of readership in Manila.[49] Some writers criticized upper-class Manilans who had the economic means to purchase works of literature yet chose not to do so. According to Yabes's "Filipinos Do Not Buy Books," cash flow alone did not drive the lack of reading culture in the Philippines. While he admits that many of the nation's citizens do not have the money to spend on books or subscriptions to magazines and literary periodicals, he excoriates the nation's richest, who "have not developed to any respectable degree the book and periodical buying and reading habit . . . [while] the middle class families—particularly those in the lower and middle substrata—are well read and informed and own decent home libraries."[50] Yabes reveals the unnerving notion that a lower- and middle-class family would cultivate better reading practices than the elite. The elite family's empty shelves mark the disintegration in class hierarchy, an erosion that promises to continue with the prospect of an increased interest in Tagalog.

While critics like Yabes located the source of low readership in the readers, others were more alarmed by the possibility that Filipino authors of English literature were failing to address the concerns of an audience that might turn from halfheartedly flipping through pages printed in English to voraciously consuming publications in Tagalog. Now that Tagalog was recognized as an official language, English writers experienced a nagging sense that the literature they were producing was disconnected from the socioeconomic realities of life in the Philippines. A. B. Rotor's "Writers without Readers," for example, contends that the elitist literature produced by English-language writers was in danger of being eclipsed by so-called popular literature published by Tagalog periodicals such as *Liwayway*. He sharply criticizes the Filipino writer for being too imitative of British and American models and exhorts his colleagues to move beyond their own privileged circles to write for the average reader. Rotor's scourging assessment blames the elite writer's separation from the masses: "They feel that they should write for themselves alone and those who can understand them. They have completely lost touch with and forgotten the great mass who had never gotten much beyond the *Saturday Evening Post*."[51]

The conflict reached a critical point in 1939, the year President Quezon and the Philippine Writers' League, headed by Salvador P. Lopez, announced the creation of the first Commonwealth Literary Awards, modeled after such honors as the Pulitzer Prize and meant to promote the literary achievements of writers in English, Spanish, and Tagalog.[52] In the end what was at stake was more than the recognition and stipend that came with the awards. The creation of the Commonwealth Literary Awards was a nationalist venture; and the leadership of the league felt charged with the weighty responsibility of both reinvigorating English literature and compelling their colleagues to renew their commitment to Philippine citizens. Acutely aware of their uncomfortable positions as members of the male authorial elite, league members like Lopez and Rotor hoped to reorient the critical stakes of Philippine literature in English as a means of claiming that the future of the nation demanded it. In their minds, "all writers worth the name are, whether they like it or not, workers in the building up of culture. Since economic injustice and political oppression are the enemies of culture, it becomes the clear duty of the writer to lend his arm to the struggle against injustice and oppression in every form in order to preserve those cultural values which generations of writers before him have built up with slow and painful effort."[53] For Rotor and Lopez, however, espousing this position was not easy. To promote a new social consciousness in their fellow writers, the league's rules for the Commonwealth Literary Awards targeted authors who incorporated what they called native features in their work.

Tensions soon arose between two groups of writers, one that championed the importance of aesthetics and literature as art and one, led by Rotor's and Lopez's group, which encouraged literature devoted to the interests of the Philippines and its masses. More than mere quibbles over aesthetics versus content, these discussions articulate the desires of male authors who, like Rotor, found their membership in an English literary elite troubling. The simmering discontent between the two camps boiled over with the publication in the *Herald Mid-Week Magazine* of Rotor's article "Our Literary Heritage" (April 10, 1940). Here, Rotor scolds authors who have failed to become actively involved in the nation's development. His entreaties speak to his awareness of the elite's potential separation from those they called the masses and the correspondence between the promotion of literature in English and the codification of an English-literate bourgeoisie. "At this moment in our history when everyone is working for a common end," he implores, "for the writer to remain aloof is for him to turn false to those very ideals about which he writes so easily. The designation 'writer' should be interpreted as a mandate to join forces with the other workers, not an excuse to shirk responsibility."[54]

Rotor encourages his fellow authors to depart from the realm of mere metaphor, to turn their eyes and pens away from the "star-studded tropical sky" to the grim realities on the ground: "Our next door neighbor . . . why it is that he has been unemployed for one year, why it is that he who has so little has to pay so much for rent, clothes and food; how it is that his sick child goes untreated when in the same block there are three physicians who do not have enough patients." Attuned to his audience and their probable responses, Rotor encourages them to address their myopic insularity, to forego their preoccupation with "literary cults and cliques" and spend a "little more time reading up on the economic paradoxes of the century, the conflict between the different ideologies, the march of progress in the other lines of human effort."[55]

The league's sponsorship of the awards prompted other Filipino writers to accuse Lopez and the organization of opening the literary world to politically motivated patronage of the arts. In response to Rotor's manifesto, authors divided according to their assumptions about the purposes of literature. Rotor, Lopez, and others defended the importance of work that would ostensibly facilitate readers' social and political edification, while others, like Jose Garcia Villa, championed the importance of aesthetic innovation above all else.[56] Authors on both sides became more and more defensive. In discussing the merits and pitfalls of the English literary tradition, guest columnists frequently taunted each other. The highly personal stakes of the conversation prompted one author to describe it as more of a "vigorous clash of personalities" than a professional disagreement over different approaches to literature.[57]

These conflicts contributed to persistent classed divisions between English literature and other literatures of the Philippines. Especially troubling, tensions between authors writing in English and in Tagalog unfortunately led to a lasting hierarchy of Filipina and Filipino languages and their literary traditions. Resil B. Mojares observes that in the 1920s a critical separation emerged between " 'high' and 'low' literature, between 'popular' and 'artistic' writing, between what at a later time would be called *pambakya* and *pampanitikan*." Although the alignment of so-called vernacular literature with pambakya and of English-language literature with pampanitikan does "not fully represent the actual situation," it does "indicate something of the unhealthy nature of this split."[58] But even the literal definition of these terms illuminates their classist dimensions. Pambakya stems from the Tagalog root word *bakya*, meaning wooden clogs or shoes. The prefix *pam-* denotes instrumentality; pambakya literally translates to "for those who wear wooden shoes," implying those in lower social classes. In contrast, the root *panitik* translates to "the ability to write," and *panitikan* means "literature": pampanitikan connotes the literate and the literary world. Not surprisingly, "among Tagalog writers," contends Bienvenido Lumbera, "there exists the resentment—not quite open maybe but nevertheless there—that their English-using colleagues regard them as poor relations. Even among readers supposedly sophisticated, the prejudice against writers in the vernacular is quite evident."[59] The widening gap between English and Tagalog contributed to a growing class divide, for "the rise of English as the language of the new intelligentsia, coupled with an education almost exclusively permeated with *sajonismo* (a liking for what is Anglo-Saxon), led to a cultural alienation that was to have far-reaching effects. The vernacular literatures dropped down the cultural scale, and almost always from the view of the new urban-oriented, university educated generation."[60] The long history of these classed divisions, which continue to structure the perception of literature in the Philippines, underscores the extent to which print culture was, and still is, a crucial midpoint of literary history and nationalist imagining. As we shall see, these intersections eventually informed the divide between Filipino and Filipina writers.

Transpacific Filipina Authors and the Borders of the Publishing World

The vehement conflict between an increasingly anxious group of male authors, worried over the importance of their craft in the face of competition by Tagalog publications, worsened the already difficult publishing environment for women, who were largely excluded from the debate. Indeed, the English literati's focus on aesthetics over politics and form versus content was closely linked to the question of *who* was authorized to produce national literature. If many male Filipino authors struggled to retain their importance in the midst of the transition from the occupation to the commonwealth, so did their female colleagues. Arguments about Philippine literature in English and its nationalist connections took on an even more contentious cast when it came to comparisons of Filipina versus Filipino authorship. Even though women were early producers of literature in English and despite the acknowledgment that a remarkable and exceptional few received, most Filipina authors faced pressing difficulties in garnering literary reception and recognition. Women writers turned to multivalent strategies to respond to the gendered elitism of Manila's publishing world. When their male colleagues questioned Filipina authors' productivity and the quality of their publications, women were neither silent nor complacent, staunchly defending their work and critiquing Filipino-authored literature. Their texts build on the efforts of Filipinas who published essays in the United States during the early part of the twentieth century, for women authors in the late 1930s and early 1940s also countered representations that attempted to contain and limit Filipinas. Their responses to the publishing world, however, also went beyond the bounds of printed ink on a page, as they formed alternative communities with other women writers to counter their exclusion from the fraternities of elite male literary nationalism.

Tensions between men and women writers found public airing in the pages of newspapers and periodicals. On May 9, 1935, the *Graphic* published an article that surveyed Filipino authors' opinions regarding the role of women writers in the literary field. Beginning with the observation that "literature, aside from other fields, has been invaded by women," Anatolio Litonjua concludes that Filipino writers ultimately "don't find cause for worry, the opinion of fascinated feminists notwithstanding." Even though women were active in writers' associations and contributed regularly to the same periodicals their male counterparts published in, Filipino authors saw themselves as the field's leaders. Refusing to be influenced by the opinions of the Filipino who is a "feminist first before he is a critic," Lopez, the same writer who had promoted literature's value as a vehicle to promote social change, was dismissive. "Will women dominate local literature?" he muses. "I don't think the question should even be raised at all. . . . Don't you see that in order to attain that dominant position the women will have to ride rough-shod over the bodies of so many capable and outstanding male writers? It is not so much that I doubt whether the women can do this, but whether the men will willingly submit to this indignity." The presumptions about women's capacity were deeply influenced by a desire to thwart the emergence of women into the profession by constructing Filipinas, in the words of Hilarion Vibal, as "light" and without "depth of thoughts," "helpless" and "tender," and "not possessing the power to be great."[61]

In January and February 1941 the discussion moved to the front pages of the *Herald Mid-Week Magazine*. A series of articles stretched the parameters of the debate to elaborate on the larger cultural threat represented by the figure of the woman writer.[62] These Filipino authors ultimately responded to a phenomenon that extended beyond their exclusive literary circle, as women graduated from universities and began to alter the demographics of the professions in Manila. In "What Is Wrong with Our Women Writers?" Yabes responds to the charge that he is a "woman-hater." Although he purports to be "no misogynist," he matter-of-factly dismisses his female colleagues. He details each class of woman writer at length, but he is most disturbed by those he calls the pedants, the Filipinas who are so intellectual that they "are as out of place in any order founded on human relationships . . . as a porker in a drawing room." This observation contradicts Yabes's earlier critique of Filipinas as gossipy and flighty, women who spend their time in "meetings [that] consist mainly of shop and drawing room talk."[63]

Yabes's criticisms focus not only on the literature produced by women, but also on a career woman's aberrant transpacific femininity, her crossing of professional and social boundaries. The debates of 1941 over the worthiness of Filipina authors dovetailed with the aftermath of women's movements in the Philippines and the 1937 act that granted suffrage to Filipinas. During this period, print and public discourse also centered on developments in transpacific Filipina femininity, altered by contact with the West (see chapter 2). Yabes's use of "at the same time" is telling; it's not just that women are producing literature, but that they are also educated, sophisticated, and rising in the Philippine social scale. His assessments are full of contradictions; according to Yabes, women are love-crazed and unable to concentrate, but they are also "prudes." Yabes's rejection of Filipina authors' potential speaks to a larger concern with transpacific Filipinas who stepped beyond the bounds of proper elite Filipina femininity. This scathing critique echoes the broad cultural anxieties over university women, the increasing numbers of Filipinas entering the workforce, and the spread of pop cultural forms produced or inspired by the United States, which were seen as threatening influences on women.

Authors such as Lydia Arguilla and Maria Luna Lopez (Salvador Lopez's wife) were quick to follow with their own retort. Their jointly authored article "Our Men Writers Are Not So Hot" takes Yabes to task for his failure to recognize his contradictory impulses and his refusal to acknowledge the gendered literary environment and the limitations that the publishing market imposed on women's production. "Women writers," Arguilla and Lopez complain, "have so long been the butt of masculine contempt and its twin, humiliating tolerance, that they cannot help being just a little apologetic for presuming to write." They bemoan a literary world in which male editors treat Filipina newspaper reporters with condescension: "Once in a while [Filipina writers] may be allowed to ghost-write messages for the Mother's Day supplement or the Xmas issue or to pump men on their ideas of the Ideal

Woman or the Dream Home. [. . .] but most of the time they stay in their little niche, getting stale and yet more stale, unhonored, and certainly unsung."[64] Arguilla and Lopez then answer Yabes by naming noteworthy male authors (including Arguilla's husband, Manuel) and exposing their lack of productivity and stagnation.

Filipina responses to the inequities of the publishing world went beyond the printed page. Women relied on close, intimate networks to counter the fraternity of nationalist authors. Ligaya Victorio (Reyes) Fruto fondly remembers this sisterhood in the essay "The Porch," published in her collection of short fiction and essays titled *Yesterday and Other Stories* (1969). Fruto's essay is a nostalgic tribute to Manuel and Lydia Arguilla, who provided a gathering place for authors in the years before the Pacific War. "The Porch" is shadowed by tragedy: Manuel, one of the Philippines' early literary prodigies, was captured and murdered by Japanese forces. Much of the essay presents the Arguillas' home and the world of authors in terms far different from the heated climate portrayed in the pages of the *Graphic* and the *Herald Mid-Week Magazine*. Read against the background of this earlier opposition, however, "The Porch" illuminates the complexities of the essay. Despite Fruto's romanticized reconstruction of the literary circle of Manila as a tightly knit clan whose members were "tolerant of beginnings" and had no "cutting jealousies," the essay brings to the surface the lingering resonances from the 1930s and 1940s portrayals of women's literary efforts as inferior and unremarkable.[65]

The essay's central metaphor is both a liminal space and a "gateway." In the opening paragraphs Fruto points to the porch as a midway, an in-between, uncertain site where oppositions meet. "It wasn't a porch, really," she admits. "Just a bit of zinc roof that jutted beyond the eaves that shaded a rectangle of mosaic-tiled floor." Having a roof of an "indeterminate shade of red" and a floor that is "a sober combination of black and white," the porch is home to potted plants that both "flowered or withered," a site where one might be either nurtured or inhibited. Yet Fruto and others nevertheless remember the porch as the "best of the parts of that lovely house," a home filled with the pleasures of cozy "living room nooks," "good crystal and china" in the large dining room," and a master bedroom that is a "book-lined sanctuary." The emphasis on indeterminacy prefaces the conflicts that arise in relations between male and female authors in the house.[66]

These tensions—what Fruto calls "just little pangs of envy sublimated in the objective appraisal of each other's work and capability"—crop up gradually in the essay. According to Fruto, the porch offered a refuge from the difficulties of the world beyond its steps; the porch was a space of quiet and solace, "with no one to break the emptiness and the silence that were panacea for a fatigued mind and bruised spirit." More importantly, the porch was a meeting place for women. These gatherings took place in the shadow of competition from their male colleagues. When Lydia Arguilla and Fruto meet to talk "desultorily," Manuel is a flurry of purposeful, productive activity. "Furiously clacking" away, he is always in the background, "hammering out a story on his typewriter, shaping it to his will. We ignored his energy." "Sometimes," Fruto remembers, "Manuel, in sly tribute to our literary pretensions, would buy some quiet by passing to us sheets of polished prose, and we, the vainest of editors, would go over lines that needed no changing, and called for no comment." Manuel's proliferation is always present: his typewriter figures as the soundtrack to the presumed comparative frivolity of the women's conversations, and he effortlessly turns out perfectly composed sentences while they, with minds "fatigued" and spirits "bruised," can only dream of success. Fruto returns again and again to her claim that the women can breezily ignore Manuel's criticism: "Once in desperate irritation, he had taken down our conversation verbatim, and he was appalled—or so he informed us—at the extreme banality of our way of thinking. This slid off our subconscious without the merest prick." But despite her insistence that such dismissals are without consequence and her confident belief in "the inefficacy of male opinion," the repetition of these small moments indicates they are not quite so easy to shrug off.[67]

Even though the divisions of the publishing world are present in the Arguillas' home, Fruto fondly remembers the porch as a haven for women. She reconstructs these experiences as happy and intimate ones, and the women establish a space in which, for a little while, at least, they can escape the confines of the predictable and be assured that their interest in their lives as mothers and wives does not necessarily detract from their potential as authors:

> There were times when what looked like women writers' social hours took a place on that porch. There we would be, a group of writing hens, busily scratching with our tongues around the edges of our little world. Our topics were not on the cosmic or the profound. Ungracefully at ease in wood or canvas chairs, or seated more or less primly on the two steps which led to the living room, Lyd [Arguilla] and I, the two Marias, Lina

[Flor], Luz, Estrella [Alfon], and, occasionally, Choling [Carmen Guerrero Nakpil] and Yay [Panlilio] would happily forget that we earned our living— mostly—by pecking at ancient typewriters and talk like women interested in women, men and children. Our laughter was free, our thoughts and words leaping from one predictable subject to an unpredictable one. In those moments we were girls again, basking in oneness with our kind before man entered the arena of our dreaming.[68]

The opposition between idyllic gathering and conflict in "The Porch" echoes the terms of the debate that divided Filipina and Filipino authors during the prewar years. Representative of the essay as a whole, the passage is rife with tension. Although Fruto ostensibly presents the porch as a sanctuary where Filipina writers can claim their experience as girls, women, and mothers to be important and valuable to literary production, any comfort and happiness is fraught and tenuous. The women are "at ease" yet "ungracefully so." Still, Fruto's nostalgic rendering of the porch testifies to the value of communities of Filipina authors, who attempted to find comfort in each other to offset the difficulties of making a living as writers in Manila.

Yesterday and Other Stories was introduced by Salvador P. Lopez, who in 1935 staunchly asserted he was not a feminist and could not be expected to "ecstasize on the literary future of the women."[69] In hindsight Lopez remembers the period as one characterized not by women's inadequacies but by their notable contributions to literature. "The new literature in English," he proclaims, "was distinguished among other things by the fact that several women were contributing to it—a radical departure from the previous cultural era. This literature was . . . marked by the acquisition of new rights by the Filipinos including the liberation of women from the restrictive monastic conventions of their Spanish past. The political emancipation of the Filipino woman had far reaching cultural implications, the most important of these being the exercise of the right of self-expression. The new literature was, in a sense, an offshoot of the new political freedom."[70]

Like "The Porch," Lopez's introduction to Fruto's collection is tinged with postwar nostalgia. The trauma of the Pacific War and the Japanese occupation recalibrated how authors remembered their interactions in the years before the war and abruptly interrupted the self-reflexive conversations about the place of Philippine literature in English. From 1942 to 1945 Japanese officials promoted strategies of linguistic restriction and manipulation that both echoed and extended those practiced by the Spanish and U.S.

regimes. Japanese officials not only encouraged the production of literature in Tagalog and other local languages, but also undertook such extreme measures as the large-scale destruction of printed materials in English. During the occupation many English-language periodicals closed or experienced periods of interruption, either because their offices and printing presses were destroyed during the bombing of Manila in December 1941 or because of the difficulties of producing newspapers that conformed to Japanese restrictions. English writers found themselves again in a compromised position. Some began publishing in other Filipino languages, others gave up writing altogether, and still others wrote in defiance of the Japanese restrictions on press freedoms. Although English literary production resurged in the decades after the war, the destruction of the archive continued to present scholarly challenges, especially during the occupation itself.

As in the case of the dismissal of Tagalog works as the literature of the masses, elite Filipinos' criticism of women writers and their work for being less productive and unworthy of publication had lasting effects on the narration of Philippine literary history. Despite frequent publication by Filipinas even in the early days of Philippine literature in English and their identification as rising stars by literary scholars (including Yabes, who became an anthology editor), many of them remained unknown until the recovery efforts of Thelma Kintanar, Edna Zapanta Manlapaz, Cristina Pantoja Hidalgo, and Soledad Reyes.[71] As a result, the list of writers of Philippine literature in English who form the canon—Manuel Arguilla, Bienvenido N. Santos, Nick Joaquin, Carlos Bulosan, N. V. M. Gonzales—does not include the names of women who were also productive at this time: Lydia Arguilla, Estrella Alfon, Ligaya Victorio Reyes Fruto, Felicidad Ocampo, and Yay Panlilio.

Class divisions between English and Tagalog writers and the gendered dynamics that influenced the publishing world of Manila are just two examples of the English literary elite's connection to broader efforts to create and maintain divisions between a Filipina and Filipino bourgeoisie enfranchised in part through their involvement, directly or indirectly, with the U.S. administration and those who were positioned beyond or outside of this privileged circle. While the rise of a new kind of Filipina femininity posed a threat to Filipinos in power, at the same time, elite Filipinas became involved in efforts to ensure their inclusion in discussions about developments in the Philippines and its national literature. As illustrated by the earliest essays written by Filipinas during the occupation and by the difficult position of women writers in literary circles, Filipinas responded to repeated attempts to contain transpacific Filipina femininity. These women formed fragile, charged alliances, with each other and with white American women. Imagining winding and often rocky paths toward opposition and resistance, Filipina authors insisted on their right to make and remake transpacific, elite Filipina identity.

Chapter Two

NATIONALISM, MODERNITY, AND FEMINISM'S
HAUNTED INTERSECTIONS

In October 1934 the proceedings at the Philippine Constitutional Convention took an unusual turn. After the successful passage of the Tydings-McDuffie Act, the Philippine commonwealth was scheduled to be formally inaugurated within a few months, and representatives at the convention spent long hours hammering out the details of the new constitution. On December 7, 1933, the ninth Philippine legislature had voted in favor of women's suffrage, set to take effect in 1935. Despite this mandate, delegates at the convention were much more hesitant. They spent days fiercely bickering over whether or not the Filipina vote should be included in the constitution. Observed by Filipina suffragists, who were prohibited from taking the floor during the proceedings, these men turned to examples from recent politics, the international feminist movement, and Philippine, U.S., and world history in making their passionate, eloquent pleas for and against the women's vote.[1] They named pathbreaking female rulers from across the globe, including Queen Victoria, Catherine the Great, and their own Princess Urduja.[2]

The debate over women's suffrage, however, was haunted by a recurring debate over four iconic Filipinas. The most recognizable was a nineteenth-century literary character turned formidable cultural figure, José Rizal's Maria Clara, the heroine of *Noli Me Tangere* (1887). By this time, Maria Clara had become synonymous with the attributes of traditional Filipina femininity, including virtuousness, dutifulness, and subservience; as one delegate argued, "[Such] sweet, delicate qualities of our women . . . find their beauty, glory and accomplishments in the person of Maria Clara."[3] Maria Clara's greatest competitor was the coed, the embodiment of a new Filipina altered by the Philippines' contact with the West. But Maria Clara's qualities were revised and recycled in romanticized versions of the precolonial, indigenous Malay woman and the barrio girl of the provinces, women who were pitched as the coed's opposites because they were immune to the polluting effects of Western influence. In debates over what made, or would make, a new Filipina, the woman who would be a citizen of a future, independent Philippines, elite Filipinas and Filipinos strove to define a national identity that was influenced by, yet ultimately independent of, the West. Adored, reviled, and revised, these competing representatives testify to the tremendous importance and instability attached to Filipina femininity in the 1930s, a period during which literary and cultural representation, nationalism, and feminism were constantly yoked together in policy and in print.

Using the context of the women's suffrage debates of the 1930s as a turning point, this chapter analyzes the varied responses—in literature, newspaper and periodical discourse, conduct manuals, and political proceedings—to the growing controversy over Maria Clara's significance (or, for some, irrelevance) amid the rise of the university-educated, Western-influenced, transpacific Filipina coed and corresponding idealizations of the precolonial Malay woman and the barrio girl.[4] The constitutional convention and women's suffrage debates served as prime settings for the airing of concerns about the Filipina's future as tied to the fate of an independent Philippines, but discussions about the transpacific Filipina's role in the commonwealth extended well beyond this arena. I argue that the 1930s saw a drawing of new lines of gendered, raced, classed, and sexed national identity in the Philippines, as elites attempted to control the terms of bourgeois, heterosexual Filipina femininity. Such versions of Filipina femininity—transpacific Filipinas and responses to threatening phantoms of transpacific women—circulate in Manila and are recurring subjects that haunt literary and cultural representation throughout the twentieth century. Certainly, they illustrate the importance of Filipina femininity to the overarching discussion of definitions of the Philippine nation at this time. Crystallized by the direct connection between the development of a new constitution and the debate over the women's vote, the ties that bound Filipinas to the nation extended well beyond such political wranglings. Conversations about these Filipinas underscore the uncertainties surrounding what it meant to be Filipina during this period and the corresponding endeavors of the elite to identify such instability as the hallmark of progressive modernity, while, on the other hand, expressing a need to rein in and control the terms of bourgeois Filipina femininity as crucial to successful national definition.

Although Maria Clara was symbolic of a certain type of Filipina femininity, the intense verbal sparring at the convention reveals that what, exactly, she signified was quite difficult to pin down. The instability stems in part from her original characterization in Rizal's novel: she was fantastic—in my analysis defined as a mixture of the "fabulous, imaginary, [and] unreal"—an apparition produced to serve multiple purposes, a woman who appeals to other characters in the novel because of her disconcerting and extraordinary mestiza beauty.[5] Although they are fascinated with Maria Clara, her status is unsettled by a horrible secret: she is the illegitimate daughter of a friar and tied to the hypocrisy of Spanish rule, and her character is thus haunted by narrative uncertainty. Later iterations of Maria Clara would bear the ghostly traces of the fantastic attached to Rizal's original. For some, she represented everything a Filipina should be: modest and chaste, loyal and servile. For others, she was the epitome of a dying tradition, symbolic of the shackles of Spanish Catholic rule, now broken by women's access to education and the rising numbers of Filipinas in the workforce, in the arts and sciences, and in academia. Another group contended that the meaning of Maria Clara herself had evolved, and Filipinas were already remaking her image in newer, modern versions, combinations of Filipina modest virtue with new women's liberated resolve.

Maria Clara's importance was enhanced by the fervor surrounding her counterpart and opposite, the transpacific Filipina coed, and the larger cultural shifts she represented. Three decades of occupation by the United States had fundamentally altered the educational and professional landscape for many Filipinas. During this period, rapidly increasing numbers of women matriculated through the new public education system, went on to graduate and professional school, and entered a wide range of careers.[6] While many hailed these developments as the long-awaited dawn of a new era, others thought they were among the many damaging effects of contact with the United States, especially on Filipina morality. The delegates at the constitutional convention, for example, were often sidetracked from the immediate question of women's voting rights to musings about Filipina morality and its consequences for the nation's future. Many claimed that because Filipina mothers would raise and guide future generations of citizens, the inclusion of women's suffrage promised to have irreversible ramifications in regard to the composition of the commonwealth and, eventually, of the nation. Enfranchising women, some held, could warp the fabric of Philippine life, for virtuous yet impressionable Filipinas would inevitably be sullied by their exposure to the grit and grime of politics. The coed soon was in the eye of this storm, as she began to signify dangerous influences and their repercussions: the import of jazz, ragtime, and Hollywood movies and the contagion of young Filipina coeds imitating what they read in magazine pages and saw on the screen. The suffrage movement intersected with multiple complex, contradictory attempts to manage Filipina sexuality. Demands were made for formal investigations of female coeds' supposedly immoral behavior in the dormitories of the University of the Philippines, and calls went up for the containment of lower-class women's sexual transgressions through the creation of a new red light district, an initiative that was supported by some of the most vocal women in the suffrage movement.[7]

In response to the coed's threatening presence and to mounting preoccupations over the sullying of Filipina morality, elite Filipinos turned to Maria Clara, extracted her idealized traits, and transferred them to the barrio girl and the Malay woman, who were ostensibly immune from the inimical dangers of urban and colonial spaces and the corruptions of the West engendered by imperialism. Allusions to this pair grounded the arguments for and against women's suffrage. Idealized illusions of the Malay woman and barrio girl were used by some to valorize a state of indigenous equality and by others to lament the loss of the traditional purity and subservience embodied by Maria Clara and warped by women's contact with urban life and American popular culture. Filipinas' and Filipinos' romanticization of women of the past and of marginalized women of the present reflects a nationalist desire to separate themselves from the residual effects of Western empire. But the romantic allure attached to these women masks an unacknowledged and self-serving motive, especially because the nationalist future envisioned by the elite excluded lower-class people and indigenous groups still living in the Philippines. As Vicente Rafael has documented, the elite, many of them urban *mestizos*, were firmly ensconced in the U.S. regime "through municipal and national offices, inclusion in the civil service, and by the 1930s, control over the entire legislative apparatus and parts of the executive and judicial branches of the government." These men "managed to monopolize the symbolic resources for imagining nationhood. Indeed, they came to regard themselves not only as a ruling class with common interests to defend but as the exclusive spokespeople for the rest of the nation."[8] Elite Filipinos were invested in reinforcing their power in the new commonwealth government. The barrio girl and the Malay woman served as rhetorical points in a debate that was really about the elite community's fight over who would define the terms of national identity, the future of the nation, and where and how the Filipina would fit into these structures.

The reappearances of these four representative women and the instability regarding what they signify are manifestations of the sprawl of empire, the ghostly traces of the imperial that reach back to the past, linger in the present, and promise to return in the future. As Rafael, Benedict Anderson, and Ann Laura Stoler have argued, empire is characterized by the spectral, the tendency of imperial legacies to haunt both colonizer and colonized.[9] Drawing upon these meditations on how empire haunts, I uncover "the familiar, strange, and unarticulated ways" in which the specters of nationalism, empire, and feminism intersect in the Philippines of the 1930s.[10] "To haunt," writes Stoler, analyzing the term's inherent multiplicity, "is 'to frequent, resort to, be familiar with,' to bear a threatening presence, to invisibly occupy, to take on changing form."[11] But the verb form of *haunt* is also "to use or employ habitually or frequently."[12] To haunt is very different from being haunted; while one can distinguish one from the other grammatically (active versus passive verb constructions), theoretically one might see the disparity between the two as rooted in will, agency, or power. Both colonizer and colonized can haunt and be haunted, and the distinction is not always easily separable. To take the example of the United States and the Philippines as a starting point, the U.S. occupation and its legacy continue to haunt the Philippines; these ghosts are manifested in the neocolonial capitalist expansion in the islands and in the continued military relationship between the two countries. But the Philippines and its colonization by the United States also haunts the United States as an often-unacknowledged absence in American public memory.[13]

Finally, haunting encompasses notions of liminality in space and time, a neither here-nor-there, neither then-nor-now. It implies overlap, the impossibility of separating one realm from the other or, in the case of the Philippines, the continually imbricated histories of this nation with those of Spain, the United States, and Japan. Elites battled with the material and ideological ghosts of what Tani E. Barlow calls "colonial modernity," a dialectical term that "accents . . . modernity's essential doubleness, for modernity and colonial or imperialist projects are in material fact inextricable."[14] Colonial modernity's integral doubleness recognizes that the rhetoric of the modern was used both to reinforce hegemony and to resist it and sometimes involved the confluence of these two imperatives. Elites struggled with this convergence in their efforts to articulate developing notions of nationalism and feminism. To be sure, empire's dynamics of power ensure that what or who haunts or is haunted by empire is always a lopsided scale, tipped in favor of the colonizer. Yet at the same time, the potential within the many meanings of haunting and its liminality leaves room for formerly colonized subjects to employ the apparitions of empire as methods of possibility and resistance.

The discussion that follows engages the tensions that emerge when we mull over what it means for empire to haunt or for one to be haunted by empire and makes visible the deeply convoluted, spectral relations that characterize the Philippines (and its colonial past and present) and elite nationalists' engagements with feminism. The tangled web that connects the specters of Maria Clara, the transpacific coed, and precolonial and barrio women encapsulates the elites' desires to reassert control over the terms of gendered national identities amid the lingering presence of one empire and the continued influence of another. Contested and celebrated figures, Maria Clara and the transpacific coed haunt the 1930s, and they in turn inform the eventual romanticization of barrio and Malay women. Such reifications represent a troubling response, for they relegate precolonial women to a romanticized Malay past and barrio women to the disenfranchised peripheries of the present and future. They isolate indigenous and barrio women to the realm of the spectral, either the ancient past or the unacknowledged and unrepresented outskirts of the present. These romanticized figures answer nationalist needs for reified, controllable female icons, yet they also serve as spectral remnants of the higher stakes attached to attempts by both Filipinas and Filipinos, prosuffrage activists, and their opponents to maintain the boundaries that defined elite national identity in response to the emergence of new forms of transpacific Filipina femininities. Therefore, even though one might view elite Filipina and Filipino nationalists as selecting and constructing the recurring symbols of Filipina women that haunt the discourses of nationalism and feminism, we are nevertheless discomforted by the uneasy phantoms of these elites' implication in the continued marginalization of indigenous and rural women.

The convergence of crucial developments in nationalism and feminism, efforts to manage unruly women's bodies, and the importance of icons of traditional femininity pitted against a modern girl are phenomena that are not unique to the Philippines. As the Modern Girl Around the World Research Group and other scholars have documented, modern girls were by this time a global regularity, appearing almost simultaneously in China, Japan, India, the United States, Great Britain, and other countries. This global phenomenon inspired multiple attempts at policing women's bodies and sexualities, often carried out as "representational project[s]" that attempted to contain unruly women.[15] Like her counterparts, the transpacific Filipina coed spurred both admiration and anxiety. Marked by her conspicuous consumption, the coed could recite lines from Hollywood films and favored the short skirts, translucent fabrics, and plucked eyebrows featured in the pages of imported American magazines. She swayed and tapped her feet to jazz rhythms. And, like these other women, she "appeared to challenge 'proper' female commitments to the nation," especially in what were seen as her transgressive expressions of sexuality.[16] She refused the watchful supervision of the *kasama*, or chaperone, sometimes kissed men and danced cheek-to-cheek with them in public, and walked the streets of Manila fearlessly. As one of these modern girls, the Filipina coed illustrates some of the tensions between the development of Philippine nationalism and the concurrent iterations of feminism and feminist practices. Frustrating attempts to delineate women's proper roles, she posed a problem for both women's suffrage activists, who were campaigning in favor of expanded equal rights, and Filipino opponents of suffrage, who clung to vestiges of controllable Filipina femininity while still claiming the Philippines was a modern nation.

In the swirling, entangled representational projects that centered on Maria Clara, transpacific coed, precolonial woman, and barrio girl, bourgeois Filipinas and Filipinos employed and reacted to the specters of colonial modernity and the intimate intersections of two empires.[17] Closely linked to efforts by elites to control the terms of citizenship, these debates in the 1930s were haunted by the traces of late nineteenth-century anxieties over Filipina sexuality. The first section focuses on these ghosts through a reading of Noli Me Tangere and its original representation of Maria Clara as a fantastic, unstable presence. I then turn to the byways of Philippine print culture to narrate the rise of the transpacific coed; I argue that the coed represented a dangerous possibility of diffusing borders that separated the Philippines' class hierarchy. Her ability to cross moral codes of bourgeois sexual propriety became all the more frightening for those who were interested in maintaining the impermeability of these borders; her capacity to both imitate and proliferate presented an especially inimical threat. Finally, I return to the spectral traces of Maria Clara and the coed in the suffrage debates. As constitutional convention delegates alternately criticized and praised the coed and idealized Maria Clara, the precolonial Malay woman, and the barrio girl, they reinforced gendered, sexed, and classed boundaries. These cyclic reappearances underscore the uncontainable aspects of the modern Filipina and her spectral others, who continue to frequent, occupy, and capture the imagination of Filipina and Filipino elites throughout twentieth-century midways of feminism, nationalism, and modernity.

Rizal's Maria Clara: The Specter of the Mestiza Body

Recognized by many literary scholars as the first novel by a Filipino or Filipina, José Rizal's Noli Me Tangere is a landmark text. Affectionately called the Noli by scholars and readers alike, this satire of Spanish imperialism in the Philippines remains firmly entrenched in the literary canon even though its author, an elite mestizo educated in Europe, wrote the novel in Spanish and published it in Germany to avoid censorship.[18] The work holds a central place in Philippine letters because of its articulation of evolving nationalism in the waning days of Spanish rule, its continued relevance (the author, his novels, and his characters are frequent points of reference even today), and Rizal's beloved status in the Philippines as a national hero.[19]

The Noli is something of a literary enigma in its merging of melodramatic, satirical, and realist modes; its proliferation from the original Spanish to multiple translated and edited versions; the speculation surrounding its intended audience; and, most important, its slippery narration.[20] Any attempt to encapsulate the novel overly simplifies its divergent, multilayered plot, but the text's undeniable core is the failed romance between Maria Clara and Crisóstomo Ibarra, a mestizo who returns to the Philippines after years abroad with a European education and a desire to spread reform by establishing a new school in his hometown. The book tracks the beginnings of Crisóstomo's nationalist consciousness and his growing awareness of the difficulties faced by people in the Philippines. Ibarra's school never materializes, for he becomes implicated in both familial and revolutionary plots that interrupt his ambitious plans and end his engagement to Maria Clara. In the concluding chapters, the lustful Padre Salví, consumed by desire for Maria Clara, tells her that her true father is the man she has known only as a godfather, Padre Damaso. Horrified, she hides this shameful truth, reveals the secret only to Crisóstomo, and encourages him to flee from Salví while he still has time. Believing that Ibarra has died, she enters a convent that Padre Salví frequently visits, and suffers unspeakable violations within its walls.

To provide a backdrop to the discussion below of the importance of Maria Clara in the women's suffrage debates, I want to examine her complex representation in Noli Me Tangere as the foundation of comparison for the iconic versions of her that are so important in the 1930s. Idealizations of Maria Clara actually misread the novel, for they take elements meant to be satirical or critical—such as her weakness, isolation, lack of political consciousness, and her dutiful acceptance of patriarchal rule—as hallmarks of ideal Filipina femininity. A decade or two later, the writers Salvador P. Lopez, Carmen Guerrero Nakpil, and Nick Joaquin would notice as much. All three mock the transformation of Maria Clara into a cult figure by the "aggressive iconoclasts of the 1930s."[21] For Lopez, writing in 1941, the cultural knowledge of Maria Clara is so ingrained in Filipinas and Filipinos that it is transferred as if "imbibed with . . . mother's milk."[22] Even if, as Joaquin dryly observes in 1952, "nobody reads Rizal," Maria Clara still enjoyed "folk-figure" status and, as Guerrero Nakpil notes, was a phenomenon that affected "millions of Filipinas."[23] By the 1950s she is "loyal to the point of selflessness, modest to the point of weakness," a "sentimental stock figure," "saccharine idealization," "namby pamby," and, sniffs Guerrero Nakpil in 1956, perhaps "the greatest misfortune that has befallen Filipina women in the last one hundred years."[24]

Although integral to the Noli's critique of friar rule and a community's failure to question Spanish hypocrisy, Maria Clara is important precisely because she is a fantastic, indeterminate presence, one that troubles the developing nationalist consciousness at the heart of the novel. Rizal's narrative strategies—structural irony, the satirical narrator, and the representation of Maria Clara and the community—undermine her idealization by those around her and by the novel's readers.[25] Her ignorance, vapid response to the world, naïveté, and desire to follow parental and filial order represent all that Rizal despised about friar rule and its enslavement of his people. The uncertainties surrounding her character and the ironies attached to her representation are informed by anxieties surrounding bourgeois femininity in the Philippines of the late nineteenth century. Like the elites of the 1930s, men like Rizal were heavily invested in controlling men's and women's sexuality as a means of maintaining racial, gendered, and classed boundaries.[26] Such investments seep into the representation of

Maria Clara and are the spectral precursors to similar concerns about trans-pacific Filipinas that will later trouble elite nationalists and feminists.

Maria Clara's eventual valorization as the embodiment of "the Filipino woman" illustrates tremendous shifts in concepts of Filipina and Filipino identity from the late nineteenth century to the early twentieth, as the terms *Filipino* and *Filipina* began to encompass multiple racial, religious, and class-based categories. Distinctions among people in the Philippines during the days of Spanish rule shifted during this period. Both Crisóstomo and Maria Clara are of the mestizo class, a distinctive category that, as Anderson notes, was lost in twentieth-century translations and scholarship.[27] The capitalization of Filipino, versus *filipino* during the Spanish regime, illustrates the arrival in the twentieth century of a category that began to meld a varied population—including *indios* (indigenes of the Philippines), *peninsulares* (people born in Spain), *filipinos* or *criollos* (Spanish people born in the Philippines), *chinos* (Chinese), and *mestizos* (people whose ancestry included indio and Spanish or Chinese or both)—into a singular national identity. Peninsulares would have viewed filipinos and mestizos as racially inferior, even though many of them became landowners, were educated, and in time formed the foundation of the twentieth-century elite.[28] Anderson sees a fundamental difference between the Noli's brand of late nineteenth-century nationalism and twentieth-century iterations; Rizal's version "has to do with love of *patria* [country, fatherland, motherland], not with race: 'Filipino' in the twentieth-century ethnoracial sense never appears [in the Noli]." Most discussions of Philippine nationalism in the Noli do not account for what Anderson calls a "*creole-mestizo* world" that is "hard to imagine" for contemporary critics, who define nationalism along lines of racialized or cultural unification.[29]

Departing from Anderson's work, I pay close attention to gender, sex, and race in the Noli's "*creole-mestizo* world."[30] Although Rizal may not have thought about racial mixture in the Philippines in the same terms as those one might use to describe, for example, nineteenth-century race relations in the United States, it is undeniable that in the world of the Noli race does matter, especially when it comes to Maria Clara. The representation of mestiza femininity in the novel is deeply complicated and tied to Rizal's campaign against friar rule and Spanish oppression. Most visible in her "blanca, demasiado blanca tal vez" (white, perhaps too white) skin, Maria Clara's mestiza heritage is the source of both the spectacle of her fantastic, disarming body and her haunting uncertainty in the novel; she is, in the words of one scholar, "an alien figure who is at the same time universally recognizable," both foreign and familiar.[31] Characters may praise and envy Maria Clara because she is extraordinarily beautiful, a woman who is an "ídolo de todos" (40; everyone's idol), but Rizal undermines this celebration through the narrator's constant equivocation.

Rizal himself would phrase the critique of submissive Filipinas much more directly in his oft-cited "A Letter to the Young Women of Malolos," a document that became a banner text for the suffrage movement. Originally drafted in 1889 when he was in Europe (two years after the publication of the Noli), the letter was Rizal's response to Filipinas who organized to support the creation of a Spanish-language school for women. Teodoro Kalaw, the director of the National Library in Manila, reprinted the text and translated versions in Spanish and English in 1932, at the height of the suffrage debates. In this treatise Rizal finds examples of brave and courageous Filipinas to be rare; he says most elite women have been so indoctrinated by the religious codes of the Spanish regime that they remain ignorant, unquestioning, and bound to the rules of convent and church. The type of woman whom he describes is eerily similar to Maria Clara. In the Philippines he has encountered "an abundance of girls with agreeable manners, beautiful ways, and modest demeanor," and women with "excessive kindness, modesty, or perhaps, ignorance. They seemed faded plants sown and reared in darkness, having flowers without perfume and fruits without sap." These women are in no position, he contends, to be the mothers of an enlightened nation. He blames the limitations on women's education and the restrictions of Spanish rule for enslaving his people. Even though the "power and good judgment of the woman of the Philippines are well known," it is precisely because of these qualities that the Spanish have fostered Filipina servility and religiosity. For Rizal these restrictions have been essential to imperial rule: the Filipina has "been hoodwinked, and tied, and rendered pusillanimous, and now her enslavers rest at ease, because so long as they can keep the Filipina mother a slave, so long will they be able to make slaves of her children." He extends this argument, tying the oppression of women in the Philippines to a broader pattern of ignorance that limits Asia. "The cause of the backwardness of Asia," he writes, "lies in the fact that there the women are ignorant, are slaves; while Europe and America are powerful because there the women are free and well educated and endowed with lucid intellect and a strong will."[32]

Armed with Rizal's arguments against the enslavement of women, prosuffrage activists and feminists in the 1930s quoted often from the letter to argue that the national hero did, in fact, heartily support women's equality.[33] Yet Rizal's gender politics are a bit more complicated than that. As Raquel A. G. Reyes convincingly argues in *Love, Passion, and Patriotism: Sexuality and the Philippine Propaganda Movement, 1882–1892*, even though Rizal and other Filipino *ilustrados*—the enlightened ones, or elite men educated in Europe— may have "advocated the most progressive thinking about womanhood, and while their contact with modern femininity in Europe shaped that thinking, the Modern Woman also engendered anxiety and hostility, posing a disturbing challenge to the ilustrado male identity." Reyes ties late nineteenth-century ilustrados' fears of modern femininity to the earlier development of notions of *urbanidad*, a way of life that coincided with the rise of a new middle class in Manila and the "messy reality of Manila's culturally hybrid urban environment where people of all classes lived together, maintained a range of sexual arrangements and followed fluid, sometimes conflicting forms of desire." Urbanidad coalesced around a series of social behavioral codes and capital accumulation as the display of bourgeois life, the signs that "distinguished the person of property, propriety, and social polish" from the lower classes in Manila and also from other peoples in the Philippines.[34] Urbanidad also centered on creating and maintaining borders of class, gender, sex, and nation, of rendering fluid and diffuse relations calcified and impermeable.

The maintenance of such divisions was especially important to ilustrados like Rizal, who were building the case for the Philippines' independence from Spain. In one salient example, Reyes examines Rizal's alarmed response to a mention of the Philippines by the sexologist Richard von Krafft-Ebbing in his *Psychopathia sexualis* (1886). In distinguishing between civilized and uncivilized peoples, Krafft-Ebbing turned to sexual behaviors and practices as indicators of civilization. He adduced the Philippines' Malays as an example of a savage race. Rizal and other ilustrados, argues Reyes, would have found this categorization extremely disturbing. Many elites claimed Malay ancestry and saw distinct differences between the Malays and the groups usually associated with savagery: the Moros of the southern Philippines, highland peoples like the Igorots, and the Negritos. In response, Rizal produced his own annotated edition (1890) of Antonio de Morga's *Sucesos de las islas Filipinas* (1609), a chronicle often cited by European anthropologists. Reyes asserts that Rizal's version is a nationalist exercise, an attempt to write Philippine history, but that Rizal's text intervenes in the categorization of Malays as savage. Although his footnotes often reframe descriptions of Malay women's sexuality, he tellingly does not interfere with Morga's descriptions of other Philippine groups. To Reyes such choices are crucial, for they reveal Rizal's investment in recuperating notions surrounding the ethnic group claimed by elites while failing to question racist presumptions about other Philippine peoples.[35]

Like other ilustrados, Rizal was concerned with maintaining racial divisions that cemented notions that some people in the Philippines were more civilized than others. The bourgeois woman was central to the shoring up of these divisions, and from the ilustrado period to the mid-twentieth century, elites were haunted by a desire to discipline and check what they saw as Filipinas' aberrant sexual behaviors, especially in the wake of education, new opportunities for women, changing codes of conduct, and the influx of popular culture from the United States. Despite Rizal's view that women needed access to education and his plea to Filipinas to depart from blindly following Spanish friar rule, he believed women should behave with "spotless conduct."[36] Anxiety over Filipina femininity and sexuality is evident in the Noli, and it circles frenetically around Maria Clara's mestiza body as the object of desire.

As a mixed-race female body, Maria Clara stands in for the ilustrados' desire to regulate elite femininity. A mestiza who was part Spanish peninsular would have been a member of the upper classes, but Maria Clara is also associated with taboo sex, coerced by a corrupt friar. The novel's characters and narrator are preoccupied with the haunting spectacle of her mixed-race body, which is consistently associated with the fantastic and unreal. The narrator's first description pivots on a central metaphor of the spectacular to stress the mestiza's attractive yet disconcerting beauty:

Si el joven hubiera estado menos preocupado y, más curioso, hubiese querido ver con la ayuda de unos gemelos lo que pasaba en aquella atmósfera de luz, habría admirado una de esas fantásticas visiones, una de esas apariciones mágicas que a veces se ven en los grandes teatros de Europa, en que a las apagadas melodías de una orquesta se veía aparecer en medio de una lluvia de luz, de una cascada de diamantes y oro, en una decoración oriental, envuelta en vaporosa gasa, una deidad, una sílfide que avanza sin tocar casi el suelo, rodeada y acompañada de un luminoso nimbo: a su presencia brotan las flores, retoza la danza, se despiertan armonías, y coros de diablos, ninfas, sátiros, genios, zagalas, ángeles y pastores bailan. . . . Ibarra habría visto una joven hermosísima, esbelta, vestida con el pintoresco traje de las hijas de Filipinas, en el centro de un semicírculo formado de toda clase de personas, gesticulando y moviéndose con animación: allí había chinos, españoles, filipinos, militares, curas, viejas, jóvenes, etc. (30)

If the young man had been less preoccupied and more curious, he would have wanted to see with the aid of opera glasses what was taking place in that atmosphere of light. He would have admired one of those fantastic visions, one of those magical apparitions which at times are seen in the great theatres of Europe, in which to the muted sounds of an orchestra, in a shower of light and a cascade of diamonds and gold, in an oriental setting, and enveloped in transparent gauze, can be seen to appear a deity, a sylph, advancing without touching the floor, circled and surrounded by a luminous halo. At her presence the flowers bloom, the dance frolics, melodies awaken, and a choir of devils, nymphs, satyrs, genii, maidens, angels and shepherds, dance. . . . Ibarra would have seen a young and most beautiful maiden, svelte, attired in the picturesque costume of the daughters of the Philippines in the center of the semi-circle formed by all sorts of persons, talking and gesticulating with animation. There were Chinese, Spaniards, [creoles], soldiers, priests, old women, young ones, etc.[37]

Here Maria Clara, while exceedingly beautiful, is also decidedly made visible through the theatrical. The text emphasizes the boundaries between this stage and the reader-viewer; we see Maria Clara only through multiple frames: two windows and Ibarra's desire for opera glasses. This passage remains in the realm of possibility only, as the conditional tense serves as a constant reminder that this is what Crisóstomo "habría visto" (would have seen) only if a number of prerequisites were met: the desire, the opera glasses, and the frame of mind to notice what occurs across the street. Rizal also fixes Maria Clara with the dual male gaze, as an object that might be viewed, a body that performs for the pleasure of the male viewer. The narrator resituates Europe's staging of colonial others and relocates the European reproduction of a "decoración oriental" (oriental setting) to a house in Manila, just across the street from where the reader and narrator sit with Ibarra. The likening of this scene to a theatrically produced panorama on an Orientalist European stage is at odds with Maria Clara's appearance in costume as a supposedly authentic "hija de las Filipinas" (daughter of the Philippines); the narrator stresses that this moment is staged and performed, rather than authentically represented as real. The layering of description heightens the fascinating uncertainty surrounding the mestiza body as the central figure of an endless proliferation of unbelievable mixtures. The narrator moves from comparing Maria Clara's assembly to an amazing spectacle of "coros de diablos, ninfas, sátiros, genios, zagalas, ángeles y pastores" (choirs of devils, nymphs, satyrs, genii, maidens, angels, and shepherds) to an analogous, even more fantastic, sight of race and class mixture in Manila. Maria Clara appears amidst "chinos, españoles, filipinos," a crowd of all classes (toda clase de personas) whose seemingly endless proliferation is underscored by the marker "etc."[38]

The men and women of the Noli are so captivated by Maria Clara that, rather than recognizing the obvious signs of her Spanish paternity, they willingly believe and perpetuate the fantastic story of her birth. Rizal's narrator mocks those who participate in the fantasy of Spanish imperial benevolence. Revealed to the reader, the disclosure of Maria Clara's suspiciously miraculous birth and supposedly blessed conception excoriates the townspeople's acceptance of the unbelievable. The story is indeed amazing. When Maria Clara's mother and father, Doña Pía and Captain Tiago, have difficulty conceiving a child, she confides in their trusted confessor, Padre Damaso, who advises her to make a pilgrimage to a festival devoted to fertility. After her encounter with Padre Damaso, Doña Pía becomes pregnant and gives birth to Maria Clara. Soon after she falls victim to depression and dies. Here, the narrator juxtaposes the fabricated story of the miracle with a false allusion (one of several in the novel):[39] "Gracias a este sabio Consejo, Doña Pía se sintió madre, . . . ¡ay!, como el pescador aquel de que habla Shakespeare en Macbeth, el cual cesó de cantar cuando encontró un tesoro, ella perdió la alegría, se puso muy triste y no se la vio ya más sonreír" (39; Thanks to this wise advice, Doña Pía became a mother. . . . Ah! like the fisherman alluded to by Shakespeare in Macbeth, who stopped singing when he found a treasure, she lost her joy, her heart was very sad and they no longer saw her smile). There is no allusion to fishermen in Macbeth, and the narrator moves directly from this falsity to an escalating series of rationalizing maneuvers, providing a list-like account of Maria Clara's relatives and their attribution of her "facciones semieuropeas" (39; semi-European features, L-L, 39) to Doña Pía's "antojos" (39; whims), her prayers to various Saints, and even "influencias planetarias" (39; planetary influences). The same relatives "que encontraban el rasgo de paternidad de Capitán Tiago en las pequeñas y bien modeladas orejas de María Clara" (39; who find traces of Captain Tiago's paternity in Maria Clara's small, well-formed ears) praise her fair hair and white skin. In these descriptions the townspeople's willingness to erase Maria Clara's obvious mestiza heritage becomes increasingly ridiculous. As long as her true parentage remains unacknowledged, others can celebrate her white skin as part of her exceptional beauty (rather than as a sign of Spanish paternity), and she can remain "ídolo de todos" (40). The community's acceptance of this fantastic story banishes the specter of rape and replaces this abuse with a need to believe in benevolent miracles.

Twentieth-century readers who turn Maria Clara into an icon bypass such recurring examples of narrative instability when they transform her into a nationalist model of femininity. These later readings of Maria Clara undoubtedly draw on her romance with Crisóstomo Ibarra. Yet representations of this romance drip with satire and emphasize a haunting uncertainty attached to the gendered divisions of male versus female nationalist roles. The couple's meeting on the *azotea* (terrace), for example, provides the necessary elements for later readings of Maria Clara as a model of nationalist, idealized femininity; here Crisóstomo draws links between his beloved and his fond memories of the Philippines.[40] This scene fashions a gendered divide between Crisóstomo, the worldly man who is educated, travels extensively, and speaks multiple languages, and Maria Clara, the provincial woman who is uninterested in education and is left behind in the Philippines. The opening epigraph links the pair to the erotic biblical Song of Songs (with its overarching metaphor of the bride and bridegroom) and highlights the chapter's play with tropes of nationalist masculinity and femininity. The exchange between the Noli's lovers begins by constructing Maria Clara as a "hermana de Caín" (sister of Cain) and "celosa" (43; jealous woman), left behind by her wayward lover and worried about his travels; as soon as they are alone she asks him, "¿Has pensado siempre en mí? ¿No me has olvidado en tus viajes? ¡Tantas grandes ciudades con tantas mujeres hermosas!" (43; Have you thought often of me? You haven't forgotten me in your many travels? So many large cities with so many beautiful women!). Crisóstomo assures her that he, like the bridegroom in the Song of Songs, sees her, hears her, and is haunted by her image, manifested by the natural world. His assurances are as much a dizzying documentation of his travels as an accounting of his devotion; he moves from the beaches of Manila to the forests of Germany, to Italy and Andalucía, the banks of the Rhine, and the rock of the Lorelei. While Crisóstomo's ornately wrought answer to Maria Clara's jealous questions accentuates his privileged male mobility, her satisfied response places her as his female opposite: "Yo no he viajado como tú, no conozco más que tu pueblo, Manila y Antipolo" (45; I have not traveled like you, I only know your town, Manila, and Antipolo). She recalls blissful moments of their childhood. Crisóstomo studied at Ateneo, a private school in the Philippines, and tried to teach Maria Clara Spanish and Latin when they played together, but she, preferring to chase butterflies and dragonflies, paid no attention.

Later readings of Maria Clara as Rizal's intended model of Filipina femininity undoubtedly draw from the azotea scene; Crisóstomo immediately equates woman with homeland, and Maria Clara becomes an agent of salvation for the lost and troubled Ibarra. Yet the inflated nationalist rhetoric of this scene is haunted by Maria Clara's unacknowledged mestiza femininity. Crisóstomo constructs the memory of the woman in the Philippines as a comforting reification that attenuates the challenges of exile. He becomes the educated, cosmopolitan traveler, while Maria Clara emerges as the homebound beauty. In isolation, the description indeed elevates her as an incarnation of Mother Filipinas. But the links between Maria Clara and patria are much more complicated, for her embodiment of Mother Filipinas depends upon what Crisóstomo sees as her blending of the best qualities of metropole and colony, Spain and the Philippines:

> ¿Podía yo olvidarte? Tu recuerdo me ha acompañado siempre, me ha salvado de los peligros del camino, ha sido mi consuelo en la soledad de mi alma en los países extranjeros; ¡tu recuerdo ha neutralizado el efecto del loto de Europa, que borra de la memoria de muchos paisanos las esperanzas y la desgracia de la Patria! . . . Me parecía que eras el hada, el espíritu, la encarnación poética de mi Patria, hermosa, sencilla, amable, candorosa, hija de Filipinas, de ese hermoso país que une a las grandes virtudes de la Madre España las bellas cualidades de un pueblo joven, como se unen en todo tu ser todo lo hermoso y bello que adornan ambas razas, y por esto tu amor y el que profeso a mi Patria se funden en uno solo. (44)

> Can I forget you? Your memory has always kept me company; it has saved me from dangers along the way; it has been my comfort in the solitude of my soul in foreign countries; your memory has negated the effect of the European lotus, which effaces from the remembrance of many of our countrymen the hopes and the sorrows of the Motherland. . . . You

seemed to me the nymph, the spirit, the poetic incarnation of my [Motherland]: lovely, simple, amiable, full of candor, daughter of the Philippines, of this beautiful country which unites with the great virtues of Mother Spain the lovely qualities of a young [people]—just as all that is lovely and fair and adorns both races is united in your being. Hence my love for you and that which I profess for my Motherland are blended into a single love. (trans. based on L-L, 44–45)

Crisóstomo remembers Maria Clara as daughter of the Philippines, but his cherished memory centers on her mixture of "las bellas cualidades de un pueblo joven" (the best qualities of a young people) with "Madre España" (Mother Spain) and ultimately of the two "razas" (races). Crisóstomo's celebration of Spain here is important; Rizal did not necessarily oppose assimilation. The movement from qualities to people and races puts the ironic valence of Crisóstomo's musings in sharp relief; although neither he nor Maria Clara knows the secret of her birth, the reader recognizes that Maria Clara's blending of Spain and Philippines goes beyond her cualidades (qualities). The irony in this passage satirically marks the complexity of the mestiza figure. Ibarra's claim that Maria Clara is an ideal combination of the traits belonging to land, people, countries, and races is undercut by his ignorance of her illegitimate birth and Spanish heritage.

Although Rizal's use of irony does not completely negate the gendered implications of the couple's characterization, the framing of the azotea scene and the narrator's understated yet meaningful revelations subvert much of the exchange. Like the first glimpse of Maria Clara, this scene is carefully layered and complicated. Crisóstomo's hyperbolic language is prefaced by the narrator's invocation to the flowers, the breeze, and the sunlight to "contadlo" (43), or tell, what transpires between the couple. The narrator poses as an incompetent, confessing "que yo sólo sé referir prosaicas locuras" (43; I only know how to recount prosaic madness). A long series of entreaties and apologies is followed by a one-sentence paragraph: "Pero ya que no lo queréis hacer, lo voy a intentar yo mismo" (43; But since you refuse to do so, I will myself endeavor to do it). The admission of incompetence calls attention to the azotea scene as overheard and retold; the posture of a supposed lack of omniscience identifies the scene as a fictive reconstruction. The remainder of the scene pits Crisóstomo's highly metaphoric language against the narrator's brief, pithy asides. These interjections overtly question Crisóstomo's sincerity; immediately before the poetic tribute to Maria Clara begins, the narrator admits that Crisóstomo, "otro hermano de Caín, sabe eludir las preguntas [de Maria Clara] y es un poco mentiroso, por eso" (44; [Crisóstomo,] another relative of Cain, knows how to ward off [Maria Clara's] questions, and is a bit of a [liar] on that account, L-L, 44).[41] Neither Maria Clara nor Crisóstomo is idealized by Rizal; both are "hermanos de Caín," relatives of Adam and Eve's son, who murdered his brother, Abel. Given the multiple ironic valences in this scene, Ibarra's exaggerated praise becomes immediately suspect, even though, according to the narrator, Crisóstomo convinces Maria Clara to believe "todo cuanto él le cuenta" (45; everything he tells her). Almost always extracted from the azotea scene, however, is not Rizal's narrative play with these lovers, their very human flaws, and their manipulation of each other's jealousies, but Ibarra's willing participation in the creation of a fantasy.

As Alicia Arrizón and Rafael note, the Noli's characterization of Maria Clara carries the spectral traces of the Virgin Mary, an icon of femininity of incalculable importance to Spanish Catholic rule.[42] The comparisons between Maria Clara and images of la Virgen contribute to Maria Clara's fantastic representation as unstable and eerie in what Rafael calls her combination of the foreign and the familiar.[43] On one hand, Maria Clara's alignment with the Virgin can be linked to the ilustrados' preoccupation with defining bourgeois women's sexuality. Indeed, Filipino elite of the 1930s will pick up on these traits and use them to crystallize codes of women's sexual behavior; the crossing of Maria Clara with the Virgin Mary recurs in twentieth-century iconic versions that celebrate a Filipina's virginal grace, chastity, and sexual purity. The elite summons the ghosts of one empire to exorcise the polluting influence of another, as the turn to Spanish Catholic codes of feminine propriety becomes the new standard for protecting bourgeois women from the immorality produced by the United States. This persistent focus on Maria Clara's sexual purity seeps into later twentieth-century translations of the novel. Even in Soledad Lacson-Locsin's hands, the line "La nueva vida se reflejaba en todo el ser de la joven: todo lo encontraba bueno y bello; manifestaba su amor con esa gracia virginal que no viendo más que pensamientos puros, no conoce el porqué de los falsos rubores" (156) becomes "The young woman's whole being was vibrant with new life; she found everything good and beautiful; she manifested her love with that *virginal chastity* which knows only pure thoughts and is unaware of the reasons for false modesty" (L-L, 183–84, emphasis added). Perhaps because of the phrase that describes Maria Clara's "pure thoughts," Lacson-Locsin translates "gracia virginal" to "virginal chastity" rather than "virginal grace," even though the novel compares Maria Clara to the Virgin Mary (often hailed as full of grace) a few paragraphs later.

While Rizal may have been interested in codifying women's proper behavior, he found the thoughtless acceptance of Catholicism's religious behaviors quite disturbing and one of the factors that limited the development of nationalist consciousness. Unlike Crisóstomo, who becomes more and more convinced of the need to help his countrymen and women, Maria Clara and her comparison to the compassionate Virgin Mary point to her incompetence when it comes to participating in nationalist ventures. Though remarkably beautiful, idolized by all, and sacrificially loyal to Ibarra, Maria Clara, with her lack of compassion, naïveté, and empty rehearsal of Spanish religiosity, is the precursor to the Filipinas whose blind submission Rizal will dismiss in "A Letter to the Women of Malolos." She is vacuous, selfish, and uninterested in helping the many impoverished indios who suffer countless abuses at the hands of the friars and the ruling upper classes.

Maria Clara is presumably the symbol of generosity and kindness, but the narrator criticizes her easy distraction by the pettiness of social gatherings. The description of her virginal grace is followed closely by her interaction with a leper in the streets of Manila. Again, Rizal's setup of this scene is quite important. In the same chapter, Maria Clara's father gives her "un hermoso relicario de oro con brillantes y esmeraldas, conteniendo una astilla de la barca de S. Pedro, donde se había sentado N.S. durante la pesca" (155; a beautiful gold locket with diamonds and emeralds, containing a chip of St. Peter's boat, where Our Savior sat during fishing trips). While most translations render *relicario* as "locket," the term also applies to a religious relic, which describes the locket's sacred contents and its status as a fetish object linked to Jesus Christ. After the narrator describes Maria Clara as being filled with pure thoughts and grace, Maria Clara and her companion encounter a leper in the streets. As she watches others give food to the leper, her companion relates the leper's sad tale. Forbidden to touch others, the man was whipped because he saved a child who had fallen into a ditch. It was awful, says her companion. As the leper ran from the whipping, the Gobernadorcillo (municipal leader) shouted after him, "¡Aprende! Más vale que uno se ahogue que no se enferme como tú" (159), or "Learn! It is better for one to drown than to get sick like you!" (L-L, 187). Maria Clara murmurs, "¡Es verdad!" (159; It's true!).

Again, Rizal's text is characteristically unclear. While a more forgiving reader might argue that Maria Clara's "¡Es verdad!" echoes her companion's sympathy, her reaction, which appears immediately after the Gobernadorcillo's cruel pronouncement, also registers her agreement with him. After hearing the story, she approaches the man and "sin darse cuenta de lo que hacía" (159; without thinking about what she was doing) drops the relic into his basket. Although her friends, reasoning that the man would prefer food, mock her thoughtlessness, the leper gratefully falls to his knees before Maria Clara. After this encounter she becomes despondent and decides to return home, observing, "¡También hay gentes que no son felices!" (160; There are also people who are not happy!). But only a few sentences later, she forgets about her brush with the less fortunate and returns to her haven above the streets, removed from the impoverished: "María Clara subió las escaleras pensando en lo aburrido que son los días de fiesta cuando vienen las visitas de los forasteros" (160; Maria Clara climbed the stairs, thinking how boring the days of the fiesta would be, when strangers would come visiting, L-L, 188). There are multiple layers of irony in this scene. Maria Clara's locket carries a fetishized object that stands in for Jesus Christ, and she has recently been compared to the Virgin Mary. Yet instead of approaching the leper with compassion and empathy, she is interested in the man as a curiosity, and she performs her act of charity thoughtlessly. Her epiphany about the sorrows of others disappears as she climbs the stairs to her home, and she is easily distracted by the prospect of a boring fiesta. The Noli parallels her lack of self-consciousness with Ibarra's growing cognizance of the plight of his people, and the novel fails to imagine an active role for this mestiza in the dawning nationalist awareness.

The Noli's treatment of Maria Clara becomes even more problematic as the text progresses, for its tragic ending depends on her sexual violation. The novel projects the apparition of the sinless Virgin onto a body haunted, again and again, by its connections to imperial sin. The later emphasis on Maria Clara's Catholic-influenced virginal purity thus overlooks Rizal's satire of Spanish Catholic friar rule, especially its use of hierarchical dynamics of sin and redemption, and the exploitation of these hierarchies by the corrupt. In terms of plot, the ultimate evils of friar rule are revealed by this woman's violation, eventual isolation, and a community that in the end forgets her. The epilogue focuses on Maria Clara as the iconic, suffering figure of the dangerous process of erasure: "De María Clara no se volvió a saber nada más" (354; We do not know any more about Maria Clara), for in the convent of Santa Clara "nadie nos ha querido decir una sola palabra"

(354; no one was willing to say a single word). The novel closes with two specters of Maria Clara's violated body: a ghostlike white woman standing in the rain, raising her arms "al cielo . . . como implorándole" (355; toward heaven as if imploring); and a nun with a drenched, torn habit pleading with the visiting government official to protect her from the hypocritical violence and horror within the convent. While Rizal cautions against the rationalizations that allow for forgetting Maria Clara, her disturbing image depends upon her body as the abject sign of both the hypocrisies of friar rule and the tragic refusal of the townspeople (and readers) to acknowledge or change these terrible acts. Ultimately, Maria Clara's fate is to become, once again, a fantastic spectacle, a beautiful but damned mixture.

The ending, which closes with the victim of imperial erasure and its haunting reminders, highlights the Noli's vexed treatment of the role of women in developing forms of elite nationalism. In the 1930s the representation of Maria Clara's fantastic mestiza body, although enveloped by satire and narrative instability in the Noli, would eventually be recycled. Simplifying the complexities of Rizal's novel, elites suppress its satire and the troubling spectacle of the mestiza's relegation to the margins of bourgeois nationalism. The later importance of Rizal as a nationalist figure, the canonization of the Noli as the foundational text of Philippine nationalism, and the recurring appearance of Maria Clara in twentieth-century conversations about Filipinas and their future in the new nation are nevertheless plagued by the spectral returns of imperial legacies, class anxiety, and the difficult midways of modernity, nationalism, and feminism, embodied anew in another spectacular figure—the transpacific Filipina coed.

The Rise of the Filipina Coed

In the years leading up to the passage of women's suffrage, Maria Clara faced some serious competition, as the most fervent and heated conversations about the future of women and the nation coalesced around the figure of a transpacific Filipina alternately called the Filipino girl, coed, or modern girl. With the passage of the Tydings-McDuffie Act in 1934 and its provisions for the creation of a commonwealth as a transition to a republic, the struggle for independence from the United States seemed to be coming to an end. The convergence of the advent of the commonwealth and the urgent call for women's suffrage led to a recurring interest in defining and categorizing the Filipina and especially in assessing how thirty years of ties to the United

States had altered Filipina womanhood, for better or for worse. In articles published in English-language, Manila-based periodicals, the coed was the object of consistent public scrutiny. This coverage lambasted her aberrant sexual behavior, which was less about actual sex acts than about her public flouting of middle- and upper-class norms of propriety: her unchaperoned outings in Manila and her daring modes of dress. In a political and cultural climate in which many were thinking about the Philippines and its promise, the coed was a pivotal figure in discussions about how women would shape that future.

The controversy surrounding the transpacific Filipina coed as a spectacle was a reminder of the residual effects of U.S. empire, Spanish rule, and their conflicting coexistence. Indeed, the public interest in the coed resonates with the multiple meanings of haunting. Uncontained and variable, threatening yet full of potential, she symbolizes the overlap of two regimes and their resonances. To some admiring observers the coed was the epitome of positive changes resulting from the interaction with the United States, a woman symbolic of a new era in the Philippines, one of independence and equality between men and women. To others the coed represented the evils of American modernity and its threat to proper Filipina bourgeois heterosexual femininity.[44] These divergent readings of the young coed crop up repeatedly in debates about the potential future of Filipinas and their role in national definition, as the coed became a frequently used icon, a figure who haunted Manila and the imaginations of the elites, while at the same time embodying their preoccupation with the specters of Spanish and U.S. empire.

One crucial feature makes the transpacific Filipina coed different from other global modern girls. Although she eagerly consumed global capital and American popular culture, as her name alone implies, her access to university education was a determining factor, and the university itself was the site of her dangerous replication. The connection to the university links the coed to the narrative of benevolent modernity that characterized the U.S. occupation. A university education was supposedly a hallmark of modernity brought to men and women of the islands. The administration established a public university only a few years into the occupation, and the creation of a large-scale educational system was important to the argument that rationalized the acquisition of the islands as an act of benevolence rather than aggression. The university was also a point of comparison between the Spanish and American regimes: while Spain limited access to higher education to elite men, the United States argued that the occupation was opening up avenues of education to the Philippines at large, including Filipinas.

In contrast to Maria Clara's cloistered and confined life, bound to the convent or the home, Filipinas and Filipinos cast the modern coed as constantly moving and surrounded by multiple options and choices (figure 9). Articles align her with the symbols of modernity in flux: the sleek automobile, the bustling crowd, the packed theater, the overflowing dance floor. "You see them," observes the author of "What Interest [sic] Them Most" (1937), "pouring out of street cars, to office or school; or driving past, sleek and proud in their fathers' cars, to some party or other, to the modiste or the hair-dresser's—young, marriageable girls all of them—in ages between 18 and 25; living in a more or less emancipated era that accepts co-education, working women, and suffrage."[45] This is a new class of women, more full of pride than of modesty. They are ebullient, and they spill out into Manila's bustling streets. They are part of the teeming masses of twentieth-century crowds; they are bodies aligned with modernity's overflow and excess.

Vicente Barranco's 1939 article, "The Filipino Girl—Model 1939" pits the ever-moving, Americanized coed against the traditional Filipina, a woman he describes as "meek, wonder-eyed, doubtful, and lost, baffled by the petty facts of life." These oppositions contrast inside versus outside, static versus mobile, enervated versus energetic, past versus future. A "completely new model, gears, wheels, and all," Barranco's coed is happy-go-lucky and active; she looks, sounds, and acts like "a copy of that modern glorified American outdoor youth, Sunkist, breezy, and airy of movement." She "goes in for sports in a grand way," "chews gum as she follows the cheerleaders," and "has swing." Her romances are influenced by pulp magazines; she dreams of "the nice looking guy who heaves the winning goal during the last few seconds of a basketball game." The coed is undoubtedly influenced by the circulation of American goods: U.S. stamped and imported oranges fuel her body, pulp literature and Hollywood movies inspire her desires, and the rhythms of American music encourage her to dance. Barranco also places the coed amid a constant swirl of activity. This transpacific Filipina can neither be pinned down nor contained. She is most at home in the whirling public spaces and rushing crowds of modern cityscapes, and she mixes fluidly among others in "the crowd at the jammed box-office of a downtown theater, caring not if her dress gets bedraggled; she holds on to a pal in the melee and skips around a victory bonfire, and likes it immensely, too; she loves to be in the crowded bus during the week-end rush to the province."

9. "What Interest [sic] Them Most," *Graphic*, March 4, 1937, 28
(Courtesy of *Philippines Graphic*).

Ultimately, all of these characteristics stem from her independence, for "it's obviously because she can take of herself that she loves all these."[46]

Not everyone was so enamored of or inspired by the coed's independence. Periodical texts illustrate growing public dismay over her behavior, as Filipinas and Filipinos reacted to a new class of women thought to be unruly and out of control, improper and immoral. Their lack of inhibition was attributed most directly to the influence of the United States, not only to the establishment of the educational system that produced the coed, but also to the circulation of an alternative system of morals and behavior. These reactions were complicated by the context of Philippine nationalism. Those who criticized the coed sought to distance themselves and the Philippines from the United States and its supposedly magnanimous transfer of modernity to the islands. For these Filipinas and Filipinos, the occupation brought not benevolent tutelage but lack of resolve, lack of control, and selfishness, traits that would again become controversial during the Pacific War years. The more benign articles argued that coeds were frivolous and lacking resolve. Even a mild article like "Those Co-eds' Resolutions: They Range from Promises to Write Regularly to the Folks Back Home to Resolves Not to Have Anything More to Do with Men" (1933), which gently scolds the coed for her inability to stick to her New Year's promises, centers on a dynamic that had become a hot topic of debate: the coed's ventures beyond the home and her family and her relationships with men. Authors chastised coeds for their lack of self-control and their susceptibility to the fantasy world of film

10. Albano Pacis, "Should the Women Continue Being Libertarian Tramps?" *Herald Mid-Week Magazine*, July 12, 1939, 16.

(figures 10, 11, and 12); they were too easily swayed by the magnetic pull of balls and parties, the promise of romance, and the temptations of movies "starring Ramón Novarro, Janet Gaynor, Greta Garbo, Jean Harlow, Norma Shearer, Joan Crawford, Clark Gable, and such other popular stars of the magic world of make-believe."[47]

The controversy over the coed's alleged immoral behavior gained energy as early as 1930, when Perfecto Laguio, one of the most vocal critics of the type, published a series of scathing articles that blamed the coed for the disintegration of Philippine morality. These treatises resulted in calls for an investigation of the dormitories at the University of the Philippines, which Laguio asserted were hotbeds of sex, licentiousness, and immoral behavior.[48] The investigation never materialized, but that Laguio was able to gain the support of political representatives underscores the importance of the coed to the political and cultural climate of the time. After an interview of Laguio was published in the *Tribune*, his comments made him somewhat of a celebrity in Manila. He spoke at length about why he would prefer eternal bachelorhood over marriage to a coed. Filipinas reacted angrily and vociferously.[49] Reacting to the public outcries, Laguio elaborated even further, and he eventually collected his essays and articles in the volume *Our Modern Woman: A National Problem* (1932). To Laguio the transpacific coed is a woman who is not only disruptive to Philippine life but also so altered by her imbibing of Western influence that she has become foreign to the Philippines. She sticks out, "does not harmonize with her surroundings." A "discordant

11. "Our Romeos and Juliets/Nuestros Romeos y Julietas," *Philippines Free Press*, October 2, 1920, 1 (Courtesy of *Philippines Free Press*).

detail against the native background," she has altered so dramatically that she is now an "alien," an "importation" incompatible with native soil.[50] Laguio's work, while hyperbolic and purposely incendiary, illustrates the growing cultural importance and weight attached to the iconic coed. More than just an adventurous and carefree twentysomething, this transpacific Filipina now represented persistent anxieties over women who refused to be controlled and failed to follow bourgeois dictates of proper behavior, guidelines that were ultimately linked to notions of authentic national identity.

While an author like Vicente Barranco would celebrate the modern coed for her adventurous spirit and carefree independence in 1939, Laguio's earlier work cast these traits as threatening. To Laguio, the modern coed's transgressive sexuality threatened to dismantle the Philippines' moral foundation. She was a flaw that needed correction. "Decency and morality among our youths," he claimed, "specially among our coeds, has undergone a truly radical change during the last decade. The modern girls are a new creature." These tremendous shifts stem from the advent of modernity and its pop cultural evils: the "talkies; the dime novels; the breezy sex-story magazines; the highly seductive passion-rousing jazz music; and the lewd suggestive dances, coupled with the feverish life that the machine age, under which we live demands, have exerted an influence upon our youths far from being desirable." To Laguio, the Filipina's problem is her lack of discernment. She is too easily swayed by what she watches and reads. To make matters worse

12. "Our 'Flaming Youth'/Nuestra 'Ardiente Juventud,'" *Philippines Free Press*, June 25, 1932 (Courtesy of *Philippines Free Press*).

she copies these behaviors. He emphasizes the coeds' display of their bodies; they wear dresses that leave "almost nothing of woman's mystery for the imagination to explore," expose themselves in "low-necked dresses of transparent silk, so tight-fitting as to reveal every curve of the body; with flesh-colored stockings." According to Laguio, the coed carefully plans this exposure in a dangerous scheme that is the beginning of a downward moral spiral, "all calculated to excite the animal instinct in man." "No wonder sex crimes have greatly increased," he declares, and he prophesies that they "will continue to increase so long as women play to the baser instincts of men."[51]

Laguio's rhetoric relies on a vocabulary of racial and sexual degeneracy and devolution to limn the coed as a threat to the Philippines' democratic future. Here he mimics the racist, imperialist logic that cast Filipinas and Filipinos as uncivilized savages in need of democratization. His preoccupation with the coed is similar to the nineteenth-century ilustrados' need to reinforce boundaries of race and gender to make a case for their own enlightenment. As "moral Bolsheviks," coeds threaten to spread their way of life like communist wildfire and are "just as dangerous" to the structure of Philippine life and society as "communists with headquarters in Moscow."

Laguio even parrots imperial rhetoric about the effect of climate on native passion: one of the key dissimilarities between American and Filipina coeds, he argues, is the temperate versus tropical climate. Hot weather in the Philippines "makes her highly temperamental" and affects her "discipline and judgment." He catalogues numerous sexual transgressions, from "neck-[ing] promiscuously, even in public places" to being picked up and swept away in strangers' automobiles to "vamping professors" in exchange for higher grades. These women are "sex-mad," "flaming youth," "exploding into conflagration when they come in contact with men." In Laguio's view, these behaviors will only spur continued sexual and societal degeneration. Coeds' behavior will ultimately prevent Filipino men from marrying them, resulting in a rising number of women who marry without wanting children or leading to "increased cases of homosexual life." Laguio envisions a Philippines populated by menacing "old maids," "busybodies, the purveyors of gossip, the direct cause of dislocation in social amenities, the inspirers of feuds in peaceful communities; the organizers of movements that meddle with everybody and everything." The slippage in these terms is important, as Laguio moves from promiscuous display of the body to a society rapidly moving toward "race suicide" at the hands of a transpacific Filipina who refuses to cooperate. The extremes of heterosexual behavior, sex gone mad, lead to further sexual aberrations like same-sex desire, the rejection of procreation, and the choice to live a single life (figure 13). In Laguio's plot, the coed matures into a bitter old woman, one who becomes an activist and organizer for disruptive change. This painting of Filipina suffrage as a movement orchestrated by meddling old maids is at the heart of Laguio's discontent with the coed as a sign of a Philippines forever altered by feminism.[52]

In the face of critiques like Laguio's, Filipina feminists advocated for a revised view of the coed, and they sought to normalize her in materials ranging from columns devoted to advice for the college girl to conduct manuals. These elite Filipinas called for recognition of the coed's potential to positively influence her community, but they also reinforced the Filipina's importance as guardian of the nation's morality. Asuncion Perez and Maria Paz Mendoza-Guazon agree: without question, the coed must accept the burden of her "tremendous responsibility" as a public figure and behave accordingly. Perez urged the elite college girl to become more aware of the privileges that come with education. A responsible coed must become a leader in the community. Perez's comments mark her intense awareness of the coed's entrance into a new class. She maintains that "while a college girl

13. "The Lady of the Hour/La Chica de Moda," *Philippines Free Press,*
February 10, 1940, 128 (Courtesy of *Philippines Free Press*).

should be envied, and the station in life she occupies is coveted, acquiring an
education alone and going through college without having any definite aim
in view and without appreciation for the social values of education, becomes
useless, if not dangerous to the student as well as to the community as a
whole." Perez reminds the coed that she must model proper behavior, serve
as an example of economy rather than frivolity, and work hard to promote
"public opinion against excessive good times which generally occupy the
mind of the youth." Most important, she can participate only in "wholesome, clean, and desirable social contact with boys, selecting the good ones
and eliminating the bad." She responds to Laguio's preoccupation with the
coed's sexual display—a body scantily clad in tight, transparent clothing; an
uninhibited woman dancing lewdly and necking in public—with a contrast-
ing performance that exhibits the coed's leadership potential and her acceptance of "wholesome, clean, and desirable" sexual contact.[53]

As Perez's article illustrates, even the coed's defenders subscribed to the
notion that Filipina college girls should behave according to bourgeois standards of heterosexual propriety and morality. These elite women created a
climate of observation and scrutiny; a coed, in their eyes, was always being

watched by a curious, sometimes nasty, public and had to be especially careful to project an appropriate persona. In *My Ideal Filipino Girl* (1931), a volume that is part collection of speeches and part conduct manual dedicated to young Filipinas, Mendoza-Guazon similarly cautions coeds to always be aware of their actions "because people expect much of you and observe you with keen interest when you least suspect that you are being observed. They judge you by your behavior, according to the things you do and say or fail to do and say."[54]

The discussion of conduct was intent on encouraging practices that would distinguish a Filipina from an American girl. Indeed, while Laguio argues that the Filipina coed is a perversion of the American university student, the product of aping American behaviors gone awry in the tropical Philippine climate, Mendoza-Guazon and others maintain that the Filipina coed must embrace what makes her unlike her American counterparts. Often, these women fall back on Orientalist notions of Asian modesty; for example, in the article "The East Views the American Coed: Her Freedom Is Admirable But Isn't She Somewhat Too Independent?" (1936), Pura Santillan Castrence observes that the American girl's "open preference for the company of the opposite sex is often shocking to the more inhibited Chinese, Japanese, or Filipino girl."[55] In its outlining of proper etiquette and behaviors, *My Ideal Filipina Girl* confronts the impact of the American film icon. Mendoza-Guazon's rules are culled from conduct manuals in Spanish and English, but her specific attention to Hollywood's hold on the impressionable Filipina is important. In the section on dancing, rule four, she offers these words of advice: "Well-bred people do not care to imitate the way stage or film actors and actresses dance. They are paid to make stunts; you are not." Filipinas should "avoid pouting and making gestures. These are proper for vaudeville or film actresses. You are not." Part of the problem, in Mendoza-Guazon's reasoning, is that imitating Hollywood is an attempt at class passing, for the coed represents the potential slippage of class divisions in Manila. Mendoza-Guazon wants to nullify this threat by admonishing those who do not dress "according to your means. A poor boy or girl who exhibits dresses that only the well-to-do can afford arouses suspicion." Instead, well-bred women, according to rule eight in the dress section, should not "ape other people in their dresses particularly the film actresses."[56]

Filipina feminists were keenly aware of the difficulties coeds presented for developing versions of nationalism and feminism. In their concern over the behavior of Filipina coeds, feminists, too, are haunted by their younger counterparts' potential to threaten the outcome of the suffrage movement. They recognized that the coed, as a Filipina that promised to spin out beyond their control, needed to be remade in order to be included within the larger body of the nation. Like many Filipino elites, Filipina suffragists were interested in sifting out the messy sediment resulting from the erosion of class divisions in Manila. The increased social and professional mixing of men and women has accorded women a "new status" and "greater freedom," which require "a new standard of conduct and new legislations." "The unrest we are observing in the present generation," notes Mendoza-Guazon in *My Ideal Filipino Girl*, "is due to the conflicts between the old and the new standards, and this conflict, this unsettled condition, this revolt, characterizes the period of transition of any country." Filipina feminists grappled with the unsettling overlap of old and new and the merging of the traces of the Spanish and U.S. regimes. With the promise of an independent Philippines flickering on the horizon, controlling the transpacific Filipina coed and what she represented became all the more important.[57]

Spectral Isolation, Past and Present: New Maria Claras, Malay Women, and Barrio Girls

The discussions of the 1930s about irrevocable changes in Filipina femininity—represented by the convenient specter of the coed's misbehaving body—peaked in the years leading up to women's suffrage. By 1934 the debate had become polemical, a focal point of life and politics in Manila. In the words of the constitutional convention delegate Sevilla, the question of whether or not to grant women voting rights had become one of the most "extensively discussed subjects that have ever occupied the minds of our people, men and women alike. Schools, colleges, and universities have time and again chosen it as a proposition for their debates. The press has dissected the subject and editorialized it from every conceivable angle until all thinkable arguments for and against it have almost been exhausted."[58] During the convention proceedings—which themselves were an example of overlapping empires because delegates spoke in Spanish and English—most of the speeches against extending voting rights to women echoed the lines of reasoning employed by suffrage opponents in other countries around the globe: delegates affirmed that women's rightful place was in the home, vilified bourgeois Filipinas as selfish and not representative of the country as a whole, and contended that they were unprepared and unfit for true independence. If this new league of women was uninterested in marriage and motherhood (or not fit for marriage or motherhood), the delegates asked, who would raise Filipino families and maintain Filipino homes? Only a small percentage, they argued, really wanted suffrage; and it was wrong to pin the future of all Filipinas to the desires of a few women living in Manila. Others reasoned that Filipinas, who were really not meant to exercise thoughts independent from men, would merely duplicate their husbands' votes and did not need to vote themselves.

Given the recurring preoccupation with women who were stepping beyond the bounds of home and family, it is not surprising that suffrage opponents in the 1930s would return to the iconic image of the dutiful, homebound Maria Clara and valorize her as the epitome of proper women's conduct. The discussion around Maria Clara, however, although an important feature of the debate, is not so easy to pin down. Although she certainly served as a symbol of chaste, devoted, servile, and weak Filipina femininity, during the suffrage proceedings themselves her name was invoked for multiple, sometimes opposing motives. Flitting in and out of the delegates' arguments, she haunted the convention with her multiple forms. While some praised Maria Clara as the embodiment of the Filipina's true spirit, others argued in favor of revising Rizal's version. Not unlike the model coed championed by Mendoza-Guazon, the new Maria Clara was a woman who still had the virtuous demeanor of the nineteenth-century original but was nonetheless a modern woman. Some located the model Filipina in the precolonial Malay woman. Others praised yet another new Maria Clara, embodied not by the girls, coeds, and women of Manila but found instead in the idealized women who lived in barrios and provinces, the regions beyond the reach of the polluting influence of the city.

This parade of "new" Maria Claras, Malay women, and barrio girls solved the problem posed by unruly transpacific Filipina coeds. These multiple forms of transpacific femininities illuminate just how important it was for Filipino delegates to regain control over Filipina femininity during this troubled period of national definition. In her foundational study of the Philippine Constitutional Convention, Mina Roces tracks the dichotomous production of Maria Clara as a Spanish-influenced model of femininity against an Americanized new Filipina. Roces argues that the idealization of Maria Clara was heavily influenced by Filipino Hispanophiles, who promoted a "Spanish construction of 'the Filipino woman': isolated from knowledge of politics and kept in the domestic sphere."[59] Extending Roces's claims, I contend that representations of Filipina women were much more complex than this opposition. Distancing the Philippines from the West—both Europe and the United States—was also important to the Filipino politicians who vetted Filipina suffrage during the constitutional convention. The delegates' frantic search for models of Filipina femininity in Maria Claras, precolonial women, and barrio girls is a negotiation of colonial modernity in the Philippines, made even more complex by the convergence of Spanish and American influences and the problems this overlap produced for the elite. But those who romanticized barrio and precolonial women in due time banished these Filipinas to the realm of the spectral past and present.

In arguments against the inclusion of the Filipina vote, features of the coed controversy reappeared. The dangerous influence of the foreign, the Filipina's inability to make decisions that would protect her from such perils, and the moral degradation of the Philippines once again cropped up as frequent points of concern. The delegates were deeply suspicious of the so-called benefits of contact with the United States, especially when it came to losing control over Filipinas. In a strategy linked to defining the Philippines as independent from its colonial rulers, the delegates consciously distanced Filipinas from American women and claimed their role as protectors. Since many suffragettes directly pointed to the example of the American women's movement to make their case, their opponents in turn examined the United States for evidence of a downward spiral of marriage, the home, and family life caused by women's suffrage. Delegate Escareal was one of several representatives who blamed women's suffrage for the disintegration of American morality. In his eyes, granting women the vote had fostered a climate in which wives no longer cared for their husbands or for the upkeep of their marriages. "What is the situation there?" he asked. "What is the mental attitude of all American women? Many American women do not care if they get separated from their husbands. In fact, once in a while, they get a divorce and a brand-new husband, as they get a brand-new automobile."[60] Delegate José de Guzman argued that "there is really one great weakness of the Filipino race, more especially true of our Filipino women, and this is our susceptibility to everything foreign. When we see that there is something in vogue in other countries, especially in Occidental cities, our craving for it becomes so intense that we do not only imitate but go beyond it."[61] Imitation is not merely the problem but also its proliferation. This out-of-control spread was again framed as being similar to the rise of communism or the outbreak of disease; according to Delegate Grafilo, "The destructive effects of suffrage upon our women, home and nation will be worse than the evil effects of plagues, Reds, or Bolsheviks."[62]

For many of the representatives, Filipina morality, already susceptible to evil influences, would be further threatened by admittance to the political world. These arguments have their foundation in an elite Filipino desire to control women's behavior, especially amid the increasing numbers of transpacific women who flouted such restrictions. According to these allegations, politics was a dirty business, one characterized by humiliation, risk, and filth, and women's entrance into this arena would subject them to certain ruin and degradation. Others, however, claimed that women would act as agents of morality in politics. Speaking in rhymed tetrameter, Sr. Bocar proclaims, "Politics here is dirty / Black with corruption so nasty / . . . When women vote, those cannot be."[63] More than one representative used the Spanish-language verb *mancillarse* (literally, to "taint" or "stain") to describe the dangerous effect that suffrage would have on women.[64] Emphasizing their chivalrous responsibility to protect Filipina women from "verbal battles of calumnies, mutual hurlings of insults, scandalous vituperations and defamations" and a "political arena . . . too risky, too unsightly, too filthy for our women to participate in," the men cast Filipina women as needing male protection and portrayed the withholding of the vote as an act of chivalry. "I hold our women so dear and precious," contended Delegado Grafilo, "that I do not want them to be vulgar or cheap."[65] Argued Delegate Carin: "Instead of being the flower whose exquisite tenderness is the object of our love and adoration, they will become the miserable object of humiliation and pity, their petals no longer of the immaculate whiteness of virtue, but thrown to the ground, trampled upon by inconsiderate enemies, disfigured and mutilated."[66] The obsession with protecting the delicate flower of Filipina virginity bears traces of the ilustrados' preoccupation with writing the terms of women's heterosexuality by encouraging self-control rather than base, savage passion. Chivalry here is a veneer that barely conceals a desire to reassert patriarchal power.

In response to the threat that the women's vote posed to Filipina morality, opponents of women's suffrage summoned the ghost of Maria Clara as the standard bearer, the epitome of Filipina femininity worthy of being carefully guarded. Those who invoked Maria Clara during the suffrage debates did so with muddled objectives, a testament to the instability of how Filipina femininity figured in political and nationalist debate at this time and the importance of the woman question to national definition. A dominant version celebrated Maria Clara as sweet and delicate, a woman of "sublime virtues" who was chaste, homebound and subservient, self-sacrificing and loyal.[67] Eliminating the novel's satirical context, the apotheosis of Maria Clara turned her ignorance, her lack of interest in the political, and her situation outside of Ibarra's growing involvement in revolution into virtues.

But some prosuffrage delegates chose to revise the image of Maria Clara, to specifically refer to Rizal's heroine in the name of recognizing Filipinas' role in national progress. While Maria Clara still served as a stand-in for the Filipina woman, these representatives rejected the "assumption that our women of today are the Maria Claras of yesterday," and a woman "in seclusion, frail and fragile, taken care of" was a "false premise . . . a false assumption," and an "insult to progress and civilization."[68] The delegates remake Maria Clara, a woman still virtuous but also quite different. Delegado Cuaderno implores his colleagues to recognize that the "Maria Clara that inspires us today is not the pale, delicate flower that she was in the days gone by, conscious only of the things within the four walls of her home; we have come to admire the changes that have come to her sisters of today: their athletic bearing, their culture, the courage of their conviction—all of which make them the understanding, intelligent, and companionable wives of today."[69] Yet similar to the Filipina feminists who wanted the coed to revise her improper behavior, even those delegates who argued against a long-gone, outdated version of the secluded Maria Clara maintain the importance of guarding a woman's virtue as a quality central to her identity.

Delegates who invoked Maria Clara, however, were careful to release their version of her from affiliation with Spanish colonization. To further distinguish themselves from the vestiges of Spanish empire, representatives on both sides of the debate found ideals of Filipina femininity in Malay, precolonial origins. Grafilo proclaims, "There is not in the Orient a more precious gem than our modest maiden, clothed in *Malay-Balintawak* chastity, the prized Maria Clara of the masculine Filipino heart. How many a Filipino Romeo with a throbbing heart is dreaming to woo and win her!"[70] This description of Maria Clara illustrates her transformation from Rizal's Spanish mestiza to an icon of nationalist Filipina femininity. To Grafilo this new Maria Clara has no affiliation with the West other than her name; he locates her solely within the Orient and stresses her virtue as being unique to the Philippines through the reference to Malay heritage and *balintawak*, or traditional Filipina dress.[71] Grafilo continues by articulating the expansive differences between East and West, or, more accurately, between Filipino and white, for "if [he] were an American, if [he] were a European—a white man—[he] would not hesitate to give [his] vote in favor of woman suffrage," but his origins in the "Far East" compel him to vote against suffrage.[72] He constructs an indigenous history that justifies his opposition to suffrage, a precolonial mythology in which virtuous Malay and Oriental women are happy to be prized by men. Representatives who championed women's suffrage also turned to the iconic precolonial woman. Delegate Palma argued that the true tradition of the Filipina was not one of "dependencia y sumisión" (dependency and submission) but one of liberty and equality. The legacy of a woman's submission to a man was itself a foreign import, one that arrived on Philippine shores with Christianity. Those representatives who called for a return to tradition, then, had no choice: "de modo que si vamos a invocar la tradicíon, tenemos que otorgar el sufragio feminino, puesto que la mujer en nuestra antigüedad disfrutaba de la misma libertad y los mismos privilegios que los hombres en el hogar" (so if we are going to invoke tradition, we must grant women's suffrage, since the woman in our antiquity enjoyed the same liberty and the same privileges as men in the home).[73]

Grafilo and Palma referred to such women as either the embodiment of traditional virtue or as forgotten precursors to women's equality. In reaching back to antiquity and the Malay past, these elites chose to align themselves with a specific version of indigeneity. Like Rizal and the other ilustrados, the delegates at the convention prized Malay ancestry as their precolonial heritage, and they differentiated themselves from other native peoples who were still marginalized. In a glaring example from his speech opposing women's suffrage, Delegate Escareal eschewed the argument that all men and women in the Philippines had natural, inalienable rights and reasserted the disparities between educated, elite Filipinos and other groups. Granting suffrage to women, he argued, would open the floodgates to enfranchising others who did not deserve the vote: "What difference is there between the Filipino, who is ignorant, whose sole qualification is that of property, and the ignorant Tinguian, the ignorant Bagobo, the ignorant Negrito? I say that there is none. The fact, Gentlemen, is that nowadays there is no such thing as natural rights."[74]

Delegates also found the true Maria Clara in an idealized barrio woman, a model of provincial femininity that had roots in Rizal's description of his character as a sheltered, confined girl. The reconstruction of Maria Clara as a barrio woman identifies the threat that the more cosmopolitan, transpacific Filipina poses for the home, family, and a gendered nationalist hierarchy. Carin confidently declares, "I know that the ways of Maria Clara, whose feminine virtues were beautifully sung by our national hero" are still practiced "today among the overwhelming number of women in the barrios —women who, conscious of their sacred duties and responsibilities as mothers or daughters, do not presumptuously claim equality and do not want suffrage."[75] Characterizing the suffrage movement as orchestrated by city-dwelling elite women, these men reject the urban, modern, transpacific Filipina for a romanticized barrio girl. Carin's barrio woman is sacred, virtuous, and dutiful and most often found not in dangerous, crowded cities but in outlying villages. In praising the "overwhelming number" of Filipinas from the barrio, Carin responds to the proliferation of transpacific Filipinas in the city. These urban women are ultimately outnumbered by the women of the provinces, who still uphold ideals of feminine virtue.[76]

The transfer of Maria Clara's character traits—her loyalty and self-sacrifice —into the bodies of barrio women had already occurred several years before the constitutional convention. The delegates echo Laguio's observation that women like Maria Clara "exist only in books of fiction. Only in remote barrios which have not been reached and spoiled by the wave of jazz civilization can their images in the flesh be now found."[77] In a survey by the *Graphic* of Filipinos who had married college women, some of the men interviewed say that, were they to choose a wife again, they would "unhesitatingly take as wives simple country girls who, in spite of their lack of college training, are, nevertheless, wiser, more human, more sympathetic, and loving." In contrast to his disloyal, negligent, college-educated wife, one attorney wistfully sighs, "A barrio girl . . . could have sacrificed for me and could have stood by my side—for better or for worse."[78]

The translation of Maria Clara into the barrio girl is a process that exercises class, gender, and sex control. This idealization of a dutiful barrio woman was undoubtedly appealing to men who were interested in limiting Filipinas' participation in the new commonwealth. The arguments against suffrage and the consistent desire for new icons of Filipina femininity were attempts to monitor who could and could not enter the world of the politically enfranchised, elite sphere. The romanticization of the barrio woman, while valorizing her traits as a "simple country girl," also necessarily confines her within the landscape of the provincial and the realm of the disempowered. She expresses no desire to vote or to become involved in politics. She is unspoiled and untainted by city life, but at the same time, she is safely sequestered within the barrio. As the transpacific coed's complete opposite, the barrio girl is static rather than mobile, contained rather than multiplying, completely servile rather than liberated, virtuously chaste rather than sexually independent. Most important, the men paint her as being blissfully happy in this state. For representatives at the convention who were anxious about the entrance of women into the political sphere, the barrio girl presented a perfect alternative to the unruly transpacific Filipina coed; like Maria Clara in the Noli, she refuses to question the men who surround her and is malleable and dutiful.

In the end the suffrage debate closed with a compromise. Many delegates remained unconvinced by prosuffrage arguments, but the representatives eventually decided to conduct a preliminary plebiscite to determine how many Filipinas and Filipinos supported the initiative. The constitution of the commonwealth was ratified on May 14, 1935, without the inclusion of women's suffrage. In April 1937 hundreds of thousands went to the polls to extend voting rights to Filipinas, and almost four decades after the foundation of the first collective of Filipina women, the Asociación Feminista Filipina, women in the Philippines could finally vote alongside men.

Yet the broader cultural legacy of the women's suffrage debates and of the controversies of the 1930s over what made a Filipina extended well beyond the political arena. As we have seen, the rhetorical search for icons of Filipina femininity, from Maria Clara to the coed to the precolonial woman to barrio girl, were influenced by the spectral traces of the Spanish and U.S. empires and by past tensions that affected the definition of bourgeois heterosexual Filipina femininity. Spurred by the debate surrounding the transpacific Filipina coed, representational projects focused on Filipina women became a means of both questioning and reinforcing boundaries of class, sex, and nation. Despite attempts to define Filipina femininity, to calm the uneasiness produced by the transpacific coed with idealized versions from the past or the provinces, such endeavors were plagued by complications and continued instability. Indeed, controversies over what made and should make a modern Filipina were characterized by disagreement, marked by uncertainty, and shaped by the phantoms of the residual legacies of Spanish empire and the continued involvement with the United States.

Elite authors' efforts to control the terms of a new nation's citizenry and the desire to determine who was enfranchised within that citizenry were haunted by the specters of long-standing race and class hierarchies that lingered in the Philippines of the twentieth century. Although Filipinas and

Filipinos involved in this work imagined and determined a new national community, they were also quite interested in retaining power. They celebrated women who were ostensibly immune from the damaging influence of the West and beyond the polluting contact of the colonial. Yet the idealization of the Malay woman preserved classed and raced hierarchies and distinguished between an elite descended from Malays and other indigenous peoples living in the Philippines. The romantic notion of the barrio woman, unquestioning and docile, servile and happily bound within the domestic, presented a counterpart to the mobile, unruly transpacific coed yet also cast provincial women as forever disenfranchised. And in claiming these women in the name of opposing women's suffrage, bourgeois Filipinas and Filipinos also attempted to limit Filipina political engagement. These tendencies are disturbing reminders of the difficulties of resisting empire and of reconciling nationalism and feminism. The confluence in the 1930s of efforts to imagine an independent Philippines and the identities of its members and the examination of how Filipina women would contribute to this community brought these specters to the foreground.

Cyclic Hauntings

The four types of women reappear throughout the twentieth century as the representational apparitions of colonial modernity, nationalism, feminism, and their complex intersections. They are the traces of a persistent cycle, as elite Filipina and Filipino authors continue to debate the terms of Filipina femininity and the national community during the Japanese occupation, after the Pacific War, and into the years of the Cold War. The decades that followed would vault the Philippines into even more complicated imbrications of colonial modernities. During the Japanese occupation (1942–45), Japan's administration encouraged and, in many cases, legislated a break from the Philippines' political and cultural ties to the United States. After the Pacific War ended and the Republic of the Philippines was finally recognized by the United States in 1946, the United States effectively rewrote imperial history and recast U.S.–Philippine relations as one of equal allies against the Japanese. Chapters 4 and 5 argue that in these shifts from the hands of one empire to another, transpacific femininities would continue to be a focal point of debate and discussion, for elites would persistently remake the Filipina as a means of retaining control over a nation and national identities in flux. The tendency to relegate provincial and precolonial women to a romanticized past or to the outskirts of the present also recurs. These two chapters treat the complicated involvement of Filipina feminists in their responses to representations of the transpacific Filipina and their use of these women to further notions of transpacific Filipinas as active players in wartime and postwar relations.

I have been seeking here to draw attention to how and why certain types of femininity become idealized, to consider the long-standing implications of such icons, and to contend that these representative figures exist in contrast to the perceived threat of their mobile, transpacific opposites. Rizal's late nineteenth-century novel, periodical coverage in the 1930s, conduct manuals, and women's suffrage debates demonstrate the many ways that discussions of the nation's future were vexed by the specters of imperial legacies and the presence of new Filipina women. Attention to the haunting multiplicity of Filipina figures during this period underscores the importance of instability over stability, of what cannot be tidily contained and what exceeds representation as the fuel and the fodder for the reified icon. In the spectral return of Maria Clara and the cyclical emphasis on precolonial and elite femininity, we see examples of elites who saw themselves as modern, produced themselves as agents of modernity, and navigated the midways of modernity, nationalism, and feminism. They chose which aspects of which empire to ally themselves with (and which to critique or excise) and limited access to the definition of the modern by determining the representation of women. One cannot discuss the intersection of nationalism and modernity without paying attention to such female figures, to the pressing importance of ways to mediate and control women who defied developing notions of proper femininity.

The spectral women of the Philippines of the 1930s are also reminiscent of the iconic women who reappear in discussions of literary nationalism across multiple fields. I return here to one definition of to haunt—to use or to employ frequently—to reexamine the entrenched prevalence of recurring disciplinary narratives attached to iconic female figures in nationalist literatures. The cult figure status of Maria Clara, the barrio girl and Malay woman, and even the idealized, suffering mother figure in a text like Carlos Bulosan's America Is in the Heart (1946) have their counterparts in other postcolonial, ethnic American, and diasporic literatures.

Much scholarship pivots on analyses of the woman as allegorical figure of the nation, the suffering mother, a woman bound and immobile within the homeland, or the memory of a raped and violated body. Laura Kang describes these tendencies as a "rootedness" that "confine[s] women 'at home'–in the private sphere, in the patriarchal family with its matrix of compulsory heterosexuality, and in terms of a singular ethnonational loyalty."[79] Similarly, Michelle Stephens, recalling feminist scholarship on the black diaspora, identifies a dominant "paradigm of home" that structures male-authored, Caribbean revolutionary texts, which construct "black female subjectivity as immobile and bound to region, island, nation, or any other conception of home."[80] These two salient examples, one taken from Asian American studies and the other from work on the black diaspora, speak to the breadth and reach of alignments of the immobile, domestic-bound woman with nation as disciplinary preoccupations that uncover the crystallization of female subjectivities and their proper behaviors, commitments, and allegiances.[81]

Without denying the importance of these paradigmatic women, the above discussion of the mestiza Maria Clara and the transpacific coed as fascinating yet potentially threatening spectacles demonstrates that the development of an iconic woman-as-nation was a response to the more pervasive preoccupation with mobile, variable, and unruly women like the transpacific coed. My intention here is not to counter the importance of iconic women to nationalist narratives but to suggest that the turn to the iconic female figure has itself become reified. As a complementary mode of inquiry, then, we might also consider what haunts iconic femininity; to search for other versions that flicker in the archive, between the lines of text, or unrecognized in the registers of our critical scopes; and to interrogate the multiple processes that relegated these other versions to the ghostly realms of the unacknowledged.

Rather than constructing a celebratory account of Filipina and Filipino elites rising up in resistance against the lingering traces of Spanish and U.S. empire, I want to end on a more cautious note, for the production of modern Filipina femininity was still shaped by previous codes of elitism, racism, and normative sexuality. Although elites use the very phantoms of empire to imagine independence from Spain and the United States, even these attempts are circumscribed by their own troubling adherence to preexisting hierarchies and to the acceptance of bourgeois scripts for women's sexuality and morality. Those who idealized Maria Clara or the barrio girl were resisting notions of Western superiority, even though such resistance enacted itself at the expense of women's rights. Those who celebrated the coed or argued for Filipina suffrage had to balance their praise against a plot that staged Western colonialism as benevolent. Even in claiming the Philippines as a modern, independent nation and in delineating the identities of its citizens, elite Filipina and Filipino authors found it quite important to excise others from their newly defined version of modernity. The Philippines of the 1930s, then, serves as a disconcerting reminder of the overlapping and inextricable power relations that make thinking about what haunts or is haunted by empire an unresolved process. The suffrage debates, the coed controversy, and the spectral return of Maria Clara and her counterparts illustrate the broad reach of empire's hauntings and their extensive, grappling hold on the representational, critical, and political practices of nationalism and feminism. These are ghosts that cannot be exorcised, lingering specters that clamor to be seen and heard.

Chapter Three

PLOTTING A TRANSPACIFIC FILIPINA'S DESTINY

ROMANCES OF ELITE EXCEPTIONALISM

Although the title of Maximo M. Kalaw's *The Filipino Rebel: A Romance of American Occupation in the Philippines* (ca. 1930) appears to extol the virtues of a male hero, the novel's true hero is undoubtedly a woman: Josefa, a Filipina from the barrio who becomes a revolutionary during the Philippine–American War.[1] After falling in love with a future Filipino politician and moving to the city to acquire an education that she hopes will prepare her to become his wife, Josefa eventually travels to the United States with her white American teachers and becomes an advocate for women's rights and Philippine independence. The concluding pages of *The Filipino Rebel* encourage the romance's "gentle reader[s]" to remember her example: Josefa "lives on" in "her firm and decisive march towards her manifest political destiny beyond the Stars and Stripes" (210). This closing encapsulates Kalaw's allegorical treatment of the evolution of Philippine nationalism through the figure of an exceptional, elite Filipina who is transpacific, trilingual, politically active, mobile, and feminist. The romance's tenuous articulation of a new version of manifest destiny—one that would move "beyond the stars and stripes"— challenges the rationalization of American expansionism and exceptionalism, yet still imagines a Philippine nationalism that can be both transpacific and feminist.

Published a few years later in the United States, Felicidad Ocampo's *The Brown Maiden* (1932) also envisions an exceptional transpacific Filipina's destiny as being intimately entwined with the future of the Philippines, but with a very different ending. While Kalaw's Josefa directly ties her transpacific feminism to the promotion of an independent nation, in Ocampo's version of a Filipina's romantic and political fate, transpacific experience and education lead to her voluntary repatriation to the Philippines. In *The Brown Maiden*, Carmen Gonzales, the daughter of the Philippine speaker of the house, elopes with a white American captain from the U.S. South who eventually abandons her just before she gives birth to their son. Even though she is deeply disturbed by "race prejudice" in the United States, Carmen remains there for much of the novel, until she decides to return to the Philippines with a Filipino doctor whom she plans to marry.[2] In the final pages she realizes that her future is to accept her partnership to a man of her race and to take up her proper role at home: "In obedience to the law of her nature, which decreed she should move swiftly and directly toward the end of her destiny, she was returning to Dr. Villegas as resolutely, as unswervingly, as she had fled from her own country" (123–24).

The Filipino Rebel and *The Brown Maiden* are noteworthy not only as two of the earliest English novels published by a Filipino and Filipina in the Philippines and the United States,[3] respectively, but also because of their remarkable representations of transpacific femininities and their critique of U.S. imperial benevolence. Both novels, however, have been critically dismissed as works of questionable literary merit for their unwieldy, plodding plots and sentimentality, hallmarks of the popular romance. Jaime An-Lim calls Kalaw's novel "terribly flawed" by the "fumbling unevenness of an apprentice," and Kalaw is remembered not as the authors of one of the first English novels in Philippine literature but for his work as a political theorist and independence activist.[4] Ocampo was remarkably prolific as a writer, but her contributions to transpacific Philippine and U.S. literature were quickly forgotten. *The Brown Maiden* received a one-sentence mention in the *New York Times*, which vaguely summarizes the novel as "a story of the Philippines."[5] In "Brown Maiden Writes," a review published in the Philippines, Junius II diagnoses some of the formal problems with Ocampo's first novel, *The Lonesome Cabin*: "Characterization is poor; conversation somewhat stilted; and her use of English gives one the impression that she herself has not completely mastered it. The story is clean and moral, and one will find it an entertaining little tale, providing he does not read it with too critical an attitude." Junius II's review doesn't completely miss the mark: Ocampo's English grammar is often imperfect; characters appear and disappear briefly, for no particular purpose and without explanation; and her descriptions are sometimes distractingly repetitive. Although Junius II notes that "it would be a safe wager to bet that a very small per cent of the Filipinos have ever heard of her," he recognizes the importance of her work, and he blames Philippine "booksellers and publishers in Manila" for "fail[ing] to call attention to what is being published in and about the Philippines."[6]

But what if we were to reexamine *The Filipino Rebel* and *The Brown Maiden*—with their unsettling representations, their overt sentimentality and dramatic plot turns, and their presumably simple endings—as characteristic not of their failings as works of literature but as illustrative of the instability surrounding the Filipina's future in transpacific relations during the 1930s and as crucial to how elite authors strategically employed the genre of romance and narratives of exceptionalism to respond to these uncertainties? To forecast the transpacific Filipina's fate in the Philippines, *The Filipino Rebel* and *The Brown Maiden* translate the iconic women who dominated cultural discourse in Manila in the 1920s and 1930s—Maria Clara, barrio girl, and coed—into romantic heroines. Kalaw's and Ocampo's novels are part of a larger phenomenon, as elite Filipino and Filipina authors made and remade the transpacific Filipina to recalibrate a class hierarchy that was continuously fluctuating because of imperial and national shifts. While intersecting negotiations appeared, as we have already seen, in multiple cultural sites—from the pages of periodicals in the United States and the Philippines, to the conflict between Filipina and Filipino members of Manila's literati, to the heated debates about women's suffrage and the coed—dramas related to the transpacific Filipina's future also played out, as I discuss below, on the pages of studies of the Philippines, histories written by the elite, and novels.

Kalaw's and Ocampo's novels are complicated interventions into a broader imperial narrative that romanticized American benevolence in the Philippines and posited the education of exceptional elites like Ocampo and Kalaw as idealized models, evidence of the successful transfer of American modernity to its colonial subjects.[7] The closing lines of both novels recall and revise this rhetorical plot of exceptional, manifest destiny, the romanticized justification of westward expansion as an imperial nation. Intervening in this march toward a future—imagined and orchestrated by the United States—for the islands, which had been held as an unincorporated territory for almost three decades, the novels employ transpacific femininities as a means of negotiating unclear and indeterminate national fates. Throughout this chapter, I use *exceptional* and *exceptionalism* quite purposefully, for both are terms that characterize the multivalent rationale for American global expansion as supposedly distinct from other forms of occupation and empire. In U.S. political and cultural discourse, *exceptional* and *exceptionalism* are mutually informative: American exceptionalism relies upon the fiction of the United States as a liberal democratic state (despite its domestic racism and violent foreign policy) to justify expansion, and this fiction has historically been reinforced by the supposed creation and production of exceptional colonial subjects as exemplary of America's benevolence.

As Martin Joseph Ponce notes, however, the educational and political practice that was known as benevolent assimilation was not, in the end, about the actual incorporation of Filipinas and Filipinos within the United States, especially because the acquisition of the islands exacerbated fears about the potential influx of brown bodies into the United States.[8] Therefore many of the educational initiatives in the islands were meant to produce subjects who, like Josefa and Carmen, would eventually return to the Philippines. As I discussed in the first chapter, the Filipina's desire was especially important to constructs of imperial benevolence in multiple ways: in the representation of people from the Philippines as eager for tutelage and in the use of educational ventures in the Philippines and abroad as a method of producing more desirable colonial subjects, that is, those who would accept the supremacy of American rule yet who would not be included as citizens.

Employing benevolent education and romance—the very tropes that were crucial to the justification of U.S. empire—The Filipino Rebel and The Brown Maiden are texts that respond to contemporaneous discussions about the debate over Philippine independence and women's suffrage and the increasingly tense climate of race and labor relations in the United States— stemming in part from the growing numbers of Filipino migrants throughout the 1920s. Kalaw, who published political appeals for independence and histories of the Philippines for American audiences, turns to the romance to expose the absence of women from Filipino nationalist historiography and to reverse their exclusion from the workings of Philippine nationalism. Ocampo's novel wrestles with the codes of race, gender, sex, and nation in the Philippines and the United States, as both countries become uninhabitable for a Filipina protagonist who flouts these dictates through her involvement with a white American man. As their spotty critical reception illustrates, Kalaw's and Ocampo's plottings of the transpacific Filipina's destiny feature unsettled and unsettling contours, fissures, and tensions. Their protagonists are undeniably connected to U.S. educational imperatives and to characterizations of exceptional elite women as beneficiaries of white American feminist uplift. In light of such vexed connections to U.S. empire, both authors contend that the transpacific Filipina's reeducation is crucial to her future ability to entwine nationalism and feminism. Reeducation implies not the formal university education or study abroad that was officially promoted by the U.S. regime (although the heroines do participate in these ventures), but rather the women's recognition of the dangers of naïve idealization and a rejection of the plot that would write the Filipina as an easily molded colonial subject.

In both novels romance serves as both trope and form for an imagining of elite Filipina exceptionalism. My reading of romance as genre and as imperial metaphor draws upon the complicated treatment of popular romance in studies of U.S. empire and in scholarship on ethnic American and Philippine nationalist literatures. Critics have analyzed popular and historical romances as occupying two sides of the same coin: as a genre that promotes and disseminates imperial narratives and structures and as a literary mode that imagines the subversion of such hegemonic formations. On one hand, in scholarship on late nineteenth- and early twentieth-century American novels, popular and historical romances have been read as reinforcing normative depictions of masculinity and femininity and as rationalizations of imperialist expansion. Amy Kaplan and Andrew Hebard, for example, have convincingly argued that nineteenth-century popular romances published in the United States buttressed hegemonic constructs of nation, empire, and proper heterosexual male and female commitments to these entities. Kaplan links the historical romance to the discursive production of a narrative of U.S. empire as benevolent and to the larger cultural representation of U.S. imperial endeavors as reinvigorating white American masculinity. In this analysis, the white female heroine of popular historical romances also serves as an allegory, a protagonist who provides the impetus for what Kaplan calls a "chivalric rescue narrative," which depends on the "liberation and subjugation of the willing heroine," who represents "a composite figure" of two potentially unruly populations: the "New Woman at home and the subjects of the new empire abroad."[9] This treatment of the white romance heroine thus writes her containment, her submission to white male imperialist ventures. While we can read the American historical romance as a genre tied to hegemonic processes and to the empire abroad, similar ends also appear in postcolonial readings of romances as allegorizing the development of an elite male nationalist consciousness through male–female relations, such as in the readings of José Rizal's Noli Me Tangere (1887) discussed in chapter 2.

On the other hand, romance has been read as a literary mode with the potential to unravel the dominance of hegemonic narratives, to imagine alternate political formations, and to destabilize normative codes of heterosexual masculinity and femininity. Asian American and African American literary scholars such as Hazel Carby, Viet Thanh Nguyen, Claudia Tate, and, more recently, Dominika Ferens, Dohra Ahmad, and Yogita Goyal have contended that the genre itself presents the possibility of subverting imperialist and racist structures in its focus on women, its treatment of the domestic, its employ of sentiment as a method of appeal, and its formal strategies. These scholars contest the dismissal of romances and sentimental novels written by ethnic American writers, many of which were initially rejected as antithetical to the political motives that energized the creation of ethnic American canons because of their overly sentimental constructs and their troubled connection to the middle class. The publication of the popular romance thus becomes a mode of resistance, a means for the ethnic American author to use what Nguyen has called "flexible strategies" to break into a primarily white publishing market while at the same time imagining ethnic American protagonists' affiliation with a middlebrow reading audience.[10] Still, these critics recognize that the romance's capacity to both imagine and normalize seemingly fantastic or unreal circumstances provides an outlet for resistance, as authors subvert representations of white bourgeois femininity or appropriate the genre's employ of the fabulous and the unreal to imagine a world and a politics not yet existent.[11]

Philippine literary criticism similarly identifies a long tradition of Tagalog and Spanish popular romances as critiques of oppressive Spanish and American regimes. According to Soledad Reyes, some of the first novels in the Philippines (including *Noli Me Tangere*) were influenced by the romance modes common in the popular *awit* or *corrido*, verse poems in Tagalog and Spanish, respectively.[12] Reyes reads the tradition of Philippine romance and its "escapist" tendencies as responses to Spanish imperialism; the awit's and corrido's "simplified ideological pattern" and conventional happy ending produced conclusions that would be unattainable amid the injustices of Spanish rule. During the American occupation the use of romantic allegories to imagine idealized worlds was a recurring strategy for Tagalog novelists responding to an "ideology that had spawned a secular, individualistic and materialistic outlook."[13] Tagalog novels published during the early decades of the occupation projected what Reyes identifies as a conservative response to Americanization; "westernized Filipinos" are "objects of caricature," and plots featured the upholding of traditional values of family and marriage.[14]

Kalaw's and Ocampo's novels are caught somewhere between these two critical poles—romance as empire building versus romance as subversive. But *The Filipino Rebel* and *The Brown Maiden* are also linked to notions of romance in broader metaphorical terms, tied to the sentimental production of the civilizing mission of the United States in the Philippines, the imperial administration's supposedly benevolent motives, and the dependence on writing the elite Filipina as the desiring subject, the heroine of a plot that ends with the exceptional elite's embrace of modernity as constructed by the United States. Written by authors who could themselves be seen as model colonials, the novels illustrate the extent to which the development of Philippine literature in English was closely, uncomfortably tied to the U.S. occupation. Kalaw and Ocampo were both intimately connected to U.S. imperial endeavors and can themselves be seen as evidence of the proper workings of the U.S. regime's production of subjects who represented the best and brightest effects of imperial benevolence. The repercussions of this complex involvement seep into Ocampo's critique of race prejudice in the United States and trouble Kalaw's appeal for Philippine independence.

Kalaw's biographical highlights offer a glimpse into his connections to U.S. empire. Maximo Kalaw and his more widely known brother, Teodoro, were key figures in Philippine academics and politics during the period of transition from Spanish colonial rule to U.S. occupation. They were members of a coterie of Filipino intellectuals who saw their work as being heavily invested in the definition of a nascent Philippine nation. Maximo attended the University of the Philippines, where he eventually became a professor, chaired the political science department, and served as dean of the College of Letters and Sciences. As the personal secretary of the future Philippine president Manuel Quezon, Kalaw traveled to Washington, D.C. He received a bachelor's degree in law from Georgetown University and an honorary doctorate from the University of Michigan. He was a notable political essayist and published book-length works on the politics of the Philippines and the cause of independence in both countries. He remained active in academic and political life, serving as an exchange professor at the University of Michigan and as a representative for Batangas in the Philippines.[15]

Although we know much less about Ocampo, her life similarly features transpacific education and experience. She attended schools in Manila and studied nursing and law at the National University. In 1924 she journeyed to the United States, where accounts place her at Columbia University as a special student in law. She later practiced as a divorce lawyer in Reno, Nevada. Her travels and professional life took her throughout the country, including to Seattle and Tacoma in Washington; Albany, New York; Oklahoma; and Berkeley, California, where she reportedly received a master's degree in social work. She spent a period of time working for the Bureau of Indian Affairs and published her observations of Native American communities in the Manila-based The Philippine Forum. Ocampo was a prolific writer: in the United States she published The Lonesome Cabin (1931), The Brown Maiden (1932), and reportedly another novel, The Woman Lawyer, although there appears to be no surviving record of this text. Some records place her in Los Angeles as a screenwriter, and one account suggests that Metro Goldwyn Mayer was scheduled to film a version of The Brown Maiden. She returned to the Philippines in the mid-1930s and published serial novels such as Portia and A Woman Doctor. Her whereabouts after the late 1930s are unknown.[16]

That the two authors—who themselves represent Filipina and Filipino success stories within the plot of benevolence and its emphasis on the exceptional elite's desire for an American university education, travel to the United States, and eventual repatriation—would choose to base their protagonists on similar experiences is not surprising. Yet Kalaw's and Ocampo's novels also tell a more complicated tale. These books are not merely the products of willing colonial subjects, and they are much more than simple parrotings of the benefits of U.S. occupation. The novels are examinations of the potential benefits that might be gleaned from education and travel in the United States, but they remain wary of the imperial regime. Rather than narrating these perspectives from the elite male viewpoint (one that was prominent in the late 1920s and early 1930s, the era of nationalist definition), Kalaw and Ocampo use different versions of transpacific femininity to subvert the romantic and sentimental rhetoric of benevolence, to project nationalist and feminist outcomes of an American education and experience, and to imagine the uncertain yet crucial role of elite and exceptional Filipinas.

Nationalist Historiography and Its Limits

The Filipino Rebel begins on the eve of the outbreak of the Spanish–American War, traces the American acquisition of the Philippines, spans the occupation and the development of a supposedly independent Philippine government, and tracks the tensions between corrupt Filipino politicians and the nationalist movement for independence. Within this historical framework, Kalaw's novel follows the romance between Juanito, a revolutionary who eventually becomes a greedy, corrupt politician, and Josefa, the beautiful barrio girl who inspires him with her fervent love for her country. The pair meets during the early days of the Philippine–American War, when Juanito dramatically bursts into Josefa's family's home to escape pursuit by U.S. soldiers. Josefa attempts to save him by pretending they are husband and wife, but the Americans see through their ruse and capture them. The couple escapes and becomes involved in the resistance. Although they do not have a formal wedding, Juanito swears that their bond is formalized by their shared love of the Philippines. He eventually decides to work for the government established by the Americans; meanwhile, she pledges to become worthy of her politician husband and promises to join him after she has completed her education. But Juanito, consumed by his desire for political power and corrupted by his collaboration with the Americans, ultimately rejects Josefa because of her peasant origins. Instead, to advance his political goals he marries the daughter of Don Pedro, a beloved Filipino revolutionary. Heartbroken, Josefa finally reveals that she is the mother of his child. After she learns of his marriage, she and her son travel to the United States with her American teachers. She rechristens herself Juana Liwanag (liwanag is "light" in Tagalog) and returns at the conclusion as an activist for both women's rights and Philippine independence.

Kalaw's "romance of the American occupation" questions the gendered impulses of Philippine historiography, offers a counternarrative to the benevolent romance of U.S. empire, and imagines the exceptional transpacific Filipina as the most appealing voice for the cause of Philippine independence. Although Kalaw himself participated in the production of Philippine nationalist historiography, his work and his comments about The Filipino Rebel highlight a multifaceted critique of the intersection between the narration of Philippine history and nationalism. First, The Filipino Rebel exposes previous accounts of Philippine–U.S. relations for their reliance on idealized rhetoric that dangerously occludes the inimical effects of the occupation. The novel's project is one of reeducation; it both illuminates and undermines a flawed educational system promoted by the United States and encourages a Philippine and American readership to recognize the dangers of naïve idealization. Second, Kalaw stresses the importance of transpacific Filipinas, who were absent from the pages of most histories written by

Filipinos, including his own earlier work. Instead, he suggests that the transpacific Filipina's future is indispensable to a successful, independent nation.

Kalaw's career as an independence activist and political theorist was devoted to addressing the deficiencies in public knowledge of the situation in the Philippines. In two volumes published in the United States, *The Case for the Filipinos* (1916) and *Self-Government in the Philippines* (1919), he offers evidence in favor of Philippine independence for a transpacific public. The two appeals are part political treatise and part history; they are primers for the American reader who has not received the correct information about the independence debates and for a Filipina and Filipino audience that also needs this knowledge as they establish their autonomy. These works not only retell past events but also include relevant documents for the American reader's information, ranging from transcripts of political speeches to texts of proposed legislation. For Kalaw an awareness of the development of the debate in both countries, however, is not just important for an American audience's recognition of the Philippines' valid right to independence. Rather, this material is also central to the people's nationalist formation, for "such knowledge is necessary not only because it is a part of their history as a nation, but also because it is indispensable to them in their present task of developing their country and preparing it for the ever-widening opportunities of the future." *The Case for the Filipinos* is "not intended solely for Americans. It is hoped that through this volume the Filipino people may have a glimpse of the drama of their national future as it is staged in America." Extending the revision work that is at the heart of *The Case for the Filipinos*, Kalaw followed this book with *Self-Government in the Philippines* to argue for the continued importance of the cause for Philippine independence (especially after the Philippines' support of the United States in the First World War).[17]

With their careful documentation of Philippine history as a foundation for a case for self-government, Kalaw's transpacific appeals were linked to larger efforts by Filipino historians, who recorded and narrated the history of the nation in the first three decades of the twentieth century. Anxieties that stemmed from the effects of American education on a new generation of Filipinos influenced the production of modern Philippine historiography in Spanish and English. In these works Filipino historians responded to the prolific circulation of material related to the Philippines produced by American authors during the first few decades of the occupation. As we saw in chapter 1, the writing of history was a technology of imperial management, of dividing and categorizing, making sense of the unfamiliar, and constructing and reinforcing rhetoric that justified the involvement of the United States in the Philippines.[18] Across the Pacific, Filipino historians used the growing demand for histories of the Philippines not only to define the terms of national community and identity, but also to reaffirm their place as the authors of this history, even during and despite their connection to the occupation. Through the production of studies in Spanish and, later, English, these intellectuals reclaimed the ability to tell the story of the nation. With the influx of mass-produced history books in English, produced first by Americans and later by Filipinos such as Kalaw, the "conventionalization, circulation, and reproduction of a dominant national narrative was underway," a construct that Resil B. Mojares argues was "romanticized, glorified, and sanitized."[19] In Mojares's diagnosis, Filipino intellectuals mourned the rise of a younger generation heavily swayed by the proliferation of foreign-produced books, and in historiography they sought to rectify what they saw as a generational lapse, as a "new U.S.-era generation was increasingly alienated from the past."[20] As a result, "writings on the Revolution take on the quality of romantic, almost antiquarian attempts to preserve for posterity a vanishing past."[21]

In promoting themselves as authors of the past, present, and future of the Philippine nation, Philippine historians valorized a male elite intelligentsia that had a precedent in the *ilustrados*.[22] The production of national history at this moment was therefore linked to the codification of a rapidly growing class of elite and exceptional men who were affiliated with the United States. The first Filipino architects of national histories were cosmopolitan, highly educated, well traveled, and versed not just in English and Spanish but also other foreign languages. Quezon's preface to *The Case for the Filipinos* makes these requirements explicit. The prefatory material describes Kalaw as one of these truly noteworthy men, for the book is "the first attempt of a young Filipino educated in American schools to write in the English language." He hails Kalaw as the harbinger of an elite, male nationalism; Kalaw is part of a "generation of Filipinos that has grown to maturity" who are "about to become an important factor in shaping the future of the archipelago."[23] The preface establishes Kalaw as a model Filipino: because of his education in the United States and fluency in English, he is uniquely able to reach an American and an elite Philippine audience.

Such trends in Philippine historiography help explain Kalaw's persistent interest in classing himself and, later, his fictional characters as being able to cull the benefits of an American education without sacrificing their nationalist loyalties. His first venture in popular literature constitutes another strategic appeal. The historical romance draws renewed attention to the central events and people of Philippine history and simultaneously enacts a critique of the romantic rhetoric that characterized the entwined destinies of the United States and the Philippines. The Filipino Rebel begins by undermining narratives of manifest destiny and benevolent assimilation. The novel opens with a reversal of the presumed fate of the United States as an imperial power, as the narrator asks, "What was America in the Filipino concept of 1898? Practically an unknown nation, noted for its economic strides, it was true, but without colonial history and no reputation as a strong power" (1). Kalaw's response to the circulation of flawed U.S. historiography is the romance, which he links directly to nationalist ventures by situating himself and the novel squarely within the tradition of the brand of literary nationalism practiced in the nineteenth century by José Rizal. In the introduction to The Filipino Rebel, Kalaw explicitly connects his romance to the legacy of Rizal's Noli Me Tangere, the text that, as we saw in the previous chapter, originated Maria Clara as an icon of elite Filipina femininity.

Locating his work alongside the Rizal tradition of producing fiction in the colonizer's language as a fundamentally nationalist project, Kalaw focuses on the political purpose of rendering historical events as a romance. In the preface he demonstrates his awareness of the ability of romance to generate an affective response. Philippine life since the war of 1898 is a story that presents Kalaw with an "abundance of materials," "intense drama of tremendous literary possibilities," and "a wealth of heroic deeds, romantic episodes and dramatic changes which could be made the background of many novels" (xvii). Yet even with the potential of the major events leading up to and continuing through the U.S. occupation of the Philippines, Kalaw maintains the importance of historical authenticity; while entertaining as fiction, his romance is nevertheless grounded in sociopolitical circumstances, for "the events and facts presented, although presented in the garb of fiction, are authentic in substance" (xvii).

In his turn from history to romance, Kalaw implicitly critiques male elite historiography for its failure to include women in the narration of a new Philippines. The same period of historical production saw the beginnings of publications about the history and development of the Filipina.[24] Remarkably, despite the concurrent production of volumes devoted to either Philippine history or developments in women's suffrage, these topics were often treated separately. Kalaw himself initially participated in this tendency to overlook the Filipina's role in the future of the nation; *Self-Government in the Philippines* includes, almost as an afterthought, only a few paragraphs devoted to the importance of Filipinas. After all, he notes, "a survey of the promise of the Philippines would not be complete without saying something of the Filipino woman. The position of the Filipino woman in the Orient is unique."[25] After quoting from Emma Sarepta Yule's observations on Filipina feminism (see chapter 1), he concludes by emphasizing the central role of education, which "has broadened her scope in life and is making her more interested in the civic activities of the Philippines." In 1919 Kalaw was fairly blasé about women's suffrage and its possibilities. "While there is no strong agitation for suffrage," he remarks, "it is doubtful whether, when they demand it, their brothers will deny it to them."[26]

Kalaw's optimism at that time was, unfortunately, inaccurate. Writing about a decade later, after the passage of suffrage for women in the United States and in the midst of growing traction for women's independence movements in the Philippines and across the globe, he had altered his view of Filipina women. The opening pages of *The Filipino Rebel* suggest that Philippine and American audiences now also need to be reeducated to recognize the importance of Filipinas to the past, present, and future of the Philippines. Implicitly questioning the lack of Filipina representation in nationalist narratives, the second paragraph of the preface carefully includes men and women: "I began cherishing the hope of presenting to our people and to the world a sketch of our national life through the lives of heroes and heroines whose destinies have been for the last three decades bound up with the fate of their country. The romance of Josefa, the political career of Juanito, the forced expatriation of Don Pedro, who chose to live beyond the pale of the Stars and Stripes . . . are the outcome. . . . *My heroes and heroines speak for themselves*" (xvii, emphasis added).

Although Kalaw's gender-inclusive use of "heroes and heroines" initially may not seem notable, there are two other moments in the preface that highlight "the romance of Josefa" as crucial to the novel's countering of the predominant focus on figures like Rizal and Emilio Aguinaldo, the president of the first Philippine Republic. Kalaw contrasts the "heroes and heroines" of *The Filipino Rebel* with the male heroes in Rizal's *Noli* and includes Rizal's quoted response to the criticism of his novel's fictionalization of history: "If the author of a novel should be responsible for everything that his heroes might say, great God, where would we be!" (xvii). The choice of this particular quote is key, for it compares Rizal's male heroes with Kalaw's own emphasis on both heroes and heroines. The preface then lists the "prominent historical figures of the period" (all of them men) and situates *The Filipino Rebel* in response to a masculine lineage of Philippine nationalist history, from Rizal, the father of Philippine nationalism, to Aguinaldo, to Quezon and Sergio Osmeña, the contemporary leaders of the 1920s.

With this gendered critique of nationalist historiography established in the novel's preface and opening pages, *The Filipino Rebel* turns to narrate the amazing story of an exceptional transpacific Filipina, her relationship to U.S. imperial benevolence, and her role in reimagining Philippine nationalism. The romance novel provides an avenue for telling the story of a woman and her contributions to history alongside those of men. Taking up the decade's fascination with iconic Filipinas like the barrio girl and the coed, the plot at the heart of the novel is this woman's remarkable rise and her idealized combination of true devotion to the Philippines with the benefits of transpacific education.

Manifest Destiny and the Transpacific Filipina

The center of Kalaw's revision of both the narrative of U.S. benevolence and the impulses of Filipino nationalist historiography is the novel's representation of transpacific femininity. Through Josefa's rise from simple peasant girl to elite activist, *The Filipino Rebel* charts a trajectory that interweaves the fates of barrio girl, Maria Clara, and transpacific coed. Kalaw draws upon the tangled, unresolved drama of competing versions of transpacific Filipinas and their idealized opposites. As I discussed in chapter 2, the 1920s and 1930s featured recurring debates over versions of Filipina femininity, especially in response to the women's suffrage movement, and the corresponding uncertainty over the emergence of the urban, transpacific coed, a woman who flouted elite norms of proper heterosexual femininity. Maria Clara and the barrio girl became symbols of a nostalgic, lost Filipina femininity as naïve, untainted by colonial and urban influence, controllable, and, most important, excluded from political involvement in the nation's future through their iconic containment within the domestic space or isolation within the barrio or rural space. *The Filipino Rebel* is haunted by the specters of these iconic women, and they fuse in Josefa's shifting characterization and her rise in class hierarchy.

Kalaw initially illuminates Josefa, his simple girl from the countryside, with the warm, soft glow of the ideal, as the novel celebrates her potential. The work is nevertheless riddled with complexity, as Kalaw juggles his praise of Josefa with an appeal for an independent Philippines and his call for the creation of a more ethical government. The romance's allegory imagines the barrio girl's entrance into the future of the Philippines, but she can rewrite her fate and claim a different destiny only by erasing her rural origins, passing as an elite coed, and aptly performing as an exceptional model. The barrio girl's enfranchisement demands her matriculation through the American educational system, mentorship by white American teachers, and travel to the United States. Josefa's rise to enlightenment as a transpacific feminist and her success as an activist depend on her successful demonstration of the benefits of American benevolence. Her actions and triumphant return have her following the plan for elites espoused by the administration of the United States. To be sure, Kalaw was undoubtedly aware of his audience, which includes other elites (many of whom would have taken advantage of opportunities provided by the United States) and potential American readers. Even though romance presents the conditions of possibility for the emergence of new forms of transpacific femininity, ultimately the implications of Josefa's dependence on American structures, the return to language of the iconic, and the romance's predictability itself complicate this potential.

The importance of women's suffrage debates and the increased fervor surrounding the coed (and recurring discussion among Manila's elite about her destabilization of the codes of heterosexual propriety) informed Kalaw's careful representations of Josefa, especially early in the novel. He constructs clear divisions between Philippine and American notions of proper feminine behavior; these borders will later become more porous as the novel progresses. Although Josefa eventually moves to the city and becomes an urban, educated Filipina, Kalaw clarifies that she is no U.S.-influenced, immoral coed. Descriptions of Josefa parallel differences between city and country with accompanying dichotomies of the "artificial" (51) versus the "real" (56), transgressive heterosexuality versus innocent virginity, and American versus Filipina girl. "There was nothing of the flirt and the wanton in [Josefa's] behaviour," Juanito observes, for the "face that suddenly dropped under his fixed gaze was that of an innocent but intelligent country girl, somewhat tanned and unpowdered, but beautifully shaped . . . unmarred by any artificial devices" (51). Ultimately, the text conflates "wanton" and "artificial" femininity with "American," while a similar slippage merges "real" and "innocent" with "Filipino." Thus Juanito, who has traveled in the

United States, wonders at her evasiveness in their interactions, for "he did not know that no real Filipino woman will dare admit her love even if she were really in love, after only a day or two of courtship" (56). Descriptions of her transformation carefully underscore the difference between this "real Filipino woman" and the "American girl," even after Josefa gains access to both urban life and American education: "From the rustic country maiden of the revolution—unschooled, but with inherent intelligence, charming in her simplicity, and unaffected by city life—she developed into a refined and well-educated city girl, speaking both Spanish and English fairly well. She did not adopt the free ways of the American girl." Josefa may navigate the ins and outs of elite Manila and take advantage of "every opportunity" (96–97), including schooling, experience of city life, and interactions with the Americans, but at heart she remains a real Filipina.

Such rules and codes of conduct are at first quite important, for Josefa must follow them in order to enter the realm of the Filipina and Filipino elite. Yet while Kalaw seems to uphold the codes of heteronormative propriety, he contends that these guidelines are not only unrealistic but also unessential to the workings of true Philippine nationalism. Josefa's revolutionary past and her previous relationship with Juanito hinder her ability to pass as a member of the elite, for during the war she succumbs to his entreaties and conceives his son. These actions and their consequences, the novel tells us, can and should be excused because they took place in the passionate context of the revolution. Rather than punishing Josefa for failing to fit within the codes of elite Filipina conduct, Kalaw constructs her approach to single motherhood and her relationship with Juanito as a sign of her ethical nationalism. He also draws upon the Philippine cultural tradition of employing and reconfiguring Spanish Catholic metaphors and narratives as a tool for imagining nationalist revolution.[27] Josefa trusts that even though her marriage is not legal or sanctified by the church, their union is nevertheless bound by a higher, more moral justice. In a confrontation with Juanito's legal wife, Leonor, Josefa claims that "in justice, by the law of God, [Juanito] should belong to [her]" (114). She believes that the moral codes of the revolutionary days have now been tainted by the "law of men" like Juanito (114), who have been corrupted by collaboration with the United States and consistently rationalize their immoral, unpatriotic choices. The romantic plot links Juanito's rejection of Josefa to his political ambitions and rise to power within the U.S. regime, and he is swayed by the material benefits of collusion with American business interests, just as he easily reneges on his pledge to care for Josefa.

Josefa's ethical Filipina nationalism and her overwhelming commitment to Philippine independence complicate any attempt to read her as a model, desiring colonial subject, a woman eager for the benefits of tutelage. Indeed, *The Filipino Rebel* acknowledges that this profile and the plot of a woman's uplift through white American guidance are both pervasive and even seductively compelling. In the scene in which Josefa arranges her trip to the United States with her American teachers, Mr. and Mrs. Jones, Kalaw exposes the illusive characterization of the United States as the Philippines' heaven-sent benefactor. Josefa finds herself believing that "the Joneses would save her from her predicament; and when the idea of her going to the States was brought to her unsolicited by Mrs. Jones herself, she decided that after all there was a God with a bounteous heart and boundless kindness!" (109). Josefa tells the couple she would like to travel to the United States in order to prove what someone from her position and background can do. But later she revises this statement. When Mrs. Jones praises her exceptional student for her "intelligence and industry" and offers to "make a lady out of [her] in the States," Josefa's response proudly reveals her barrio origins and exposes the American woman's prejudices toward people from the lower classes. To Mrs. Jones's surprise, Josefa answers, "I would like to correct you, Mrs. Jones. I belong to the class that you have always thought very low in standard, ignorant, superstitious, and unprogressive" (110). In this scene, Josefa asserts that her origins in the barrio and her devotion to Philippine nationalism underwrite her desire to obtain an education in the United States. Although she may want to serve as an inspirational "example" (110), her goals are linked to her hope of changing how an American audience views Filipinos from the barrio: "I would like to show you and your people that the people in the barrio can, if given the opportunity, progress. . . . I am going as far as the highest university work and I will also make it my task to tell your people what I know of my people" (110–11).

The novel acknowledges that the United States may offer options for women that are not available in the Philippines, but Kalaw still highlights the dangers of overromanticizing these opportunities, as evidenced by Josefa's response to the Joneses' desire to view themselves as her benefactors. Moreover, Kalaw consistently returns to the just and fair goal of Philippine independence and to the value of nationalists' continued loyalty to this utmost objective, which can be achieved only through constant attention, hard work, an awareness of the dangers of any involvement with the United States not resulting in benefits for the Philippines, and a belief in patriotism as a political practice rather than a mere romantic ideal. Josefa's vigilant dedication to the Philippine cause constitutes the principal difference between her relationship to U.S. empire and Juanito's naïveté. In contrast to his blithe, unquestioning readings of U.S. history, she is loyal to the Philippines above all other allegiances and causes. While he fails to question the Americans' motives and is corrupted easily by capitalist greed, she avoids the pitfalls of taking U.S. sponsorship too far. "I received favors from America, especially from those Americans who have helped me," she tells him, "yet when it comes to the cause of my country, I place it above any other consideration" (203). According to Josefa/Juana, the downfall of Philippine nationalism stems from empty idealism like Juanito's: "We Filipinos always speak of patriotism without knowing what Filipino patriotism should be" (178). What is true patriotism? Josefa's model of elite exceptionalism returns to the importance of truth telling; in her words, patriotism is "loyalty and adherence to the history of our country and to the deeds of our heroes" (178). True patriotism can be achieved only by those who merge an awareness of the country's history with political action that serves the principle of "our liberty and independence" (178). In the end, it is not idealism itself that is a problem, but that the "triumph of an ideal" (178) is too often waylaid by self-serving motives.

Although Josefa's benefactors echo imperialist rhetoric by picturing tutelage as fostering an obedient, well-trained colonial subject, education instead sharpens the activist consciousness of an independent and self-reliant Filipina national. Romance, a genre linked to both empire building and its undoing, here serves as a form that can imagine these linked oppositions. The romantic plot, which would seemingly turn Josefa into the ill-fated romance heroine, results in a new exceptional elite and catalyzes the awakening of her transpacific, feminist nationalism and her rebirth as the political activist Juana Liwanag. After Juanito's betrayal, she views the chance to continue her education abroad as an avenue to escape the destiny of the tragic romance heroine: "What should she do now? Must she resign herself completely to fate, admit her defeat and continue to live merely to exist and to feed her boy? Somehow, there was something in her nature that revolted at such an idea . . . she remembered the principle her teachers Mr. and Mrs.

Jones were constantly preaching, the principle of self-reliance, of the new opportunities for women. The picture, time and again painted to her, of America, as the land of opportunity, began to fill her mind with a new possibility. Why not go to America? There, in the land of opportunity, would be her chance to show what she could accomplish" (108). While an American education presents a problem to the nationalist consciousness of those who, like Juanito, are naïve consumers, Kalaw suggests that it does offer possibilities to women, but only with a caveat. Here, the novel attempts to figure American principles as being used not to justify the manifest destiny of an ever-westward moving colonial power, but as providing a Filipina woman from the barrio the opportunity to claim an alternate fate. Josefa fashions Emersonian self-reliance into a foundation for feminist consciousness. The novel thus complicates the plot of the desiring Filipina subject, who in this case strategically uses educational opportunity to merge feminism and nationalism.

By the end of the novel, male politicians have failed, and the novel's valorization of Josefa underscores the potential of transpacific Filipinas to broker independence and a new form of strategic tactical collaboration between the two countries. The most successful Philippine–U.S. partnership is not with men in politics or government but between Filipinas and American women. With this turn to coalitions of women, the text capitalizes on the sentimentalized appeal of romance as a form. The concluding pages of the novel move from revising history to the importance of truth telling, especially when voiced by a Filipina. Josefa's fluency in the languages of colonial rule, Spanish and English, offers her the opportunity to promote independence in a way that will compel an international audience to recognize the cause. As a woman suffragist and independence activist, she has "addressed more American audiences than Quezon or any other Filipino" (201). As she explains to Juanito and Don Pedro at the end of the novel, "I tell you, my friends, the Americans are a just and liberty-loving people. It is only a question of telling them the facts" (203). In returning to the importance of reconstructing colonial history, the novel finds special power in telling the facts to readers who are especially sympathetic, the "women of America," who "are eager to help us in our campaign for women's rights. They are also willing to help us, in return for our cooperation, in our struggle for the emancipation of our country" (208–9). "We should not forget," she continues, "that the women of America have equal rights with men, and that they can be of tremendous help in winning America to our cause" (209). Kalaw not only highlights the potential of members of an English-speaking elite to speak to an American audience but also accords special value to Josefa's unique intertwining of transpacific femininity, nationalism, and feminism. Her success as an independence and women's rights activist stems from her ability to merge East and West. Josefa's final words in the novel emphasize her continued political activism, and the plot of elite exceptionalism for this transpacific Filipina ends not with a contained and managed colonial femininity, but with a turn to the promise of transpacific feminism as a global venture.

Yet the novel does not end in Josefa's voice. Even though Kalaw imagines the potential of transpacific femininity, contradictions in the novel's final moments underscore the difficulties of enacting these midways of transpacific feminism and nationalism. In one of these scenes, Juanito sits in a room whose walls are covered with photographs from *Liwayway*, the popular Tagalog magazine, and the English newspaper the *Tribune*. The most "prominent" are "pictures of American movie actresses and of Quezon, Osmeña, Harrison and Stimson." But another stands out: "The blurred picture of a Filipino woman, a Miss Juana Liwanag, with an account of a Filipino convention at San Francisco, where, it seemed, the lady took a rather prominent part. The following subheading attracted his attention: 'Filipino Woman Patriotism'" (178). Here Kalaw contrasts the challenge of representing Liwanag with more discrete, easily containable models of either femininity or Philippine and American male government officials. The out-of-focus photograph of Juana Liwanag is an anomaly amid the clarity of the Hollywood movie actresses and Philippine (Quezon and Osmeña) and U.S. officials (Harrison and Stimson). Unlike the easily representable, well-circulated images of Hollywood film stars and male political figures, the transpacific Filipina nationalist, although she "took a rather prominent part," cannot be captured by photographic representation.

The romance narrative itself closes without happy resolution; Juanito dies of a heart attack soon after he realizes that Juana Liwanag is his former love, and she reads about his death in a newspaper. Following the format established by Rizal's epilogue to the *Noli*, Kalaw's closing begins with a reference to "our gentle reader" (210), who may be questioning the novel's conclusion; here his authorial voice reemerges to remind us that any happy ending must be suspended because the story of the struggle for an independent Philippines is unresolved:

But Josefa lives on, "with a smile on her lips and a tear in her eyes!" She lives on . . . showing by her personal example that the freedom and permanent happiness of the country must be sought across the field of sorrow and sacrifice.

She is the veritable image of her beautiful Philippines, who, though ever courted by misfortune, betrayed by her friends, with her beloved Republic torn from her, with the false gods, to effect her permanent downfall, dangling gold and pleasures before her, continues working, hoping, struggling, braving a thousand perils and disappointments in her firm and decisive march towards her manifest political destiny, beyond the Stars and Stripes. (210)

In the epilogue, Kalaw casts Josefa as a reproducible type. Her "personal example" becomes iconic, the "veritable image of her beautiful Philippines." This production is intimately tied to Josefa's status as a romantic heroine; the phrase, "with a smile on her lips and a tear in her eyes!" is a quotation from Sir Walter Scott's historical verse romance *Marmion* (1808).[28] But even though the language is quite similar to the earlier idealized, naïve terms used by Juanito's claiming of Josefa as "the very symbol of his beloved land" (61) and by Rizal's Crisóstomo Ibarra and his promotion of Maria Clara as the spirit of the Philippines, this iconic woman is different. Instead of serving as a passive symbol of the homeland, she is mobile rather than static and steadfastly marching beyond the imperial reach of the United States.

Still, the epilogue lacks conclusiveness, and the final "veritable image" of Josefa's transpacific femininity is riddled with complexity. The novel's closing pages present an unwieldy conclusion for a text so concerned with promoting the transpacific Filipina's potential, as the iconic language of the epilogue entwines both possibility and foreclosure. Amazingly, the epilogue's final three paragraphs abruptly identify the "true Filipino rebel" in the body of Josefa's son, who has been "anonymous" but will soon emerge as a leader "if you are generous enough" (211). For Martin Joseph Ponce, this sudden turn to Josefa's heir represents the novel's problematic reaffirmation of a necessary link between heterosexual, biological reproductiveness and Philippine nationalism.[29] Indeed, this reinforcement of heteronormative nationalism has unsettling repercussions. The ethics of "working, hoping, struggling, [and] braving," so central to the success of Philippine independence, end not with the triumphant Filipina feminist we saw only pages earlier, but with the ever-sacrificing Filipina mother.

The nuances in The Filipino Rebel provide an avenue for exploring the complexities of narrating the intersections of nationalism and transpacific feminism. The oscillation between Josefa's subversive characterization throughout The Filipino Rebel and the turn to iconography in its final pages encapsulates the difficulty of projecting the transpacific Filipina's destiny. Josefa occupies an uncertain space between model colonial subjectivity (that of a woman who accepts and desires new opportunity as represented by American sponsorship) and a formulation of Filipina feminism that attempts to be both nationalist and transpacific. These complexities arise not only from tensions between colonizer and colonized, but also from the ways in which Filipino intellectuals like Kalaw chose to reconstruct and narrate the pasts and futures of exceptional transpacific Filipinas and the Philippine nation.

Exceptionalism and the Brown Elite

A few years after Kalaw published The Filipino Rebel, Felicidad Ocampo produced The Brown Maiden, a novel that imagines what was offstage for its predecessor: the transpacific Filipina's education and experience in the United States. At the beginning of the romance, Carmen Gonzales, a member of a rich, powerful Spanish mestizo family, is a sheltered, naïve young girl, a woman similar to Rizal's virginal, cloistered Maria Clara. But she soon rebels against this typology and elopes with Nolan, an American officer stationed in the Philippines and "a Southerner with a strong antipathy for the colored race and who boasted of ancestors who had come to this country on the Mayflower" (11). The couple moves to the United States, where Nolan's family immediately ostracizes Carmen. He quickly abandons his pregnant wife, and their child dies in infancy. Carmen briefly travels back to the Philippines, where she encounters a different type of race prejudice, for she is alienated by former friends and associates because of her interracial marriage. Returning to the States, she attends the University of California at Berkeley and becomes a social worker. Through these U.S. experiences, Ocampo expands upon an important aspect of transpacific education: Carmen witnesses firsthand the hardships of the working class, immigrants, and people of color. Nolan returns briefly at the close of the novel, but rather than projecting a happy future with a white man, Ocampo ends with her heroine's decision to return to the Philippines in the arms of a Filipino doctor.

Like Kalaw, Ocampo was affected by transpacific shifts that prompted a recalibration of who could claim elite privilege in the Philippines and in the United States. Her making of a transpacific Filipina's elite exceptionalism is inextricably tied to a representational strategy that manages racial fear in the United States and the destabilization of class boundaries in the Philippines. She situates her romance against the backdrop of rising numbers of Filipino men in the United States, continued debates over the future of the Philippines, and lingering discourses of primitivism, and she is quite interested in protecting the elite from lingering notions of savagery still attached to discursive constructions of brown bodies. To critique American race prejudice, *The Brown Maiden* reconsolidates the differences between elite Filipinas and Filipinos and the working class in the United States and indigenous peoples in the Philippines. In doing so, Ocampo consistently emphasizes Carmen's exceptional status, and the novel's grounding contention is that race prejudice is especially dangerous because it erases important class distinctions that would ostensibly separate Filipinas and Filipinos.

While the more overt objective of the book might be to criticize racism, the novel implicitly questions a story that would plot the United States as the endpoint of a transpacific Filipina's destiny, and Ocampo's version of elite exceptionalism also rejects representations of women as desiring colonial subjects. Carmen serves as a stand-in for the elite Filipina who at first naïvely accepts the romance of U.S. occupation, gradually becomes aware of its dangers, and finally recognizes her nationalist destiny with a man of her race and class by returning to the Philippines. If Kalaw's representation of Josefa in *The Filipino Rebel* critiques romantic notions of benevolent U.S. empire as a civilizing and philanthropic mission, Ocampo's Carmen expands this project by complicating the frequent turn to white American and Filipina sisterhood as a pivotal metaphor in the rhetoric of global feminist uplift.

In marketing *The Brown Maiden*, Meador, the publisher, fused the appeal of popular romance with the political critique of racism in the United States. The description of the novel on the dust jacket bills it as "a highly-romantic novel replete with tense dramatic situations and the pulsating emotions of a young, unsophisticated Filipino girl, in love with love." Moving from the dynamics of the generic features of romance, the description highlights its sociopolitical concerns. "East meets West," the jacket alluringly promises, "with the eventual clash of ideals," yet "when the scene changes to a liberal America, further complications arise and a distraught lady, despite her wealth and high position in her country, becomes the victim of circumstances created by a hard and fast convention that draws the color line." The jacket copy highlights the conundrum at the heart of the novel, for rather than contesting racism writ large, Ocampo contends that American readers should be sympathetic toward the elite, exceptional Filipina, who is wrongly judged because of her brown skin.

The novel's title and recurring anxiety over brown skin color indicate Ocampo's awareness of the American public's increasingly negative reaction to the presence of brown male laborers in the United States. As Rhacel Salazar Parreñas, Richard Baldoz, Linda España-Maram, Mae Ngai, and Leti Volpp have argued, tensions surrounding the presence of Filipinos in the United States during the late 1920s and early 1930s stemmed from a complex imbrication of raced, national, gendered, and sexualized discourses.[30] These decades were marked by a dramatic increase in the numbers of Filipino migrants in the United States, which was a matter of great concern, especially on the West Coast. A number of factors contributed to the surge in Filipino migration, especially previous exclusions of Chinese and Japanese laborers, the active recruitment of Filipinos by agricultural industries, and the convenient status of Filipinos as nationals, which exempted them from other immigration restrictions. Filipinos were soon viewed as an especially threatening force on multiple fronts, as growing concerns about trade competition from the Philippines, depressed labor markets, and anxiety surrounding intermarriage and miscegenation fueled anti-Filipino sentiment.[31] Rising tensions in the West led to juridical, political, and legislative measures that sought to solve the perceived problem of these communities of men. Even worse, anti-Filipino sentiment contributed to race riots and violence. The situation escalated when Filipino laborers began to form coalitions with Latino migrant workers to lobby for labor rights. Crossing the bounds of race and nation, such unions only exacerbated a now-familiar debate about the dangers of employing nonwhite Americans and immigrants, an argument that became more forceful during the Great Depression. This political climate soon affected discussions about the status of Philippine independence; indeed, the two issues were so interwoven that by the time legislation sanctioning the transition to independence was passed, provisions that limited Filipino immigration to fifty a year were included, and a corresponding Repatriation Act offered to pay the expenses of Filipinas and Filipinos who volunteered to return.[32]

But concerns over Filipino labor were also fueled by older fears regarding masses of primitive brown bodies. As I discuss in chapter 1, during the early years of the occupation the American public was increasingly fearful of people from the Philippines, as proimperialist arguments depended upon casting the islands' native inhabitants as uncivilized, incapable of national organization, and in need of democratic tutelage. Such notions were reconstituted in the 1920s and 1930s, and they were distilled in controversies over Filipino men's sexual contact with white taxi dancers and antimiscegenation debates. To many Americans, Filipinos were men of base, unbridled passion, dangerous and threatening to white women. In part, the dire situation was attributed to the lack of Filipinas in the United States; according to the work of sociologists, journalists, and anti-immigration advocates, Filipino men, desperate for interaction with women, turned to lower-class white women and Latinas in the taxi dance hall, sites that turned interracial desire into media spectacles.[33] Many wondered what made Filipinos so attractive to women outside of their race. These concerns led to a perceived need to manage and control unruly Filipino migrant masculinities. Anti-Filipino sentiment soon led to contemporaneous conversations about intermarriage. A series of California court cases from 1925 to 1932 (the same year that Ocampo published *The Brown Maiden*) eventually led to *Roldan v. Los Angeles*, in which the California Court of Appeals finally defined Filipinas and Filipinos as Mongolians and thus ineligible for marriage with whites.[34]

The worries over Filipino migrant laborers created rifts within the transpacific community, as elites were extremely careful in their efforts to distinguish themselves from the migrant community and avert the fear of uncontrollable brown bodies. Ocampo would have been in the United States at the height of these discussions. She was well aware of the persistent discourse of the primitive, and especially the traces that linked Philippine peoples to Native Americans in the United States. In 1936 she published an article entitled "The Red Men" in the Manila-based periodical *The Philippine Forum* that clarifies her position on indigenous populations. In the article she catalogues her observations after working with Native American communities and presents her opinions of their customs, beliefs, and medical practices. The beginning sounds a note of sympathy: "Never in the history of the world has the extermination of people been so complete as that of the American Indians during the past three hundred years." She is quite clear about who is to blame for this decimation, for "they are being so systematically reduced by the white man's vices that another century may mark the last of their race." "The average white man," she proclaims, "knows little or nothing about the Indians," who "are not understood much less appreciated" in the United States. Attempting to correct assumptions about Native Americans her Filipina and Filipino readers may have, she acknowledges common stereotypes of Indian savagery: "The general impression is that Indians are cruel to their enemies, even torturing them at the stake in extreme cases; that they know nothing about forgiving their foes." While Ocampo contends that there may be some truth to these perceptions, she argues that in comparison to the evils of the West, especially those perpetrated in the name of Christianity, the "Indians are much less cruel." "There is no Indian massacre," she observes, "that compares in horror with that of St. Bartholomew's Eve, or the Massacre of Glencoe. None compares with the records of the Inquisition, or Queen Mary's persecution in England, or the later James II abominations. And there was no torture by the Indians that was not used by the Spaniards." Ocampo ends the article by asserting an unacknowledged truth: "Every frontiersman of the Indian days knows that, in every outbreak the white men were the aggressors, and that in every robbery, torture, and massacre, the Red Men did exactly as the white men did."[35]

The more transparent politics of Ocampo's views of the West's crimes against Native Americans (both in their decimation of these peoples and the continued, unquestioned perpetuation of notions of American Indian savagery) is at odds with her more hesitant practices in representing indigenous and working-class groups in The Brown Maiden. Both genre and place inform these diverse representational strategies; while Ocampo can quite frankly excoriate the West and white men in a journal article geared to a Philippine audience, she has a much more uneasy relationship to her American readers. In response to the lingering connection between brown skin and the primitive and concerns about interracial marriage, Ocampo constructs a transpacific Filipina with an awareness of an American readership that was already anxious about growing numbers of brown (Filipino and Latino) bodies in the United States, fearful of interracial mixing, and for whom repatriation was a desired goal. The Brown Maiden thus consistently aligns its heroine with the lingering traces of the Philippine Spanish elite. The opening of the novel compares her to European models of beauty like the Venus de Milo. A Spanish mestiza, Carmen, like the Maria Clara figure, is cloistered and sheltered at home, protected from dangerous influences and fascinated with romance. Subject to codes of elite Filipina heterosexuality, Carmen craves exposure to a more adventurous life, which she gleans from the "novels pertaining to love affairs" (9) that her parents and Catholic convent school teachers try to keep her from reading. In love with love and with the romance novel as a form, she questions why she is "always compelled to read books dealing with history and religion and denied the novels of love and thrilling episode" (10), and she eagerly consumes "books from every source dealing with love and romance," which she "devour[s] with the hunger of an aching heart" (19). Naïve, sentimental, and melodramatic, Carmen sighs and trembles, throws fits and tantrums, and initially plays the role of the popular romance heroine well.

By emphasizing Carmen's aristocratic and Spanish origins, Ocampo decouples race and class. Molding her heroine for an American readership, she distances Carmen from the discussions of Filipinos as Asian or Mongolian and from possible connections to Latino and Mexican laborers. Her fond memories of home link beauty to European aristocracy; her villa in the Philippines is "a modern structure of Spanish architecture rich in beauty and full of pleasantness, her rooms spacious, and full of treasures her grandfather had brought from Spain" (31). Once she is in the United States, Carmen's class origins produce much confusion over her racial and national identification. One character muses that her "ancestors must be Spanish. Perhaps she's Castillian [sic], but proud to be a Filipino" (41). The same character alters her opinion in the sentences that follow, declaring that Carmen's father "admitted he was a Filipino" but is also supposedly "from Sevilla" and even later says Carmen's mother is "a Cuban" (41–42). In one of Carmen's first encounters with racism in the United States, she visits Nolan's aunt, who refuses to invite her into the house because she is a Filipina. Nolan and his cousin, Mabel, respond by describing Carmen's exceptionalism. Nolan explains that her "father is a high official in Manila, the Speaker of the House in the Philippine Assembly; she is a well educated girl, and they are not ordinary people" (27), and he finishes by saying that "Carmen does not look like a Filipino" (28). Carmen is "the daughter of a big man in the Philippines, a very rich man who owns big sugar plantations" (28), adds Mabel, who also extends Carmen's extraordinariness to her relatively fairer skin: she "is the only heir almost white, so why discriminate?" (28). Throughout the novel other characters echo these sentiments, and Carmen's elite class position becomes inseparable from her near whiteness.

Even though Ocampo sometimes privileges whiteness, skin color in The Brown Maiden is itself changeable, and Carmen's alluring "brown, velvety skin" (9) is a shifting signifier. Rather than linking brown skin color to Filipino or Latino migrants on the West Coast, Ocampo recasts differences in skin tones (and by extension, ostensibly race-based characteristics) as products of environmental rather than biological factors. Carmen explains matter-of-factly to her acquaintances that Americans can become brown, and Filipinos are not always brown to begin with: "You see we live on the other side of the equator, and even Americans who go there get brown, too. The sunshine tans them, and they all get brown. When I was a little girl my mother told me I was very fair, but when I grew up I, too, became brown" (26). Even with the novel's multiple reminders that Carmen is a "brown maiden," there is textual ambiguity regarding exactly how brown she is; one character observes that Carmen is "a bit brown but fair in comparison to some" (42). The stock terms that make her legible as a romantic and melodramatic heroine often render her skin white. At one moment she is "white as a ghost" (43), at another "as yielding as a white rose" (110). These changeable skin colors illustrate her racial and class instability in the text, which makes her all the more attractive to those around her. White Americans find her beautiful not only because she defies what they think a Filipina should "look like" (84), but also because she unmoors linkages between race and presumptions about sexed and classed white and brown bodies. She is both brown and "virginal," yet also white and "oddly exotic" (42).

Even in the face of such uncertainties, Ocampo's use of Carmen's elite status as a strategy for critiquing race prejudice ends up cementing raced, gendered, and classed disparities in the United States and the Philippines; in the end, the book contends that racism prevents the recognition of Filipina exceptionalism. Carmen's brief encounter with a Filipino laborer in San Francisco underscores disparity rather than affiliation. While Americans admire her mastery of English (34), the Filipino bellboy she meets finds "the simplest English names . . . baffling" (25). This incidental moment in the text is, amazingly, the only point of interaction between Carmen and a Filipino laborer. Indeed, in the novel's geography, elite Filipina and migrant laborer are so unalike that they do not occupy the same spaces. After Nolan abandons Carmen and then guiltily decides to search for her on the West Coast, he "comb[s] every street and every place where there was a Filipino" but cannot find her in this population, who inhabits "the main streets and the poorest districts of the city" (75). Accentuating Carmen's link to the elite women who participated in U.S. educational programs, Ocampo widens the gap between the two groups of Filipinos with the observation, "It was seldom a brown maiden came to the United States unless she came for the purpose of going to college" (75).

Carmen's elite status is also predicated on her difference from indigenous peoples in the Philippines. In keeping with other texts circulated in the United States and the Philippines, Ocampo repeatedly refers to the Igorots as a stand-in for the primitive. In comparison to Philippine indigenous peoples, Carmen and her family exert control over the Igorots, and this ostensibly marks the Gonzales family's relative civilization. Echoing a hierarchy of race-based supremacy that existed in both Spanish and U.S. regimes, the novel asserts that an American audience should think of Filipinas and Filipinos like Carmen and her family as fundamentally different from Igorots: the book figures Igorots as less civilized, un-Christian, and necessarily controlled by an elite ruling class. These descriptions evoke American racial constructions of indigenous populations and slavery in the South. Carmen's rebellious thoughts are "as unruly as wild igorots" (25) and she remembers fondly her father's home in Baguio, where he "owned two hundred acres and had a hundred Igorot tenants" and where she could amuse herself with the activities of "horse-back riding and teach[ing] the Igorots about praying" (31). At this point in the novel, Carmen might have been read by Ocampo's American readers as successfully enacting the logic of benevolent assimilation; the Gonzales family serves as Filipina and Filipino managers and as a civilizing force. With the exceptionalism of the brown elite established, the novel then moves to unravel the presumed importance of their connection to the United States.

Plotting the Transpacific Filipina's Return

As the romance comes to a close, Ocampo reinforces the preeminence of class elitism but also plots an important critique of the narrative of U.S. imperial benevolence, its emphasis on the Filipina as a desiring colonial subject, and uncomplicated representations of transpacific sisterhood. Carmen becomes an unruly transpacific coed, and she begins to rebel against norms of elite Filipina heterosexuality. Her membership in the elite quickly disintegrates after her interracial marriage and move to the United States. In the last half of the novel she rapidly changes, as her university education and exposure to the working-class, single woman's life begins to convince her that the freedom and adventure she once associated with experience in the United States are perhaps not quite what she thought they were. Carmen sees herself as a model not only for Igorots in the Philippines, but also for the poor and working-class people of the United States, and when she reflects upon her good deeds among marginalized lower-class white and immigrant communities, she revels in her superiority. In addition to "training her mind and storing it with facts," Carmen's social work exposes her to "the poorest districts in town" (95); she visits impoverished children and people living in shanties and even in the streets. While Kalaw's Josefa used education in the United States to rise from her barrio heritage, Carmen's descent into the masses allows her to "test her powers" (95). She falls into the trap of self-congratulation and repeatedly praises herself for her work: "It was good to be alive. It was good to help the poor; it was good to think she could help sick women, men and children in the hospitals. It was good to know the problems of poor people in the factory district; to help and guide them" (100). Her mantra-like recognition of her magnanimity performs both an enactment and reversal of the self-aggrandizing rhetoric of benevolent assimilation engaged in by the United States.

The rhetoric of benevolence, however, also informed notions of racial uplift in the global feminist movement. While the end of Kalaw's The Filipino Rebel unmistakably endorses the political potential of collaborative partnerships between Filipinas and white women, Ocampo's ambiguous treatment of transpacific sisterhood reveals the difficulty of collaboration between women of different races and classes. Her novel expands upon the early Filipina feminist writers I featured in chapter 1: elite Spanish mestizas who vilified working-class white women as a means of reinforcing their own upper-class status, on one hand, and as a rejection of representations that cast Filipinas as desiring subjects, on the other. The promise of such coalitions is complicated not only because the boundaries of nation, race, and class interfere, but also because historically these alliances have been linked to assumptions about the elite Filipina's desire to become like her white, supposedly more modern and more liberated sisters. Instead, the novel identifies transpacific sisterhood as difficult and uneasy, and it critiques uncomplicated links that would equate white American or Western-defined modernity, transpacific sisterhood, and achieving the objectives of global feminism.

Throughout the novel white women befriend Carmen and facilitate her passage to housing, education, and work. Despite these gestures of kindness, Carmen is extremely uncomfortable and often disturbed by their lives, even though they enjoy the independence she ostensibly desires. In the novel white working-class women's labor leads to unhappiness, unfulfilled dreams, bitterness, and even physical ugliness, as these women represent what the novel sees as the perverse outcome of single womanhood. The sight of older women like Miss Amelia, the proprietress of the YWCA who shelters Carmen, horrifies her. "It was hard," thinks Carmen, "to realize Miss Amelia had once been young and beautiful. She seemed so grotesque and sexless, with her eyes empty of dreams and memories; her face gray and sinister as a shadow" (44). The encounter with Miss Amelia parallels other scenes with similar outlines: Carmen encounters a single woman, who befriends or offers to help her; Carmen listens to the woman's story of heartache and loneliness and resolves to "make [her life] different by the strength and the effectiveness of her resistance" (73). She swears to "never submit as other women submitted," to "never become, through inertia, a part of the ugliness that enveloped her" (73) and to not be enveloped by the depressing difficulties of working-class life.

Ocampo distances herself from her heroine's judgmental view of white working-class women through her narration (*The Brown Maiden* is, after all, dedicated to the directress of the Elizabeth Sommer YWCA in Washington, D.C.). The novel does not completely preclude the possibility of coalitions between white working-class women and Filipinas, but it does question the potential meaning and easy valorization of these moments. Without explicitly chastising Carmen, the narrator's commentary exposes her insensitivity. After hearing one woman's heartbreaking life story, Carmen oscillates in her reactions: "Poor thing, thought Carmen, she exaggerates, dreadfully. That is what comes from being an old maid. Like most women whose love had ended not in denial, but in satiety and bitterness, she was inclined to belittle the supreme importance of the divine passion in the scheme of life. As a deserted wife and a brown maiden, she felt that she could live for years without it, even without the thought of romance. . . . Later Carmen sat and pondered Miss Benton's story. Yes, she could understand the yearning of one who had never known love" (101–2). Such moments of self-realization often occur immediately after her most judgmental observations, which she states with a great deal of conviction. She either has no compassion for white, unmarried women or, often only a few paragraphs later, acts as a self-reflexive, empathetic woman who has been similarly scorned by her lover. This equivocation is essential to the novel's take on transpacific sisterhood. Ocampo's heroine resists the role of desiring Filipina, anxious for the tutelage of her white female superiors. She questions the overarching results of women's independence in the United States, and although she once longed for liberation and freedom from her sheltered life, the plight of single white women so troubles her that, despite temporary moments of understanding between them, such connections are in the end ephemeral.

Carmen's increasingly overwhelming anxiety that she, too, will wake up as lonely and alone as the white women surrounding her leads her to realize the nationalist destiny that the romance projects for the exceptional trans-pacific Filipina. Ocampo connects Carmen's failed relationship with Nolan to her naïve idealization of the United States, and her recognition of this failure stands in for her newfound awareness of this trap. She understands that her partnership with a white man was the great mistake in her life, a "mad and headstrong folly" (72) that has led to a life of hardship and sadness, for "if she had only waited and married a man of her own people, who understood her, she would have been happy, and her whole life would have been different" (94). Her relationship with a white man is a problem in both countries, and Americans and Filipinos alike reject the couple for strikingly similar reasons. Nolan's family is of southern, slave-owning, aristocratic heritage; he tells Carmen of fond memories of "his plantation" and the "Negro mammy who had raised him" (13), and his mother angrily reacts to his relationship to Carmen because of what it might do to the family's "pride and name" (38). Ocampo emphasizes Carmen's ignorance of the long history of racism and the idealization not only of imperial ventures in the Philippines, but also of slavery in the South. This reeducation enables her decision to repatriate as a woman aware of the folly of benevolent notions of U.S. empire.

Interracial marriage weakens the ties that bind Carmen to the Philippines, to such an extent that she and other Filipinas and Filipinos become mutually foreign to one another. The text alternately represents Manila and the United States as idyllic spaces of opportunity that eventually turn strange and foreign to Carmen as soon as she marries Nolan. San Francisco at first seems "to her an enchanted land" and "like a Fairy Tale" (23), but the city soon becomes uninhabitable. Carmen idealizes the memory of her home in the Philippines, which, in contrast to the United States, stands "for peace, and beatitude" and is "a tranquil land, smiling, dreamy, wistful" (78). Yet upon her initial return to Manila, Carmen finds that her romanticized "land of sunshine" is now "inexplicable" (78): "Her own people were strange. She would have enjoyed it all, immensely, as Carmen Gonzales the Brown Maiden, but not as Carmen who had married an American. Furthermore, her own people were as foreign to her as she would be to them. She spoke the same language, had intellectual contacts with them but they would remain as unsympathetic and as aloof as the Igorotes [sic]. Her wealth, her father's high standing, would not help, nobody would believe that she was one of them, they would resent her" (78). Just as her identification as a "Brown Maiden" excluded her from familial relationships in the United States, so Carmen's new identity as a woman "who had married an American" initially prevents her from rejoining the Philippine national community.

The transpacific Filipina gains a form of independence and knowledge in the United States, but this experience ultimately leads to her reacceptance of her place in the Philippines. To stress the grave importance of transpacific Filipinas' reconstitution within the national community, Ocampo turns to recurring tropes of everlasting youth, references to fate, and metaphors of bodily suffering and aging. As the romance comes to a close, Carmen's story of self-development and discovery culminates in her realization that true happiness depends on marriage to a Filipino man and return to the Philippines. In keeping with the genre's interest in star-crossed fates, Carmen's reacquaintance with Dr. Villegas involves a melodramatic series of plot twists, chance meetings, and fortunate coincidences. After she has moved to San Francisco and reestablishes her life, she once again encounters Nolan, who is dying. Even though she feels some obligation to help her former husband, she knows their relationship was a mistake; she helps him but feels "no compassion in her heart" (107). As Nolan lies on his deathbed, she calls a doctor, who sends Dr. Villegas instead. Unbeknownst to Carmen, her parents had arranged for her to marry him, and he has been searching for her in the United States. The novel projects the favorable outcome of this marriage in completely unambiguous terms, as Carmen observes, "He holds the key to my future; he, alone, is capable of renewing my youth" (124). The thought of remaining in the United States is soon somatically displayed by her body; she feels an "oppression, the feeling of being slowly smothered" (120), becomes "exhausted" by the "oppressive heat," experiences a "curious sensation of smothering," and notes a "contraction in her throat as if she had become suddenly paralyzed" (122–23). But marrying a "man of her people" promises a fairy-tale ending and eternal youth: "She was young again with the imperishable youth of magic and enchantment. To love, to hope, to strive—this was both romance and adventure" (116).

The rewards of lasting youth, adventure, and romance express the benefits of the transpacific Filipina's reincorporation within the national community. Carmen's marriage to Villegas and return to the Philippines imply that she will regain her status among the elite. Their partnership potentially recuperates this unruly coed within the norms of elite Filipina heterosexuality. In the novel's final moments, Carmen's former interest in flouting the rules of tradition and convention disappears; Dr. Villegas registers his surprise at Carmen's violent reaction after he kisses her before proposing marriage, because she had "been in this country long enough to be broad minded, and [to] know that kissing is an indication of affection" (119). Yet Villegas appreciates his prospective wife's display of "the true Filipino spirit and the real Filipino pride" (119). The narrator's commentary identifies Carmen's return to elite codes of Filipina heterosexuality as an expression of her "primitive" nature, for she "was still the primitive woman with primitive tendencies, and measured love in accordance with the standards of her race and her people" (119). With a seemingly instinctive reacceptance of the dictates of proper heterosexuality, the willing Filipina subject now accepts her national fate: "In obedience to the law of her nature, which decreed she should move swiftly and directly toward the end of her destiny, she was returning to Dr. Villegas as resolutely, as unswervingly, as she had fled from her own country" (123–24).

Even though Ocampo's romance concludes in a way that would have been perhaps comforting to her American readers (the couple with "primitive tendencies" repatriates, and Carmen's and Nolan's ill-fated, dark-haired, blue-eyed, and mixed-race infant dies long before the novel ends), the closing line of the novel—"it was all so simple at last" (126)—oversimplifies the romance's implications and the instabilities that are so crucial to the representation of the tenuous connections that tie together transpacific Filipinas, nationalism, and feminism. Ocampo's oblique representational strategies could certainly be read as the result of her lack of control as a writer, or as her capitulation to an American market. It is important, however, to read the novel both through and against its resolution. Its final pages might project a transpacific Filipina's rejection of single womanhood and her return to the Philippines, but this ending also questions an uncomplicated narrative of benevolent education and white female sponsorship in the United States. Carmen's repatriation and marriage might accomplish the goals of educating the exceptional elite Filipina without assimilating her into the American nation, but in the end her choices are not spurred by U.S.-sponsored initiatives, but via her self-education and her experience of a very different type of life in the United States. Certainly the destiny of Ocampo's transpacific Filipina in the Philippines is distinct from Josefa's. Carmen does not become a political activist advocating on behalf of her nation's right for independence, nor does she promote the importance of transpacific feminist networks. Rather, she hopes to "devote her time to social work; teaching her people what she had learned in the United States" (124). But exactly what has Carmen learned? As she and her fiancé embrace on a boat bound for the Philippines, she takes with her an awareness of racism, a recognition that her easy romance with white people was a "mad and headstrong folly" (72), and a suspicion of easy narratives of feminist uplift and transpacific sisterhood. The resolution of Ocampo's *The Brown Maiden* is, in the end, hardly simple.

Literary Fates

Some might see the provocative endings of *The Filipino Rebel* and *The Brown Maiden* as evidence of the failures of their educational projects. For Kalaw, the rise of the barrio girl to the elite transpacific feminist could be read as shoring up the very idealizations of U.S. imperial history that he critiques for much of the novel. Similarly, Ocampo's ire toward racism in the United States and her criticism of the narrative of benevolent uplift are undercut by her protagonist's elitism, her reinforcement of brown exceptionalism, and the novel's projection of a future in which the transpacific Filipina must repatriate. These novels, then, do not fit easily within versions of nationalist resistance that would demand readily discernible and enacted political agendas. Indeed, the multiple strands of romance's potential—to narrate imperialist ideologies and to imagine the subversion of these structures— are inextricably woven together in these two novels. Kalaw's and Ocampo's works shift back and forth between what Viet Thanh Nguyen has called dichotomies of resistance and accommodation, the categorization of Asian American authors based on perceptions about authorial and textual political perspectives of the United States.[36] With their complicated relations to the U.S. regime and because the romance was out of step with the aesthetic innovation celebrated in both the Philippines and the United States, Kalaw, Ocampo, and their novels had no place in the evolution of a tradition of Philippine literature in English or in formations in the 1960s and 1970s of an Asian American literary canon that privileged authors with politics in keeping with developments in Asian American cultural nationalism.[37]

Thinking of Kalaw's and Ocampo's novels in terms of success and failure ignores the very complexity that makes these works absolutely crucial to the narrative of Philippine–U.S. relations and to the transpacific Filipina's role within this history. We might, then, reconsider the destinies not only of

Josefa and Carmen, but also of these two novels and their authors—their dismissal and eventual forgetting—and connect them to the elite Filipina's and Filipino's elision from most American-based accounts of early to mid-twentieth-century transpacific history and cultural production. Catherine Ceniza Choy, Augusto Espiritu, and Cynthia Tolentino have begun to address this critical lacuna.[38] In part because of the greater number of materials reflecting migrant laborers' experience, the majority of Filipina and Filipino American studies of the early twentieth century have focused on the male Filipino migrant, with an unintended yet serious consequence: Filipinas are either absent from this history or relegated to status symbol, evocative of the migrant laborer's loneliness and longing for home. Produced at the height of intersecting debates over Philippine independence and the surge of migrant Filipino laborers in the United States, *The Filipino Rebel* and *The Brown Maiden* prompt us to consider what has been lost in their absence from the archive: the importance of Filipina femininity to the transpacific community in the Philippines and the United States, to the story of developing Philippine–U.S. connections, and to the continued unsettled tensions within diverse groups of Filipinas and Filipinos in the United States.

Ocampo's and Kalaw's transpacific Filipina elites—who, on one hand, seem to be examples of a romantic, idealized narrative of imperial benevolence, but who, on the other hand, are also exceptional precisely because of their eventual rejection of these plots—reveal the literary production of Filipina and Filipino authors as part of a larger meditation on the difficulties and complexities of imagining and enacting opposition. They share important and unacknowledged connections with other postcolonial and diasporic intellectuals, and they are linked to the global phenomenon of burgeoning nationalist and anticolonial movements.[39] Their undermining of benevolent education and plots of imperial and global feminist uplift also historicizes and extends other narrative patterns that have been recently examined by Asian American scholars.[40] For example, Lisa Lowe's treatment of the fraught development of modern humanism, Nguyen's exploration of the good and bad subjects of Asian American resistance movements, Kandice Chuh's imperative to imagine Asian American subjectivities and critique otherwise, and David Eng's analysis of neoliberal capitalism and its effect on what he calls queer liberalism all underscore one similar and troubling cycle: the acquisition of liberation, or a façade of liberation, presumably achieved via one's acquiescence to and implicit perpetuation of the very ideological structures that have created dynamics of oppression.[41]

The Filipino Rebel and The Brown Maiden mark their authors' own troubled links to U.S. occupation and encapsulate why literature produced during this period is compelling—because of, and not in spite of, its difficult-to-read connections with imperial objectives. Kalaw and Ocampo exemplify how colonial subjects posited women as crucial to national identity and counter notions of an elite nationalism solely envisioned and furthered by men. The two romances present a synergy that should not be ignored, as they tie the transpacific Filipina's destiny to imaginings of the Philippines, the United States, and their postimperial futures. In The Filipino Rebel and The Brown Maiden, she serves as an experimental prototype, as her authors, exceptional elites themselves, use romance to assert control over the protean and unsettled dynamics of transpacific relations and as an avenue to create alternative destinies, however complicated and uncertain, for the Filipina and the Philippines.

In projecting the transpacific Filipina's destiny, the conclusions to both romances end with an appeal to sentiment, to the hearts and minds of "gentle readers." This emphasis on the heart—both that of the transpacific woman and of her audience—will become even more important, as we shall see, in the 1940s and 1950s, when sentimental constructs and revisions of transpacific sisterhood—and new plots for the transpacific Filipina and her destiny—emerge as dominant strategies during the Pacific War and the Cold War.

Chapter Four

NEW ORDER PRACTICALITY

AND GUERRILLA DOMESTICITY

THE PACIFIC WAR'S FILIPINA

In the article "Collaboration Begins at Home," published in January 1943, the columnist writing under the pen name M. L. I. offered a New Year's resolution for Filipina housewives. The stakes were high, which seemed appropriate for a nation and its citizens, both reeling from the turmoil of war and occupation. In the course of a year, Filipinas and Filipinos had undergone an especially difficult transition from a fledgling commonwealth only a few years away from official independence from the United States to a once-again occupied country with a new imperial master. When M. L. I.'s "Collaboration Begins at Home" was published, the Japanese regime had been in the country for over a year. The debate over whether or not Filipinas and Filipinos should work with or resist the Japanese was a hot button topic, complicated by a collision of two empires who both promised liberation for the Philippines. With M. L. I.'s article, one of the few remaining Philippine periodicals still in print, the *Sunday Tribune Magazine*, brought the dilemma of a divided country directly to the reader's heart and home: the wartime hearth managed and cared for by the Filipina housewife.

Written under the watchful eyes of Japanese supervision, M. L. I.'s plan is weighted with the responsibility of wartime difficulty. It also turns to the promise of possibility, a call for Filipinas to embrace their potential, to write the terms of a new future:

> For us housewives, in particular, the new year is like a big book, with clean unwritten pages, for us to fill with what we will. It is up to us to say whether the pages shall be full of days usefully and gainfully spent, or

otherwise. For instance, no end of possibilities lie before us in sharing in the work of building up a greater New Philippines, a fact which may possibly surprise some of us, who may be immersed in household and family. But the humblest of us has a role to play, and more so to the housewife, who traditionally holds the family purse and practically decides the way of living for her family.[1]

Casting the unfolding new year as a book with pages yet to be filled and the Filipina housewife as its author, this extract from "Collaboration Begins at Home" illustrates some of the key patterns that dominate the discourse of Philippine English periodicals during the Japanese occupation. In articles, columns, and essays, Filipina authors reclaim the humble housewife's importance to the Philippines' future and challenge women to rise to the occasion, to reject the flippant frivolities associated with the West and instead direct their energies to "useful" and "gainful" activities, and to accept their responsibility as major contributors during a time of national possibility and potential.

In her final days as a columnist for the *Philippine Herald*, one of the newspapers whose offices were destroyed early in the war and eventually closed for the duration of the occupation, the Filipina–Irish American journalist Yay Panlilio also presented women with an urgent imperative. Writing "advice for the women" in one of her columns, Panlilio, too, reminded her readers of the high stakes of national crisis: "Let your children look back," she insists, "and remember how their mothers faced the war."[2] While authors like M. L. I. would continue producing material in English under the supervision of the Japanese administration, others, like Panlilio, would forego their writing careers for the moment and join the growing guerrilla resistance movement against the Japanese. Panlilio soon became a colonel and an important strategist in one of the most successful guerrilla operations in the Philippines. When the war was over, she resumed her career as a writer, using her talents to appeal to an American audience on behalf of Filipinas and Filipinos who anxiously awaited the recognition, compensation, and veterans' benefits promised to them by the United States. Panlilio's memoir, *The Crucible: An Autobiography by "Colonel Yay"* (1950), is, on one hand, an appeal to the hearts and minds of an American public and, on the other hand, a case for the recognition of women's contributions during the war amid discursive productions that overwhelmingly celebrated the wartime exploits of men.

These two examples capture the focus of this chapter, which turns to yet another archival byway to analyze the broad spectrum of how Filipina writers recrafted transpacific femininities in response to rapid shifts in their country's relations with Japan and the United States during and immediately after the Pacific War. In the years of the occupation and the postwar period, Filipina and Filipino authors once again remade the Filipina to negotiate their country's changing status in Asia and the Pacific. This chapter draws attention to the previously unrecognized importance of Filipinas in the Pacific War and analyzes the complex midways of gender, nationalism, and feminism in the 1940s. In the first half, I examine occupation-era periodical work that was redefining the terms of bourgeois Filipina femininity. In essays published from 1943 to 1945 women use the venue of English print culture to determine the Filipina's place in the Japanese New Order. The war years saw the reconfiguration of the home and housewife, for the Japanese regime and its supporters promulgate the woman's return to the domestic realm as part of a larger cultural liberation from the damaging effects of Western influence, embodied in the tensions of the 1930s surrounding the coed. Cropping up repeatedly in the pages of these periodicals, the bodies of these revised, New Order Filipinas reconstruct the terms of identity and the nation during the Pacific War, amid the competing influences of United States, Japan, and Philippine nationalisms.

The New Order Filipina was entangled in the web of Japanese propaganda, which actively sought to strengthen ties between the Philippines and other so-called Oriental nations while deemphasizing the influence of Western and Allied nations like the United States and Great Britain. The rhetorical use of the Orient was strategic; the term broadly encapsulated notions of pan-Asian unity but also marked the argument that the Japanese could foster Philippine nationalism while at the same time furthering imperialist expansion. Although many of the texts I focus on were produced under duress (for periodicals like the *Sunday Tribune Magazine* that were under the direct supervision of Japanese administrators and censors), this collection of work nevertheless testifies to how Filipina authors responded to the war and the occupation. During the war, elite women who had begun to work outside the domestic sphere began to define the home as a space to enact forms of nationalism and feminism. The three years of the occupation were the runup to the reclamation of the caring Filipina heart as important to home and nation, which became a dominant representational pattern in the postwar period.

The chapter's second half focuses on Panlilio's memoir, *The Crucible*, published by Macmillan in the United States. This book takes up wartime tropes popularized in the Philippines and the United States as part of its appeal to readers to reconsider the contribution of guerrillas to the war and to recognize the efforts of women. Panlilio recounts her life as "Mother of the Guerrillas" and "Guerrilla Wife." Through this representation of what I call guerrilla domesticity, she manipulates the emphasis on the maternal and the home that was central to pro-Japanese texts. Panlilio constructs a new, resistant Filipina femininity that is both martial and domestic. Her memoir, however, is also conversant with wartime and postwar propaganda circulating in the United States, which emphasized brotherhood between Filipinos and U.S. GIs, a construction that depended ultimately on casting women as helpless victims suffering at the hands of demonized Japanese villains. Instead of representing the Filipina mother as being paralyzed or victimized by war, Panlilio views her guerrilla mother and wife as more than just metaphor, and guerrilla domesticity itself as a form of military strategy.

Building on the analyses in previous chapters of Filipina elites' fraught representations of transpacific networks of women, I examine wartime and postwar imaginings of coalitions of women and read the shifting, unstable production of transpacific sisterhood against the dominant metaphor of wartime brotherhood. All of the writers featured here use new formations of transpacific sisterhood—between Filipinas and Asian women in the essays written during the occupation and between Americans and Filipinas for Panlilio—as a method of nationalist, patriotic, and feminist practice to circumvent masculine imperial and nationalist discourse. Ultimately, these methods are also strategies for surviving the war and its aftermath. Whereas the essays and romances I discussed above are more hesitant in their representations of transpacific sisterhood, Pacific wartime writers explore the positive—and politically advantageous—potential of coalitions with women in other Asian nations and in the United States. During the years of the Japanese occupation, Filipina writers found it important to reclaim rather than reject Asian sisterhood. These authors suggest that such collaborations do not preclude their allegiance to the cause of Philippine nationalism. While the periodical essays stress the value of Filipina and pan-Asian sisterhood, Panlilio encourages emotional networks between Filipinas and American women to capture the sympathies of readers in the United States.

In part, this chapter historicizes developments in transpacific feminism during the Pacific War and the postwar era and studies their contours, which, like the authorial and representational approaches featured in earlier chapters, do not fit easily within dynamics of resistance or subversion. Because of the circumstances of the war, these women encountered pressing difficulties that affected their unfolding practices of feminism. Rather than attempt to pin them down as either resisting or collaborating with Japan or the United States, I extend Viet Thanh Nguyen's delineation of "flexible strategies" of authorship and view their work through two overlapping lenses.[3] The first is what Lina Flor Trinidad in 1944 called "practical patriotism," the end product of those "usefully and gainfully spent" domestic energies suggested by M. L. I.[4] Expanding upon the meaning of "practical patriotism," I examine the complex rhetorical maneuvers authors must rely on for their professional and literal survival during the occupation and in the postwar years. The second is Panlilio's term, "tightrope and triple-talk," a vexed performance of Filipina domestic femininity that is central to her manipulation of both male privilege in military complexes and her appeal to American readers. What follows, then, is also an exercise in the practical, an examination of how these women managed to walk the tightrope of battling empires and "triple-talk" their way through extraordinary difficulties against all odds—to earn a living as a writer under the watchful eyes of Japanese censors, to actively resist Japanese forces as a guerrilla, and to make new forms of Filipina femininity and transpacific sisterhood amid imperial and national shifts.

The Japanese Occupation and Its Critical Contours

The motives that have shaped scholarship on the war in the Philippines and on the triangulated relations connecting the United States, the Philippines, and Japan are deeply entrenched in larger disciplinary and cultural narratives. Within the U.S. academy, consideration of the Pacific expansion of the Japanese empire remains a somewhat uncomfortable topic, one that has until fairly recently been avoided within Asian American studies.[5] What would it mean for the political coalition among Asians that energized the development of Asian American studies as a discipline if one were to reconsider Japanese empire and to compare U.S. and Japanese imperial endeavors? Indeed, such comparisons would problematize political unities formed across ethnic and national borders, which were so crucial to the emergence in the 1960s and 1970s of Asian American cultural nationalism. Despite the rhetoric of racial equality that was so important to the justification of Japanese expansion, the regime was marked by extreme violence and aggression, and victims of the Japanese empire are still wrestling with trauma and debates over reparations.[6] Scholarship on the occupation is further compromised by wartime and postwar revisions of U.S.–Philippine relations. During the war, Japan figured as the universal enemy of the United States and the Philippines, and prior tensions—such as the presence of Filipino laborers in the United States, the occupation of the Philippines, and the long struggle for independence—dissolved in the wake of public discourse that celebrated unity between Filipinas and Filipinos and Americans.

In comparison to Spanish and U.S. imperialisms in the Philippines, the Japanese occupation was short-lived (1942–44). In part because of the Japanese regime's relative brevity, developments in Philippine letters during this period remain relatively unstudied.[7] Analyses of occupation literature have also been bounded by two mitigating factors: archival limitations caused by the destruction of materials during the war, and the dismissal of the merit of the work itself. Indeed, scholars point to the war years as a low period for Philippine literature in English, as limited publishing opportunities gave way to what many see as a corresponding efflorescence of Tagalog literature.[8] But even though English literature produced during the war may be politically compromised by its appearance in newspapers and magazines directed or supervised by Japanese censors, these texts document the indispensable role of cultural propaganda in the implementation of Japanese objectives.

Like their American predecessors, Japanese officials saw the reeducation and indoctrination of Filipinas and Filipinos as essential to the occupation's success, and the regime emphasized the importance of reconnecting citizens to their Asian identities. Efforts included attempts to reassert Tagalog and Nippongo/Nihongo as national languages, a corresponding devaluation of English, an overhaul of the educational system to purge Western influence, and rigid control of media outlets.[9] The cultural restrictions and changes instituted by the Japanese administration reconfigured Philippine nationalism and national identity. Marcelino Foronda's assessment of this period is insightful: "While the Occupation ended too soon, and, therefore, its impact seems minimal, the return-to-the-Orient movement that it engendered entered into the Filipino racial consciousness, thus also bringing about pride in being Filipino and a love for things Philippine."[10]

To achieve widespread cultural indoctrination, Japanese officials early on marshaled the efforts of Filipinas and encouraged them to foster the interests of the Greater East Asia Co-Prosperity Sphere. Most scholars have yet to seriously consider the importance of women to the occupation.[11] My study of the gendered dynamics in this period expands upon recent attention to the occupation of Japan by the United States and to the role of American and Japanese women in wartime occupation. Building upon frequent comparisons between the occupation of Iraq and the narrative of the success of the United States in Japan, Mire Koikari and Lisa Yoneyama have reconsidered the American involvement in Japan and the frequent discursive emphasis on American women saving Japanese women from oppression. These representations of the U.S. occupation of Japan, then, became the foundation for later Cold War rhetoric that centers on the spread of democracy, the eradication of communist oppression, and the management of both white American women at home and women abroad as allies in Cold War expansion.[12] One might compare such developments in the U.S. administration of Japan with endeavors by the Japanese administration in the Philippines, for Japanese media outlets and official policies during these few years stress the importance of the role of women and argue that Filipinas must reject the oppressive forces of the West.

The Japanese invasion of the Philippines began within days of the bombing of Pearl Harbor on December 7, 1941.[13] Japanese forces entered Manila on January 2, 1942, and immediately moved to institute political, economic, and cultural control over the city. The military administration rationalized the occupation as a liberation of the country from its Western oppressors and the welcoming of the Philippines as a member in the Greater East Asia Co-Prosperity Sphere. Japanese propaganda urged the populace to reject its previous ties to the United States and Great Britain and to reformulate connections to other Asian nations. Lt. Gen. Masaharu Homma, commander in chief of the Imperial Japanese Forces, ordered that measures be taken to reeducate Filipinas and Filipinos as to their place in the empire, eliminate their dependence on the West, develop a new Filipino consciousness as fellow Orientals, correct a cultural overemphasis on materialism, learn the Japanese language (along with Tagalog as a national language), and be inspired by a new love of labor.[14]

To cement perceptions of their benevolent aims, in October of 1943 the Japanese freed the Philippines, staging the proclamation, complete with an orchestrated flag-waving crowd for prime photo opportunities, of a supposedly independent republic governed by José Laurel as president. Meanwhile, the situation in Manila became increasingly difficult, as the nation as a whole faced critical unrest, market panic, food shortages, unemployment, and poverty. Things became worse as the war continued, putting even more pressure on propaganda outlets to disseminate a business-as-usual outlook and to reenergize the spirits of the city's inhabitants.[15]

Japanese officials began controlling educational ventures and media outlets immediately. Libraries were raided, and many books were destroyed. The textbook examining committee censored educational materials, and new policies ensured that only Filipinos could teach history, the national language, and subjects related to "character education."[16] Radio stations offered lessons in Japanese.[17] Approaches to reining in print media were extreme. The main office of the *Philippine Herald* was destroyed in the initial days of bombing. Soon after entering the city, Japanese forces closed the offices of two independent papers, the *Bulletin* and the *Philippines Free Press*.[18] New periodicals—among them *Pillars*, a monthly periodical edited by Filipinos under Japanese supervision, the bilingual monthly women's magazine *Filipina*, and the academically oriented *Philippine Review*—were founded during the occupation, but all presses were subject to print restrictions, and the publishers were required to apply for a permit before publishing.[19] After limiting which presses could publish, the Japanese *Sendenbu*, or Propaganda Corps (later renamed the *Hodobu*, or Department of Information), initiated a widespread propaganda campaign, of which the *Tribune* was an arm. The pieces published in the *Tribune*, notes Ricardo Trota Jose, "were all logical corollaries which stemmed from the basic policy plans. They were building Japan up as a leader of Asia, emphasizing Japanese culture, turning back to traditional Philippine culture and nurturing nationalism, portraying the evils of western and especially American culture."[20] The *Tribune*'s articles were translated and republished in the Spanish-language *La Vanguardia* and the Tagalog *Taliba*.

Filipina and Filipino authors, shaken by the bombings of Manila and the sudden takeover of the city, found themselves in an arduous position. In his seminal study of life during the Japanese occupation, Teodoro Agoncillo describes this time as one of "opportunity and hypocrisy." English, as I argued in chapter 1, was hotly debated as a viable choice for literary production in the 1930s, and now it once again came under scrutiny. Those writing in English found themselves in a dilemma with no clear options. Some started publishing in Tagalog, while some had their work translated for them. The situation, recalls Cristino Jamias, was dire: a "total intellectual blackout. The threads of the literary clothwebs snapped. The writings in English did not count. The writers who came to their own in the '30s who were compelled to say anything in print just kept up appearances. . . . It was a talent to hide, but lying low for those who were known to be able to write was almost a death. The enemy was everywhere." Even in the work that was published, writers had to be extremely careful, especially since "the Japanese *Hodobu* had censors who wielded their blue pencils as ruthlessly as their officers the *samurai* swords." The authors of pro–New Order articles, stories, and essays responded to criticism by saying their actions stemmed from economic need rather than desire. After the war many of these writers would conveniently forget the ties to the East for which they had at one point vociferously lobbied. Yet many prominent Philippine journalists rejected these terms, disappeared from the literary scene altogether, or joined the resistance.[21]

These texts, produced in Japanese-monitored publications, are indeed entangled with the motives of the Japanese administration, but they attest to a hitherto ignored feature of the occupation, namely, the importance of Filipinas in building the new republic. A drama played out on the pages of the sanctioned periodicals. Indeed, almost immediately Japanese officials deemed that women could and should be involved in the cultural life, political administration, and education of the new Philippines. The attention to women was surely strategic, since Filipinas had earned suffrage in the Philippines only five years earlier. Japanese administrators created a Women's Bureau staffed by leading Filipinas in Manila. To supplement this formal political body, newspapers focused on outlining directives for Filipina women, from encouraging them to become actively involved in the moral uplift of the nation to offering practical advice to housewives for conserving resources and food.

A Call for Practical Patriotism: Filipinas of the New Order

Beginning in January 1943, newspapers and periodicals in Manila issued an urgent call to action. The stakes were high, the tasks numerous and difficult. These initial pleas directly link the Philippines' destiny to that of the rest of Asia. In order to enact that future, elite women such as M. L. I., Encarnación Alzona, Francisca Tirona Benitez, and Mrs. Leon Ma. Gonzales argue that this time, like no other, is one of "new needs and new situations," a period of "serious responsibilities"[22] that demands the "active participation" of its women in a task of "paramount importance."[23] Their language is prophetic, millennial, tinged with the same rhetoric used by the Japanese to justify their imperialist expansion. Tirona Benitez, the director of the Women's Bureau, for example, in an article that outlines new educational initiatives for girls and women, urges them to take part in claiming the "ultimate destiny of the Filipino people as an Oriental nation."[24] In these terms, the Filipina housewife becomes both the representative of the Philippines as a whole and a principal player in its restructuring. Yet the women also acknowledge that these times, while offering the Filipina opportunities to embrace her true potential, call for nationwide sacrifice and hardship. The Filipina housewife is responsible for the education and caring of the nation and its citizens and additionally is called to duty beyond the bounds of the home, to willingly sacrifice herself for her nation. "We want Filipino women," said President Laurel in 1944, "who, if necessary, will go out of their homes, unite with the Filipino men, and if necessary be crucified with them on the cross of national salvation, so that we may either rise together, men and women, Filipinos alike, or fall together, men and women, Filipinos alike."[25] In these texts, war becomes the great equalizer, as men and women, all "Filipinos alike," stand and fall together, presumably united in their resistance to Allied forces.[26]

A survey of essays and articles published by Filipinos and Filipinas in some of the main periodicals of the Japanese occupation—the Tribune and Sunday Tribune Magazine, Filipina, and the Philippine Review—reveals several recurring trends in the preoccupation with the Filipina's role in the New Order. Many authors encourage women to foster sisterhood with other Asian women. To build the case for transpacific Asian sisterhood, some writers turn to an ethical argument, pointing to racism and classism in the United States and invoking a long history of American exploitation not only of Filipinos, but also of other people of color. Others use a more metaphysical approach and insist that Filipinas and Filipinos are in need of spiritual regeneration, a resurrection of the Oriental soul. For some, this regeneration must be accessed through a return to a construction resurrected from the women's suffrage debates of the 1930s: the idealization of precolonial Malay heritage and culture. For others, salvation depends on becoming more aware of Christian duties to one's neighbors and modeling the Victorian ideal of the angel in the house. But the most dominant rhetorical argument centers on what might be called the evolution of Trinidad's notion of practical patriotism. Drawing on the old vilification of the transpacific coed, these authors overwhelmingly satirize the prewar Filipina as being far too frivolous, shamelessly Westernized, and distracted by the allure of Hollywood glamour. Arguing that this version of transpacific femininity has no place in the Japanese-occupied Philippines, they remake the frivolous elite

Filipina into a reformed icon, a New Order Filipina who rejects the flippant attitudes and careless pastimes of the prewar days and instead devotes herself to practical and nationalist concerns such as improving her family and fostering a community of fellow citizens.

To reinforce connections between the Philippines and other Asian nations, writers during the occupation repeatedly call attention to examples of racism as practiced in the United States. Echoing Japanese imperial logic, they counter the triumphant rhetoric of Filipino–American brotherhood that dominates American public discourse during the war; they instead promote coalition among Asian nations and praise Japan for freeing oppressed peoples of Asia from the bonds of Western domination (an argument that only served to shore up Japanese imperial expansion). In their criticism of racism, the essayists turn to an easy target: the experience of African Americans in the United States. They also define race, class, and labor disparities as long-standing, widespread problems. The writers use rhetorical terms that differ starkly from those employed by elite authors in the first three decades of the twentieth century, who carefully distanced themselves from African Americans, Mexicans, other people of color in the United States, and the indigenous peoples of the Philippines. In "The Dawn of a New Era" (1942), A. Perico reminds his readers that "prejudice is directed not only against the Negro but also against all brown and Oriental peoples." After pointing to the example of "a Filipino physician who was nearly lynched by an outraged white mob because he married an American girl from a little town in Virginia," Perico then connects this seemingly isolated example to a broader pattern. "Even the Italian, because of his olive skin," notes Perico, "has been discriminated against, as the 'Wop'; and the Mexican, the South American and the Spaniard have been treated as inferior and labeled 'Spic.' "[27]

Writing in 1943, O. Marajas is much more scathing. Marajas references the race riots in Watsonville, California, in 1930 to bitterly critique so-called brotherly U.S.–Filipino relations:

"Brown brothers" they had been called. But since white and brown in a discriminating country like the United States are as distant as the poles, the word brother becomes a euphemistic term for "hewers of wood and drawers of water," which in their painful nakedness, the browns would surely resent. Like the Negroes the Filipinos had never been looked upon as the equals of the Euro-Americans. Their "spheres of influence" were the kitchens and orchards, for, as a rule, they have never been given better jobs than as fruit-pickers, dish-washers, laborers and servants. Prosperity was alien to them; so was dignity.[28]

Contextualizing race-based discrimination and labor disparities, Marajas highlights a longer, more inimical history and exposes Filipino–American brotherhood as a fiction that occludes the exploitation of Filipino labor in the United States. The reference to the term "spheres of influence," the phrase frequently used in the late nineteenth century to justify the carving up of Africa among competing imperial interests, links African American and Filipina and Filipino experience as mutually shaped by imperial expansion. The relationship between the United States and the Philippines, argue Marajas and Perico, was strained long before the contemporary moment. Such conflict and tension set the stage for the reformation of relations between the Philippines and the Greater East Asia Co-Prosperity Sphere.

In confronting this rapidly shifting political landscape, authors faced a crossroads. In what ways might the Philippines and its citizens meet the potential offered by the war and repair their frayed ties to their Asian brothers and sisters? The heart of the problem, according to many of the writers, is metaphysical, what Lady Pungol calls "the full realization of the spiritual values of the East."[29] Spiritual regeneration, some argue, is necessary to refashion connections between Filipinas and their sisters in Asia. For these authors, well-cared-for homes and Filipina housewives are perfect locations and architects of this reawakening. Tirona Benitez observes, "The keynote of our spiritual regeneration is the revival and strengthening of Oriental virtues and good old Filipino traits, and the weeding out of Occidental ways and attitudes opposed to these virtues and detrimental to our well-being. The home is the starting place for spiritual regeneration."[30] Writing for the periodical Filipina in 1944, Lady Pungol agrees and adds that much of the problem stems exactly from transpacific interaction, the creation of a hybrid Filipina identity that is neither Western nor Asian. Filipinas and Filipinos find themselves in a conundrum, for "in our effort to Westernise our Oriental soul, we have fairly enough succeeded in becoming neither one nor the other." She then enumerates a list of polluting Western influences: the "outlandish names we may give our children," "languages other than our own we may have learned to speak to perfection," and "imported stuffs we may have learned to eat or drink or use with ease and elegance."[31]

In the view of these authors, the spiritual reinvigoration of the Filipina and Filipino soul and the shedding of superficial Western trappings will return men and women to states of equality. These claims contradict arguments recurring throughout much of the early to mid-twentieth century that stress the distance between Filipinos and other Asians and the affinity between the Philippines and the West. Such differences, although influenced by the disparate contexts of the Philippine independence debates and the Japanese occupation, nevertheless should be reread amid this broader history of transpacific relations. As I argued in chapter 1, for most of the twentieth century advocates for independence envisioned a democratic Philippines as the successor to the United States. Given the tensions between the United States and China and Japan, authors chose to emphasize difference over similarity.[32] Now, with the rise of a new imperial regime, writers in the Philippines once again faced the dilemma of which colonial bedfellow to choose. Articles published during the occupation rewrite these terms, as writers must manipulate their claims and their censors by using New Order rhetoric. The reliance on the soul stresses that Filipinas' and Filipinos' Asian identity can be recovered, reconverted, and transformed, even after over 350 years of contact with the West.

In a move to differentiate the New Order Filipina from long-standing stereotypes of Japanese women as being weak and oppressed, authors justify their new relationship to the rest of Asia with idealizations of their precolonial, indigenous background. Both men and women writers use strategies similar to those employed by feminist Filipinas in the 1930s, who underscored examples of Malay equality to argue for the existence of liberated women in precolonial times. Seeking to correct those who might think that modern women's equality was a result of American influence, Maria Kalaw Katigbak suggests that the problem stems from "an inadequate background on the history of the Filipino woman."[33] The regeneration of the Filipina soul, then, is not just a wholesale acceptance of Japanese models of masculinity and femininity. Indeed, there is much discussion by those who worry about the acceptance of Japanese women's immediate deference to men. To circumvent this opposition to Asian sisterhood, the authors maintain that Filipinas and Filipinos, unlike their counterparts in Japan, have long established a system of equality between men and women because of a Malayan legacy that embraces "the principle of equality of man and woman," a "noble tradition" that has been "preserved" and "cherish[ed]" by "modern Filipinos."[34] Arturo M. Tolentino goes even further. The "apparent divergence" between Filipinas and Japanese women, he writes, is actually a much "later development," for "in ancient times, Japan too accorded a very high place to women."[35]

If Filipina women are and have been equal to men, what does the Filipina who accepts spiritual regeneration gain? Repeatedly, these articles assert that elite Filipinas of the New Order must forsake the frivolity of their Americanized predecessors. Presenting a scathing critique of prewar transpacific women who are the products of American colonial influence—the "so-called 'smart set,'" "large city faddists" and "civilised modernes"[36]—the authors decry those who fail to live up to their wartime duties. This type of woman, scolds Alzona, "delights in aping scandalously the gay, artificial life of Hollywood stars as portrayed on the screen." Both men and women in the cities "have shamelessly adopted the worst features of the decadent western civilization." But lest her readers think this phenomenon is widespread, Alzona assures them that these women are a minority, the "idiotic wives and daughters of a few rich men."[37] The call to accept wartime responsibility, then, is also a call to reject imitation and to avoid especially the dangerous continuing circulation of American capital consumption. Fernandina Cariño Rosal, like Alzona, presents her case in moral terms. She states that Filipinas must reject the evils of the West and embrace the hard work and productivity of their Eastern sisters. She adduces many counterexamples of New Order Filipinas who are doing so: "Our women have never been as active in national affairs than as they are today. In pre-war times, their most important activities were balls, parlor games, parties, and picnics. Today, they are engaged in more serious tasks, helping people help themselves."[38]

The women give high praise to those who have rejected the damaging influence of the ideologies of materialism, individualism, and capitalism—which, in their minds, have torn an already threadbare fabric of national unity that now must be repaired. They remake the transpacific Filipina as one self-conscious of her duty and responsibility to a new Philippines, allied with other Asian Pacific nations rather than the West. In a fictional letter to her daughter, the personified one-year-old new republic under the Japanese occupation, Trinidad summarizes the major divergences between the women (and the nation) of yesterday and those of the future. Espousing her practical patriotism, Trinidad's treatise sums up the dominant direction of this series of essays, a pattern that appears in multiple periodicals and spans the range of the war years. Elite women of the new Philippines will

> be brought up with a sense of values that does not give too much importance to material things. You will be brought up with a firm belief that individualism is a selfish stand and that anything selfish is not beneficial

in the end. You will learn to act and speak with a keen regard for other people. You will do things that will not primarily benefit yourself alone, nor even just your immediate family. You will accept without a doubt the fact that when citizens, male or female, strive to work with common zeal and without materialistic aims, a perfect harmony will be effected and this harmony will hasten the perfection of the work.[39]

Trinidad's musings reflect the dominant critique of Western materialism and individualism. The New Order Filipina recognizes that individualism is always a selfish venture and that such self-interest has no place in a nation rebuilding itself. This Filipina, they say, has grown up, matured, wearied of the petty distractions of "balls, parlor games, parties, and picnics," and turned to more "serious tasks, helping people help themselves."[40]

But practical patriotism, while certainly influenced by the dramatically different circumstances of the war, nevertheless depends on the bourgeois woman's moral responsibility to shape the family and the nation. Trinidad's imagining of the new nation as a daughter is telling. The writers' wartime Filipina gladly foregoes individual pleasure to concentrate instead on her family, her community, and the nation. She rejects material comforts in favor of spiritual salvation. She realizes the importance of being "more constructive," choosing charity work and activities "so that their benevolence is not simply of the heart but also of the mind, and the recipient of their help receives benefits not only for the body but also for the spirit."[41] And she relishes her responsibility to cultivate communal values, the "higher demands of family, nation, race and humanity."[42]

The idealization of the Filipina as the foundation of ethical upbringing and the caretaker of a future nation's citizens is manifested differently in Josefa Gonzales de Estrada's 1944 reference to the Victorian angel in the house. Turning not to the traditions of the East but to an icon popularized in the West in the nineteenth century, Gonzales de Estrada's allusion to the angel in the house draws together some of the thematic language of occupation-era articles: the canonization of the New Order Filipina, the emphasis on practicality and martyrdom, the construction of the woman as defender of the family and the nation. The Filipina as "WIFE and MOTHER" is a woman "who must be stable like Mother Earth, wise like the Mother of Jesus, and vigilant, long suffering, utterly reliable; all understanding and love . . . she must be the material representation of an unseen Guardian Angel, with the small failings of a human being who is not yet a saint, but is on the way to canonization in the hearts of her brood as soon as ever death touches her."[43] Combining earth mother with the Virgin Mary, Gonzales de Estrada's angel is rooted in Philippine soil and Christian spirit, both saint and martyr, strong and able. Given the overwhelming number of Catholics in the Philippines, de Estrada's Christian references are carefully planned. She strings together a narrative of spiritual salvation with a call for charitable action and a valorization of the martyred mother figure.

Ultimately, the term practical patriotism describes more than the writers' reimagined, New Order Filipina. In this period authors struggled not only with the transition from one imperial master to the next, but also with the hard everyday realities of a nation both occupied and at war: the destruction of their homes and communities, the loss of loved ones, growing poverty levels, food and resource shortages, divided loyalties, and a nagging sense of their nation's uncertain future. In these essays, we see authors navigating such uncertain political and ontological terrain through the recreation of a distinct type of transpacific femininity. Taken as a whole, the results are difficult to pin down. Although most of the texts welcome the opportunity to reconnect ties between Asia and the Philippines, the details of such linkages remain in conflict. The transpacific Filipina, while the touchstone for the articulation of these connections, is imagined as having variable commitments and influences: moral and spiritual regeneration and a return to precolonial values; equality between men and women, yet a grateful return to the home as her rightful place; and a rejection of individual desire combined with a renewed commitment to community responsibility.

In espousing practical patriotism—for themselves and for their subjects—occupation authors might be easily dismissed as regurgitating propaganda. To be sure, the production of these essays in Japanese-supervised periodicals does much to explain their anti-Western stance and their praise of the opportunities provided by the Greater East Asia Co-Prosperity Sphere. Yet at the same time, we must be cautious in our treatment of these authors and their work, for they valorize practical patriotism in order to imagine seemingly impossible, complicated intersections of nationalism and feminism. The rejection of individualism as practiced in the United States in favor of pan-Asian sisterhood was, on one hand, a concerted effort to break from the Western-influenced Filipina coed of the 1930s and a narrative that idealized the United States as the gatekeeper to her liberation. On the other hand, practical patriotism is also eerily prophetic, for despite these authors' desires to distance themselves from the West, their praise of women's central role as the nation's heart is a predecessor to the rhetoric circulating in the postwar and Cold War years.

Tightroping and Triple-Talking:
Intersections of Transpacific Feminism and Nationalism

While the notion of pan-Asian sisterhood was crucial to the coprosperity of Asian nations under the New Order, the trope of sisterly ties was also conversant with the dominant wartime metaphor of Filipino–American brotherhood. Panlilio's The Crucible reimagines such familial relations to craft a feminist plea for recognition by the United States and the Philippines alike. Panlilio's text recovers the importance not only of Filipino guerrillas but also of Filipinas and their contributions to the war. Like the authors working during the Japanese occupation, Panlilio faces a nation in flux, one with indeterminate status, and the corresponding opportunity to claim a space for women in actively rewriting the terms of the new nation and its future relations with the United States. In The Crucible Panlilio deploys a technique she calls "tightrope and triple-talk" to respond to the recurring tropes that are so important to the discursive production of the Filipina in the United States and the Philippines during the Pacific War: sisterhood and victimization, the power of the home and the family, and the woman's duty to contribute. Taking up these patterns, Panlilio reasserts them in the name of the guerrilla resistance and its recognition. At the same time, she underscores how women's contributions to the war extended well beyond their construction as symbolic icons by both pro-Japanese and pro-American discourse (respectively, the iconic mother at home and the suffering, violated woman in the hands of evil Japanese forces). Revising earlier imaginings of transpacific coalitions of women, Panlilio rewrites the terms of transpacific sisterhood, which she constructs as existing between Filipinas and American female readers, not, like that of her previous counterparts, between Filipinas and other Asian women.

The early events of the war supplied ample material for the idealization of familial Philippine–U.S. relations. The bombings of Pearl Harbor and of Clark Field in the Philippines within days of each other, the joint surrender of Filipino and U.S. forces in April of 1942, and the suffering of these troops at the hands of Japanese soldiers as they marched from the Bataan province to the Camp O'Donnell military prison all fueled a supposed reaffirmation of equality between the Philippines and the United States. In the United

States, emotional tides were quickly turning, and Filipinos, who were once seen as an immigration nuisance and dangerous competition for American laborers, were now hailed as friends, allies, and brothers. After all, both countries had suffered at the hands of a mutual Japanese enemy. Both had reason to seek vengeance, and the two were united as allies in the war.

But after the triumphant days of the war's end and the Philippines' liberation from the Japanese by the United States (an irony that has not been lost on scholars in that the United States effectively liberated a nation it had held as a territory for almost fifty years), the warm brotherly relations began to cool.[44] The controversy received public airing in 1945, when congressional debates over the amount of war reparations and the logistics of paying benefits to Filipino veterans took center stage in both countries. Filipinas and Filipinos had to rebuild a nation torn apart by war. As tense discussions over benefits and reparations took place, the economic situation in the Philippines was steadily declining. Given the request for aid to their country on the congressional docket, Filipinas and Filipinos in the Philippines vehemently responded to criticism from abroad about the state of their nation. The journal *Philippine-American*, for example, published a series of appeals by Filipinas, Filipinos, and American expatriates that asked GIs to be careful in their representation of the Philippines to their congressional representatives at home. Articles gently remind the "unthinking" and "hasty GI" to take care, to stop sending "unjust, thoughtless letters to his congressman," and to remember their responsibility to the Philippines.[45] The authors built a case on the foundation of the dire need for aid in their country. They also manipulated the postwar rhetoric in the United States of the spread of global democracy and raised the specter of racism to remind their American counterparts of the urgency of the situation and of Americans' moral and ethical responsibility to their brothers and sisters.[46]

In these repeated calls to do the right thing, the amount and extent of benefits for war veterans and guerrillas was a repeated point of contention. Those who had served as part of the U.S. Armed Forces of the Far East and those in the guerrilla resistance were ready for the back pay and compensation promised when they were recruited. In 1946 Salvador P. Lopez devoted his column in the *Philippine-American* to the fading glimmer of what he called "Filamerican magic," which seemed especially lackluster from the perspective of those who had served in the war: "It is an odd commentary on Philippine–American relations that today no group of Filipinos feels more deeply aggrieved towards the United States than the very men who cemented those relations with blood and fire. Through four long years of common struggle and sacrifice under the magic spell of Filamerican ideals, there was every good reason to expect that nothing would ever impair the strength of those relations. But victory has been won, the war is over, and the once potent Filamerican magic is fast becoming spent."[47] The souring of relations was exacerbated by those in the United States who balked at giving veterans the full benefits they were promised (in the initial days of the war, Filipinas and Filipinos were to receive the same benefits as U.S. citizens in the armed forces). Citing such differences as the unequal rate of exchange between the Filipino peso and the U.S. dollar, Congress left the issue of reparations unresolved, launching a Filipino veterans' rights movement that lasted over fifty years.[48] When those who served in the guerrilla forces also began asking for their benefits, the situation became very complicated, especially because it was extraordinarily difficult to determine the authenticity of guerrilla outfits and whether or not they had truly served on the side of the United States.[49]

Panlilio lost no time in adding her voice to this appeal. She wrote urgently on behalf of those who had served and would soon expand her audience to include readers in the United States. Panlilio was born in the United States and returned to the Philippines as a teenager. Working as a photographer and reporter for the *Philippine Herald*, she became well known in Manila as the city's fearless woman journalist. Caught in Manila at the outbreak of the war, Panlilio was swept up in resistance efforts. She eventually joined one of the most successful guerrilla outfits in the Philippines, Marking's Guerrillas, and became both a colonel and the lover of their general, Marcos V. "Marking" Agustin.

Panlilio was disturbed by the developing controversies over the recognition of guerrilla troops. Many of her efforts were explicitly devoted to gaining acknowledgment for guerrillas and their families, especially after the Army Forces Western Pacific (AFWESPAC) issued guidelines for monetary compensation that excluded the families of those who had served. Writing a "Letter to a War Widow" (1946), addressed to her good friend and fellow guerrilla Lydia Arguilla, Panlilio angrily cites AFWESPAC's unfair fifth guideline: "*Members of a unit must have devoted their entire efforts, while in the unit, to military activity in the field, to the exclusion of normal civilian pursuits and family obligations. Persons who lived at home, supporting their families by means of farming or other civilian pursuits, and who assisted guerrilla units on a part-time basis are not considered as guerrillas entitled to recognition and pay.*" Panlilio's consternation and repugnance at the "unjust and petty" exclusion of guerrilla families are unequivocal. "Short of the Japanese occupation itself," she "can't see anything more unjust than that," for "*the widows they discriminate against are those whose husbands died most honorably and bravely of all.*" Panlilio chastises the United States for what she sees as morally reprehensible actions, for the nation was shirking its responsibility. The AFWESPAC guidelines deprive those like Arguilla, who not only served as a guerrilla but also lost her husband, the author Manuel Arguilla. These surviving family members suffered during the war and continue to mourn their losses. "What more," ponders Panlilio, "could America ask. . . . You'd think our people had done enough, having done for America what America could not do."[50]

Early appeals like "Letter to a War Widow" form the backdrop for *The Crucible*. In the opening chapter of the memoir, Panlilio establishes the importance of the "tightrope and triple-talk" that pervades the public forum of her radio broadcasts. Her description of these strategies, however, also is a primer for reading the entirety of *The Crucible*. Tightroping and triple-talking describe other acts and maneuvers: throughout the memoir, seemingly casual chitchat, subtle implications and clues, and performance of domestic tropes that subvert wartime male hierarchies. Panlilio stresses that the use of language itself—written and spoken, private and public—offers opportunities for resistance:

> While I waited, I tightroped and triple-talked in and out of the Japanese-censored scripts, trying to accomplish three things: advise the truculent, unarmed Manilans to look before they leaped; tip off [the radio show] the Voice of Freedom what to say instead of what it was saying; inform the Filipino-American forces by the most delicate innuendo what was going on behind enemy lines, innuendo so obscure sometimes that only mental telepathy could decode it. Between broadcasts I chittered and chattered with the Japs, covering my tracks in advance by looking and sounding even more of a fool than I was. (11)

In this passage Panlilio attests to her ability to outwit multiple male censors —Japanese, Filipino, and American. Tightroping and triple-talk accomplish what the officials of the United States Army cannot, even though they do not immediately recognize her contributions. Listening to her radio broadcast, even the war heroes Douglas MacArthur and Carlos Romulo can't quite figure it out: " 'Damn that woman!' the great MacArthur had burst out, turning on his aide, Major Carlos Romulo, who as Manila newspaper owner before the invasion had been my boss. 'Isn't that *your* Yay?' The boss hung his head, and I, talking my way to a saber execution, would have kicked him by television if I'd known it"(12).[51] This episode with Romulo and Mac-Arthur is one of several scenes in *The Crucible* that exemplify the incompetence of most military men and their inability to perform the acts of interpretation required to recognize a woman's involvement in the war.[52] The portrayal of men as incompetent listeners and interpreters is vital to the appeal of the memoir, as the scene foregrounds an audience of women as being potentially more understanding and more careful readers.

As a metaphor, tightrope and triple-talk also waffles between the delicate steps of a balancing act and the razzle-dazzle of circus performance. And indeed, such equivocation is exactly what Panlilio marshals throughout *The Crucible*. Unlike the practical patriotism of occupation-era articles and their use of pro–New Order rhetoric, Panlilio's memoir at first is unabashedly and, in light of her critical views in "Letter to a War Widow," embarrassingly pro-American and anti-Japanese. Yet if one views tightrope and triple-talk as a narrative ruse, the pro-American sensibilities become a bit more complicated. Indeed, Panlilio handles her American readers with great care. Macmillan published *The Crucible* in 1950, at the height of developments in Cold War sentimental rhetoric. As I discuss in chapter 5, and as Mary Dudziak, Jodi Kim, Christina Klein, Penny Von Eschen, Thomas Borstelmann, and others have documented, public and political discourse in the United States, on one hand, romanticized earlier imperial endeavors to justify contemporary expansion (and effectively rewrote the American involvement in the Philippines) and, on the other hand, popularized racial metaphors like the melting pot to recast the violent history of racism and injustice in the United States into a narrative of benevolence.[53]

But in terms of the ideological, the equivocation necessary in tightroping and triple-talking illustrates the difficulties Panlilio encounters as she attempts to construct her guerrilla identity as transpacific, feminist, and nationalist while remaining within the bounds of her appeal. This is no easy task, and the process is riddled with questions, twists and turns, and complications that sit uncomfortably with clearly cut definitions of opposition. Panlilio uses her mixed-race background as a biological basis for her ability to speak as both Filipina and American. "Colonel Yay" also attributes her refusal to conform to models of the dutiful, subservient wife and mother to her mixed Filipina and American heritage. But read within the context of *mestizaje* in the Philippines, Panlilio's claim that her "half-and-half" (63) racial identity is also the foundation of her transpacific *and* nationalist feminism, which markedly differs from a long-standing cultural ambivalence toward the mestiza woman's place in earlier Philippine nationalist texts.[54] The challenges of combining Panlilio's nationalist and feminist objectives are, as we shall see, best illustrated by the balancing act she performs throughout the text, with varying levels of success. The potential power of tightroping and triple-talking, of walking a fine, taut line—one that tenuously strings together her Filipina American identity, her fierce devotion to the Philippines' independence, and her desire to claim a feminist stance through her performance of guerrilla wife and motherhood—is compromised by repeated challenges to her feminist identity. These difficulties stem sometimes from external sources—such as the violent behavior of Agustin—and sometimes from Panlilio herself, as she constantly wavers between her use of romance and motherhood to further her appeal and her suspicion of a domestic family narrative that would require her subservience to a man.

"Like America": The Philippines Is a Melting Pot

Panlilio published *The Crucible* within a few years of the establishment of the Philippine republic, a time when the memory of the debates over reparations and veterans' benefits was still fresh. During this period, war memoirs were immensely popular in the United States; readers were eager to have testaments of the real, lived experience of a war in the Pacific that seemed far away and difficult to imagine. The front matter markets the book to an American audience.[55] The foreword by the journalist Kate Holliday is one of two documents that ostensibly authenticate the main text, the other being reprinted material from the U.S. military that officially recognizes the guerrilla regiment. The foreword constructs an implied reader who deserves to know not only about the previously unacknowledged guerrilla movement, but also the unique story of a Filipina's bravery in war. Holliday recognizes that while "Yay . . . wanted to tell the citizens of the country in which she was born about her 'boys'" (5–6), Panlilio's American audience must understand that Filipinas were also involved in resisting Japanese forces; the book will thus "let the people of America balance their part in the winning of the war against hers" (5). Still, Holliday emphasizes that this story is much more than a straightforward account, and she offers a prologue to the representational manipulation Panlilio employs throughout the narrative. "Yay," she tells us, "has underplayed herself in every page of what you are about to read. Such is Yay. For the story, as she saw it, was the men in the outfit and what they endured. She only allowed herself to enter when it was necessary for her to fight with them for 'principle,' for 'the American way' which is so very dear to her" (6). Instead of proclaiming her own glories in battle, Panlilio, in Holliday's eyes, is ever "humble. Her importance in Marking's outfit has to be inferred. She makes herself a shrew, if anything, a gnat singing about them all" (6). Holliday's foreword thereby acts as a preface to the acts of tightrope and triple-talk that are central to The Crucible, for Panlilio's casting of herself as a nagging, shrewish wife becomes a method for developing control over the guerrilla camp.

In keeping with the postwar idealization of the United States as a melting pot of cultures and a site of racial harmony, the foreword bridges a Filipina author and her American audience through the presumption of shared American principles, conveniently and biologically matched by Panlilio's racially mixed heritage. The relationship Holliday describes is one of both friendship and professional collegiality in that both women are journalists. She glowingly praises the woman she warmly calls by her first name and says that this story "was lived by one of the most gallant women of our time" (5). Panlilio's biological mixture of Irish American and Filipino heritage, as Holliday regards it, makes her an apt representative of a new unity between the Philippines and the United States; she is both "what the Islands call a 'mestiza,' a mixture" and "a woman of whom two nations should be proud" (5). In this logic, mestiza identity is the basis for Panlilio's idealized blending of Philippine and American principles, the best of both nations: "Born in Denver of an Irish Father and a Filipino mother, she grew up in the freedom of the United States, and she took with her into the hills of Luzon not only the American ideals of justice and pride but the Filipino traits of courage and unselfish devotion" (5). Similarly, Holliday maps character qualities onto physiological features, and Panlilio's "Filipino heritage" is phenotypically expressed by her "small, too thin" body and "olive skin and black hair and eyes," while "the Irish in her comes out in delicate bone structure, long-fingered hands, a pointed chin, a casual yet fluid manner of using her body, an intensity of mind" (5). The slippage between traits and body parts, racial characteristics and national ideals underscores the use of racial mixture as the biological crucible for future Philippine–U.S. relations. This slippage, though, also marks a lapse in Holliday's praise of hybridity and reveals the limits of melting pot ideology, which depended upon the recognition of racial difference to imagine the absorption of racial others into an assimilated mixture.

In the text of *The Crucible*, Panlilio employs notions of biological blending. She evokes even the iconic image of the melting pot as melding the best qualities of multiple nations. In a description prefatory to her account of the exceptional bravery of Allen, a "Malay-American-negro," Panlilio compares the crucible of race in the Philippines to that of the United States. Assuring her readers that the Philippines, "like America," is a melting pot, she takes care to explain and define what it means to be a mestiza or a mestizo in the Philippines. But Panlilio's description of the melting pot in the Philippines reveals how savvy she is about race in transpacific contexts. Despite narratives of democratic inclusion represented by the melting pot, she recognizes that racial strains and mixtures are nevertheless classed within a hierarchy:

> There are *mestizos* and *mestizos*. Like America, the Philippines is a melting pot. The tapestry of blood-blends is rich, with the Malay the strong, ever-present warp and all the world's strains as the color and design of the woof. Chinese blood gives a fair, fine-textured skin. Spanish heightens the bone structure and, like Portuguese and Italian, makes for beautiful eyes; only the Hindu, called "Bombay," bequeaths a larger, deeper, more lustrous eye. German and Swiss blood is weak and usually loses to the Malay, but English and American half-breeds are strikingly occidental-ized, so much so that they sometimes lack the piquant, petite charm of the oriental. Parents of mixed blend can expect and take delight in the variation among their children, especially such throwbacks as crop out. (167)

Panlilio's lengthy explanation of *mestizaje* illustrates her awareness of racial hierarchy in the United States. Instead of clarifying the important order of mestizos in the Philippines, which would have placed Spanish and Chinese mestizos in an aristocratic class that was very different from the American mestizos, she bases her explanation on a racial classification system that would resonate with a post–Second World War reader in the United States. This is especially important given the recent experience of the Pacific War, seen by both Americans and Japanese as motivated in part by doctrines of racial domination. In this hierarchy, German and Swiss blood is weak and easily overtaken by the Malay, while English and American can successfully and beneficially alter mestizos to the extent that they are "strikingly occidentalized." Indeed, as one of the "English and American half-breeds," Panlilio claims her own special status (after all, "there are *mestizos* and *mestizos*").

The description of "Mestizo Allen" and his uncommon bravery illustrates Panlilio's awareness of what goes unacknowledged in postwar discourses of race. Despite celebrations of the United States as a site of harmonious racial blending, the American public was still deeply suspicious of miscegenation; interracial marriages were culturally taboo and legally prohibited in most states.[56] In the Philippines, Mestizo Allen might be "least conspicuous of all blends," but his "dark, chocolate brown" skin would have distinctly marked his difference in the United States (167). Sidestepping Allen's darkness, Panlilio moves on to emphasize his exceptional devotion to the guerrilla cause and his exemplary behavior; he is "well built, well educated, courteous and patriotic" (167). He illustrates "the fact that Americanism is not a nationality but a code of ethics" (168), as U.S. qualities of courage and patriotism become the idealized expressions of racial mixture. What lies beneath this description, though, is an assertion that both Allen and Panlilio are exceptions to the rule, ideal racial mixtures because of their dedication to an American "code of ethics."

Participating in a postwar narrative that erases former colonial injustice and violence, Panlilio often aligns the United States with ethical practices and principles. Like authors before her, she reminds her American readers of their moral responsibility to fulfill promises to the Philippines. During a heated disagreement with Marking, she threatens to kill herself rather than compromise what she believes is the best course for the guerrillas to take. For Panlilio, this is the only option: "It's American. Filipinos will die for love, and Americans will die for principle. I am half-and-half. I die the same way" (63). Her rhetorical conflations illustrate the ambiguities of this midway of transpacific identity, nationalism, and feminism. The assertion that she is "half-and-half" and thus will "die the same way" roots her ability to blend Filipina love with American principle in the already popular rhetoric of the melting pot and Cold War sentimentalism.

Guerrilla Domesticity and Its Limits

To appeal to American readers' sympathies, Panlilio uses such combinations of the sentimental and the exceptional in her representation of guerrilla mother and wife. Throughout the opening chapter, she tightropes and triple-talks to undermine the rigid boundaries of male space. Recalling the popularized, exclusive brotherhood of American and Filipino men, she maps a gendered cartography of wartime Manila that excludes women's military action. With the siege of Bataan underway, U.S. forces repeatedly deny Panlilio the opportunity to accompany them into battle. She pleads with several colleagues to take her with them on trucks bound for Bataan, yet gets nothing but refusals: "From Keeler in Intelligence: *Stick around.* From Diller close to MacArthur: *Go home.* From Glass: *Save the country if you can.* And again from Keeler: *Wait for orders. We'll send you orders*" (9). Panlilio focuses especially on the limits this military bureaucracy places on women: women must remain within the domestic, familiar space of home and passively wait for direction. War ossifies boundaries that she has formerly been able to cross easily as a woman reporter and agent working for U.S. intelligence. Instead, she must outmaneuver the gendered limits of wartime Manila by putting on the trappings of hyper-subservient femininity. Formerly known throughout Manila as a tomboy, she escapes from the city with a price on her head by passing as a clinging, simpering woman: "And the disguise that passed friend after friend, sentry after sentry, was simply girls' clothes—worn for the first time in years. A masculine escort, lipstick, powder, a dress. . . . I simpered, clinging to my escort's arm" (13).

Panlilio's most extensive balancing act, however, is the construction of her new identity as a "guerrilla mother," which takes up the domestic to claim a position of military power in an environment that would render a woman's active involvement in war impossible. Panlilio's initial unfamiliarity with domestic duties punctuates her uneasy approach to the behaviors of motherhood; she confesses that "not even a handkerchief had I washed for years before the war" (35), and she must quickly learn to care for an entire camp of men: "Nagging, scolding, pounding at them, I wondered what had happened to me. Where was the girl who had wandered far and fast and been reprimanded by Romulo at the top of his lungs in the days when he was no general and the *Herald* was the liveliest paper in town? No reckless scrapes for me any more, and no reckless scrapes allowed even those around me. With or without bosoms, a fretful, no-good-end predicting Mamma. Gone my once jaunty shoulders. Gone even a sense of humor" (128). Although Panlilio may not have what she envisions as the stereotypical body of a "Mamma," her behavior makes her one. By nagging and scolding her guerrilla children, the impetuous and tomboy reporter rises to a leadership role that was not previously possible. Combining maternal influence with military power, she claims control of the camp, declaring it "my house, by God"

(15). While the men initially resist Panlilio's authority, complaining that "now we take orders from a woman" (15), their objections subside as she assumes the role of protector. She relies upon racialized representations of motherhood, especially the black mammy figure. As "Mammy" (74) and "Mother of the Guerrillas" (75), Panlilio describes the men's gradual recognition of her power within the camp, especially over their general, Marking: "Through three years I was to spread my skirts protectively between Marking and one or another of his best men" (58). In her "practiced heavy-mother role," Panlilio reinscribes gendered and racial stereotypes of maternal bodies: "I had to smile because I don't have a great, bulging bosom upon which to pillow a troubled head, and if I don't ooze with kindness I look thin, dark, and mean" (126).

Although Panlilio's guerrilla Mammy maintains a leadership role in the camp, fulfilling this role does not ultimately challenge constructs that would confine Filipinas to the domestic realm, nurturing nationalism at home while the men leave to fight. Some of the most interesting textual moments are those in which Panlilio leaves camp, commands her men, and wields a gun. In these scenes she reveals that her involvement in the guerrilla resistance extended beyond the domestic space of the camp, as she plays a primary role in military action. Unlike her accounts of learning to act like a mother, which are plagued by frustration, she participates in the outfit's exploits with little conflict.

Panlilio triumphantly represents guerrilla motherhood as a way for a woman to claim power during the war, but there are still limits to these acts of tightrope and triple-talk. Her persistent discomfort with whether or not motherhood is truly resistant is best illustrated by the stark difference between her mothering of the guerrillas and of her own children. While she instinctively accepts and aptly performs the role of guerrilla motherhood, her sure footing trembles around her biological children. Her sons and daughter are in hiding for much of the war, yet when they do appear she cannot translate her care for the guerrillas to her own children. When her teenage daughter, Rae, is carried off with some of the guerrillas, Panlilio carefully and somewhat nervously insists that she can easily resolve the conflict between a normal and a guerrilla mother's reaction: "I knew that as a normal mother I should worry, yet, as a guerrilla mother, I knew into whose care the splitting of the trails had given my blooming child. I slept well. I worked well. Rae would roll in when the fighters rolled in" (290–91). Rae eventually returns safely, but in the next chapter Panlilio again struggles when she and her children return to the United States. When her youngest, Kerty, begins crying because he cannot read a menu, the guerrilla woman who is so calm in the face of battle becomes nervous as she quiets her child "and little beads of sweat formed on [her] forehead and nose" (302).

The gap between a "normal" and a guerrilla mother is accentuated further by the contrast between Panlilio and her own Filipina mother's concept of proper maternal behavior.[57] Her mother chastises Panlilio for "curs[ing] in front of the children" and instinctively cares for them; despite her mother's illness, she is "in her element" as she bustles around the kitchen preparing a meal (304). She also immediately begins to parent the children by assigning chores, teaching them table manners, refereeing arguments between brother and sister, and "patiently instruct[ing] her granddaughter in good house-keeping and her grandsons on the neat, dust-laying way of cleaning a floor" (304). While Panlilio can command and protect an entire camp of men, in the presence of her mother she becomes little more than a casual observer.

Throughout The Crucible nationalism and feminism are often at odds, and this conflict plays out most visibly in domestic spaces. Panlilio's efforts to advance the greater cause of Philippine independence consistently clash with her resistance to taking orders from and submitting to a man, especially because the family metaphors that she and the other guerrillas use to describe the camp's dynamic are conflated with actual military hierarchy. Scenes with her lover and commanding officer, Marking, reflect serious limits in her for-mation of guerrilla domesticity. As mother, second-in-command, and wife, Panlilio struggles with her supposed subservience to the guerrillas' "Pappy" and general; finding herself "constantly, never-endingly . . . at his beck and call—forever 'on duty,' " she describes herself as being "almost insane with it" (62).

But Panlilio's dilemma is more than just a matter of taking orders. Guer-rilla wifehood has especially disturbing physical and sexual dimensions, for she also becomes the object of Marking's sexual aggression and of his emo-tional and physical violence. In her recounting of her first night with the guerrillas, she recognizes her endangered position as the lone woman among a large group of men. Gratefully, she accepts Marking's offer to have her sleep next to him as a form of protection from sexual violation. Marking responds by taking advantage of this position himself. Initially rejecting his advances by pointing to the importance of the guerrilla cause ("Man, man, get away from me. We have work to do. We need sleep," 26), she eventually capitulates when he reminds her, "Tomorrow might not come" (26). Faced with this grim possibility, she succumbs. She also posits a woman's involvement in the nationalist venture as unfortunately also requiring her emotional, physical, and sexual subservience to a man: "Tomorrow might not come . . . When a man gives his life for his country, how little a woman's heart! I turned my head, to meet his lips. War was our marriage, the guerrillas our sons" (26). As she repeats his reasoning, the ellipses both erase her earlier fear of rape and mark a gap in logical reasoning; she suddenly accepts a relationship that posits a woman's little emotional resolve as giving in to a man's greater desire. This rationalization of rape is glossed over by her sacrificial rhetoric of nationalist duty to one's country.

Panlilio still criticizes cultural narratives that restrict Filipina femininity, especially those that define the Filipina as one ruled by the whims of her Filipino husband. She identifies both the United States and the Philippines as sites that produce limited roles for women through a critique of various sources: U.S. magazines and commercial products and Marking's oral version of family history. In one of her first interactions with Marking, she describes her attempt to play the dutiful wife as he narrates the story of his childhood. Marking's version of his family history centers on managing an unruly version of Filipina femininity. He describes what he sees as one of the more defining moments of his upbringing: the persistent battle between his father, who held a position of authority in the community, and his disobedient wife, who repeatedly shamed the family with her gambling habit. Marking's father sanctions his wife's arrest and imprisonment. Holding the key to her freedom, he finally manipulates her to the point that he can "put her to bed like his child" (91). Marking describes this as a formative event. He tells Panlilio that she fulfills his father's prophecy that Marking will one day meet a mestiza woman who will become his wife.[58] With Panlilio at his side, he can confidently proclaim, "Now I am my father's son, and my father's word was prophecy. I am more lucky than my father. I have a better woman than my mother" (92).

As Panlilio relates the experience of listening to this story, she is clearly uncomfortable, for, like her unfamiliarity with motherhood, the behaviors appropriate to a Filipina wife are not second nature. Instead, she turns to her memory of notions of proper femininity gained from American women's magazines, advice columns, and even commercial packaging for guidance: "Somewhere I had read, in a Macfadden [sic] story title or subhead, perhaps in the Ladies' Home Journal or a medicine wrapper, that the best way to hold a man is to make him talk and avoid interrupting him. Also, not to sleep in his face" (88). Following these guidelines, she at first becomes the silent Filipina listener. This episode markedly differs from her interaction with Marking throughout the rest of the memoir, in which she consistently questions his decisions and criticizes his actions. Although she protests when she hears Marking's dismissal of his mother ("Don't say that. . . . She was your mother," 92), she describes being momentarily caught up in the dynamic of dominant husband and subservient wife: "He slipped his lean, strong arm under my knees and lifted me to his lap to cuddle me there. I smiled within. My friends would have stood mouths agape to see me cuddling. I liked it, too. I cuddled for all I was worth, and felt weak and sweet in the arms of a real man, woo-woo" (92). The overall tone throughout this interaction, however, is ridiculous, from the content of the instructions regarding proper wifely behavior to the "woo-woo" that ends the scene. The irony that underwrites this recounting illustrates Panlilio's careful manipulation of gendered forms of romance and memoir.

Marking and Panlilio's relationship becomes progressively more disturbing, as his angry responses to what he sees as her disobedience give way to bouts of emotional and physical violence. Although he allows her to reason with him about guerrilla operations, as soon as he sees her interacting with another man he becomes enraged. These fits of jealousy are consistent, a never-ending cycle of violent abuse and aggression that is frightening for Panlilio. She repeatedly describes being near death and a victim powerless against his animal-like strength. She recognizes the problem that Marking's abusive violence presents for her formulation of resistant femininity; the man's ability to exercise repeated violence on the Filipina body is an extreme articulation of her ultimate subordination.

Triple-Talk at Home and Abroad: A Transpacific Community of Women

In light of Marking's behavior, it is not surprising that the community of women in *The Crucible* is so important to Panlilio's reconstruction of the Filipina mother and wife as a military, nationalist figure. These women actively contribute to military resistance, from combat, to espionage, to sending money and food to the camps. Like Panlilio, Filipina guerrillas such as Trinidad Diaz "stood out" "against the background of tradition and the gentle, bashful womanhood around her" (30). *The Crucible* mentions several female guerrillas, but the most important one is Lydia Arguilla, the same woman to whom Panlilio addresses her "Letter to a War Widow." The two women form a sisterly bond strengthened by their work in the camp: "We were friends and fellow writers before the war; we stood shoulder to shoulder in the guerrilla" (191). Panlilio has high praise for Lyd and her ability to adapt to the guerrilla camp world. As a character in *The Crucible*, the elite Arguilla is a foil to Panlilio, who spent her childhood in poverty (Panlilio later reveals that as a child she "lived in tenements, box-cars, ranch shacks . . . a canvas tent," 303). Through her account of Lyd's involvement with the guerrillas, Panlilio contends that even the elite transpacific Filipina was an important part of nationalist resistance. Lydia's bourgeois sensibilities are valuable and essential to the guerrillas. As a woman who is "fastidious, choosy, leaning to Shakespeare and classical music, Lyd brought new worlds into the lost guerrilla world—discussion, comment, sophisticated humor, intellectual stimulation, a new kind of comradeship" (190).

Tightroping and triple-talking give Panlilio opportunities to build such sisterly relationships among women in the Philippines and abroad. Using her talents as a writer, she writes letter after letter to "prominent citizens in Manila, to rich people, to loyal people, to keenly intelligent people" (22); these missives solicit support for the guerrillas' cause, and many of them are addressed to women. Yet another balancing act, letter writing allows Panlilio to elude censors and intelligence agents and remind women of past friendships and affiliations. She cautiously "wrote into [the letter] just enough to identify myself to the receiver beyond a doubt: 'Remember the day your baby was born? No matter what I thought, I said he was beautiful, didn't I?' . . . She would know the letter could be from none but me, and she would intercede with her influential, wealthy father for information or money for the resisting forces" (22). The "keenly intelligent" women here can accomplish what Romulo and MacArthur cannot do through the radio broadcast, for the mother is able to read between the lines. The reader of the letters, however, also stands in for the readers of *The Crucible*, especially those who can interpret carefully, correctly, and with sympathy, as letter writing and letter reading form a special relationship between Panlilio and her female audience in the United States. Panlilio reaches out to mothers across the Pacific to remind them of their ability and responsibility to intercede on behalf of their sisters and friends in the Philippines.

The importance of sisterhood in the Philippines is matched by *The Crucible*'s emphasis on a potentially powerful female readership in the United States. Panlilio's imagining of sisterhood reconfigures the troubled relationship between elite Filipinas and white American women that I tracked in chapters 1 and 3. The Crucible's version of transpacific sisterhood also represents a carefully orchestrated break from the pan-Asian coalitions that were so central to Filipina authors during the Japanese occupation. While the Bataan Brotherhood uses the traumatic memory of Bataan to effect sentimental ties between American and Filipino men, The Crucible refers to this experience to construct affective, triangulated ties among a Filipina mother, a GI, and the absent figure of an American mother. The outfit shelters a GI who stumbles upon the guerrilla camp after escaping from a Japanese military prison. In this scene Panlilio sympathetically cares for an "American mother's son," who represents "a little of the flesh and bone that had survived" the events in Bataan (126). While the guerrillas warn Panlilio that the man may be a spy, she recognizes his experience of the horrors of Bataan and decides to protect him. She feeds and clothes him and, after noticing that he watches her "helplessly" (129), teaches him how to eat Filipino food that is unfamiliar to him. Formerly hunted and afraid, the GI responds to Panlilio's efforts, joins the other men in calling her Mammy, and becomes one of her guerrilla sons. Panlilio envelops him within an assessment of the underestimated guerrillas ignored and unaccounted for by others, constructing herself as having a special ability to recognize the unique potential of those who "maybe . . . looked like nothing to anybody else, but mother's eyes are sharp, and it is the world that is blind" (128). In recognizing the needs of the "American boy" who becomes yet "another one" of "too damn many sons" (128), Panlilio forms an affiliation not only between the GI and the group of guerrillas who welcome him as one of them but also between herself and her female audience in the United States.

Panlilio's awareness of her American readers undoubtedly influences her representation of the United States as a site in which she can reformulate her feminist identity, which she can ostensibly accomplish only at a remove from both the Philippines and Marking. This choice has a complicated discursive history, especially given the recurring rhetorical models of American benevolence that have dominated narratives of Philippine–U.S. history. In the end her attempt to weave together nationalism and transpacific feminism requires her to return to the United States in order to escape the restrictive definition of womanhood in the Philippines. Her repatriation at the end of The Crucible is predicated on a confrontation with Marking after yet another of his uncontrollable jealous rages. She leaves the Philippines with her brother, a United States Army corporal, and vows never to return to Marking again. While she is in the United States, Marking sends her letter after letter, documenting the exploits of the guerrilla outfit—now officially recognized by the United States Army as the Yay Regiment—and pleading with her to return home. Initially rejecting the description that Arguilla tells her is "as thrilling as a pulp-magazine love story" (311), Panlilio reports that she eventually "broke down" (314) after reading Marking's entreaties and the many letters from guerrillas also asking her to return. After learning that Marking is traveling to the United States, she interprets her acceptance of his courtship as differing from her former relationship. Her proud declaration that she will "teach him a lesson he'd never forget" by "marry[ing] him" (315) reverses the disciplinary narrative of the marriage between Marking's mother and father, as Panlilio vows to reeducate him.

Given the account of her challenging relationship with Marking, *The Crucible* ends oddly with this optimistic and idealized heterosexual marriage as promoting, rather than hindering, a formulation of transpacific, feminist nationalism. Panlilio's assured claim that she can teach Marking through marriage erases her previous resistance to the role of dutiful wife. Indeed, without explaining exactly how marriage will alter the previous dynamic of their relationship, her three-sentence summary of the legal proceedings imagines them as somehow instantly creating a foundation of gender equality, as the couple leaves "the two lawyers in El Paso, flipping coins to see who would be the bride and who the groom. We had our picture taken, to preserve our happiness forever" (315). She stresses even the marriage proceedings as a merging of borders; the couple's ceremony takes place in the borderlands of El Paso, brokered by American and Mexican attorneys (315). The picture-perfect happy ending leaves no trace of her previous difficulties in mothering her children, as the couple's children from other marriages become just another aspect of paperwork, a "legal mess" that is "untangl[ed]" by their lawyers (315). With the marriage finalized, she closes with the reconstruction of a domestic family narrative and the promise of a new future: "Then, all wars ended, we started home, to build the peace" (315).

On one hand, these final pages present yet another performance, another version of tightrope and triple-talk that capitalizes on the book's "pulp-magazine love story" appeal to construct a satisfying ending for a reader readily familiar with other sentimental versions of U.S.–Philippine relations. Yet in a fashion similar to the final paragraphs of Felicidad Ocampo's and Maximo Kalaw's romances, the closing of the memoir—with its reaffirmation of the couple's love and allegorical confirmation of benevolent relations between the United States and the Philippines, now jointly victorious over Japan—nevertheless reads uneasily, for it provides an overly simple solution to the book's many complexities. The blissful final lines undermine the urgency of the plea for guerrilla recognition and disguise the challenges that are the heart of the memoir's exploration of transpacific feminism and nationalism. And in the end, the conclusion envisioned by The Crucible would turn out to be more fantasy than reality. Panlilio and Marking eventually divorced, and she returned to the United States. And even though The Crucible was published by a major American press, Panlilio's story and public knowledge about the role of guerrillas in the Pacific War would soon fade from Americans' public memory. Filipino veterans labored for decades to receive full recognition and compensation from the U.S. government, only to receive a fraction of what was promised. Panlilio's name, like those of the Filipina authors who filled the pages of wartime periodicals with directives for New Order Filipinas, would eventually be forgotten, overshadowed by the grand, masculinized narratives and grainy film images that circulated in the years after the war: General MacArthur triumphantly returning to the shores of the Philippines, the suffering and glory of the Bataan brothers, and the reformation of the Japanese into good democratic subjects after the supposedly resounding success of the occupation by the United States.

Resolutions and Returns

Working against the predominant ways in which we remember and tell the story of relations between the United States, the Philippines, and Japan during and immediately after the war, I end this chapter with a return to the resolution and call to action posed by two Filipina columnists in the early days of the Japanese occupation and their very different outcomes, imagined as a book with blank pages yet to be filled, and the provocative question, "How will your children remember your efforts during the war?" Ultimately, the content produced on those pages and the answers both imagined and enacted by these women are uneasy and unstable. Filipina authors who published for periodicals like the Sunday Tribune Magazine, Filipina, and Philippine Review inevitably might continue to be lost in obscurity, dismissed as mindless propagandists. Similarly, Panlilio's The Crucible may also remain unread because of its pro-American moments or because of her acceptance of an abusive relationship and a sentimentalized, domestic narrative, which create deep fissures in her proud claiming of feminist independence.

Yet this lack of easy triumphs and unquestioned victories is important.

Overall it is this uneasiness that works against the romantic, nationalist discourse of war pursued both by Japan and the United States. The Japanese regime couched its expansion into Asia under the rubric of equality and liberation, as they supposedly welcomed their newly freed Asian brothers and sisters into the pan-Asian family. This rhetoric only masked the violence, aggression, and atrocities that marked the regime.[59] Similarly, the United States turned to the rhetoric of the family, to brotherhood between equals—a construct and narrative readily embraced by Filipinas, Filipinos, and Americans alike in the years after the war. This sentimental story and the iconic love between male equals has continued in its dominance, even though it was deeply undermined in the years following the war by the unsettled questions of Filipino veterans' rights, the continued use of the Philippines for military base agreements, and the steep cost of war reparations.

Most important, these texts ask us not only to recognize the role of Filipinas in the war efforts, but also to reconsider how we have narrated the Pacific War itself as a masculine enterprise, a duel of two imperial nations struggling to impose control over a feminized Philippines. Instead, these texts are remarkable because they offer a counternarrative to a male-dominated field of war—in historical memory and academic scholarship—and because they pivot on the importance of the family, on sisterhood, on imagining domesticity as having wider, transpacific influence.

Panlilio's *The Crucible* and the periodical materials produced during the Pacific War are important transitional points that connect the 1940s to the decade that followed. They are an apt preview of Cold War discourse in the Philippines and the United States in which transpacific relations are staged as a drama of sentiment, in which the Filipina's heart and mind become pivotal to definitions of Filipina and Filipino communities at home and abroad. Yet the texts produced during and immediately after the Pacific War are themselves a volatile crucible. The essays contextualize the dominant turn to the Malay precolonial woman—a figure in the 1930s during the suffrage debates, resurrected during the Japanese occupation, and a recurring feature of print material in the 1950s. As we will see in the next chapter, the feminist claiming of the Malay woman during the Cold War becomes increasingly troubled, especially as it becomes linked to a sentimentalized discourse in the Cold War that elides racist terminology and treatment of indigenous peoples in the Philippines. The debates surrounding the transpacific, American-influenced Filipina were also far from over, as American pedagogical enterprises in the 1950s would again turn to educational opportunities abroad to encourage the creation of model, Americanized Filipinas and Filipinos as willing partners in U.S. democratic expansion. In imagining delicate balancing acts, Panlilio's memoir and occupation-era texts constitute the beginnings of a repeated sentimental engagement, a valorization of home and hearth, mind and heart, and a romanticization of the Filipina's potential to determine national and transpacific relations.

Chapter Five

"POINTING TO THE HEART"

COLD WAR MAKINGS OF THE TRANSPACIFIC FILIPINA

The drama of Bienvenido N. Santos's much-anthologized short story "Scent of Apples" pivots on a difficult question and a compromised answer. During the Second World War a young Filipino narrator travels through the frozen Midwest on a public relations tour for the U.S. War Department. A representative of the Philippines, he is charged with the task of comforting families whose sons are fighting a war in the "faraway lands" of the Pacific.[1] Stopping in Kalamazoo, Michigan, to deliver a lecture, the narrator is stymied by a query posed by Celestino Fabia, who introduces himself as "just a Filipino farmer" (139). Fabia's question is straightforward: "Are our Filipino women the same like they were twenty years ago?" (139). After pausing briefly, the narrator decides to lie. His hesitation registers both his sympathetic affiliation with Fabia as a fellow Filipino and an intense awareness of their class, educational, and generational differences. Hoping his answer will not disrupt Fabia's "certain ideals, certain beliefs, even illusions peculiar to the exile" (139), he assures the older man that although modern Filipinas may be different, this "'change, however, has been on the outside only. Inside, here,' pointing to the heart, 'they are the same as they were twenty years ago, God-fearing, faithful, modest, and *nice*'" (139).

The dramatic impetus of the story's plot, Fabia's query and the narrator's cautiously formulated response, represent the linchpins of this chapter: the construction of Filipina femininity altered by transpacific contact; the Filipina's troubled but integral relation to formations of Filipino heterosexual masculinity; the role of elite Filipinas and Filipinos in rewriting postwar transpacific relations; and the turn to sentiment—the pointing to the Filipina's heart—as the emotional stuff that constitutes these revisions.[2] I examine a recurring fascination with the transpacific Filipina in several texts: "Scent of Apples" and its companion pieces "Brown Coterie" and "So Many Things" from Santos's collection of short stories *You Lovely People* (1955); and the nonfiction work of three Filipina feminists, Carmen Guerrero Nakpil's essay "The Filipino Woman" (1952), Maria Paz Mendoza-Guazon's *Development and Progress of the Filipino Woman* (revised and expanded in 1951), and Trinidad Tarrosa Subido's *The Feminist Movement in the Philippines, 1905–1955* (1961). Published in the Philippines during the Cold War and in close temporal proximity to the 1955 conference in Bandung, Indonesia (where African and Asian nations declared their aligned or nonaligned status), these texts document responses to broader concerns about the role of transpacific Filipinas in the postwar climate, the years in which Filipina and Filipino authors assessed the past and projected the future of American influence in the Philippines.[3] These writers provide a means of rethinking the gendered, sexed, raced, and classed dynamics of postwar and Cold War discursive productions, for they stage a drama in which questions about transpacific Filipinas—and their fraught answers—are necessary to the narrative reformation of Filipina and Filipino identities and communities and to the imagining of Philippine–U.S. relations.

Building upon the previous chapter's discussion of how elite authors in the Philippines participated in larger acts of transpacific rewriting during and immediately after the Pacific War, here I extend previous scholarship on the raced and gendered constructs of the Cold War and the accompanying employ of sentiment in discourse of the 1950s.[4] In *Cold War Orientalism: Asia in the Middlebrow Imagination, 1945–1961*, Christina Klein argues that the entwined postwar and Cold War imaginaries of containment and integration necessarily depended on pedagogical and ideological projects that served to reeducate the American public. While a heroic model cast the spread of democracy abroad by the United States as the effort of an individual nation, the sentimental version necessarily depended on public appeals to communal responsibility in which Americans became connected to others' hearts and minds in the global fight against communism. Klein's formation complicates the project of Edward Said's theorization of Orientalism, the epistemological binary that opposes dominant West versus its other, the passive and exoticized East, a dichotomy that, for Said, ultimately grounds imperialist and global hegemonies.[5] In Klein's analysis, rather than practices that articulated and reified differences between East and West, middlebrow cultural productions from the 1940s to the 1960s turned to sentimental integration, "narrated the knitting of ties between the United States and noncommunist Asia, and were infused with a structure of feeling that privileged precisely the values of interdependence, sympathy, and hybridity" that instead of "undermining the global assertion of U.S. power, often supported it."[6] The dual justification of U.S. foreign policy and the spread of American interests into Southeast Asia, Asia, and the Pacific depended on disseminating and marshaling a sentimentalized American responsibility, a need to restrain the inimical spread of communism, pitched as antithetical to the very stuff of American-ness.

As Klein and others have noted, the warm glow of an American melting pot was tarnished by a long history of past and present conflicts, especially long-standing struggles by people of color, women, and queer communities for legal rights, an end to systems of oppression, and equality; and the violences of colonial and neocolonial expansion. Mary Dudziak, Jodi Kim, Scott Kurashige, Melanie McAlister, Penny Von Eschen, Ellen Wu, and others have articulated the complexity of how the dynamics of race, nation, class, gender, and sex shaped Cold War politics and cultural formations and the intricacies of deployments of sentiment at home and abroad; they have also highlighted the efforts and practices of those who attempted to resist or subvert the ideological reach of Cold War containment.[7] I both build upon and depart from this foundation. For U.S.–Asian relations, the overarching plot of Cold War containment often centers on white, male American power managing the threat of feminized Asian nations. Rather than examining a geopolitical dynamic ostensibly produced by a dominant male-coded West and perpetrated on a submissive female-coded East, I argue that elite Filipinos and Filipinas also played with the gendered rhetoric of sentiment to imagine transpacific identities, communities, and interactions.[8] Santos's, Mendoza-Guazon's, Guerrero Nakpil's, and Tarrosa Subido's works underscore the fact that postwar and Cold War renegotiations were not one-sided, for Filipinas and Filipinos were crucially engaged, even in sometimes vexed ways, in these processes of revision.

In an extension of the byways mapped throughout *Transpacific Femininities*, this chapter's archival cartography broadens our knowledge of Filipinas' transpacific experience in the 1950s, illuminates fluctuating class and gender dynamics, and complicates how we have narrated Asian American relations during the Cold War.[9] Remakings of the transpacific Filipina in the works of these four authors illustrate the importance of these women to how elites in the Philippines engaged with and actively constructed Cold War relations, contended with the lingering legacies of U.S. empire, and responded to continued instabilities in raced, classed, and gendered hierarchies. As previous chapters have illustrated, the large numbers of Filipino men migrating to the United States in the first half of the twentieth century intersected with the rise of elite Filipinas, cosmopolitan women who traveled to or were educated in the United States. The class tensions between the Filipino migrant laborer and an elite community in Santos's stories, usually read in the context of exilic Filipino masculinity, are thus conversant with a broader discussion about the transpacific Filipina and her future.[10] A reexamination of Santos's stories alongside Guerrero Nakpil's, Mendoza-Guazon's, and Tarrosa Subido's feminist studies reveals that these texts respond not merely to the *scarcity* of women, but also to the *proliferation* of transpacific Filipinas, perceived by some as a threat, the unruly, unmanageable product of American involvement in the Philippines, and celebrated by others as icons of feminist progress, often problematically linked to representations of U.S. imperial benevolence.

These four writers grapple with the tangled, messy threads that link the 1950s moment to a discursive tapestry that weaves together elite responses to sentimental constructions, supposedly benevolent pedagogical initiatives, and strategies that both rationalized and recast empire. The reeducation of the American public during the Cold War has important and hitherto unrecognized connections to the rhetorical turns to the heart and the family, that, as we have seen, were strategies for masking imperial domination in the Philippines and for obscuring the violence of the occupation. In the 1950s, public discourse in the United States elided a history of imperial and racist violence in the islands and revalorized a familial relationship between the two countries. Such rhetoric drew upon long-lived justifications of American expansion via narratives that sentimentalized the spread of democracy abroad.

In the Cold War period, the new Republic of the Philippines was politically unstable, as government leaders dealt with continuing opposition from communist factions, recovered from infrastructural and economic damages incurred during the war, and coped with the imbricated legacies of the U.S. and Japanese occupations. These dynamics proved to be advantageous to U.S. foreign policy. As the United States became interested in reinforcing a stronghold in the Pacific Rim to manage and check the threat of communism in Asia, the Philippines figured as a crucial site. During these transitional years, American expansion and control in the region still depended on constructions of close, familial ties, which have proved to be remarkably entrenched. Even after the formal recognition of the Philippines as an independent republic, the U.S. government continued to cultivate the so-called special relationship with the islands that has persisted for over sixty years. The partnership between the administrations of George W. Bush and Gloria Macapagal Arroyo in the "war on terror" had its foundation in the Americans' use of the Philippines as a strategic site for military and economic domination in the Pacific.[11] This enduring involvement has included free trade agreements, the maintenance of military bases, the sponsorship of government leaders who were supportive of U.S. foreign policy, and continued neocolonial domination furthered by the circulation of American capital and business in the islands.

Caught in this overlap of imperial past and a new nation's future, transpacific elites found themselves in a complex position because of their connections to the United States. The Cold War era saw renewed attention to multiple educational ventures that historically targeted elites.[12] The outbreak of the Pacific War interrupted initiatives like the *pensionado* program that allowed the writers featured in chapters 1 and 3 to travel to the United States, but similar opportunities, including the Exchange Visitor Program, cropped up again in the 1940s and 1950s.[13] Postwar fellowship and exchange programs assembled reproducible examples of American benevolence with new motives: to testify to the benefits of the spread of U.S. democratic and pedagogical ideologies as a justification for Cold War expansion into the Pacific.[14] Under the auspices of these programs, people like Santos and Mendoza-Guazon traveled to the United States, earned graduate degrees, and ostensibly were to return as Americanized triumphs. Yet, as Cynthia Tolentino observes, some of these "professional Filipino knowledge producer[s]" who were responsible for circulating information about Filipinos and the Philippines as "experts on Americanization" subversively countered prevailing sociological and racial notions about the Philippines and its people.[15]

Transpacific fellowship and exchange programs also focused on recruiting women. And indeed, this strategy was neither accidental nor original; notions of America's benevolence heavily depended on the argument that the United States was expanding rights for women. By the 1950s the number of Filipinas attending universities, participating in study abroad opportunities, and entering the workforce had risen dramatically. The same programs that would have produced the elite narrator of "Scent of Apples," a man educated in an American university, also trained a corps of Filipina nurses and a cadre of Filipinas funded by fellowships and educated in universities. The mass migration of Filipina nurses, argues Catherine Ceniza Choy, was therefore an "unintended, though historically significant, outcome of U.S. cold war agendas and post–World War II labor shortages," and the education, development, and recruitment of Filipina nurses were crucial to changing twentieth-century relations between the Philippines and the United States.[16] In Filipina and Filipino literary production, these transpacific women soon became representative figures who embodied the intersections of sentimental productions, benevolent pedagogies, and imperial erasures during the Cold War.

Turning to a sampling of texts, the sections that follow stress the four authors' fascination with transpacific femininities, placed at the heart of discussions about national identity in the Cold War era, class rifts that divided Filipina and Filipino communities in the United States, and the future of the Philippines. The texts summon ghosts we have seen before, the spectral traces of earlier formations of transpacific femininities and their complexities. They are examples of how Filipinas and Filipinos reimagined Filipina femininity as a means of negotiating the terms of shifting gender and class hierarchies in the Philippines and in the United States during the Cold War period. The first sections examine Santos's "So Many Things," "Brown Coterie," and "Scent of Apples," stories that pit vilified Filipinas—the nurse and the *pensionada*, or the fellowship-funded university coed—against their idealized opposites. Drawing upon previous work by Filipina and Filipino postcolonial, feminist, and queer theorists and on scholarship on Filipina diasporic migration and constructions of gender and sexuality, I link the development of an idealized Filipina caregiver to mid-twentieth-century anxieties over her nonnormative, transpacific counterparts.[17] A reading of these texts exposes a series of anxieties, for the privilege of acquiring a university education in the United States has led to perversions: a nurse who cares for her patient but who lacks compassion beyond the walls of the hospital, and a generation of younger, snobby women who commit multiple crimes, ranging from forgoing their national affiliation to questioning the scripts of heterosexual femininity to, worst of all, trying to redefine Filipina and Filipino identities abroad. In a revision of the sentimentalized rhetoric that justified America's imperialist and global expansion, Santos's stories point toward an alternative pedagogy, one that stresses care and concern between men of different classes as a means of curbing the transpacific Filipina's threat.

The second half of the chapter connects Santos's texts to the largely unstudied work of his contemporaries Guerrero Nakpil, Mendoza-Guazon, and Tarrosa Subido, Filipina feminists who argue for the importance of women as actors on the national and global stage. While Santos's fiction delimits the transpacific Filipina, these scholars underline her potential, albeit with complicated results. Guerrero Nakpil presents a twisting, complex argument that claims that the transpacific Filipina is defined precisely by her constant escaping of definition. Mendoza-Guazon and Tarrosa Subido link the Filipina's development to feminist historiography that identifies the precolonial indigenous woman, or india, as a model of women's equality. At the same time, they contend that the postwar Filipina's hybridity—and difference from her Asian sisters—qualifies her as an architect of transpacific relations and a leader in naming the terms of new femininity.[18] These studies situate the transpacific Filipina as part of a narrative of universal ethics and morality that was important to the U.S.–Philippine coalition in the Cold War. Filipina feminists appropriate a Cold War, sentimental rhetoric of democracy and universal freedom not to contain a communist or feminist threat, but to champion women's rights. My analysis, however, also aims to divulge the deep complexities of Mendoza-Guazon's and Tarrosa Subido's intersections of nationalism and transpacific feminism, which are troubled by their perpetuation of benevolence and their marginalization of other women of color. Santos, Guerrero Nakpil, Mendoza-Guazon, and Tarrosa Subido offer varied responses to a question that, like Fabia's query in "Scent of Apples," leads to uncertain, compromised answers: What place should Filipinas have in the rewriting of transpacific relations?

The Unmanageable Coed and the Uncaring Nurse

The first of Santos's many collected works, You Lovely People, was published in Manila in 1955. The collection entwines multiple points of view, including the first person elite narrator, Ben, who works in Washington, D.C., and travels as a representative of the Philippines (best known as the narrator of "Scent of Apples," although he is not named in this story); Ambo, the elderly Filipino laborer who befriends Ben; and a third person, omniscient, and often highly satirical unnamed narrator.[19] These stories, many of which originally circulated in the 1940s and early 1950s in Philippine periodicals, are the products of Santos's experience abroad in the United States as a graduate student and later as an employee of the U.S. War Department.

Santos later republished many of the stories as part of the American version of *Scent of Apples* (1979), which cemented his place in the Asian American canon; in her review Maxine Hong Kingston notes, "Filipino-Americans now have a book."[20]

Santos would later describe *You Lovely People* as more novel than collection.[21] Although the male narrators link the individual pieces, what truly ties the collection together is the stories' focus on women. The Filipinas of *You Lovely People* are described by the Filipino writer N. V. M. Gonzales as the core of the work: "It is this concept which gives the book a center and a heroine, the Filipino woman. Obviously, she is what no woman in the flesh can ever be; still, the hurt men are as if possessed. . . . We clutch at fireflies in the dark in the hope of seeing why they glow, and we are terribly disappointed when afterwards the light goes off."[22] Representations of women in the collection are indeed vexed and varied. Augusto Espiritu's biographical and historical treatment of Santos helpfully diagnoses the author's idealization of a maternal Filipina, the vilification of a cosmopolitan Filipina influenced by life in the United States, and the displaced figure of white femininity as a flawed copy of an idealized Filipina. Via an analysis that links such stories as "Scent of Apples" to Santos's own transnational and expatriate experience, Espiritu tracks the writer's personal disappointment in the cosmopolitan woman's "apparently 'shameless' display of self-confidence and sexuality."[23] In letters, short stories, and interviews, Espiritu tells us, Santos "would express his displeasure at . . . modern, liberated women who, in effect, betrayed the national idea."[24]

Santos's charged imaginings of transpacific Filipinas are conversant with a larger fascination with the Filipina nurse and coed. The ethics of care at work in these stories posit the Filipina heart as responsible for caring for the nation and its bodies. These women presumably nurture home, country, and community in the Philippines and abroad. Texts from the Cold War years, then, provide the representational setup of a naturalized link between Filipina women and what sociologists have called a "chain of care." While scholars like Rhacel Salazar Parreñas have extensively analyzed the gendered repercussions of globalized Filipina labor, theorists such as Martin Manalansan IV, Allan Punzalan Isaac, and Kale Bantigue Fajardo have contended that a discourse of naturalization galvanizes the links in a chain that connects women's bodies to the role of mother and nurturer and to the emotional responsibility of care.[25] These feminist and queer theorists call for greater awareness of these naturalized assumptions in discussions of Filipina migrants and for the recognition of other forms of diasporic migration. Indeed, the Filipina as an icon of care emerges not only in critical discourse on migrant female workers, but also in mid-twentieth-century discursive productions that remake the Filipina's heart in the face of her queer transpacific others, women like the nurses and coeds of Santos's stories: single women who were not wives or mothers, whose desires exceeded male-orchestrated rubrics, and who departed from the image of woman as caring mother of the nation.

According to Santos, education and experience in the United States create flawed, corrupt Filipinas, represented by the nurse and the coed, who can neither construct nor maintain proper affective relations with Filipinos abroad. These women are dangerous threats that must be contained, for they have the potential to circulate as unauthorized and inauthentic representatives. Santos's stories feature the gendered and sexed differentials of these relationships in the creation of normative, male-controlled transpacific spaces. The women stand in for the many ways in which he hypothesizes transpacific Filipinas as, on one hand, disruptive to the emotional affiliations that connect men of different classes and, on the other hand, as absolutely central to the reimagining of the transpacific Filipina and Filipino community and Philippine–U.S. postwar relations. Santos capitalizes on the shift in the 1940s and 1950s toward sentiment to reclaim the elite Filipino's control over defining the terms of transpacific identities and communities.

The nurse and the coed in "So Many Things" torment Ambo, an elderly, working-class Filipino who longs for the company of his countrywomen. In Ambo's world, Filipinas are seldom seen and crucially linked to memories of home. "There were very few Filipino women in the United States," he recalls; "there was a time when he didn't see one for years and years" (108–15, 113). As his roommate is about to leave for the Pacific War, Ambo meets two prospective renters to take his place, Mrs. Morales and her daughter Emilia, who, like Ambo, are from the Visayas, a southern region of the Philippines. After coming to the United States on scholarship, Emilia now works at the Pentagon. The meeting sours when Ambo overhears Emilia complaining to her mother about the prospect of living with him. This painful rejection spurs memories of Remedios, a Filipina nurse who once cared for him in a hospital in Chicago and who initially seems to be Emilia's opposite. But in a series of flashbacks we learn of Ambo's obsession with the nurse, who rejects his letters, flowers, and invitations to dinner. At the end of the story, he is lost, despondent, and isolated from the Filipina and Filipino community.

While the discourse of the 1940s and 1950s in the United States centered on brotherly relations with the Philippines, Santos's "So Many Things" emphasizes the material traces of Filipino objectification in a capitalist and military complex that relies on and then discards Filipino laborers. Ambo's friends and roommates are pawns of the U.S. military; he can only watch as the "Army took the boys . . . one by one" (108). What can a Filipino do in this hostile environment, especially when his exile and alienation are made worse by wartime isolation and Filipinas' cruelty? The nurse and the coed only heighten Ambo's difficulties. He collects objects, memories, and the narratives that are attached to them to manage both his loneliness in the United States and the transpacific Filipinas who refuse to comply with his ideals of femininity. He temporarily fashions a connection to home by romanticizing his brief relationship with Remedios, but his cherished Filipina is unattainable, a dream destroyed by heartless women who no longer have any affiliation with their distraught countryman and who cannot and do not want to fulfill his imagined ideals.

The story's persistent obsession with things, a term that describes both sentimental objects and memories, recalls Americans' interests in reproducing models of a supposedly benevolent empire. The opening paragraphs introduce the recurring slippage in the meaning of *things*. Ambo's apartment, a central meeting place for Filipinos through much of *You Lovely People*, becomes a repository for left-behind possessions. Appearing twice in the story's initial paragraphs, the word *things* first refers to the boys' "personal belongings" and the "few things they treasured" (108): a father's gold watch, a packet of letters from home. But in the second paragraph, the meaning of *things* shifts from the tangible to the ephemeral. One Filipino uses the word to describe heart-wrenching visions of farewells and departures—such as the mental snapshot of his friend saying goodbye to "that blondie" who was "crying on his shoulders as though his going were the end of the world for her" (108–9). In this story, objects spark memories, yet memories can become "such things [that] break my heart" (109). The thing, then, ultimately serves as a palpable iteration of sentiment, one that represents both Filipino disenfranchisement (as the men are gradually taken by the army and leave behind only a meager collection of objects) and loneliness (as they constantly worry that, should they die in the war, no one will mourn their loss).

Ambo is the keeper of such discarded possessions and memories. But the story's list-like register of his possessions has larger significance: this depressing collection of objects is a coping strategy for the Filipino laborer.

Ambo's hoarding of memories and souvenirs reflects what Susan Stewart has theorized as a means of using sentimentalized object and narrative acts to attenuate the lonely, alienating present.[26] Santos surrounds Ambo with a seemingly inexhaustible listing of objects that are old and useless: rusty razors, broken suitcases, an empty water glass, well-worn clothing. Both objects and owner are "dubious," "dusty," "out of place," "useless," and "old" (111). He gazes at his things to categorize multiple excesses; in an attempt to organize and control, he classifies the clutter, his loss, and his alienation in one sweep.

The text's elite transpacific Filipina, who refuses to provide comfort to her fellow *compañero* (countryman), exacerbates his alienation. The first meeting between Ambo and the Morales family accentuates the class, educational, and gendered tensions between the Filipino laborer and the transpacific Filipina. The contrast between Emilia and her mother, Mrs. Morales, reveals the transpacific Filipina's education in the United States as the root of her problematic femininity. Like the text's rendering of the U.S. military's extraction of the Filipinos, the representation of Ambo's encounter with Mrs. Morales and her daughter is intrusive and excruciating. Different from her young, educated, and cruel child, Mrs. Morales speaks Visayan and establishes an instant camaraderie with Ambo. In contrast, Emilia rejects such regional and linguistic affiliations. As the story progresses, her vilification intensifies. She repeatedly insults Ambo when she knows he is in hearing distance, despite her mother's embarrassed attempts to stop her. The young woman is unruly and unabashed, a predator, "curled up like a tigress on the couch" (112).

In response to the coed's heartlessness, Ambo, like Fabia in "Scent of Apples," clings to a beloved memory of a Filipina in what turns out to be a futile attempt to create a shared cultural and national affiliation. The story turns to the iconic Filipina nurse, Remedios, the kind woman who attended to Ambo during his stay in the hospital. The flashback that describes his interaction with Remedios contrasts her with the disdainful Emilia. Santos points toward the importance of the elite Filipina's heart, for Ambo constructs his relationship with Remedios as a romance. Instead of Emilia's rejection, Remedios, at least in Ambo's mind, immediately expresses concern for him. He believes her response is grounded both in her empathy and in their shared, collective identity as Filipina and Filipino: "When she saw him being brought in, she came over, and inquired in the dialect if he felt very sick. True, she was Filipino. And she knew that he was a Filipino! Shame on him for doubting, for not being so sure" (113). Through this idealized, caring nurse, Ambo can remember what it is like to be home, as she brings with her the recognizable smell of "coconut milk and pressed camia flowers" (114). For Ambo, this woman—aptly named after the Spanish word for cure—carries the aura of home and comfort, salves to his wounded pride and loneliness. The power of the romance narrative transforms Remedios into objects and feelings that are beloved, evocative of the Philippines, and unattainable in the United States.

The story's turn to heterosexual romance is a Filipino laborer's desperate attempt to craft an idealized version of Filipina femininity as a remedy for the pain caused by her transpacific opposite. The romance narrative turns Remedios into Ambo's talisman against the present. But the use of the conditional tense to mark unfulfilled potential reveals the failure of such sentimental productions: "Ambo wanted to take her hand. But all he did, all he could do was to look at her, and through his fevered mind, she was his sister, she was his mother, she was his sweetheart, she was his wife, ministering to him, talking to him with love, and he was home again. The faces of the other men and women appeared indistinct. He was home, and someone—this Filipina girl—loved him. She would be very sad, she would weep over him if he should die" (113–14). Marked by the mix of past tense and conditional future, this memory collapses time and space; the description projects both into the future and back into the past and travels between a foreign country and the Philippine homeland. In the space of a few sentences, Remedios becomes representative of multiple types of emotional affiliations, renders all others "indistinct" and meaningless, and returns Ambo home. The comma splices, parallel structure, and repetition present a list of multiple blurred women, all of whom figuratively belong to Ambo, love him, and serve his needs—ministering to him as a nurse when he is sick, whispering words of care, and mourning his death. Yet this fantasy idealizes Remedios to the extent that she becomes untouchable: "All he could do was to look at her."

The broken, unrequited romance represents the failure of sentimental narrative acts, which cannot restrain the incorrigible transpacific Filipina. Ambo eventually recognizes his folly and the "many silly things he did afterwards," but he remains plagued by unanswered questions: "Was there anything wrong in being grateful? Why didn't she acknowledge his letters and the flowers? And when he stood there at the main door of the House, smiling at her, why did she not stop to talk to him?" (115). Santos recognizes Ambo's unrealistic attachment to Remedios, but his sympathies nonetheless lie with his brokenhearted character. He accentuates Remedios's heart-lessness, her lack of empathy for her fellow countryman. In the end, the Filipina nurse is all too similar to the coed. Like Emilia, Remedios has come to the United States on a scholarship and stays at the "International House" (114). Like Emilia, her education and affiliation with other international students distance her from Ambo. The exchange program may prepare a coed for a job in the State Department and train a nurse, but transpacific education also disrupts the ties that should affectively bind a Filipina to her countrymen. The Filipino's moment of comfort is fleeting, for this nurse leaves him only with things that break his heart—memories of "letters unanswered and flowers returned" (115).

The Proliferation and Containment of Heartlessness

Santos's preoccupation with the nurse and the coed speaks to a broader cultural fascination with these figures as representatives of how transpacific relations altered Filipina femininity and deepened class rifts between migrant and elite Filipina and Filipino communities. If the nurse was crucial to the promotion of educational opportunities in the United States, as we saw in chapter 2, in the early to mid-twentieth-century Philippines, the coed emerged as a stand-in for alterations in Filipina femininity brought about by interaction with the West. Constructions of the coed illustrate the unsteady midways of Philippine nationalism, transpacific relations, and feminist movements. Chapter 2 tracked the peak of her iconic status in the 1930s, when pro- and anti-Filipina suffrage activists heatedly debated her merits and flaws (Filipinas gained the right to vote in 1937).[27]

The coed reappears in periodicals of the post–Second World War years with marked differences. According to her supporters, such as Avelina Cabanilla Orallo, the postwar coed was hardly flighty or materialistic, but the epitome of strength and survival, a woman who had faced both "the hardships and privations of a Japanese occupied country" and "the influence of fun-loving, happy-go-lucky [American] GIs." Orallo's article "The Post War Coed" (1948) identifies this woman's ubiquitous presence in Manila: "You see her everywhere, on the campus, in an office, behind a counter, in buses or in jeeps. You can easily recognize her anywhere, with her red lips, red nails, fresh coiffure, and a bag slung over her shoulders. She sports anything from the cat's goggles to the slit-skirts, down to the Chinese heel-less shoes." Orallo responds to critiques that the coed of the 1940s is "artificial and shallow . . . cold and materialistic" by arguing that this new Filipina is smart, self-sufficient, and engaged in national and international politics. Despite her Hollywood hairstyle, slit skirt, red pout, and perfumed wrists, "underneath . . . she is just the same. She indulges in the same sweet hopes and secret dreams. She has the same disappointments and frustrations. Just as the coed of yesterday had failures and heartaches, so does the coed of today." Orallo's language is strikingly similar to that used by the narrator of "Scent of Apples," whose assessment of the Filipina opens this essay; both emphasize sameness and stability amid sweeping changes. Like the narrator of "Scent of Apples," Orallo maintains that the coed, on the inside, still has a heart. But while Santos's narrator lies to Fabia and, in doing so, edifies an iconic woman as being faithful and nice to argue that the Filipina in reality does not have any of these qualities, Orallo warmly praises the beating heart and the humanity that lie beneath the image.[28]

Such divergent readings of the coed are not surprising, especially given the treatment of women in nationalist contexts. "Women," observes Cynthia Enloe with wry certitude, "haven't had an easy relationship with nationalism."[29] Enloe's matter-of-fact assessment—of the patriarchal tendencies of nationalist movements and the resulting marginalization of women's involvement and feminist objectives—diagnoses broad patterns manifested in multiple sites, from the Philippines to India, the African diaspora to the Chicana and Chicano borderlands. Indeed, as feminist scholars like Enloe, Lisa Lowe, Laura Kang, Gloria Anzaldúa, and Chandra Talpade Mohanty remind us, cultural nationalist movements often idealize feminine icons of land, home, or nation, while vilifying women who do not fit these models.[30] The desire to control models of femininity resonates with Cold War constructions of white American women as being crucial to cultural nationalism in the United States; we need think only of the apron-clad, pie-baking, meticulously coiffed white American housewife pitted against a desexualized, Soviet female other.[31] One might recast patterns of patriarchal nationalism versus feminism, then, as discursively connected to the twofold oppositions that determined Cold War ideologies. And such configurations fit, to some extent, the debates of the 1930s to the 1950s surrounding the coed, figured as either a model of new Filipina strength or dangerous threat.

I draw here on the above contexts to examine the proliferation and containment of the coed in Santos's stories, which don't quite match the oppositional binaries described above. "Brown Coterie" and "Scent of Apples" disrupt normative constructs of migration in multiple and charged ways.

Santos's critique of U.S. empire and its wide-ranging detrimental effects centers on managing the threat posed by transpacific Filipinas, whose queer bodies do not fit within idealized and iconic constructs of woman as mother and caregiver. As illustrated by the way in which "So Many Things" ends, even though Santos sympathizes with the Filipino laborer's need to romanticize Filipinas, he is quite aware that such idealizations are illusions. Yet his stories contain the transpacific Filipinas' heartlessness in order to reclaim the right of the Filipino elite and working-class male to control their identity amid attempts to imagine Filipinos as models of benevolent empire or willing allies in U.S. foreign policy. The stories' critique is subtle, but the works divulge how sentimentalized benevolence masks the exploitation of Filipino labor and upsets normative gender relations between transpacific Filipinas and Filipinos. Santos's "Brown Coterie" and "Scent of Apples" reject both pedagogies of benevolence and heteronormative nationalist constructs that depend on transpacific Filipinas and instead regard homosocial coalitions between elite and working-class men as the more productive alternative for forming national community.[32]

"Brown Coterie," which follows "So Many Things," returns to the inimical cosmopolitan coed, located in the Virginia suburbs of Washington. These transpacific women have advanced degrees from elite research universities, speak multiple languages, and work for the U.S. government. The story sanctions what Santos posits as particularly insidious: Filipinas who attempt to define the terms of postwar national identities and communities. In "Brown Coterie," experience abroad has resulted in Filipinas' failure to integrate transpacific communities and their disruption of the chain of care. They not only lack sympathy for Filipino laborers but also forego their own affiliation with the Philippines. To make matters worse, they reconstruct the terms of Filipina femininity.

The collection progresses from the laborer's loss and dispossession to the elite's excess and privilege. The coterie of Filipinas and Filipinos who hold cushiony jobs with the U.S. government and enjoy plush cosmopolitan lifestyles have the luxury of trivializing both the Pacific War and its implications for Asians in the nation and abroad. Santos's narrative voice is snide, showing little of the sympathy that characterizes Ambo in "So Many Things." The narrator's irritation is directed toward the coterie's class and intellectual snobbery and their desire to affiliate with the West.

Yet such portrayals pale in comparison to the narrator's portrait of the coterie's Filipinas, who consistently step beyond normative boundaries.

While the men are interested in European tragedies or Western philosophers, the women take this preoccupation beyond scholarly passion or casual hobby. Here, the disparities between these coeds and their earlier incarnations in Remedios and Emilia are in high relief. Actively attempting to forego national and racial identifications, the women play the dangerous game of racial and national passing:

All the girls reeked with gray matter and were now trying hard to make it quite obvious, except Clarita who was doing her best to be happy and succeeding only in being gay. There were two sisters from Ann Arbor, Pilar and Tecla, one with a Ph.D. in chemistry and the other seriously threatening to get one in a year. Both looked underfed and they certainly were short-sighted. Hilda, always heavily perfumed and primly accoutered, had graduated with honors, but she was the only one, aside from Clarita, who looked nice enough to make a man forget that she had brains. Rosa had obviously some Spanish blood and further accentuated it by shifting to Spanish with no provocation at all. She was light-skinned and had often been mistaken for a South American. That to her was most flattering as it must be to a group of Filipinos who haunted the International House in New York City, seeking game and passing themselves off as South Americans, and getting away with it, too. The rest of the girls at Clarita's had to be content with being mistaken for Chinese or Hindu or truly identified as Filipino. . . . [Maria] was short and wore loose dresses that seemed too long for the fashion of the day, but she was rich. Her family's wealth was safely out of the Philippines. She drove a huge Buick and rarely, not quite alone. Helen was tall but flat-breasted. Every time she opened her mouth, she said "statistics." Angela had a Phi Betta [sic] Kappa pin and a pair of the most immoral legs you ever stared at. (116–26, 118–19)

Whereas "So Many Things" vilifies the transpacific Filipina for her failure to maintain emotional bonds with her countrymen, "Brown Coterie" fleshes out the unmanageable coed and emphasizes her desire to reject outright her identification as Filipina. The above passage negotiates the complexities of race, nation, and class in the midcentury Philippines and United States; passing is not just a matter of race, for national and class affiliations clearly matter. There is a hierarchy of acceptable choices, and Japanese is never an option. In choosing South American as the most enviable alternative, Santos's Filipinas distance themselves from groups associated with migrant labor, such as the large numbers of Asians arriving in the United States in the nineteenth and early twentieth centuries, and Mexican workers recruited into the Bracero program. They also align themselves with the (often lighter-skinned) elite in the Philippines, who trace their racial heritage to the Spanish ruling class. The title of the story underscores Santos's satire: no matter the women's advanced degrees, honor society memberships, and lighter skin, in the United States this coterie is brown.

Through long and complex sentences that become unmanageable and difficult to parse, the above passage also uncovers the transpacific Filipinas' dangerous proliferation. The women's education produces not models but perversions; the passage jumbles together their unconscionable interest in the game of passing with transgressive and distorted sexualities. Advanced degrees lead to "underfed," "primly" dressed women, only one of whom "looked nice enough to make a man forget that she had brains." The text emphasizes the women's aberrant sexualities in the last three sentences, which include a series of modifications that outline incongruous and out-of-place bodies: Helen stands out as "tall but flat-breasted," and Angela has "immoral" body parts. Modifying phrases and an interplay between essential and nonessential clauses disrupt sentence order and reflect the women's destabilization of raced, gendered, and national identity. In the sentence "Hilda, always heavily perfumed and primly accoutered, had graduated with honors, but she was the only one, aside from Clarita, who looked nice enough to make a man forget that she had brains," grammar reflects a tension between essential (subject and predicate) and nonessential (appositives) aspects of femininity. Essential: Hilda's status as a graduate and her beauty. Nonessential: her primness and perfume. The interruptive moments, however, also mark the threat of these Filipinas' transgressive bodies and create an expanding scale of disorder.

The Filipinas in the coterie not only destabilize heterosexual femininity, but also stubbornly refuse to imagine a community that crosses class lines. In a reversal of Ambo's romanticized memory of Remedios, the women reify a figure of working-class Filipino masculinity, the Pinoy, for destructive ends. "This party would be complete," says one Filipina, "if we had one real Pinoy in the crowd, don't you think so?" When a Filipino asks her to clarify, the others quickly chime in, " 'You're not Pinoys,' the sisters from Michigan chorused. 'You're not the real McCoys,' said Helen. 'You're synthetic' " (120). Here, the Filipinas use a derogatory term that Filipino laborers in the book never use to describe themselves. To Santos, the Filipinas' objectification of the laborer is evidence of their heartless elitism. The women take the slang term Pinoy and, in the next sentence, equate it with the popular colloquialism that connotes the genuine and authentic: the "real McCoy." This dichotomy between synthetic and real reveals the women's troubling desire to claim authority by constructing Filipino subjects. To the women, laboring Filipinos are party accoutrements, the objects of cruel jokes. They callously produce a reified Filipino subject and by doing so break sentimental, affective ties that should knit together transpacific Filipina and Filipino communities.

"Brown Coterie" further sanctions the women for constructing alternate formations of Filipina and white heterosexual femininity. The story recalls the snapshot image of the memory that opens "So Many Things"—that of a Filipino and his "blondie," who weeps uncontrollably at the thought of her boyfriend's departure. The blondie returns in "Brown Coterie" in the body of Eric's girlfriend, Virginia, who instantly becomes the object of the women's disdain. Here, the white woman's return prompts another critique, of the Filipinas' encroachment into a sphere that should presumably be controlled only by Filipinos, as the women attempt to define the terms of heterosexual femininity. When Eric and Virginia leave the party to go on private walks or kiss and cuddle before the others, the Filipinas angrily respond. After enduring the women's thinly veiled insults for much of the afternoon, Virginia finally leaves the group under the pretense that she has a headache; when she retires to a separate room, the tension surrounding Eric's relationship with a white woman explodes. In the heated discussion, the Filipina women script the terms of Filipina and white women's heterosexuality. According to them, the key difference between the two has everything to do with sex: "The trouble with you boys, . . . you're blonde conscious. . . . Not only that, you prefer dating them instead of, say, one of us, because . . . well . . . to put it bluntly, you know that with us, you won't get any nearer than first base, whereas with them, you surely get your money's worth" (123). Amid the prevalence of relations between white women and Filipinos, the Filipinas idealize their own femininity as more modest and chaste than that of the hypersexual blonde.[33] Like Ambo of "So Many Things" and Fabia of "Scent of Apples," the women of the coterie champion Filipina modesty. Yet "Brown Coterie" rejects the women's assertion of such control. By the end of the story, Santos casts his transpacific Filipinas as ridiculous, mean-spirited, lonely, and rejected by the eligible bachelors in their set; they can only passively wait for and accept the attention of Filipino men. The story contains these women by granting them only two options: either embodying the qualities of the dutiful wife or exhibiting a volatile, Americanized heterosexual desire that has no outlet for expression.

In response to the threat posed by transpacific Filipinas, "Brown Coterie" and "Scent of Apples" revise the narrative of benevolent instruction that was so important to America's imperial endeavors. The stories develop sentimental pedagogies that, instead of rationalizing global expansion, offer alternative ways of fostering emotional bonds for Filipinos abroad. "Brown Coterie" illuminates the transpacific Filipina as the ghostly context for Celestino Fabia's nostalgic idealization of women in "Scent of Apples." In these two texts we see a recurring pattern: in contrast to Filipina heartlessness, understanding between men of different classes mitigates pain and alienation. Santos develops an exemplary relationship between elite Filipino and laborer in "Scent of Apples," as the narrator of the story gradually understands a Filipino farmer's difficulties. After his lecture, he accepts Fabia's invitation to visit his home. The two main objects in "Scent of Apples"—the piles of rotting fruit in Fabia's house and the fading photograph of a Filipina—return to the importance of objects and their symbolic import. As Fabia and the narrator enter the house, they are overpowered by the smell of apples. Filling half of a back room in the house and permeating the air with their fragrance, the apples highlight the laborer's useless, excessive presence in the economies of U.S. capitalist empire. Fabia explains that the abundance stems from the failing market: "Prices have been low. I've been losing on the trips" (144). His hoarding of apples is a futile endeavor to become both a controller and consumer of what he produces.

In a system that renders Filipino labor useless and excessive, Fabia, like Ambo, first finds comfort in his nostalgic idealization of women in the Philippines. He clings to a discarded photograph of a Filipina, "yellow and soiled with many fingerings" (144), that he discovers in Chicago (where Ambo meets Remedios). The face of the woman is now unrecognizable. In a manner similar to Ambo's feverish dream of Remedios becoming all women —mother, sister, and lover—Fabia's cherished photo represents his emotional attachment to the memory of women back home. The narrator assumes that the object must be a family heirloom, but Fabia's quick confession ("I don't know who she is") reveals the fallacy of this idealization. Through the "blur" (144) where the woman's face should be, the text exposes this Filipina as vanished, unrealistic, and ultimately, as a destabilized act of representation.

The narrator does what the uncaring nurse and the unmanageable coed in *You Lovely People* are unwilling to do: he pays attention to and mends the broken heart of a Filipino laborer and forms a sympathetic bond that crosses class divisions. His response to Fabia's question, "Are our Filipino women the same like they were twenty years ago?" pointedly contrasts with the transpacific Filipinas' heartless dismissals. Fully aware of the potential consequences of his actions, the narrator explains, "I weighed my answer carefully. I did not want to tell a lie yet I did not want to say anything that would seem platitudinous, insincere. But more important than these considerations, it seemed to me that moment as I looked towards my countryman, I must give him an answer that would not make him so unhappy" (139). In this interaction, the narrator decides to perpetuate the illusion of a Filipina whose "heart" and "inside" are unchanged. The narrator's trip cements this relationship. By the end he has come full circle. Gripping Fabia's hand, the narrator bids the older man farewell and says, "Tell Ruth and Roger [Fabia's wife and son] . . . I love them" (146).

In pointing not just to this narrator's heart but to the figurative Filipina and Filipino heart, Santos engages in a larger sentimental rewriting of transpacific relations. These stories ultimately expose the Filipina's failure to manage her heart correctly and to care for the hearts of others. They also examine the importance of new forms of sentimental education, as the narrator from "Scent of Apples" models the necessity of caring for the working-class men in the United States who have been left behind and are alienated by both elite expatriates and the American capitalist and military system that depends on Filipino labor. The stories do much more than represent amicable Philippine–U.S. relations and much more than showcase the best and brightest examples of what an education in the United States can produce. They teach the meaningfulness of sentiment and responsibility and exemplify models of care for and awareness of other Filipinos, especially on shifting and uncertain transpacific ground.

The ethic at work in Santos's stories demands that the Filipina be pigeonholed into the role of caring for Filipinos abroad. Women either serve as romantic ideals or are vilified for their lack of empathy and concern. Transpacific women, for Santos, have only these two options, and the lesson at the heart of the stories depends upon the vilification of women whose nonnormative bodies step beyond these bounds. These texts twist notions of Cold War sentimental pedagogy and serve as a reminder of the plight of Filipino laborers, who are lost in the sweep of the broad terms of developing American international relations. Unfortunately, this critique ultimately depends on a different form of narrative heartlessness, one that leaves Filipinas with limited options.

The Unpredictable Filipina: A Feminist Critique

Three years before Santos published *You Lovely People*, Carmen Guerrero Nakpil's essay "The Filipino Woman" appeared in the magazine *Philippine Quarterly*. Because of the popularity of Guerrero Nakpil and her work the essay was reprinted in her collection *Woman Enough and Other Essays* (1963). Like Santos's stories, Guerrero Nakpil's essay wrestles with the question of how to remake transpacific femininities amid national shifts in the 1950s. "The Filipino Woman" presents a counterpoint to Santos's anxious critique of the transpacific Filipina and to his stories' containment of unruly Filipina women within iconic versions of uncaring nurse and heartless coed. Guerrero Nakpil's answer to Celestino Fabia's question, "Are our Filipino women the same . . . ?" is a resounding yes, although for reasons that differ starkly from those explored in Santos's collection. What if, as Guerrero Nakpil asserts, one were to see the Filipino woman as defined precisely by her inability to be defined? While Santos would distill his Filipinas into the status of the iconic and limit the coterie's elite women, Guerrero Nakpil imagines another Filipina, one whose very nature in terms of psychology, influence, and even biology resists such limitation. In "The Filipino Woman" Guerrero Nakpil contends that the Filipina is, at heart, the same because her essential quality is unpredictability. In an illustration of what Lisa Lowe has called heterogeneity, hybridity, and multiplicity, the essay pictures a Filipina who is indeterminate, variable, and inconstant. The insistence on Filipinas' hybridity, ranging from genetic diversity to the varied results that stem from the effects of trade and empire, counters a version that would view the liberated Filipina as solely a product of American benevolence.[34] Like other works by Filipina feminists, "The Filipino Woman" presents the Filipina with a challenge. Will she, as Guerrero Nakpil hopes, resist pressure to be defined by Spain, the United States, or Japan and break from the stodginess of old forms?

The essay features multiple instabilities, which are crucial to its response to anxieties about transpacific Filipina femininity. Both the content of "The Filipino Woman" and its form revel in an argument that itself remains mutable. The first sentence, for example, recognizes the challenges posed by trying to define the Filipina of the 1950s and immediately undermines a project of rigid classification: "To assume an abstraction and call it 'the

Filipino Woman' is, I realize, a dangerous thing to do" (6). Guerrero Nakpil, wary of oversimplifying "the nine million Filipino women who do not measure up, or who will prove, by just being what they are, that my generalizations have vilified, venerated, apologized, or merely been hasty" (6), resists a definite characterization of her subject. Her lack of resolution is a tenuous performance that mimics the uncertainty she finds in Filipina femininity. Indeed, "The Filipino Woman" is rife with contradictions. Doublespeak and satire complicate an argument that twists and turns, that resists being pinned down. The essay leads the reader into rhetorical dead ends and opposing conclusions—all to refuse predictability and stasis. Such serpentine rhetoric models a feminist critique of stability, a reaction to attempts to limit, define, and contain the Filipino woman.

Similar contradictions appear throughout the opening. The essay begins with a premise that celebrates the Filipina's inherent malleability, her chameleon-like capacity to be and become whatever is most desirable. Her body is marked by racial and national instability; when abroad, she "is always being taken for a Chinese, a Siamese, an Indonesian, an Indian, a Mexican, or a South American" (6). Such hybridity lends itself to multiple interpretations, and "she seems to give each according to his need" (6), no matter what racial or national affiliation. "Chinese men find in her eyes the necessary upslant," observes Guerrero Nakpil, "the Japanese think her correctly small; . . . the Latins trace her sanguine grace to their own blood, and the white Anglo-Saxon, like that first chronicler of the Filipino woman, the sixteenth-century Pigafetta, comforts himself by saying that 'she is almost as large and as white as our girls'" (7). The Filipina, it seems, is able to fulfill the desires of the beholder. Her inscrutability, however, is also the physical expression of genetic diversity, for "far from being unique and distinctive, Filipino beauty is a subtle compound of Malay, Chinese, Spanish strains flavored by half a dozen others" (7). At this point the essay draws on imperial constructions that characterized Filipinas as objects of desire.[35] Guerrero Nakpil acknowledges the same trend we see in Santos—the male desire to read and control the terms of Filipina femininity—except that in her view such desire extends to other Asian men and to white European and American men. Guerrero Nakpil's Filipina, like Santos's coterie women, can pass when abroad.

After establishing the Filipina as presumably easily molded by men, a body to be read and interpreted however the viewer sees fit, the rest of the essay meditates on the question, Is the Filipina really what she seems to be?

To answer this query, Guerrero Nakpil allegorizes women's experience from the precolonial islands, to the Spanish, American, and Japanese regimes, to the emergence of the new Republic of the Philippines. She writes a new history of the Filipina, narrating her development through the trope of successive romances with "three men in [her] life: her Asiatic ancestor, the Spanish friar, and the Americano" (7). The essay culminates in a dizzying account of the results of multiple colonizations that reclaims hybridity not only as being central to the Filipina's national character, but also as an aspect that itself should not be limited. The Filipina cannot be defined precisely because of her multiple characteristics, exhibited in her genetics and the physical aspects of the body and in her character and psychology. The terms used to describe the modern Filipina read like a laundry list of the varied and the multiple: she has "polygenetic ancestry" (6); is "heterogeneous" (6), "various" (6), and a "subtle compound" (7) of a "polychromatic" past (7); "a sort of compromise" with a "composite" make-up (12), "split personality" (19), and "hybrid character."

Yet interwoven with this celebration of the transpacific Filipina's multiplicity is a critique of the modern Filipina's self-imposed limitations. To Guerrero Nakpil, it is not, in the end, definition by others or cultural mores and social restrictions that limit the elite Filipina, but rather her acceptance of these terms. "The Filipino Woman" presents an urgent call for Filipinas to break free from their adherence to "sets of forms handed down from grandmother's grandmother" (15). Yet while Guerrero Nakpil certainly has sharp words for the woman who clings to a performance of virtue (such as the quality of being perceived as *mahinhin*, a Tagalog word for "demureness, reticence, reserve," 15) she is also critical of those who believe that merely putting on the trappings of the West—or, in Santos's terms, playing the game of national and racial passing—alone equals liberation. She satirizes Filipinas who wear the costume and practice the habits of the Westernized woman, only to remain hampered by codes of conduct that constrain women in both the Philippines and in the United States:

> Part of her has remained the innocent, poetic, vulnerable home-body that she was at the close of the Spanish era; the other part tries hard to catch up with the modern American woman who can drive a car, and bear children only when she wants to. . . . She goes to church in the morning, and gives her opinions on free love to a magazine reporter in the afternoon; she secretly yearns for the libertine codes of Hollywood movie

stars, but refuses to let her *novio* kiss her. She has learned to blow cigaret [sic] smoke into her eyes and to hold an eight-hour job in Manila's downtown, but she has to be home before dusk or Mama will be angry. She wears a chemise under her daring sun-back dress, and a large towel over her bathing suit. She goes to ball games and prize fights, but faints in the excitement. She drinks ginger ale at nightclubs, so everyone will think it is a Scotch highball, but is indignant if anyone gossips at her drinking. She is always talking about birth control, but she has an average of five children to prove that all she does is talk. She still has not decided which is more fearful, hellfire or social disgrace, and neither is she sure whom to follow, Emily Post or the catechism. (18–19)

Here the emphasis on the many parts of a Filipina is freighted with contradictions between the daring (aligned with the modern American woman) and the conservative. The satire focuses on the Filipina's consuming fear: on one hand, while she relishes opportunities to wear low-backed dresses, to smoke cigarettes and sip mocktails, and to fantasize about living the life she sees on the silver screen, she remains controlled by the lingering restrictions of Spanish Catholicism, the social graces of Manila elite society, and the codes of etiquette as prescribed by Emily Post. The satiric tone works to mediate the tension surrounding the transpacific Filipina. Although Guerrero Nakpil is undecided regarding the benefits of hybridity and is especially critical of Filipinas who cling to what she calls the forms of conventional femininity, the bemused tone of the essay is crucial in that humor, while indicating the intriguing challenges of the complex, impossible-to-pindown Filipina, figures this woman as not threatening.

To illustrate the diversity of the Filipino woman, the essay closes by resorting to categorization. Guerrero Nakpil offers a catalogue of the many types of women in the Philippines. But in doing so she chooses to link these women to ethnoregional types in ways that are similar to the descriptions of the "Four Faces of Maria Clara" that will appear in *Wedding Essentials* over fifty years later. The cosmopolitan, city-based Filipina "is a glib, irreverent coed, at home with Proust and contraceptives; or an intolerably alien bobby-soxer who acts much like American teen-agers except that she takes no narcotics and more baths; or a society matron off to Europe twice a year for her wardrobe's health" (20). In contrast, the woman of the "barrios . . . is earthy, native, hardworking, smelling of loam and a new rice" (20). She describes the woman living in "the Mountain Province" as an "aboriginal beauty, squat and red-cheeked, bringing forth a baby while she grips a tree trunk" (20). While Guerrero Nakpil wants these examples to read as added evidence for her argument that there is no uniform body that one might distill into the Filipino Woman, nevertheless, her devolution into types undermines the essay's emphasis on hybridity.

But instead of reading this closing as an unfortunate turn in the argument, a failure in Guerrero Nakpil's theorization of transpacific femininity, we must contextualize this move as being linked to rhetorical strategies we have already seen. Such contradictions are themselves a model of feminist practice. To Guerrero Nakpil, the transpacific Filipina's future is still cloudy and undetermined. "The Filipino Woman" moves constantly back and forth; the essay presents an argument that itself cannot be contained, limited, and defined. And with herself writing in the voice and from the viewpoint of an ever-changing Filipina, Guerrero Nakpil crafts a rhetorical argument that repeatedly returns to possibilities that are unrealized, to hypotheses that cannot be proved, to scenarios that might be played out and imagined yet not, in the end, confirmed. For in the closing lines of the essay Guerrero Nakpil returns to the many pressures that would turn the Filipina into a "clear, pure, internally calm, symmetrical personality with definite facets in the predictable planes" (20). "Perhaps, in time," she muses in the final paragraph, "the different strains which now war within her in mongrel contradictions will have been assimilated into a thoroughbred homogeneity. But when that happens, the Filipino woman will have lost the infinite unexpectedness, the abrupt contrariness, the plural predictability which now make her both so womanly and so Filipino" (20–21). In modeling the unpredictable over the predictable and contrariness over resolution, Guerrero Nakpil is hopeful about the transpacific Filipina's ability to resist limitation and containment.

A Feeling for Global Responsibility

The publication of *You Lovely People* and "The Filipino Woman" was matched by the production of texts authored by Filipina feminists who narrated and historicized their own complicated answers to the question, "Are our Filipino women the same like they were twenty years ago?" For women in the Philippines, 1955 was a landmark year. By then, five decades had passed since the formal inauguration of the feminist movement in the Philippines, marked by the founding of the Asociación Feminista Filipina.[36] In the years before and after the anniversary, Filipina and Filipino scholars assessed the state of women in the Philippines in essays, pamphlets, theses, government-funded documents, and books.[37] Overall, their verdict was clear: the Filipina feminist movement was alive and well and embodied by the lives of women who had had much to contribute to Philippine life, culture, and politics. The timing of these studies, however, intersects with important national landmarks. The officially recognized Philippine republic was approaching its tenth anniversary. These years, then, afforded ample opportunity for critical reflection on the status of women and the nation, phrased via Cold War discourses of the transpacific Filipina's heart.

Trinidad Tarrosa Subido's *The Feminist Movement in the Philippines (1905–1955)* and Maria Paz Mendoza-Guazon's *Development and Progress of the Filipino Woman* claim transpacific Filipinas' importance to Philippine life, culture, and politics. If Santos reacts to the proliferation of transpacific women with a critique of the uncaring nurse and the unreasonable coed, Tarrosa Subido and Mendoza-Guazon point not only to the transpacific Filipina's crucial role in the development and progress of the nation, but also to the Philippines' evolving relations with other countries. The new transpacific Filipinas documented by Mendoza-Guazon and Tarrosa Subido are a far cry from Santos's flippant women. "The Filipino woman of the modern type," notes Mendoza-Guazon, "cares less for flattery, but demands more respect; she prefers to be considered a human being, capable of helping in the progress of humanity, rather than to be looked upon as a doll, of muscles and bones."[38] The two writers underscore the advancements of elite transpacific Filipinas in the fields of medicine, nursing, social science, and the humanities as well as their rightful place as leaders in the new Philippines.

Both writers marshal Cold War rhetoric in the name of feminism. Their efforts, however, are not without cost. While studies like Tarrosa Subido's and Mendoza-Guazon's view the transpacific Filipina's hybridity as an asset to the nation, they reinforce some constructions that are both familiar and troubling, for their work echoes earlier tensions in the representational strategies of the elite. Biographically, the two women were undoubtedly the product of an Americanized pedagogy, and the rhetoric of American benevolence (so important to the interests of Cold War expansion) filters into their prose. The texts' praise of the transpacific Filipina and their call to recognize her importance amid developing Cold War relations are complicated by their reliance on narratives of Western-initiated progress and their accompanying erasure of American colonial and racist violence. Although Tarrosa Subido and Mendoza-Guazon temper their praise of the West by romanticizing the precolonial india in the Philippines as the precursor to modern Filipina feminism, they also obscure the marginalization of indigenous peoples. Drawing on the scholarship of Filipina feminists based in the United States and the Philippines, such as Delia Aguilar, Melinda L. de Jesús, and Neferti Tadiar, I engage these difficulties here, for such imaginings of transpacific Filipina feminism are messily, inextricably tangled with the very notions of American benevolence and superiority that rationalized U.S. empire, Cold War expansion into the Pacific, and the continued oppression of Philippine ethnic groups.[39]

Mendoza-Guazon's and Tarrosa Subido's studies begin at a similar point: a recap of the history of imperial contact and the contention that the Filipina was independent in the indigenous, Malay past. Philippine feminism, they believe, began well before the formal establishment of the Asociación Feminista Filipina in 1905, the rise of women's clubs, collaborations with white American feminists, and the campaign for Filipina suffrage. The two works feature precolonial, indigenous women as models of feminism; triumphant rhetoric valorizes indias and distances them from Orientalized versions.[40] The studies respond to the anxieties of those who, like Santos, posit the Filipina's Westernization or Americanization as contributing to the production of unruly transpacific women. Tarrosa Subido and Mendoza-Guazon sentimentalize the past as one in which indias had unquestioned equality. In these native Philippine societies, the woman, "we are told, was her brother's equal in the home, in society, in government. She could hold positions of honor and prestige like him."[41] Their works imagine the indigenous woman as quintessentially independent, liberated, and modern well before the days of Spanish and American occupation.

The reference to indigenous Philippine societies works not only to trace the transpacific Filipina's feminist roots back to an idyllic, precolonial past; it also revises the more contentious relationship between Filipino men and the movement and responds to a long history of popularized representations that confined elite women to home and family. Men's willing acceptance and welcoming of women's leadership are frequently mentioned in the story of Malay women's equality in the islands. Because they see equal relations between women and men as historically grounded in precolonial societies, Tarrosa Subido and Mendoza-Guazon, in their version of the feminist movement, can breezily recast male opposition to the transpacific Filipina and assert that "as a whole, the men of the country have been sympathetic to the feminist movement, and have not once begrudged their womenfolk any of their triumphs."[42] Both writers turn to indigenous societies to reconfigure frequent valorizations of elite women's roles in the home. Even educated bourgeois women were expected to remain within domestic spheres during the Spanish regime, and, more recently, Japanese New Order discourse idealized a woman's contributions to her home and family as part of a reclamation of Oriental sisterhood.[43] When compared to Tarrosa Subido's and Mendoza-Guazon's narration of the presumably long history of men who embraced women's power in Philippine communities, critiques of transpacific Filipinas' role in 1950s politics, the workforce, and outside the home can therefore be easily dismissed as anomalies.

As Catherine Ceniza Choy has demonstrated in her study of Encarnación Alzona (a feminist scholar who was a contemporary of Mendoza-Guazon and Tarrosa Subido), feminist scholarship in the 1950s perpetuated Orientalist stereotypes that ultimately viewed other Asian women as inferior to their Western counterparts.[44] Tarrosa Subido's observation is typical: "More than one historian has inferred that the pre-Spanish Filipina had never known the restrictions usual to most other women of her times, like the bound feet of the Chinese, or the veiled faces of Middle East women, or the enforced seclusion of most Oriental women" (1). Both women draw attention to the female body and the physical restrictions through which other Asian cultures limit their women: feet tightly wrapped, veils that shroud the face and body, forced containment. They use a vocabulary of physical restriction and argue that these assumptions about women are, for their Asian neighbors, tied to biological assumptions about women's abilities. In keeping with such tendencies, Mendoza-Guazon begins her study by saying her work is a direct response to the argument that "to Orientals the natural inferiority of females is self-evident" (9). This making of the Filipina as differing from other Oriental women has emerged before. Like the Filipina essayists featured in chapter 1, Tarrosa Subido and Mendoza-Guazon take issue not with the blanket characterization of Asian women as oppressed, but with the enfolding of Filipinas within this assessment. Departing from the Filipina authors examined in chapter 4, who strategically linked women of the Philippines to other Asian women during the Japanese occupation, Tarrosa Subido and Mendoza-Guazon emphasize the imprisonment of Chinese and Middle Eastern women to highlight the Filipina's comparative individuality and freedom.

During the Cold War, such strategies of comparison strategically align

Filipinas with a supposedly more liberal United States, described in expansive terms, and distance the Philippines from other, nondemocratic Oriental nations (and notable sources of conflict with the United States), cast here as sites of restriction and limitation. The women construct U.S. empire as benevolent, and democratic tutelage under American colonial rule ironically becomes a catalyst for accessing women's pre-Spanish colonial feminism. Mendoza-Guazon and Tarrosa Subido have high praise for the modernizing benefits of Western education, which they contend freed Filipinas' from the "medieval way of life" (Tarrosa Subido 2) that came with Spanish rule. "There has never been in the history of the world," gushes Mendoza-Guazon, "such a noble and magnanimous program of government as that proclaimed by President McKinley on January 30, 1899" (49). Women "took advantage of every freedom granted by the American administration: the freedom to know, to speak out, to worship, to move freely, to associate, to criticize—using these basic civil liberties as springboards to more and more rights and privileges: the right to vote, the right to hold office, to equal pay for equal work, to equal dignity in the conjugal partnership, plus the privileges of favorable working conditions by reason of sex. The first springboard, happily for the cause of Feminism, was placed within easy reach of the women at the turn of the century: Popular Education" (Tarrosa Subido 2). In this narrative, Western education and benevolent assimilation release Filipinas from former restrictions and results in a cascade of liberties and rights that gives women the opportunity to fulfill feminist potential. Here, Tarrosa Subido draws attention to American education as leading not to the proliferation of unruly, unmanageable women but to a series of expanded freedoms.

This representation of the United States is a complicated example of the two women's transpacific feminism. According to Tarrosa Subido, the American administration may have contributed the steppingstones, but Filipinas were responsible for taking advantage of and extending their rights and privileges. The naming of liberty, equality, and expansion sounds a triumphant note, and the use of this rhetoric in the name of feminism both sentimentalizes the role of the U.S. colonial administration and obscures its racist, imperialist objectives. Indeed, this casting of American education as especially benevolent toward women is deeply problematic since the United States established the educational system in the Philippines in part to justify the argument that Filipinas and Filipinos were unfit for self-rule and needed the guidance of their American superiors. These terms echo the pedagogical reach of American benevolence that was so important to Cold War expansion.

Cognizant of the lingering cultural importance of domestic roles for women (especially since, in the Philippines, options to leave the home were still limited to an elite few), Mendoza-Guazon and Tarrosa Subido contend that the Filipina of the 1950s is a woman who is fantastically able to control and manage the domestic realm while remaining unthreatening to Filipinos. Here they build upon the centrality of women's domesticity featured in texts of the Pacific War era. "Despite the Filipina's expanded outside interests," notes Tarrosa Subido, "her first concern remains the home. In case of conflict between home and career, she will give up the latter; and where she holds down both jobs of homemaker and career-woman, she takes care to maintain top efficiency as homemaker by organizing her day for the comfort of husband and children. Hence, the Filipino home still enjoys the solidarity, security, and happiness that characterized it fifty years ago" (Tarrosa Subido 71).

Yet while Tarrosa Subido might claim that a modern Filipina would willingly choose home over career, *The Feminist Movement in the Philippines* repeatedly offers examples of women who did not have to make such a drastic decision. She takes care to ground her claims in the actual experiences of women. These cases are illustrated by charts and tables documenting career paths, photographs showcasing exemplary women who sport Westernized versions of traditional Philippine dress, and narrative summaries of women's talent for delicately balancing the needs of the home, their careers, and work in the community. She devotes an entire chapter to organizing and categorizing women's achievements in list form. The chapter of lists begins by indexing women's accomplishments in broad categories, including agriculture, science, the arts, invention, law, medicine, and home economics. The lists are meant to call attention to the extraordinary, both in terms of numbers of women and the specifics of their accomplishments. But the lists also illustrate how the achievements of women and their global and national effects cannot themselves be contained. Many of them are recognized for their breakthroughs; Tarrosa Subido credits in particular the country's first dentist, councilwoman, lawyer, and doctor. The list is impressive, accounting for about a hundred women and their noteworthy contributions to the Philippines.

Read in the context of stories like Santos's, of the anxiety over the proliferating transpacific Filipina, and of the corresponding desire to manage and categorize, Tarrosa Subido's book both celebrates the achievements of Filipinas and stresses that they cannot and should not be limited. Examined as a narrative, the list culminates in a category that recognizes women "who have made a name for themselves" (61); the final category is a simple accounting of names of women who excel "in All-around Socio-Civic, Moral, and Cultural Circles" (70). These women are cast as the nation's elite, the notable, the leaders of the nation's past, present, and future, women whose reach and influence are international. This is the case for the entry on Senator Geronima T. Pecson:

> Geronima T. Pecson—rose from classroom teacher to world spokeswoman on education; Chairman, Joint Congressional Committee on Education, Congress of the Philippines; author of several bills in the interest of education, teachers, and social welfare, foremost of these the Elementary Education Policy Act of 1953 and the teachers' salary acts of 1948 and 1953, raising teachers salaries; Philippine delegate to UNESCO (1950–1954), and first and only woman delegate elected by that 60-nation body (now 72 member nations) to its Executive Board; chairman of the Programmed Commission, UNESCO organizer of National Federation of Parent-Teachers Association, founder of UNESCO Philippine Educational Foundation (UPEF); active in local, national and international organizations; recipient of many public and private honors and awards. (63)

Yet even as the list categorizes the extraordinary feats of women such as Pecson, it serves to document how Filipinas exceed categorization. The title of the chapter itself, "Opportunities, Unlimited," foregrounds proliferation rather than containment. The chapter contrasts contemporary excess with the handful of women listed as having notable accomplishments in the early part of the twentieth century. In the conclusion Tarrosa Subido reminds readers that the lists "do not pretend to being [sic] exhaustive; they are offered really as an index to the limitless opportunities now open to the women of our sovereign Republic" (70).

The recognition of Filipinas' central role in international and national relations is crucial to Tarrosa Subido's and Mendoza-Guazon's feminist perspective and to their imagining of new forms of women's global coalition. They argue that the transpacific, elite Filipina's hybridity contributes to her ability to be a model to other Filipinas—not just in the home or in the Philippines but also in the reformation of international relations. The well-managed and well-cared-for home becomes the foundation of women's active involvement in the spread of universalized notions of freedom, ethics, and morality within the Philippines and abroad. Extended involvement in the international sphere is more than just a metaphor. Tarrosa Subido praises "our Filipino women abroad," who "have built a reputation for intelligence, dependability, and gracious adaptability, and have earned good will and esteem for their country wherever they are sent" (73). She acknowledges a long history of Filipina participation in educational initiatives from 1905 to 1955, and she highlights the achievements of transpacific women who "have not only won friends for their native land but have, in turn, brought back and spread amongst us a better understanding of other peoples and other cultures—which is precisely what the times call for. The same mission has been accomplished by our women overseas who are on exchange programs, in the foreign service, in UN agencies, or studying and traveling on their own" (Tarrosa Subido 73). This assessment reimagines the terms of Cold War sentimental reeducation, and she suggests that Filipinas can and should participate in global work that bridges nations and cultures. Such ambassadorship is, after all, "precisely what the times call for."

The negotiation at the heart of these works is delicate and complicated. For although American education and opportunities to travel may have been catalysts, Tarrosa Subido and Mendoza-Guazon move beyond education and experience abroad to consider women's organizing efforts and activism at home and beyond: "Our women's experiences and contacts with the women of other countries, plus their training in organized and cooperative effort over five decades of local club-work, have certainly equipped them to face the pressing international problems of: universal human rights, universal ethics, world interdependence, world understanding, and world peace" (Tarrosa Subido 75). Tarrosa Subido believes it is their meaningful activist work in the Philippines that enables transpacific Filipinas to be effective in meeting the world's current challenges. She imagines women in the Philippines as part of a larger global network. The Philippine women's club movement is portrayed as a microcosm, a model of how the collective actions of women can lead to tremendous results that extend beyond the borders of the nation. The prominence given to action, organization, and coalitions of women is an important response to other discursive constructions of the transpacific Filipina. Although these two writers incorporate the turn to sentimental responsibility in their works, they also embrace a true call to action for their fellow Filipina citizens.

Mendoza-Guazon and Tarrosa Subido call attention to the goals of "world interdependence, world understanding, and world peace" as an urgent plea to recognize the transpacific Filipina's role in shaping a global code of morality, ethics, and responsibility, one that draws upon the sentimentalized processes of American expansion during the Cold War. It is also a call to action that is difficult and troubled. Global responsibility furthers a progress narrative that features Asian and Middle Eastern women (emblematized by Chinese women with bound feet and Muslim women in hijab) who supposedly need to be saved by the West. The women's triumphant rearticulation of the transpacific Filipina depends as well on romanticizing the indigenous past and effacing how elites like Tarrosa Subido and Mendoza-Guazon were implicated in the very dynamics—those influenced by colonial rule, capitalist structures, and hierarchies that privileged elites of Manila—that relegated indigenous women to the margins of Philippine culture and society. These Filipina women represent themselves as part of a global, feminist project of uplift, one dictated by historically Western concerns.[45]

Yet one should still read Mendoza-Guazon's and Tarrosa Subido's viewpoints as more than just easy acceptance and proliferation of rhetoric originating in the United States, for their feminist claims complicate such a reading. These women's use of broad, humanist brushstrokes paint Filipinas as feminist, transpacific, and crucially involved in the power relations that determined the nation's history. They present an alternative to Santos's unmanageable, disruptive women. Mendoza-Guazon and Tarrosa Subido answer Fabia's question with their own sweeping vision of transpacific Filipinas who have the potential to care for and promote the new Philippines and its interests. Their responses certainly point to the transpacific Filipina's heart but also to her education; her involvement in organized activism; her role in shaping the life, culture, and politics of the Philippines; and, ultimately, her feminist sense of global responsibility.

Coda: Inward and Outward Turns

The appeal to sentiment, or pointing to the heart, was a recurring motif in discourse about Philippine–U.S. relations before, during, and after the Cold War. In part, sentimental narrative constructions have contributed to both the rationalization of U.S. imperial expansion and to its eventual reimagining during the Cold War, a process of revision that perpetuated neocolonial and military involvement in the Philippines under the guise of benevolence. But, as we have seen, the turn to sentiment in these transpacific narratives has had especially troubling repercussions for Filipina women, who are repeatedly written out of the broad constructs of brotherly love between nations or relegated to iconic status. The unruly coed and the uncaring nurse of

Santos's stories have no place in idealized versions of Filipina and Filipino communities in the United States, which depend instead on lingering memories, blurred and fading images of women bound to a nostalgic homeland. Filipinas who are models of feminism at home while forging transnational connections have also been forgotten, perhaps because their attempts to construct the midways of transpacific feminism and nationalism cannot be easily categorized. Studied and imagined by feminists of the 1950s like Guerrero Nakpil, Mendoza-Guazon, and Tarrosa Subido, such versions remain unread, contained within an archive with possibilities that can and should be accessed.

To be sure, in pointing to the hearts of transpacific Filipinas, Filipina and Filipino authors contend that these women were central to how intellectuals were making sense of the future of the Philippines, its citizens, and its past, present, and future connections to the United States, other Asian nations, and the world. While American sentimental discourse rewrote Philippine–U.S. relations, citizens in the Philippines participated in their own revisions and disrupted the framework of the passive, feminized East and the dominant, masculine West. Vexed and complicated, their responses represent neither easy defiance nor compliant acceptance. They emphasize how important it is to pay close attention to the particular even as we assess the overwhelmingly large, from the ideologies of the 1950s that sought to divide the globe into oppositions of West and East and First World and Third World to the contemporary sweep of transnational scholarship. In all their complexities, these textual examples demand that we turn both inward and outward to rethink the critical questions and answers that shape not only how we examine Cold War containment and the persistent binaries of dominant West and passive East, but also the framework we use in our studies of transpacific relations.

TRANSPACIFIC FEMININITIES, MULTIMEDIA ARCHIVES, AND THE GLOBAL MARKETPLACE

In 2009 David Byrne, previously of the band Talking Heads, and his collaborator Norman Cook (better known as Fatboy Slim) assembled an eclectic group of vocalists—including Florence Welch, Tori Amos, Cyndi Lauper, Sharon Jones, Natalie Merchant, Kate Pierson, Sia, Santigold, and the Filipina "jazzipino" artist Charmaine Clamor—to produce an album with a premise even more surprising and incongruous than its collaborators. Released the following year, the album, entitled *Here Lies Love*, is a song cycle that braids together the stories of Imelda Marcos, the former first lady of the Philippines, and her devoted and forgotten childhood servant, Estrella Cumpas. Imagined primarily via the perspective of these Filipinas, the album's infectious, clubby dance tracks clash with the discordant context of the regime of Ferdinand Marcos, a tragedy of U.S.-backed leadership gone terribly and violently wrong. Elected in 1965, Marcos declared martial law in 1972; he ruled the Philippines as a dictator until he, his wife, and their family were ousted by popular revolt in 1986.

Drawing upon Imelda Marcos's past as a beauty queen, her fairy-tale rise from countryside girl to first lady, her ease in global spaces, and her ambitious political persona, *Here Lies Love* capitalizes on Marcos's self-presentation as a spectacle of transpacific Filipina femininity. The Marcos era was characterized by large-scale political oppression; censorship of the press and media; the kidnapping, torture, and murder of political opponents; and extortion and theft. Although many of these crimes have yet to be resolved, today Imelda Marcos's worldwide claim to fame centers on her thousands of shoes, a collection that became a symbol of the pair's unchecked greed and corruption and eventually of Imelda's absurdity. But the former first lady was a formidable political figure in her own right, and she was a crucial player in her husband's domestic and foreign policies. Known interchangeably as Imelda, Madame, and the Iron Butterfly, names that encapsulate her variable performances, Marcos crafted a consummate persona that combined exotic appeal and demure modesty with political power.

Anticipating the head scratching that might be prompted by the album, Byrne begins the liner notes with a series of reasonable questions. "What is this?" he asks. "Why am I interested in this? Why do a series of songs about Imelda Marcos and Estrella Cumpas?" (1). His answer draws upon a cycle of making and remaking transpacific femininity: "The story I am interested in," recalls Byrne, "is more about asking what drives a powerful person— what makes them tick? How do they make and then remake themselves?" (2). Byrne categorizes the song cycle as a narrative of self-construction with Imelda at its center; for him, this Filipina is captivating not only because she was so powerful, but also because of her ability to refashion herself. Deciding early on that the first lady's monstrously absurd collection of "shoes, all 3,000+ pairs, would never be mentioned" (2), he reports that the album was designed to focus instead on a "more universal, revealing, and profound" subject through the opposition of the complexities of "Imelda's rise" against the "tragic parallel story" of her former caregiver Cumpas. This claim to universality—the desire to "imagine the former first lady in a manner unconstrained by politics or protesting voices," as Christine Bacareza Balance puts it—"highlight[s] parallel discursive streams of memorializing the Cold War years of Marcos' U.S.-backed dictatorship—either as a cultural apex or an anomaly of excess." Moreover, these justifications "simply foreclosed the possibility of understanding (1) the art of politics and (2) the political nature of art."[1]

Keeping Balance's assessment in mind, one can do more with the question that introduces and frames *Here Lies Love*. Indeed, what is this? I'd like to use Byrne's recently produced object to think about the continued global circulation of transpacific femininities in this and other twenty-first-century cultural sites. Extending both the textual and historical parameters that have been my focus, this epilogue briefly explores the contemporary recasting of transpacific femininities in light of three icons: Imelda Marcos, the overseas Filipina worker, and the mail-order bride. I document these remakings not only in the album's construction of Marcos and her devoted, tragic caregiver Estrella, but also in Filipina bloggers' and web designers' responses to digital representations of Filipinas as domestic and erotic commodities. How might one rethink these contemporary archives and icons in the context of the cycles of making and remaking I have traced throughout *Transpacific Femininities*?

My discussions have centered primarily on a print archive, one that illustrates the deeply entwined connections among the emerging new forms of Filipina femininity, Philippine literature in English, and the intersection of Spanish, American, and Japanese empires. In mapping these archival byways, I explored theoretical and analytical midways that illuminate the importance of transpacific Filipina femininities to the nexus of nationalism and feminism as the Philippines underwent a series of geopolitical transitions. These recursive patterns of making and remaking the modern transpacific Filipina were crucial to how Filipina and Filipino elites negotiated imperial and national shifts in varied cultural sites. Such cycles, however, are also marked by problematic representational and authorial practices. Influenced by the elite's interest in reasserting their claim to a bourgeois heterosexual hierarchy and their desire to differentiate themselves from working-class, poor, and indigenous peoples, Filipina and Filipino imaginings of modernity, nationalism, and feminism were often uneasy and complicated.

Far from resolved, such tensions and instabilities persist in twenty-first-century manifestations of the transpacific Filipina. Despite Byrne's claims to apolitical universality, *Here Lies Love* is a collection of material that musically remakes and recirculates Filipina femininities to commercialize and reconstruct transpacific U.S.–Philippine history. Byrne's recasting of this Filipina as entertainment links *Here Lies Love* to the long history of U.S. imperial amnesia and to representational projects that attempted to contain a transpacific Filipina's threat. The creation of the album almost a quarter of a century after the end of the Marcos regime and its predominantly positive reception speak to more than just the lasting mythos of Imelda.[2] Indeed, Imelda Marcos's tremendously affective and effective (albeit disturbing) career as a politician is as much about the power and traction of transpacific femininity itself as it is about her political ambition, talents of persuasion, and lack of moral compunction. Marcos was—and is—so memorable because she was able to manipulate and capitalize on a preexisting fascination with transpacific femininities, to translate these performances into actual political agency.

While a work like *Here Lies Love* attests to how such forms of transpacific femininity might be circulated for musical consumption, these fascinations have also informed contemporary Filipina cultural production, as feminists respond to the commodification of the transpacific Filipina's domestic and erotic potential in the iconic figures of the caregiver and the mail-order bride. Here I draw connections between these constructions not to suggest links of causation between the two, but to gesture toward their imbricated functions as globally circulated representations that are steeped in the fraught history of the making and remaking of transpacific femininities. The Marcos regime catalyzed changing patterns in the circulation of Filipina bodies and representations that, as Neferti Tadiar and Roland Tolentino have shown, persist well into the contemporary moment.[3] The overseas contract worker or overseas Filipina or Filipino worker (OCW/OFW), often imagined popularly as a woman, has become the Philippines' new national (and transpacific) heroine. The increasingly romanticized image of the Filipina caregiver builds upon the representational dynamics that, as we saw in chapter 5, were especially important to how Filipina and Filipino authors imagined postwar geopolitical transitions in the Philippines. Indeed, the Cold War rhetoric of the caring Filipina heart gives life to the contemporary overseas Filipina worker, a woman glorified as her country's most valuable export, one whose domestic employment abroad has shifted the economic power of women.[4] If the Filipina is idealized nationally and globally because of her unique ability to go above and beyond other women's abilities to provide domestic care, comfort, and cure, the Filipina mail-order bride figures as the other side of transpacific femininity as commodity, a woman imagined in the global marketplace as able to merge a Filipina's exceptional servitude with Orientalized eroticism.[5] Circulations of these iconic women undoubtedly center on presumptions about the transpacific Filipina's ability to offer (domestically or erotically) what other women cannot or are not willing to provide.

In the twenty-first century, the global interest in the mail-order bride and the caregiver might be tracked in multiple cultural forms, but they are undoubtedly most visible online. Heeding Tadiar's call to "hear . . . the alternative affective literacies of political imagination making their way through the major channels of global culture," I contrast Byrne's construction of an album as a multimedia archive with Filipina-produced efforts that offer an important counter to the online circulation of these icons.[6] Since the 1990s Filipinas have created websites, web contests, and blogs to address the circulation of the Filipina image in digital space. These women use online productions to question and critique the dominance of transpacific icons like the domestic caregiver and the mail-order bride. Imagining what they call a "newfilipina," or *Bagong Pinay*, they reframe and reconfigure patterns of female iconography that have been crucial to nationalist and feminist movements in the Philippines. They document, circulate, and assemble an online repository of their work in digital productions that bear traces of the crucial intersections among feminism, nationalism, and transpacific women in print culture. And in a contemporary revision of the networks of transpacific sisterhood that were strategically employed throughout the first half of the twentieth century, they use the hyperlinked structure of the blogosphere to form virtual communities of transpacific feminists.

But this new archive also manifests key differences. Created after the postrepublican period (1946–72) and the years of the Marcos dictatorship, after student-led protests and the rise of feminist activism in the Philippines, and after the popular revolution of 1986 that shifted the political stage, online remakings of the transpacific Filipina promote different versions of modern Filipina femininity for new ends. There is a palpable tone of urgency in these websites, as they stress that representations of the Filipina have had, and still have, disturbing offline ramifications. Rather than seeing these contemporary formations as breaking from an earlier tradition established and furthered by the elite during the first half of the twentieth century, in these closing pages I draw a continuum that connects the efforts of Filipina women's movements and organizations to these earlier attempts. Contemporary Filipinas must continuously renegotiate the terms of Filipina femininity amid the vestiges of imperial and national reformations that were important in the earlier twentieth century, and the overlapping transformations that have been and still are crucial to alterations in transpacific geopolitics. For, as we know, now the dynamics at stake are not necessarily linked to physical occupation and empire, but to the transpacific shifts produced by the globalized, capitalist, and neocolonial flows that continue to tie the Philippines and the United States to Asia and the Pacific. And while the Filipina travels, literally and discursively, beyond the bounds of the Pacific region, these contemporary movements and iterations nevertheless still trace and cross the patterns and intersections that have been my focus.

....

Fitting for an album devoted to a transpacific Filipina now synonymous with excess, *Here Lies Love* does more than just use Imelda Marcos's biography as its inspiration. This multimedia archive features mostly poppy, danceable tunes meant to recall the infectious beats of the clubs she loved to frequent in the 1970s and early 1980s, a period of music that Byrne himself recalled fondly. In constructing the songs, Byrne incorporated quoted material from Marcos's interviews; the title, for example, refers to the phrase that she hopes will one day be engraved on her tombstone. He also wrote and designed *Here Lies Love* as a concept piece, meant not to be downloaded in fragments but bought in its entirety. The result is a fascinating production. Designed to look like a book, the album includes two CDs; 120 pages of liner notes in which the songs' lyrics are juxtaposed with Byrne's personal reflections on the Marcoses and U.S.–Philippine relations; archival photographs of the Marcoses and stock images depicting the difficulties of life in the Philippines; Byrne's own photos taken while traveling in the Philippines; and his reproductions of Imelda Marcos's sketches. The album also includes a DVD in which the songs are set to a dizzying pastiche of video clips from the Marcos-sponsored propaganda film *Iginuhit Ng Tadhana: The Ferdinand Marcos Story* (1965), footage of late 1970s and early 1980s club scenes, and news clips of violence and revolt during the martial law years. Even the mythos of the album extends further than the object. *Here Lies Love* took years to make, included what Byrne describes as a "year's worth" (2) of research in the Philippines, was narrated in his personal online journal, and was preceded by a rough-draft performance staged at Carnegie Hall, with a cast of Asian performers that included Joan Almedilla, Dana Diaz-Tutaan, and Ganda Suthivarakom, all of whom were eventually recast as backup singers in the final version. "'All this,'" reports the *New York Times* review of the Carnegie Hall performance, "'is highly researched,' [Byrne] said. 'This is not artistic license. This is reporting.'"[7]

If *Here Lies Love* is an example of multimedia as an alternative method of "reporting," like many of the print archives I have already discussed, its resulting assemblage of transpacific femininities is riddled with unsettling contradictions. These instabilities have their foundation in the politically troubled history of U.S.–Philippine relations before, during, and after the Marcos years and in the manner in which these transpacific relations were both informed by and negotiated via representations of women. As the album moved from concept to staged performances to final product, it proceeded via the erasure of imperial and neocolonial violence. In transforming the Marcoses into a supposedly "universal story" for global consumption, *Here Lies Love* slicks a glossy veneer over Philippine national trauma. The Asian performers who originally voice Imelda's and Cumpas's desires disappear, and their substitution by more marketable female vocalists turns these Filipinas into portable, extracted commodities. The album blurs the lines between its "highly researched" contents, as documentary evidence appears alongside a personal photo collection and copied illustrations. This particular type of so-called reporting mimics prior constructions of Filipina femininity in late nineteenth- and early twentieth-century cultural productions that, as I argued in chapter 1, represented both a fascination with and fear of Filipina bodies and contained their excess in constructions of the Filipina as the eroticized savage or as the desiring colonial woman.

Linking Marcos to the fraught mixture of global capital and unstable models of femininity embodied by the Filipina coed of the 1930s and 1950s, the reconstructed history of *Here Lies Love* posits her as a product of the circulation of Western pop cultural forms. Through the ventriloquistic maneuvers of indie rock and pop female singers, the album also remakes the transpacific Filipina as an object for global consumption. Her subjectivity is made marketable in the pop rhythms and beats of each track and in the overall plot of the song cycle, which writes Imelda's story as a rags-to-riches fairy tale. The album constructs a sympathetic listener, one who cheers Imelda on, worries over her difficulties with her husband, dances and laughs with her in New York clubs and at celebrity-filled cocktail parties, and smiles knowingly at her effortless manipulation of state leaders. And Byrne's strategy is remarkably effective. Praising this "rags-to-kleptocracy biography" as "both loony and a stroke of genius,"[8] critics noted that *Here Lies Love* is undeniably successful in making the consumer forget the troubling history of the Marcoses, so that the listener/viewer/dancer can become a version of Imelda. "Crank the volume high enough," observes Jenny Ortuoste in *The Manila Standard*, "you forget the subject and become immersed in the music," so that, as Jessica Zafra writes in the *Philippine Star*, the album "makes you believe that you are the invincible queen of the dance floor."[9] The album's appeal to the listener's and viewer's sympathies is remarkably resonant with Marcos's own performances as a politician and, later, as a martyr, and her employ of the musical and representational constructs of suffering that, as Balance, Reynaldo Ileto, and Allan Punzalan Isaac have argued, have been central to Philippine nationalist movements.[10] The effects are both mesmerizing and disturbing and recall other texts that similarly accentuate Marcos's ability to attract and repulse, to captivate and terrify.[11]

Although the lyrics of the songs and the production of an album devoted to Imelda Marcos are certainly politically questionable, Byrne is nevertheless well aware of the horrors of the Marcos regime. His interviews and journal reflections are more explicit regarding his own sense of the Marcoses, of the role of the United States in allowing their corruption to continue, and of the connections between contemporary U.S. foreign policy and relations with the Philippines from the 1960s to the 1980s. Rather than taking on these repercussions directly, however, *Here Lies Love* relies on the screen of structural ironies to attenuate its complicated politics; according to Balance, "*Here Lies Love* continues to maintain an ironic distance from its subject, an amused detachment from the actual events that led to [Imelda Marcos's] notoriety."[12] This strategy of "amused detachment" and the album's ultimate failure to acknowledge the political repercussions of potentially glorifying and capitalizing on this violent period in Philippine history are but microcosms that recycle patterns we have seen before: imperial amnesia and a desire to write the Filipina as a desiring consumer of U.S. capital and culture, pedagogy and ideology.[13]

While the album does market transpacific Filipina femininity, at the same time, certain elements of *Here Lies Love* unsettle such commodification. The album's representation of Estrella Cumpas as a domestic caregiver is especially complex. On one hand, Byrne's inclusion of Cumpas's narrative draws attention to the poor and working-class women who, as we have seen, were often excised in the earlier formations of the transpacific Filipina as mobile, cosmopolitan models of potential. But the final product also structurally and narratively sidelines Cumpas; in the album as a whole, the songs voiced by Estrella are far fewer in comparison to those aligned with Imelda. On the other hand, Cumpas's representation in the album centers on her sacrifices as a selfless, loving, and devoted servant, a characterization that figures her as a stand-in for the nation. While early songs set Imelda up as a poor girl from the country with big, uncontainable dreams, a woman to be both pitied and admired, later tracks inevitably must come to terms with Marcos's corruption. Estrella's songs are crucial to this reckoning, for she also serves as the voice of the Filipino people. In contrast to the tremendous arc of Imelda's personal and political life, Cumpas emerges as one of the casualties of Marcos's quick rise to power. The notes for her songs are accompanied by stock photos of people in the Philippines: families navigating flooded streets (13, 14, 16); a bustling market scene (27); an older woman walking on a busy municipal street (83); two children peering out of a doorway (87). Byrne repeatedly contrasts these photos with images of Imelda, often glamorously dressed and side by side with world celebrities, diplomats, and leaders (figure 14).

14. Photo included in the liner notes of David Byrne's *Here Lies Love*. The American boxing promoter Don King dances with host and First Lady Imelda Marcos at a gala party in honor of the Muhammad Ali versus Joe Frazier "Thrilla in Manila" fight in Manila, October 1, 1975 (AP Photo/Dwight Johnson).

In its closing songs *Here Lies Love* raises the question of resistance, and Filipinas' and Filipinos' desire for and ability to overturn oppression. The Marcos years are most famous for corruption, violence, graft, and the suppression of liberties, but this period was also extraordinarily influential in shifting the dynamics of activism. "The emergence of the radical and reformist youth organizations," observes Vicente Rafael, "historically paralleled the rise of the Marcoses."[14] The youth resistance had long-lasting effects on Philippine politics; student-led protests, in Rafael's assessment, "had a considerable impact on altering the terms of political discourse in the Philippines."[15] Originating in demonstrations to promote academic freedom in response to anticommunist action, the student movement quickly gained momentum. Activists in the late 1960s and early 1970s focused on protesting against U.S. foreign policy, the Vietnam War, the Marcos government, and increasing class disparity in the Philippines.[16] The first violent clashes between youth and police occurred in 1964, and on January 26 and January 30, 1970, the events that became known as the First Quarter Storm, including police action against demonstrators that resulted in hundreds of injuries and the death of four students, "set in motion a wave of marches and rallies protesting the 'fascist' behavior of the state, many of which resulted in further violent clashes."[17]

The long-term effects of student activism in the Philippines coincided with the shifting dynamics of women's resistance and the rise of new organizations devoted to women's rights. Tracking the complex nature of these groups, feminist scholars like Tadiar and Mina Roces have explored late twentieth-century Filipina activism and its wide-reaching political and cultural resonances.[18] An offshoot of the youth movement, the organization MAKIBAKA (Malayang Kilusan ng Bagong Kababaihan, or Free Movement of New Women), a group widely recognized as "the first outrightly radical feminist organization in the republican era," had "three primary objectives: a) [to] mobilize Filipino women into greater participation in society, b) to expose cultural imperialism, and c) to liberate Filipino women from social discrimination and sexual exploitation."[19] The Concerned Women of the Philippines was formed in 1978 to oppose fraudulent elections and campaign for reform. The years following the assassination of the leading political opposition leader Benigno Aquino in 1983 saw the flowering of numerous women's activist groups and coalitions, including GABRIELA (General Assembly Binding Women for Reforms, Integrity, Equality, Leadership, and

Action), a large umbrella organization that included over one hundred women's groups.[20]

The mobilization of women in organized protest and the ties between organizations lobbying for women's rights as part of a broader campaign to address social, economic, and educational disparities paint a crucial historical and cultural backdrop for contemporary Filipina blogger production.[21] Byrne's multimedia archive of transpacific femininity temporally coincides with the rise of Filipina-produced websites and blogs that specifically address the circulation and consumption of the Filipina digital presence and its troubling repercussions. In February 2008, Women's History Month in the Philippines, the feminist website designers and bloggers of FilipinaImages .com partnered with the encyclopedia WikiPilipinas to sponsor a contest devoted to the Filipina. To correspond with this venture, Lorna Lardizabal-Dietz, Dine Racoma, and Noemi Lardizabal-Dado created a blog that addressed what they saw as the persistent problem of online representations of Filipinas. Their efforts initially sought to correct an imbalance in SERPs (search engine results) for the Filipina. The women were concerned with the number of searches spitting out dating websites, advertising mail-order brides, and commodifying the Filipina as sexualized and exotic. Arguing that the "Filipina of the Future deserves a more empowered, diverse image online," these women sought not perfection but a recognition of transpacific Filipina femininity as "multiple, complex, and whole."[22]

FilipinaImages.com was not the first or only response to representations of Filipinas online. Ten years earlier Perla Paredes Daly tried to address a similar problem with the site *Bagong Pinay* (New Filipina), a venture that was also meant to counter the digital representation of Filipinas as sexualized commodities. The inaugural issue featured an open forum (*magsalita ka!*), which featured lively debate about the identity of the "newfilipina," a neologism coined by Paredes Daly. And as a testament to the persistent linkages between online circulation and the commodification of Filipinas, the efforts of these open forums were themselves interrupted by those who mistakenly thought the site was a venue for dating or marriage.

In the twelve years since *Bagong Pinay* appeared, Filipinas have constructed numerous online responses to the corresponding increase in numbers of dating websites and marriage brokers. On the shimmering screens of these other forums in English, contemporary Filipinas remake what it means to be a Filipina. While the captivating beats and rhythms of Byrne's *Here Lies*

Love elide how the interstices of imperial history, globalization, and national corruption continue to have violent effects on Filipina women, Filipina website administrators and bloggers are acutely aware of these ramifications, and they challenge the commodification and consumption of actual and iconic Filipina bodies in the global marketplace. They are part of a long history of Filipina women who actively contested their discursive production in a wide number of media forms. The website newfilipina.com is not just a blog, but also a repository that records and catalogues these conversations and creates an online collection of contemporary Filipinas' remakings of transpacific femininities. As a contemporary archive that documents how Filipina feminists respond to late twentieth- and twenty-first-century iterations of transpacific femininity, newfilipina.com has its roots in the print productions of Maria Claras, barrio girls, coeds, modern girls, new Filipinas, and New Order women. As part of this representational continuum, the online production of modern Filipina femininity is connected to and departs from these earlier versions. In using the terms *Bagong Pinay* and *newfilipina*, these women playfully reconfigure a term that, as we have seen, was recycled throughout the twentieth century. The recurrence of the newfilipina stresses the historical and recursive paradigms that have consistently marked the production of modern Filipina femininity for the past century.

Reacting to the dominant circulation of transpacific Filipinas as sexualized objects and icons of care, the women of the blogosphere assume heterogeneous and multiple authorial personas. In their blogs many call attention to their offline identities and to the meaning of blogging to their lives. Yet bloggers like Mathe Ubaniaga also illustrate the complexities of enacting this multiplicity.[23] In her March 2008 contribution to the blog *Hot Momma: The Adventure That Is Motherhood*, Ubaniaga, writing as Mathe, contends that the "blogger image of the modern Pinay" is "one to be admired, and should be an accurate indicator of where the modern Filipina is. They write well as most of them have a good command of the English language. These Pinays who live virtual lives which are not so far from their real ones are well-educated, well-informed and well-bred in the way they carry themselves as netizens."[24] Mathe goes on to draw a transpacific cartography that stretches across the bounds of oceans, class, and continents: "Whether they are career women in the Philippines or stay-at-home moms in the US or Australia or even Overseas Filipino Workers in Europe, these Filipinas epitomize the modern woman we all would want the world to know: the ever sweet, ever sensible Pinay of the modern era—always worthy of respect, always proud of her race."[25]

Mathe's comments incorporate strains I have documented throughout this book, for she valorizes Filipina bloggers' education and intellect yet also normalizes their behavior as being "well-bred" (and thus separate from a discourse of sexualization). But while Mathe characterizes a cross-classed spectrum of bloggers that includes working women and Filipina home-workers, her own identity as a blogger is much more fragmented and even torn between these two poles. An OFW based in the United Kingdom, Ubaniaga also publishes a blog about her experiences as a worker abroad. She writes *Pinoy around the World: How Life Is Away from Home* under the name modernmaclara, a persona that rewrites the iconic Maria Clara, the character from José Rizal's *Noli Me Tangere* who was reinterpreted in the first part of the twentieth century as a model of elite, Spanish-influenced femininity—chaste, virginal, and subservient.[26] Aesthetically, the two blogs are dramatically different: *Hot Momma*'s space features bright yellows and sunflowers encircling photos of children, while *Pinoy around the World*'s dominant backdrop is white space, with muted colors and grays. While *Hot Momma* is, as Mathe describes it, primarily a "mommy blog," *Pinoy around the World* is often openly critical of the political situation in the Philippines and devoted to chronicling the difficulties of OFW life abroad. The existence of these two blogs puts into sharp relief the difficulty of holding in mind these two notions of modern Filipina femininity. Even though Mathe might claim the Filipina's and also her own ability to encompass multiple forms of femininity, the partitioning of her different personas as Mathe/Hot Momma and as a twenty-first-century modernmaclara nevertheless demonstrates what she perceives as their immiscibility.[27]

The online forum is both limiting in its dominant representations of women and potentially liberating in its possibilities, its release from isolation, and the potential the women see for creating new forms of connection and community. The blogs differ substantially from Byrne's version of transpacific femininity in *Here Lies Love*, which ultimately draws upon Imelda's incredible selfishness and her eventual rejection of cross-class coalition with Estrella Cumpas as part of the album's tragic narrative. In contrast, contemporary Filipina bloggers—in ways that are both reminiscent of and different from early to mid-twentieth-century women authors who reformulated transpacific sisterhood—actively pursue new community partnerships with other women. The WikiPilipinas contest furthered these connections through its rules, which required that the bloggers published their entries on their own blogs and posted links back to the contest. The women construct themselves as part of a larger global community that is figured in the interstices of online circulation. They see themselves alternately as global Pinays, Filipina Americans, and netizens. Writing from a network that spreads from the Philippines to the United States, the United Kingdom, and Australia, Filipinas imagine themselves as part of a community that crosses lines of class and location, one that connects a "scrapbooking mommy" to a graduate student in the United States, an OFW based abroad, to a "Bi-Cultural Pinay" who "was born and raised with Brown skin and thick black hair in middle-class, blond and brunette Midwest North America."[28]

The use of the term *Pinay* itself emphasizes the importance of cross-class alliances within these transpacific networks. As I discussed in chapter 5, Pinoy and Pinay initially referred to working-class men and women who migrated to the United States during the first half of the twentieth century. Illustrated by its usage in Bienvenido Santos's short stories, Pinoy and Pinay thus marked the disparities of class and labor experiences of transpacific men and women. In making the Pinay *bago*, or new, Filipinas reconfigure the Pinay as a global formation of identity, one that is inclusive of Filipinas and Filipina Americans and that cuts across class boundaries. This embracing of Pinay, however, also bears the traces of the activist influence of the student protests of the 1960s and 1970s in the Philippines and the development of feminist activist organizations that specifically addressed the conditions of poverty and class disparity in the Philippines. Filipina bloggers consciously envision themselves as connected to working-class and poor women in the Philippines and abroad.

The politics of cross-class alliances and global networks outlines the uniquely Philippine iterations of the bloggers' transpacific feminism. The women construct an online version of kinship politics, practices that rely on the intimate connections of family networks and associations that, according to Roces, have historically structured and enabled women's political involvement in the Philippines.[29] In positing online connections with other women and in encouraging other Filipinas to become involved in their own blogging endeavors, Filipina bloggers redefine and expand upon the political practices of kinship. Rather than the exclusive control that has historically been exercised and, in many cases, exploited by rich, powerful families like the Marcoses, this new familial and global collective promises to expand exponentially and carries with it the responsibility of maintaining an awareness of those who are disenfranchised and marginalized in both online and offline spaces.

Without question, many of the bloggers are acutely cognizant of the material disparities that allow them to access and produce these online networks. In keeping with this trajectory of activist response, FilipinaImages .com promotes concerted efforts not only to alter the circulation of online Filipina images, but also to encourage women to address the disturbing violence that stems from these representations. Many of the women emphasize what one blogger calls "offline empowerment."[30] This movement from the blogspace to offline political empowerment reflects the influence of women's resistance and political movements in the Philippines and of women-of-color feminism in the United States. A blogger named Lisa emphatically claims, "Bloggers need to raise awareness of the social injustices that jail the Filipina spirit (such as global sex trafficking, abuse of domestic workers overseas, immigration issues, and enslaving poverty) and they also need to be aggressive in their denouncement of Filipina commercialization. To enhance the online image is to affirm the authentic presence of the Filipina."[31]

In calling attention to the link between representations of women and the economic and political difficulties faced by Filipinas around the world, these women respond to the gendered repercussions of development and globalization in the Philippines. Indeed, "Filipina women," observes Tadiar, "not only have borne the costs of this war of development but also have literally become the bodily price paid for it. Prostituted women, domestic and service-sector workers, home-workers, and rural and agricultural workers as well as factory workers are the most visible, primary, national commodities that the Philippines has marketed vigorously since the 1970s in order to buy its share of economic development."[32] The feminist bloggers who created *Bagong Pinay* and *newfilipina* are acutely aware of these repercussions, for representational dynamics both stem from and make possible the conditions that have led to such real-time circumstances. Their call for awareness, then, is also a call to address how cycles of representation have led to the globalized economic flows and inequities that rely on the labor of Filipina bodies.

The dynamics of the blogosphere, however, have also opened up the site of conversation to access by the nonelite. Without overstating the potential of online or digital production, forums like magsalita ka, the site FilipinaImages .com, and the WikiPilipinas contest are archives that are less restrictive than the print and publishing circles that dominated and shaped literary production in the first half of the twentieth century.[33] These Filipinas imagine a new repository of transpacific femininities, one that responds to and signifies on an older collection of materials that still resonates in contemporary notions of transpacific Filipinas. Similar to the early to mid-twentieth-century productions of Filipinas in print culture, Filipina bloggers emphasize key instabilities. Contemporary Pinays are theorizing their new multimedia archive in ways that demand activist consciousness, community and dialogue with other women, and strategies of linking and communication. They draw upon a cross-section of Filipinas, a community that is responsive to the transpacific circulation of iconic Filipina femininity and influenced by transnational and Third World feminist movements. Through their blogs the women reconceptualize their place in the elite and revise a complicated history of transpacific Filipina feminists and their entanglements with the sometimes politically compromised, not always easy imaginings of Filipina femininities.

Echoing the Filipina bloggers' appeal, I close *Transpacific Femininities* with a sense of urgency. *Here Lies Love* and the online work of Filipina bloggers present a wide spectrum that highlights the importance of transpacific femininities in our contemporary moment. Despite their very different origins, motivations, and political repercussions, the variety of these representations reveal that the cycle of the making and remaking of transpacific femininities even now plays out in contemporary venues—from a multimedia concept piece such as *Here Lies Love* and its marketing of Filipina bodies to the feminist imaginary produced in the Filipina blogosphere that contests and questions women's commodification and consumption. Figures of transpacific Filipinas are still a means of negotiating shifts produced by geopolitical transitions, now manifested not in formal empire or occupation, but in the dynamics of neocolonialism and the global marketplace. The transpacific femininities in these multimedia archives call attention to the West's fascination with models of Filipina femininity in these new contexts. Extending the byways and midways traced throughout this book, these contemporary iterations of the modern Filipina still have traction. And the disturbing ramifications of these cycles and patterns also expand beyond the printed page, offscreen, and in real time via representational projects that, like much of *Here Lies Love*, render violence and exploitation benign and palatable. Yet despite these sobering truths, the instabilities in these versions of transpacific femininity—from the rupture of imperial forgetting that interrupts the swaying rhythms of a danceable track, or the pressing plea for change demanded and enacted by a Filipina feminist blogger—nevertheless remind us of the ongoing search for untraveled routes and unmapped connections in our archives, theories, critical practices, and pedagogies. However fraught and unstable, it is precisely our makings and remakings of these moments that both point toward and reach out for possibility.

INTRODUCTION *Transpacific Filipinas*

1. "The Four Faces of Maria Clara," *Wedding Essentials*, 164–65; Lazam, "In Maria Clara's Wardrobe," 163.

2. My spelling of this icon's name varies from Rizal's original Spanish orthography (María Clara). I use the Anglicized "Maria Clara" here and throughout the book to indicate her transformation in the twentieth century. For a more detailed discussion, see chapter 2.

3. Rizal, *Noli Me Tangere*, 30.

4. My use of the word *intimacies* in this context draws on Lowe, "The Intimacies of Four Continents," in Stoler, *Haunted by Empire*, 191–212.

5. The U.S. occupation was interrupted by the outbreak of the Pacific War in the Philippines in 1941 and the Japanese occupation.

6. In using "Philippine literature in English," I follow current terminology used by scholars in the Philippines.

7. For examples, see DeLoughrey, *Routes and Roots*; Diaz and Kauanui, "Native Pacific Cultural Studies on the Edge"; Edwards, *The Practice of Diaspora*; Gilroy, *The Black Atlantic*; Guterl, *American Mediterranean*; Hau'ofa, *We Are the Ocean*; Huang, *Transpacific Imaginations*; Isaac, *American Tropics*; Palumbo-Liu, *Asian/American*; Rowe, *Literary Culture and U.S. Imperialism*; Skwiot, *The Purposes of Paradise*; Stephens, *Black Empire*; Stillman, "Pacific-ing Asian Pacific American History"; Sumida, *And the View from the Shore*; and Wilson, *Reimagining the American Pacific*.

8. Manlapaz, *Filipino Women Writers*, 3.

9. Kaplan and Pease, *Cultures of United States Imperialism*. This collection was influential in drawing attention to U.S. empire studies.

10. Christina Klein has suggested that American studies would do well to expand its geographic boundaries. See Klein, "Why American Studies Needs to Think about Korean Cinema." Some notable exceptions to the above generalization include studies

of the Philippines, including Tadiar, *Fantasy Production* and *Things Fall Away*; Rafael, *White Love and Other Events*; Espiritu, *Five Faces of Exile*; and Hau, *Necessary Fictions*.

11. See, for example, Espiritu, *Five Faces of Exile*, and Tolentino, *America's Experts*.

12. Here and elsewhere, I use the term *Nippongo* in addition to Nihongo because it was used by Filipina and Filipino authors during the Japanese occupation.

13. Rotor, "Writers without Readers," 8.

14. While the Americans effectively increased English language fluency over a short period of time, the number of people in the Philippines who spoke Spanish was extremely small; often they were people who were Spanish or had Spanish parentage. The ability to speak Spanish marked the elite classes through the twentieth century.

15. This section is indebted to previous work on the Philippine literary tradition in English, especially the introduction to Lumbera and Nogales Lumbera, *Philippine Literature*; Hayden, *The Philippines*; Hosillos, *Philippine–American Literary Relations*; Mojares, *Origins and Rise*, chapters 6–8; Ponce, *Beyond the Nation*; and the introduction to Yabes, *Philippine Short Stories, 1925–1940*. Meg Wesling's *Empire's Proxy* offers an extended analysis of both the role of English education and the teaching of American literature during the occupation.

16. See chapter 16 of Constantino, *The Philippines*; chapter 19 of Worcester, *The Philippines Past and Present*; and chapter 3 of Wesling, *Empire's Proxy*.

17. Hayden, *The Philippines*, 534–48.

18. Many of the Filipino exiles in Espiritu's *Five Faces of Exile* were *pensionados*.

19. Mojares, *Origins and Rise*, 335. Mojares notes the rise of English-language literary production and the changing perception in the Philippine literary world of the English-language writer as a legitimate artist. See also similar observations in anthologies, such as volume 1 of Yabes, *Philippine Short Stories*, and studies of the Philippines that account for the American presence, such as Hayden's *The Philippines*.

20. Mojares, *Origins and Rise*, 335.

21. Zoilo M. Galang is generally credited for the first novel published in book form in the Philippines, *Child of Sorrow* (1921). The next literary landmark is Maximo Kalaw's *Filipino Rebel*, although publication dates for this volume are variably cited as 1927, 1929, and 1930.

22. Hayden, *The Philippines*, 603. Leopoldo Y. Yabes also observed, in 1939, that "English is the language of commerce, of government, of education, and (together with Spanish) of culture. . . . English has united the Filipinos" ("A History of Filipino Literature in English," 1).

23. See Gonzalez and Campomanes, "Filipino American Literature." For a detailed account of the publishing activity of Filipinas and Filipinos in the United States in the period before the Second World War, see chapter 5 of Hosillos, *Philippine–American Literary Relations*.

24. These writers include Jose Garcia Villa, Carlos Bulosan, Manuel Arguilla, Bienvenido Santos, and Carlos Romulo. For a listing of some of these works, see the

bibliographical entries in Gonzales and Campomanes, "Filipino American Literature."

25. This paragraph distills a number of sources, including Bautista and Bolton,
Philippine English; Bresnahan, "The Politics of Language"; Croghan, *The Development of
Philippine Literature*; Gonzalez and Campomanes, "Filipino American Literature";
Hosillos, *Philippine–American Literary Relations*; Lumbera, "The Nationalist Literary Tra-
dition" and *Writing the Nation/Pag-akda ng Bansa*; Lumbera and Nogales Lumbera,
Philippine Literature; Manuud, *Brown Heritage*; and Yabes, *Philippine Short Stories, 1925–
1940* and *Philippine Short Stories, 1941–1955*.

26. For example, in 1999 Rachel Lee theorized the possibilities that transnational
reading strategies might provide for considerations of race and gender in Asian American fiction. See the conclusion to Lee, *The Americas of Asian American Literature*. The
1990s was a period of energetic critical debate regarding what transnational frameworks might mean for the politics of Asian American studies. In the reprint version of
her seminal article "Denationalization Reconsidered," Sau-Ling Wong recaps some
of these conversations. See Wong, "Denationalization Reconsidered." See also
Palumbo-Liu, *Asian/American*, and Koshy, "The Fiction of Asian American Literature,"
and, for a representative example of a collection, Lim et al., *Transnational Asia Pacific*.
For more recent work in Asian American literary studies that thinks critically about
transnational frameworks, see Chuh, *Imagine Otherwise*; Park, *Apparitions of Asia*; Parry,
Interventions into Modernist Cultures; and Huang, *Transpacific Imaginations*.

27. The importance of transnational turns in American studies is aptly illustrated
by presidential addresses of the American Studies Association meetings during the
2000s. See Sumida, "Where in the World Is American Studies?"; Kaplan, "Violent
Belongings"; Fishkin, "Crossroads of Cultures"; Halttunen, "Groundwork"; and
Elliott, "Diversity in American Studies and Abroad." These disciplinary meditations
have been matched by an efflorescence of scholarship that embraces the comparative,
transnational and transoceanic, hemispheric, and global, especially in the past ten
years. In the writing of this book, some of the most influential works include Ander-
son, *Imagined Communities*; Chuh, *Imagine Otherwise*; Choy, *Empire of Care*; DeLoughrey,
Routes and Roots; Edwards, *The Practice of Diaspora*; Gilroy, *The Black Atlantic*; Gopinath,
Impossible Desires; Isaac, *American Tropics*; Kaplan and Pease, *Cultures of United States
Imperialism*; Kramer, *The Blood of Government*; Levander and Levine, *Hemispheric American
Studies*; Lowe, "The Intimacies of Four Continents"; Manalansan, *Global Divas*;
Palumbo-Liu, *Asian/American*; Parreñas, *Servants of Globalization* and *The Force of Domes-
ticity*; Rafael, *White Love and Other Events*; Seigel, *Uneven Encounters*; Stephens, *Black
Empire*; and Stoler, *Haunted by Empire*. This book is also indebted to the many Philippine
scholars who have long been well attuned to the lasting effects of U.S. empire. For
groundbreaking work, see Ileto, *Pasyon and Revolution* and *Filipinos and Their Revolution*;
Constantino, *The Philippines*; Campomanes, "New Formations of Asian American
Studies"; and Tadiar, *Fantasy Production* and *Things Fall Away*.

28. In chapter 5 I argue that in part this binational focus is one of the lasting legacies of the Cold War.

29. Isaac, *American Tropics*; Go and Foster, *The American Colonial State*.

30. Diaz, "To 'P' or not to 'P'?"; Stillman, "Pacific-ing Asian Pacific American History"; Diaz and Kauanui, "Native Pacific Cultural Studies on the Edge."

31. Stillman, "Pacific-ing Asian Pacific American History," 241–43.

32. See, for example, Diaz, "To 'P' or Not to 'P'?"; Diaz and Kauanui, "Native Pacific Cultural Studies on the Edge"; DeLoughrey, *Routes and Roots*; Firth, "Future Directions for Pacific Studies"; Hau'ofa, *We Are the Ocean*; Stillman, "Pacific-ing Asian Pacific American History"; Teaiwa, "Globalizing and Gendered Forces"; Thaman, "Decolonizing Pacific Studies"; and Wood, "Cultural Studies for Oceania."

33. Anderson, *The Spectre of Comparisons*, 227–63; Kramer, *The Blood of Government*, 35–86; Rafael, *White Love and Other Events*, 19–51; and Salman, *The Embarrassment of Slavery*, 1–21.

34. Kramer, *The Blood of Government*, 39.

35. See Sommer, *Foundational Fictions*; Sharpe, *Allegories of Empire*; and Pratt, *Imperial Eyes*. Laura Hyun Yi Kang examines and critiques the notion of Asian women as bound to the home and homeland in *Compositional Subjects*.

36. For key examples, see Anzaldúa, *Borderlands / La Frontera*; Gopinath, *Impossible Desires*; Kaplan, Alarcón, and Moallem, *Between Woman and Nation*; Kang, *Compositional Subjects*; Kauanui, "Native Hawaiian Decolonization"; Lowe, *Immigrant Acts*; Mohanty, *Feminism without Borders*; Shimizu, *The Hypersexuality of Race*; Smith, "American Studies without America"; and Stephens, *Black Empire*.

37. Although Isaac also sees Jessica Hagedorn and Carlos Bulosan as representative figures of the Filipina and Filipino in American culture, he does not make the same argument regarding their treatment in literary criticism. See Isaac, *American Tropics*, 121–78.

38. For representative discussions of Bulosan and *America Is in the Heart*, see San Juan Jr., "Beyond Identity Politics," and "Carlos Bulosan, Filipino Writer-Activist"; Wesling, "Colonial Education and the Politics of Knowledge"; and Gonzales, "*America Is in the Heart* as Colonial Immigrant Novel." Readings that depart from this trend include Chuh, *Imagine Otherwise*, chapter 1; Ponce, "On Becoming Socially Articulate"; and Lee, *America's Asia*, 17–44.

39. For sources that focus on Hagedorn, queerness, feminism, and the politics of resistance, see Mendoza, "A Queer Nomadology"; Gairola, "Deterritorialisations of Desire"; Twelbeck, "Beyond a Postmodern Denial"; Chang, "Masquerade, Hysteria"; and Lee, *America's Asia*, 73–105.

40. For analyses of such metonymic relationships between the politics of Asian American authors and their works, see Ling, *Narrating Nationalisms*, and Nguyen, *Race and Resistance*.

41. Recent work has recovered texts that document Filipina experience in the first half of the twentieth century, including Buell, *Twenty-Five Chickens*; Monrayo, *Tomorrow's Memories*; and McReynolds, *Almost Americans*.

42. For foundational critiques of such tendencies in second-wave and Western feminism, see Anzaldúa, *Borderlands / La Frontera*; hooks, *Feminist Theory*; Lorde, *Sister Outsider*; and Mohanty, *Feminism without Borders*. See Aguilar, *Toward a Nationalist Feminism*; de Jesús, *Pinay Power*; and Roces, *Women, Power, and Kinship Politics*.

43. Roces, "Is the Suffragist an American Colonial Construct?" 29.

44. Ibid., 29–30.

45. Ibid., 27–28.

46. Hoganson, "As Badly Off as the Filipinos," 11.

47. Ibid., 25.

48. Ibid. See also Patterson, *The American New Woman*, 5.

49. Weinbaum et al., "The Modern Girl as Heuristic Device," 2.

50. Weinbaum et al., *The Modern Girl around the World*. In this volume, see especially Weinbaum et al., "The Modern Girl as Heuristic Device" and "The Modern Girl around the World"; Dong, "Who Is Afraid of the Chinese Modern Girl?"; Ito, "'The Modern Girl' Question"; and Ramamurthy, "All-Consuming Nationalism." For further studies of new women and modern girls, see Barlow, *The Question of Women*; Brown, *Glamour in Six Dimensions*; Conor, *The Spectacular Modern Woman*; Edwards and Roces, *Women's Suffrage in Asia*; Patterson, *The American New Woman*; and Sinha, *Specters of Mother India*.

51. Weinbaum et al., "The Modern Girl as Heuristic Device," 4.

52. Ibid., 15.

53. These elite men present one answer to Rey Chow's question, "Can brown women be saved from white men by brown men?" (*Writing Diaspora*, 40). I would add, though, that these authors revise this question, to ask, "Can brown women be saved from white men *and women* by brown men?"

54. I examine these shifts more specifically in chapter 4.

55. These include Buaken, *I Have Lived with the American People*; Romulo, *I Saw the Fall of the Philippines, Mother America*, and *My Brother Americans*; and Javellana, *Without Seeing the Dawn*. In a more focused example, Bienvenido N. Santos's short story "Woman Afraid" also identifies a postwar change in Americans' views of Filipinos; the main character, Cris, observes, "These past few years there have [*sic*] been a change. Everybody is hearing now about how brave the Filipinos are, and how loyal they are to America. People did not think of that before my country fell into the hands of the Japanese and before everybody heard how we resisted bravely" ("Woman Afraid," in *You Lovely People*, 100).

ONE *Cartographies*

1. Yule, "The Woman Question in the Philippines," 7.

2. Brody, *Visualizing American Empire*, 89.

3. Stillman, "Pacific-ing Asian Pacific American History," 243.

4. In addition to Stillman's remappings of the Pacific as a means of articulating new intersections between the disciplines of Asian American and Pacific studies, this mode of critical navigation builds on important work in Pacific studies, such as Elizabeth DeLoughrey's interest in the shifting, mobile routes of Pacific literature's graphings of indigeneity, in *Routes and Roots*.

5. Definitions in this and the preceding sentence are from the *Oxford English Dictionary*, "midway, n., adv., adj., and prep.," www.oed.com.

6. Anderson, *The Spectre of Comparisons*, 227–62; Kramer, *The Blood of Government*, 35–86; Rafael, *White Love and Other Events*, 19–51; and Salman, *The Embarrassment of Slavery*.

7. Brody analyzes the connections between American Orientalism and the visual displays that were central to U.S. empire. Brody's discussion features an article that directly links Filipina women to the butterfly and Japanese geisha: "A Madame Butterfly of the Philippines" (*World*, June 7, 1903). See Brody, *Visualizing American Empire*, 74–76. See also Lye, *America's Asia*, and Lee, *Orientals*.

8. This argument extends work on resistance to such colonizing methods of organization, control, and surveillance. See Rafael, *White Love and Other Events*; Kramer, *The Blood of Government*, 229–84; and Slotkin, "Igorots and Indians."

9. For examples of readings of Philippine literature in English, see Manuud, *Brown Heritage*; Baltasar et al., *Philippine Literature*; Hosillos, *Philippine-American Literary Relations*; Mojares, *Origins and Rise of the Filipino Novel*; Abad and Manlapaz, *Man of Earth*; Yabes, *Philippine Short Stories, 1941–1955*; Croghan, *The Development of Philippine Literature*; Cruz, *The Best Philippine Short Stories*.

10. Balce, "The Filipina's Breast," 89, 92.

11. While certain modes of dress are coded as Western, as this study and as the Modern Girl Around the World Research Group have demonstrated, these styles and behavior originated simultaneously across the globe. See Weinbaum et al., *The Modern Girl around the World*.

12. See Balce, "The Filipina's Breast"; Kramer, *The Blood of Government*; Rafael, *White Love and Other Events*; and Brody, *Visualizing American Empire*.

13. In addition to Balce, "The Filipina's Breast"; Kramer, *The Blood of Government*; Rafael, *White Love and Other Events*; and Brody, *Visualizing American Empire*, see Wexler, *Tender Violence*; Delmendo, *The Star-Entangled Banner*, 21–46; and Vergara, *Displaying Filipinos*.

14. Rafael, *White Love and Other Events*, 32–38.

15. Kramer, *The Blood of Government*, 231–84; Rafael, *White Love and Other Events*; 19–51.

16. Rafael, *White Love and Other Events*, 22.

17. Kramer, *The Blood of Government*, 231–84.

18. For a reading of the homoerotics of these dynamics, see Mendoza, "Little Brown Students."

19. All quotations in this paragraph are from Comfort, "Native Tagal Women," 19.

20. Wilder, "Raising of Children Is Chief Philippine Industry," E2.

21. Ibid.

22. Balce makes a similar point, noting that "the surly Filipinas of the imperial archive are now replaced by globalized smiles of female labor, yet like colonial representations of old, their smiles belie the violence of inhuman conditions of exploitation, physical and sexual abuse, poverty, maddening loneliness, and the terror of uncertainty and deportation" (Balce, "The Filipina's Breast," 105).

23. In contrast, see Balce's discussion of images that contrasted elite Latinas from Cuba and Puerto Rico with women from the Philippines ("The Filipina's Breast," 99–102).

24. For an analysis that documents a similar pattern in a travelogue, see Brody, *Visualizing American Empire*, 10–28.

25. "Mrs. Aguinaldo's Wardrobe," 12.

26. Even after Aguinaldo was released by U.S. forces, newspapers and magazines in the United States illustrate a continued fascination with him. Brody, *Visualizing American Empire*, 64. For a fascinating reading of this cartoon's implications, see Wesling, *Empire's Proxy*, 69–103.

27. "Mrs. Aguinaldo's Wardrobe," 12.

28. For related discussions of the politics of dress, see Miller, *Slaves to Fashion*, and Roces, *Women, Power, and Kinship Politics*.

29. "Tells of the Busy Filipino Woman," 3.

30. "Four Filipino Girl Students Are Eager to Return Home," SM4. See also "Bright Girls from Far Away," V20.

31. Hoganson, "As Badly Off as the Filipinos," 16. See also Hoganson, *Fighting for American Manhood*.

32. See Ferens, *Edith and Winnifred Eaton*, 19–45; Marchetti, *Romance and the Yellow Peril*; and Nguyen, *Race and Resistance*, 33–59.

33. See Ferens, *Edith and Winnifred Eaton*, 19–45, and Shah, *Contagious Divides*.

34. Yule, "The Woman Question in the Philippines," 7.

35. I discuss this phenomenon in more detail in chapter 5.

36. Quintero de Joseph, "American and Filipino Women," 1412.

37. Ibid., 1413.

38. Ibid., 1412.

39. Quotations in this paragraph are from ibid., 1412.

40. Ibid., 1413.

41. De Veyra, "The Filipino Woman," 14.

42. Ibid.

43. Yabes, "What Is Wrong with Our Women Writers?" 1.

44. Rafael, *White Love and Other Events*, 9, emphasis in original.

45. See Pascasio, "The Language Situation in the Philippines."

46. Ibid., 242.

47. Yabes, "A History of Filipino Literature in English" and "Philippine Literature in English." See also Da Costa, "Filipino Literature in English," and Viray, "Filipino Writing in English," 12.

48. Jose Garcia Villa's "Honor Roll," which catalogued the year's best short stories, was published in the *Graphic* and followed by similar awards.

49. For examples, see Rotor, "Writers without Readers," 8; Arcellana, "Readers without Writers," 1; Lopez, "Orienting the Filipino Writer"; Yabes, "Filipinos Write Books" and "Filipinos Do Not Buy Books," 2.

50. Yabes, "Filipinos Do Not Buy Books," 2. In keeping with this assessment, Philippine scholars such as Soledad Reyes, following the lead of Petronilo Bn. Daroy, argue that literature in English was primarily written about and for the middle classes in the Philippines, those who, during the Spanish regime, would not have had access to education yet were able to attend universities during the U.S. occupation (Reyes, "The Philippine Novel"). Yabes here undoubtedly defends English literature in light of his own personal interests (after all, he, too, is a struggling writer); he later reflects upon his own experience as a literary critic in a postscript to his introduction to *Philippine Short Stories, 1925–1940*: "The truth is that the achievement of the local short story writers in a borrowed language over a period of only a little more than a decade was too obvious to ignore. But maybe the enthusiasm went beyond proper bounds, and I myself was not exempt from the euphoric feeling. . . . I was in my middle twenties and I shared the enthusiasm and hopes of my fellow writers." See Yabes, "Postscript," *Philippine Short Stories, 1925–1940*, xlv.

51. Rotor, "Writers without Readers," 8. For a response, see Lardizabal, "Presumptious Literary Heirs."

52. Lopez, "State Patronage of Letters," 1. The awards were short-lived, however, interrupted by the outbreak of the Pacific War and the Japanese occupation.

53. Ibid., 2. See also Philippine Writers' League, "Direction in Our Literature," and Lopez, "A Word on 'Proletarian Literature.'"

54. Rotor, "Our Literary Heritage," 12.

55. Quotations in this paragraph are from Rotor, "Our Literary Heritage."

56. See Jose Garcia Villa's literary pronouncements in Chua, *The Critical Villa*.

57. In "Criticism and Literary Growth" (p. 3), Yabes here refers to a comment by his fellow writer Federico Mangahas.

58. Quotes from Mojares, *Origins and Rise of the Filipino Novel*, 274.

59. Lumbera, "Philippine Literature and the Filipino Personality," 3.

60. Mojares, *Origins and Rise of the Filipino Novel*, 274.

61. Quotations in this paragraph are from Litonjua, "Is That So?" 18, 41.

62. See Yabes, "What Is Wrong with Our Women Writers?"; Arguilla and Lopez, "Our Men Writers Are Not So Hot"; and "Letter from Another Woman Writer."

63. Quotations in this paragraph are from Yabes, "What Is Wrong with Our Women Writers?" 1.

64. Arguilla and Lopez, "Our Men Writers Are Not So Hot," 1.

65. Fruto, *Yesterday and Other Stories*, 63.

66. Ibid. All quotations are from pp. 60–61.

67. Ibid. All quotations are from pp. 61, 62, and 63.

68. Ibid., 62.

69. Quoted in Litonjua, "Is That So?" 18.

70. Lopez, introduction to Fruto, *Yesterday and Other Stories*, iii.

71. Paz Marquez Benitez is a major exception to this assessment. Her short story "Dead Stars" is consistently lauded (by Yabes, himself, no less) as the first short story worthy of critical acclaim. See especially Manlapaz, *Filipino Women Writers in English*; Kintanar, *Women Reading*; Reyes, *The Romance Mode*; and work by Hidalgo, such as *Filipino Woman Writing*, *A Gentle Subversion*, and *Over a Cup of Ginger Tea*.

TWO *Feminism's Haunted Intersections*

1. At one point in the debate, one of the delegates implored the other members to give women the opportunity to speak. His entreaty was met with resounding cries of "No!" from the other delegates. *Constitutional Convention Record: Manila, Philippines* (hereafter CCR) 4, no. 78 (October 31, 1934), 507.

2. "Discurso del Señor Vinzons a Favor del Sufragio Feminino," CCR 4, no. 73 (October 25, 1934), 357–60.

3. "Discurso del Sr. Abordo Contra el Sufragio Feminino," CCR 4, no. 74 (October 26, 1934), 383.

4. This chapter is indebted to Roces, "Is the Suffragist an American Colonial Construct?" and "Women in Philippine Politics and Society."

5. *Oxford English Dictionary*, 2nd ed., "fantastic, a. and n," www.oed.com.

6. Maria Paz Mendoza-Guazon studied the numbers of women who graduated from colleges and universities in the Philippines (especially Manila). She reports the following statistics regarding the first Filipina graduates from the state university in its initial years: medicine (1912, 1), liberal arts (1913, 1), master of arts (1917, 2), pharmacy (1915, 3), law (1915, 1) tropical medicine (1916, 1), education (1917, 1), dentistry (1920, 1). After a decade had passed, she records a rise in graduates. In 1927 "there were 231 women who were awarded degrees, as follows: Medicine, 12; Dentistry, 7; Pharmacy, 22; Bachelor of Science in Pharmacy, 4; Bachelor of Science, 7; Bachelor of Science in Education, 88; Bachelor of Science in Commerce, 5; Bachelor of Philosophy, 11; and Associate in Arts, 75" (Mendoza-Guazon, *Development and Progress of the Filipino Woman*, 50). Coeds attended an array of universities, including the University of the Philippines, National University, University of Manila, Liceo de Manila, Manila College of Pharmacy, Philippine Women's College, the Centro Escolar de Señoritas, and University of Santo Tomás (ibid., 50–53).

7. Hart, "Playing with Fire," 5–7, 26; and "The Boomerang," 2–3, 32–33.

8. Rafael, *White Love and Other Events*, 108.

9. Anderson, *The Spectre of Comparisons*; Rafael, *White Love and Other Events*, 1–18; Stoler, "Intimidations of Empire," 1–22. See also the introduction to Edwards and Gaonkar, *Globalizing American Studies*.

10. Stoler, "Intimidations of Empire," 1.

11. Ibid.

12. *Oxford English Dictionary*, 2nd ed., "haunt, v.," www.oed.com.

13. See, for example, Ileto, "Philippine Wars and the Politics of Memory"; Kaplan, "Left Alone with America"; and Isaac, *American Tropics*.

14. Barlow, *The Question of Women*, 7.

15. Weinbaum et al., "The Modern Girl as Heuristic Device," 16. For other work on modern girls, see Barlow, *The Question of Women*; Brown, *Glamour in Six Dimensions*; Conor, *The Spectacular Modern Woman*; Sinha, *Specters of Mother India*; and Roces and Edwards, *Women's Suffrage in Asia*.

16. Weinbaum et al., "The Modern Girl as Heuristic Device," 15.

17. See Lowe, "The Intimacies of Four Continents."

18. While the *Noli* is often linked to turn-of-the-century Philippine nationalism (most famously by Anderson's seminal study, *Imagined Communities*), such scholars as Reynaldo Ileto and Renato Constantino have cautioned against overemphasizing Rizal and his importance. See Anderson, *Imagined Communities*; Constantino, *The Philippines*; and Ileto, *Pasyon and Revolution*.

19. Some well-known contemporary examples include Hagedorn, *Dogeaters*, and Linmark, *Rolling the R's*. Hau's *Necessary Fictions* includes an excellent examination of Rizal's national hero status and its influence on the cultural legacies of the *Noli*.

20. See Anderson, *The Spectre of Comparisons*, 230–31; Dizon, "Rizal's Novels" and "Felipinas Caliban"; Hau, *Necessary Fictions*; and Rafael, *The Promise of the Foreign*.

21. Nakpil, "Maria Clara," 31.

22. Lopez, "Maria Clara," 37.

23. Joaquin, "The Novels of Rizal," reprinted in *La Naval de Manila and Other Essays*, 59–75, 61, 70; Nakpil, "Maria Clara," 36.

24. Lopez, "Maria Clara," 38; Joaquin, "The Novels of Rizal," 66, 74–75; Nakpil, "Maria Clara," 30.

25. Benedict Anderson's work diagnoses the long critical history of bypassing the novel's fictional strategies, especially Rizal's use of structural irony. The deep reverence for Rizal as national hero and martyr contributes to readings of the novel as earnest rather than satiric. Viewing the text as a handbook for Rizal's personal views on nationalism, some scholars conflate the author with either the narrator or characters such as Ibarra. Anderson later criticizes his own impulses to do so in "Forms of Consciousness in Noli Me Tangere."

26. This argument builds on Raquel A. G. Reyes's work in *Love, Passion, and Patriotism*, which I discuss in greater detail below.

27. This paragraph summarizes the key claims of Anderson's "Hard to Imagine" in *The Spectre of Comparisons*, 235–62.

28. Rafael, *White Love and Other Events*, 6.

29. Anderson, *The Spectre of Comparisons*, 233, 259. See also Kramer, *The Blood of Government*, and Rafael, *White Love and Other Events*, 4–14.

30. Previous works on gender and the *Noli* include Rafael, "Language, Identity, and Gender"; Dizon, "Rizal's Novels" and "Felipinas Caliban"; Casas, "Noli me Tangere."

31. Rafael, *The Promise of the Foreign*, 74.

32. Rizal, "A Letter to the Young Women of Malolos," 25, 30.

33. Pura Santillan Castrence, for example, published a series on the women characters in Rizal's novels. See Castrence, "The Female Characters in Rizal's Novels"; "Women Characters in Rizal's Novels"; "The Women Characters in Rizal's Novels—Doctora Doña Victorina de Los Reyes de De Espadaña"; "The Female Characters in Rizal's Novels—Sisa"; "Women Characters of Rizal, The Tertiary Sisters, III"; "The Women Characters in Rizal's Novels—Doña Consolación."

34. Quotations from Reyes, *Love, Passion, and Patriotism*, 49, 20.

35. See ibid., 198–249.

36. Rizal, "A Letter to the Young Women of Malolos," 26.

37. I alternate using my own translations with Soledad Lacson-Locsin's excellent translation of the *Noli*. Instructed by Anderson's words of caution regarding the *Noli's* "criollo-mestizo world," here I have adjusted Lacson-Locsin's original translations, which translates "filipinos" to Filipinos. See pp. 28–29. Further references to the translation will be identified with the abbreviation "L-L."

38. For a related reading of this passage, see Rafael, *The Promise of the Foreign*, 80–81.

39. Dizon helpfully outlines some of these false references in "Rizal's Novels."

40. Rafael provides an extended discussion of this scene that does not focus on its ironic frame in "Language, Identity, and Gender in Rizal's Noli," 120–23.

41. Here I alter Lacson-Locsin's original translation, which translates "*mentiroso*" to "fibber."

42. Rafael, *The Promise of the Foreign*, 73–78; Arrizón, *Queering Mestizaje*, 119–53.

43. Rafael, *The Promise of the Foreign*, 74.

44. Here I hope to illustrate the processes that normalized Filipina heterosexuality, which were affected by the lingering influences of Spanish and U.S. colonialism. This, I hope, is not to reify heterosexual identity even further, but to complement the work of others who analyze multiple formations of sexual identities, practices, and their representations in the Filipina and Filipino diaspora. See, for example, Manalansan, *Global Divas*; Fajardo, "Transportation" and *Filipino Crosscurrents*; and Ponce, *Beyond the Nation*.

45. "What Interest [sic] Them Most," 28. See also Sevilla, "The New Filipino Woman," 16, 43.

46. All quotes in this paragraph are from Barranco, "The Filipino Girl," 8.

47. "Those Co-eds' Resolutions," 26.

48. See "Coed's Morality Should Be Investigated" in Laguio, *Our Modern Woman*, 199–200 (originally published in the *Tribune*, September 20, 1930).

49. Laguio, "The Modern Coed" (originally printed in the *Sunday Tribune*, September 7, 1930), *Our Modern Woman*, 3–11.

50. Laguio, "The Modern Woman," in *Our Modern Woman*, 16.

51. All quotes in this paragraph are from Laguio, *Our Modern Woman*, 5.

52. All quotes in this paragraph are from ibid., 5–9, 19–20. For a corresponding perspective, see Hizon, "A Letter to a Young Lady," 6, 41.

53. All quotes in this paragraph are from Perez, "The College Girl," 25.

54. Mendoza-Guazon, *My Ideal Filipino Girl*, 22.

55. Castrence, "The East Views the American Coed," 8. See also Uichanco, "The University Lady," 2, and the article, "What Every Girl Should Know," 10.

56. Mendoza-Guazon, *My Ideal Filipino Girl*, 32, 24, 31, 32.

57. Ibid., 19, 22.

58. "Discurso del Delegado Sevilla de Bulacán," 489.

59. Roces, "Is the Suffragist an American Colonial Construct?" 26.

60. *CCR* 4, no. 78 (October 31, 1934), 534.

61. "Discurso del Delegado José de Guzman," 339.

62. "Discurso del Delegado Grafilo," 370.

63. "Discurso del Sr. Bocar," 348.

64. *CCR* 4, no. 72 (October 24, 1934), 334.

65. "Discurso del Sr. Carin Contra el Sufragio Feminino," 482; "Discurso del Delegado Grafilo," 371.

66. "Discurso del Sr. Carin," 483.

67. "Discurso del Sr. Abordo Contra el Sufragio Feminino," 383.

68. "Discurso del Sr. Joven," 556.

69. "Discurso del Sr. Cuaderno a Favor del Sufragio Feminino," 566.

70. "Discurso del Delegado Grafilo," 369.

71. Roces documents the Filipina suffragists' wearing of the *balintawak* as emblematizing their attempts to differentiate themselves from American and British feminists. See Roces, "Is the Suffragist an American Colonial Construct?"

72. "Discurso del Delegado Grafilo," 373.

73. "Discurso del Sr. Palma," 435.

74. *CCR* 4, no. 78 (October 31, 1934), 533.

75. "Discurso del Sr. Carin," 488.

76. In Mina Roces's analysis, the barrio girl is an iteration of the *dalagang Filipina*, romanticized in paintings by Philippine National Artist Fernando Amorsolo, which feature rural women wearing traditional Filipina dress in idyllic rural settings. See Roces, "Is the Suffragist an American Colonial Construct?"

77. Laguio, *Our Modern Woman*, 5.

78. "College Girls for Most of Them," 4.

79. Kang, *Compositional Subjects*, 216.

80. Stephens, *Black Empire*, 61.

81. See, for example, Ramamurthy, "All-Consuming Nationalism," and Kaplan, Alarcón, and Moallem, *Between Woman and Nation*.

THREE A Transpacific Filipina's Destiny

1. Kalaw, *The Filipino Rebel*. There is some discrepancy and speculation about the novel's original publication date. The literary scholars Resil B. Mojares and Cristina Pantoja Hidalgo cite the publication date as 1927; other sources have it listed as 1930 or 1931. I follow Martin Joseph Ponce here in approximating the publication date; see the first chapter of Ponce's *Beyond the Nation*. The difficulty of knowing exactly when the novel was published may not be resolved; the only in-print copies that are readily available are the 1964 reprint editions, which do not include an original publication date.

2. Ocampo, *The Brown Maiden*, 35.

3. The first novel in English written by a Filipino was Zoilo M. Galang's *Child of Sorrow*, published in the Philippines in 1921.

4. An-Lim, "The Filipino Rebel," 91. As An-Lim notes, there has not been much published on Kalaw's work. Literary histories briefly mention the novel. Notable exceptions are McMahon, "The Malevolence of 'Benevolent Assimilation,'" and the excellent reading of heteronormative nationalism in the first chapter of Ponce's *Beyond the Nation*.

5. "Latest Books Received," BR18.

6. Junius II, "Brown Maiden Writes," 59, 60. See also Yabes, "The Filipino Novel."

7. Previous readings of *The Filipino Rebel* have characterized the novel's response to benevolent assimilation without centering on its entwined interest in transpacific feminism. See McMahon, "The Malevolence of 'Benevolent Assimilation,'" and Ponce, *Beyond the Nation*. For an extended analysis of education and benevolent assimilation, see chapter 3 of Wesling, *Empire's Proxy*.

8. See Ponce, *Beyond the Nation*.

9. Kaplan, *The Anarchy of Empire*, 95. See also Hebard, "Romantic Sovereignty," 805–30.

10. Nguyen, *Race and Resistance*, especially 33–59.

11. See Tate, *Domestic Allegories of Political Desire*; Carby, *Reconstructing Womanhood*; Nguyen, *Race and Resistance*; Ferens, *Edith and Winnifred Eaton*; Ahmad, "More than Romance"; and Goyal, *Romance, Diaspora*.

12. Reyes, "The Romance Mode," 165. Reyes' identification of the romance elements in *Noli Me Tangere* are a bit unusual, as this novel is usually identified as a beginning moment in Philippine realism or social realism.

13. Ibid., 176.

14. Ibid., 177.

15. Biographical information is culled from the introductions to *The Filipino Rebel* and Maximo Kalaw's *The Case for the Filipinos* and *Self-Government in the Philippines*, and "Maximo Kalaw," http://www.panitikan.com.ph/authors/k/mmkalaw.html (accessed April 2, 2010).

16. This paragraph draws upon biographical accounts of Ocampo in Junius II, "Brown Maiden Writes"; Galang, "Ocampo, Felicidad V."; and *The Philippine Forum*, August 1936, 5. *Portia* is the story of a woman lawyer practicing in Reno; the novel was published serially in *The Philippine Forum* from August 1936 to April 1937. *A Woman Doctor* is set in the Philippines and was serially published in *The Philippine Forum* beginning in May–June 1937.

17. Quotations in this paragraph are from Kalaw, *The Case for the Filipinos*, xv, xiv.

18. A representative example is Worcester, *The Philippines Past and Present*. For an analysis of Worcester's studies (and the larger project of U.S. censuses and surveys of the islands), see chapter 1 of Rafael's *White Love and Other Events*. For discussions of similar ventures, see Balce, "The Filipina's Breast"; Kramer, *The Blood of Government*, 229–84; Wexler, *Tender Violence*; and Delmendo, *The Star-Entangled Banner*, 21–46.

19. Mojares, "Time, Memory, and the Birth of the Nation," 287.

20. Ibid., 275.

21. Ibid.

22. The word *ilustrado*, which translates as the "enlightened ones," demonstrates this elitism. See chapter 2 for a discussion of these dynamics.

23. Manuel Quezon, introduction to *The Case for the Filipinos*, vii. Here, my reference is to W. E. B. Du Bois's idealization of the talented tenth, a small group of African American men who would be responsible for racial uplift.

24. See, for example, the 1928 edition of Mendoza-Guazon's *Development and Progress*. I discuss the production of studies of women's history more specifically in chapter 5.

25. Kalaw, *Self-Government*, 172–73.

26. Ibid., 174.

27. For the groundbreaking text that describes this tradition, see Ileto, *Pasyon and Revolution*.

28. This line appears in canto V, st. XII, line 340 of *Marmion*; Scott's version is "with a smile on her lips and a tear in her eye."

29. See Ponce, *Beyond the Nation*, 53–55.

30. This paragraph draws upon Parreñas, "White Trash"; Baldoz, *The Third Asiatic Invasion*; España-Maram, *Creating Masculinity*; Ngai, *Impossible Subjects*, 96–126; and Volpp, "American Mestizo."

31. Leti Volpp summarizes these entwined concerns: "Anxiety about what was called the 'Third Asian invasion' was expressed primarily around three sites: first, the

idea that Filipinos were destroying the wage scale for white workers; second, the idea that they were disease carriers—specifically of meningitis; and, third, the idea that they were sexually exploiting 'American and Mexican' girls." See Volpp, "American Mestizo," 805–6.

32. See Ngai, *Impossible Subjects*, 96–126.

33. See Parreñas, "White Trash"; Volpp, "American Mestizo"; and España-Maram, *Creating Masculinity*.

34. See Volpp's rigorous accounting of these cases in "American Mestizo."

35. Quotations in this paragraph are from Ocampo, "The Red Men," 71, 76.

36. Nguyen, *Race and Resistance*, 3–31.

37. See ibid., and Ling, *Narrating Nationalisms*. For content specific to Filipinas and Filipinos, see Espiritu, *Five Faces of Exile*; and Yu, "The Hand of a Chinese Master."

38. Espiritu, *Five Faces of Exile*, and Tolentino, *America's Experts*.

39. For example, Kalaw and Ocampo have affinities with the elite Caribbean and African diasporic nationals featured in Edwards's *The Practice of Diaspora* and Stephens's *Black Empire*.

40. In using the term "narrative pattern," I draw upon the introduction to Gina Marchetti, *Romance and the Yellow Peril*.

41. See Lowe, "The Intimacies of Four Continents"; Nguyen, *Race and Resistance*; Chuh, *Imagine Otherwise*; and Eng, *The Feeling of Kinship*.

FOUR *The Pacific War's Filipina*

1. M. L. I., "Collaboration Begins at Home," 3.

2. Panlilio, *The Crucible*, 9. Citations are to the Rutgers edition.

3. See the introduction to Nguyen, *Race and Resistance*.

4. Trinidad, "A Letter to My Daughter," 11.

5. A notable exception is Jodi Kim's *Ends of Empire*.

6. See Yuki Tanaka's introduction to Henson, *Comfort Woman*; Field, "War and Apology"; Hicks, *The Comfort Women*; and Kim, "History and Memory."

7. Foronda, *Cultural Life in the Philippines*, 1.

8. Agoncillo, *The Fateful Years*, 2: 555–606.

9. I use the outdated "Nippongo" in the remainder of the chapter because this is the term used by Filipina and Filipino authors.

10. Foronda, *Cultural Life in the Philippines*, 1.

11. One notable exception is Lanzona, *Amazons of the Huk Rebellion*. For representative studies of the Japanese occupation and Philippine–Japan relations, see Yu-Jose, *The Past, Love, Money*; Yu-Jose and Ikehata, *Philippines–Japan Relations*; Ikehata and Jose, *The Philippines under Japan*; Foronda, *Cultural Life in the Philippines*; and Kintanar et al., *Kuwentong Bayan*.

12. Lisa Yoneyama studies media representations of American and Japanese women during the occupation and also draws on critical feminist perspectives to outline the postwar development of what she calls "cold war feminism" (Yoneyama, "Liberation under Siege"). See also Garner, "Global Feminism and Postwar Reconstruction," and Koikari, "Exporting Democracy" and *Pedagogy of Democracy*.

13. The most comprehensive historical study of life during the Japanese occupation is Agoncillo, *The Fateful Years*.

14. Foronda, *Cultural Life in the Philippines*, 10–11.

15. Agoncillo, *The Fateful Years*, 2:477–554.

16. Foronda, *Cultural Life in the Philippines*, 11.

17. Dalmacio, "Filipinos and Nippongo," 37–41.

18. Jose, "The *Tribune* during the Japanese Occupation," 49–50. Jose details the *Tribune's* transformation from a prewar "proudly independent, reputable and a leading publication" to a newspaper so tainted by its association with the Japanese administration that after the war the publishers chose to change its name. See ibid., 45.

19. Agoncillo, *The Fateful Years*, 2:563.

20. Jose, "The *Tribune* during the Japanese Occupation," 54.

21. All material in this paragraph draws upon Agoncillo, *The Fateful Years*, 2: 602, 564, 571–72, 576, 564, 604. Quotes are from 602, 576, and 564. See also Abelardo, "Filipino Writing during the Occupation."

22. Benitez, "New Education for Girls," 54.

23. Alzona, "What of the Filipino Woman?" 33.

24. Benitez, "New Education for Girls," 57.

25. "President Urges Women to Do Their Bit for National Sacrifice," 1.

26. For similar calls, see Benitez, "The Women's Bureau"; Gonzales de Estrada, "Keeping Watch at Home"; "The Role of Women in Building a Strong and Prosperous Country," 3; P. Kalaw, "Women Can Help in the Reconstruction," 13; Torre-Guzman, "Determination among Our Women," 1, 9; Alvez, "Dear Miss Filipina."

27. Perico, "Dawn of a New Era," 1.

28. Marajas, "Remember California Watsonville Incident," 1.

29. Pungol, "Largely about Our Women," 6.

30. Benitez, "New Education for Girls," 54.

31. Pungol, "Largely about Our Women," 6.

32. For examples, see Quintero de Joseph, "American and Filipino Women," and de Veyra, "The Filipino Woman." I discuss these trends in chapter 1.

33. Katigbak, "May We Have Our Say?" 27.

34. Alzona, "What of the Filipino Woman?" 34.

35. Tolentino, "Filipinism Inspired by Nippon," 38.

36. Alzona, "What of the Filipino Woman?" 35; Pungol, "Largely about Our Women," 32.

37. Alzona, "What of the Filipino Woman?" 35.

38. Rosal, "Filipino Women," 8, 10.

39. Trinidad, "A Letter to My Daughter," 11. See also the corresponding article by Palarca, "Memo: To Mother." For some of this practical advice, see "The Housewife and the Emergency."

40. Rosal, "Filipino Women," 8.

41. Benitez, "New Education for Girls," 55.

42. Pungol, "Largely about Our Women," 7.

43. Gonzales de Estrada, "Keeping Watch at Home," 2.

44. For example, see Ileto, "Philippine Wars and the Politics of Memory."

45. Raymund, "A GI Appraisal of the Filipinos," 17. For other appeals, see Lopez, "Letter to GI Joe," Palarca, "Memo to the American People," 47; and Castrence, "Yet, I Love America."

46. "So You're Going to the States!" 28–31.

47. Lopez, "The Eagle's Eyrie," 64.

48. See Satoshi Nakano's work on Filipino veterans' rights, especially "Nation, Nationalism, and Citizenship."

49. The *Philippines Free Press* was especially active in its assessment of guerrilla outfits, which was not always favorable. See Salas, "Marking's Family—'Fightingest of All,'" 48; Ty, "Fake Heroes," and "Guerrilleras," 4; Lim, "Are All Guerrillas Heroes?" 14–15; Lim, "Guerrillas 'Didn't Steal No Chickens for Me'"; "For Mindanao's Women Guerrillas, No Recognition nor Pay," 28–29; J. B. R., "Guerrillas—Heroes or Bandits?" 6.

50. All quotes in this paragraph are from Agustin, "Letter to a War Widow," 8–10, emphases in original.

51. Although he does not name Panlilio in his memoir (she would still have been in hiding with the guerrillas when it was published), Carlos Romulo provides a different account of the same broadcasts. See Romulo, *I Saw the Fall of the Philippines*, 254.

52. Despite the critique of male readers here, Panlilio elsewhere has high praise for Romulo and his dedication. The two were friends and colleagues; one of Yay's encoded letters was to Romulo giving him information about his wife and family. See the chapters "Letters from Yay" and "In January" in Romulo, *I See the Philippines Rise*, 165–207.

53. I discuss these developments more specifically in the next chapter. See Borstelmann, *The Cold War and the Color Line*; Dudziak, *Cold War Civil Rights*; Kim, *Ends of Empire*; Klein, *Cold War Orientalism*; Von Eschen, *Race against Empire* and *Satchmo Blows Up the World*.

54. See, for example, my discussion of *Noli Me Tangere* and the character Maria Clara in chapter 2.

55. *The Crucible* received only brief mention in the United States but was reviewed much more substantially in the Philippines. See "Review of *The Crucible*," 23; Rivera, Jr., "One Woman's War"; and Jose, "Guerrilla Notes."

56. For a discussion of miscegenation in mixed-race Asian American literature, see Koshy, *Sexual Naturalization*.

57. Panlilio would later describe her conflicted relationship with her mother in the series of essays "My Filipino Mother." See Marking, *Where a Country Begins*, 2: 9–41.

58. In constructing a dynamic of fulfilled prophecy, Marking subscribes to a construction similar to (but more sexualized than) the version studied by Caroline Hau and Reynaldo Ileto in Philippine nationalist narratives, in which a woman becomes the source of inspiration for her lover or husband. See the discussion of Bulosan's character Mameng in chapter 2 of Hau's *Necessary Fictions*, and chapter 3 of Ileto, *Pasyon and Revolution*.

59. The groundbreaking study of the use of race in the Pacific War is Dower, *War without Mercy*.

FIVE *"Pointing to the Heart"*

1. Santos, "Scent of Apples," *You Lovely People*, 138.

2. The rhetoric of the heart links Santos to another well-known text written by a Filipino, Carlos Bulosan's *America Is in the Heart* (1946), a foundational work for narratives of nationalist Asian American masculinity.

3. On the significance of the Bandung conference, see Espiritu, "To Carry Water on Both Shoulders"; and Von Eschen, *Race against Empire*, 167–89.

4. See Klein, *Cold War Orientalism*, 1–17; and Wu, "America's Chinese."

5. Said, *Orientalism*.

6. Klein, *Cold War Orientalism*, 16.

7. Borstelmann, *The Cold War and the Color Line*; Dudziak, *Cold War Civil Rights*; Kim, "I'm Not Here, If This Doesn't Happen," "From *Mee-gook* to Gook," and *Ends of Empire*; Lim, "Contested Beauty," in *A Feeling of Belonging*, 121–53; McAlister, *Epic Encounters*; Von Eschen, *Race against Empire* and *Satchmo Blows Up the World*; Klein, *Cold War Orientalism*; Kurashige, *The Shifting Grounds of Race*; and Wu, "America's Chinese." See also Omi and Winant, *Racial Formation in the United States*, 95–112; and Nguyen, *Race and Resistance*, 61–85.

8. Neferti Xina M. Tadiar's observations regarding "fantasy production" are especially helpful; she argues that "while the West owns the codes of fantasy, the non-West is no less an active and willing participant in the hegemonic modes of imaginary production that are predicated on these codes." Tadiar also pays attention to the problematic results of elite fantasy productions. See *Fantasy Production*, 12.

9. As I have argued previously, in part because of the dearth of known primary materials produced by or about Asian women, in narratives of both Filipina and Filipino and Asian America, women often figure as question marks, a fuzzy yet nevertheless necessary presence in the narration of migrant male experience in the United States. Indeed, in accounts of early to mid-twentieth-century Asian American relations, what's most notable about the Filipina is her scarcity: one oft-quoted statistic emphasizes that in the early twentieth century only a small percentage of Filipinas migrated to the United States among some tens of thousands of Filipino bachelors

(Takaki, *Strangers from a Different Shore*, 58). The critical treatment of Santos's "Scent of Apples" (often read in the context of developments in Asian American and Filipino American masculinity) offers salient examples that illustrate some of these recurring tendencies. Most examinations of "Scent of Apples" center on the exile and alienation of male Filipinos in the United States and the development of sympathetic, homosocial relationships between the story's elite, educated narrators, and older Filipino farmers and laborers. See Casper, "Greater Shouting and Greater Silences"; Bayot, "Bienvenido N. Santos"; Bresnehan, *Conversations with Filipino Writers*; Bascara, "Up from Benevolent Assimilation"; and Rico "You Lovely People." For queer readings, see Chuh, *Imagine Otherwise*, chapter 1, and de Jesús, "Rereading History, Rewriting Desire." Few critics link exile in Santos to representations of women; among those who do are Rico and Espiritu, *Five Faces of Exile*, 139–78. Catherine Ceniza Choy makes a similar observation in "A Filipino Woman in America," 127–31, and *Empire of Care*, 1–14. Recent work in the United States and the Philippines has recovered important primary materials. See Buell, *Twenty-Five Chickens*; McReynolds, *Almost Americans*; Monrayo, *Tomorrow's Memories*; and the Images of America series, including Mabalon and Reyes, *Filipinos in Stockton*. See also Kintanar, *Women Reading*, and Manlapaz, "Literature in English by Filipino Women," and "Filipino Women Writers in English." Based at the Ateneo de Manila University in the Philippines, the Ateneo Library of Women's Writings (ALIWW) is a special collection that houses works by and about Filipinas. For work on women's periodical production, see Encanto, *Constructing the Filipina*.

10. For examples, see especially Campomanes, "Filipinos in the United States," and Espiritu, *Five Faces of Exile*, 139–78.

11. As Reynaldo Ileto notes, such revisions of imperial history and the elision of violence have dangerously continued into the twenty-first century (Ileto, "Philippine Wars and the Politics of Memory," 216). For a resounding critique, see D. Rodríguez, "'A Million Deaths'" and *Suspended Apocalypse*, and Bascara, "The Case of the Disappearing Filipino American Houseboy."

12. Espiritu, *Five Faces of Exile*, 3; Choy, "A Filipino Woman in America," 131, note 5. See also Roma-Sianturi, "Pedagogic Invasion."

13. Klein, *Cold War Orientalism*, 198–99; Choy, *Empire of Care*, 61–93.

14. Klein, *Cold War Orientalism*, 199–201.

15. Cynthia Tolentino helpfully links Carlos Bulosan's *America Is in the Heart* to sociological studies of racial difference and the rise of a professional class of Filipinos educated in the United States (Tolentino, "Training Center of the Skillful Servants," 383–84).

16. Choy, *Empire of Care*, 64.

17. In addition to Choy, *Empire of Care*, see Aguilar, *Toward a Nationalist Feminism*; Aguilar and Lacsamana, *Women and Globalization*; de Jesús, *Pinay Power*; Fajardo, "Transportation"; Isaac, "The Byuti"; Manalansan, "Queer Intersections"; Parreñas,

Servants of Globalization and *The Force of Domesticity*; and Tadiar, *Fantasy Production* and *Things Fall Away*.

18. This reading builds on Choy, "A Filipino Woman in America."

19. Bresnehan, "Bienvenido N. Santos," in *Conversations with Filipino Writers*, 96.

20. Kingston, "Precarious Lives," 28.

21. Grow, "The Hallowed and Hollowed Ground," and Bresnehan, "Bienvenido N. Santos," 99.

22. N. V. M. Gonzales, introduction to *You Lovely People*, vii–x; ix.

23. Espiritu, *Five Faces of Exile*, 154.

24. Ibid., 153.

25. Parreñas, *Servants of Globalization*, *The Force of Domesticity*, and *Illicit Flirtations*; Fajardo, "Transportation"; Isaac, "The Byuti"; and Manalansan, "Queer Intersections."

26. Stewart, *On Longing*, 137–39.

27. Examples include "Those Co-eds' Resolutions"; Campos, "A Filipino Co-ed in America Says College Is Fun"; Castrence, "The East Views the American Coed"; Pacis, "Should the Women Continue Being Libertarian Tramps?"; and Perez, "The College Girl."

28. All quotations in this paragraph are from Orallo, "The Post War Coed," 22, 23.

29. Enloe, *Bananas, Beaches, and Bases*, 42.

30. Anzaldúa, *Borderlands / La Frontera*; Kang, *Compositional Subjects*; Lowe, *Immigrant Acts*; Mohanty, *Feminism without Borders*.

31. Lim, *A Feeling of Belonging*, 123–26. Recent work examines how white American women questioned constructs of the suburban American housewife, either by employing this model to advance feminist politics or by actively challenging restrictions on femininity. See Meyerowitz, "Sex, Gender," and DeHart, "Containment at Home."

32. Unfortunately I do not have the space to examine at length the other alternative suggested by these stories: relations between Filipino men and white women.

33. This comparison between Filipina modesty and white women's sexuality has contemporary iterations, as studied by Espiritu in *Homebound*, 157–78.

34. This reading of hybridity is inspired by Lisa Lowe's foundational definition of the term in *Immigrant Acts*, 60–83.

35. See the discussion of the Filipina body in chapter 1.

36. This formal organization, however, should not eclipse important levels of women's activism in the Philippines, especially during the revolution against Spain and the United States.

37. For examples, see Alzona, *Rizal's Legacy to the Filipino Woman*; Bayani-Arcilla, "Development and Political Rights"; Benavides, *The Filipino Woman's Social, Economic, and Political Status*; Domingo, *Women's Rights*; Kalaw, *How the Filipina Got the Vote* and *Filipino Women*; Mendez, *The Progress of the Filipino Woman*; Pecson, *The Filipino Woman in Nation Building*; Peña, "The Rise of the Filipino Woman"; and Reyes, *Filipino Women*.

38. Mendoza-Guazon, *Development and Progress*, 61.

39. For work that historicizes and theorizes similar complexities and their continued ramifications, see Aguilar, *Toward a Nationalist Feminism*; Aguilar and Lacsamana, *Women and Globalization*; and de Jesús, *Pinay Power*.

40. Choy, "A Filipino Woman," 127–31.

41. Subido, *The Feminist Movement in the Philippines*, 1.

42. Ibid., 2.

43. I deal with these representations more specifically in chapters 2 and 4.

44. Choy, "A Filipino Woman."

45. For critiques of such tendencies in second-wave and Western feminism, see bell hooks, *Feminist Theory*; Lorde, *Sister Outsider*; and Mohanty, *Feminism without Borders*. For discussions of the rhetoric of "saving" Middle Eastern women, see Butler, *Precarious Life*, and Whitlock, *Soft Weapons*.

EPILOGUE *Transpacific Femininities*

1. Balance, "Dahil Sa Iyo," 120.

2. Although reviewers in the Philippines, the United States, and elsewhere note the potentially troubling material that grounds the album, the reception of Byrne's collection has been overwhelmingly positive. See Fusilli, "Dance Mix: Funk Meets Mrs. Marcos"; Gil, "For Love of Imelda"; Ortuoste, "Here Lies Myth"; Pareles, "Lyrics Lush and Gawky"; Wolk, "The Imelda Marcos Story"; and Zafra, "Dancing on the Grave of History."

3. See Neferti Tadiar's discussion of the dynamics of global circulation, Filipina bodies, and literary responses in *Things Fall Away*, 25–140. For discussions of Filipino American responses to diaspora and globalization, see Gonzalves, *The Day the Dancers Stayed*, and See, *The Decolonized Eye*. As Roland Tolentino observes, during his dictatorship, Marcos "mobilized the majority of national bodies—the youthful citizenry—and placed them in the service of multinational capital in the homeland and the debt servicing industry in foreign lands. . . . He also created the government infrastructures that further embedded the OCW [Overseas Contract Worker] in Philippine culture" (Tolentino, "Macho Dancing," 78). For work that complicates the gendered and sexed dynamics of how domestic caregivers have been constructed in academic and cultural discourse, see Choy, *Empire of Care*; Fajardo, "Transportation" and *Filipino Crosscurrents*; Gonzales, "Military Bases"; Isaac, "The Byuti"; Manalansan, "Queer Intersections"; Parreñas, *Servants of Globalization*, *The Force of Domesticity*, and *Illicit Flirtations*; and Rodriguez, *Migrants for Export*.

4. Choy, *Empire of Care*; Parreñas, *Servants of Globalization*, *The Force of Domesticity*, and *Illicit Flirtations*; and Manalansan, "Queer Intersections."

5. Tolentino, "Bodies, Letters, Catalogs." Other scholars have carefully analyzed the complex networks of desire and power at work in the mail-order bride's representation and circulation, and they have rightly insisted that critical analyses must not participate in constructions of these women as merely objects without agency. See ibid. and Parreñas, *The Force of Domesticity* and *Illicit Flirtations*.

6. Tadiar, "Popular Laments," 21.

7. Michel, "Extravagance (and Shoe Love) in the Rise of a Despot."

8. Pareles, "Lyrics Lush and Gawky," and Zafra, "Dancing on the Grave."

9. Ortuoste, "Here Lies Myth," and Zafra, "Dancing on the Grave."

10. Balance, "Dahil Sa Iyo"; Ileto, *Pasyon and Revolution*; and Isaac, "The Byuti."

11. In a memorable scene from Jessica Hagedorn's *Dogeaters*, Steve, a foreign journalist, interviews Madame, the character modeled after Marcos, and finds himself repeatedly flummoxed in his attempts to ask Madame about the state of corruption in her country (217–24). Reading Marcos as "a performance artist that viciously crafted her persona through the affective registers of singing and crying," Balance, for example, references Byrne and Cook's album as part of a larger catalog of recent reconstructions of Imelda over the past decade. However disturbing, there is nevertheless something, argues Balance, worth listening to in Marcos's impressive and influential catalog: from her pageantry, to her repeated employ of *kundiman* (Filipino love songs that also have affective, nationalist registers), from her enigmatic interviews to her frequent public emotional breakdowns. Balance argues that these stagings often centered on an important incongruity, especially as the Marcos's oppressive rule spun out of control and grew increasingly more violent; these "musical stunts, in fact, became their own unique form of torture" (Balance, "Dahil Sa Iyo," 121, 129).

12. Balance, "Dahil Sa Iyo," 134.

13. Reactions to Marcos in the Philippines are admittedly also complicated, for there are Filipinas and Filipinos at home and abroad who participate in her idealization. Byrne found this aspect of the Marcos story truly incredible. Indeed, Imelda's cult status is even more amazing because of her continued valorization in the Philippines, and the persistence of her loyal fans, who maintain that she has been wrongly vilified and that she contributed much to the nation as a patroness of the arts; they point to what they see as a long list of good deeds, from the construction of cultural centers to her role in furthering the Philippine image on a broader international, and global scale (Balance, "Dahil Sa Iyo").

14. Rafael, *White Love and Other Events*, 154.

15. Ibid., 152.

16. Roces, *Women, Power, and Kinship Politics*, 123–47, and Hilsdon, *Madonnas and Martyrs*, 157.

17. Rafael, *White Love and Other Events*, 155.

18. See Roces, *Women, Power, and Kinship Politics*, and the first section of Tadiar, *Things Fall Away*.

19. Quoted in Roces, *Women, Power, and Kinship Politics*, 147.

20. See ibid., 123, and Stoltzfus, "A Woman's Place."

21. As Roces notes, while Western feminist movements certainly influenced the character of feminism in the Philippines, there is also a crucial need to be more careful in assumptions of the nature and extent of this influence, to be wary of "uncritically grafting" (133) the theories of Western feminism to the Philippine context, and a need to define the importance of local practices even amid the global networks of transnational feminism. See especially the discussion of beauty in Roces, *Women, Power, and Kinship Politics*, 127–33.

22. http://filipinaimages.com/about (accessed May 31, 2011).

23. In a related example, May Friedman argues that American academics should be careful in their analysis of the "mamasphere," for "to valorize the history of the contemporary mamasphere for its multiplicity is itself simplistic, evidence that 'a new hegemony of privileged texts can emerge at any time.'" Friedman notes that most academic discourse on the blogosphere still marginalizes queer bloggers and bloggers of color (Friedman, "On Mommyblogging," 203).

24. *Hot Momma: The Adventure That Is Motherhood*, http://www.matheubaniaga.com/2008/03/let-me-share-bit-more-about-myself.html (accessed April 5, 2010).

25. Ibid.

26. http://modernmariaclara.wordpress.com/about/ (accessed February 18, 2011).

27. For feminist work on mommyblogs and definitions of motherhood, see Lopez, "The Radical Act of 'Mommy Blogging,'" and Friedman, "On Mommyblogging."

28. http://www.myecdysis.com/2008/03/bi-cultural-pinay/ (accessed March 17, 2011).

29. Roces, *Women, Power, and Kinship Politics*, 124–33. Roces rightly urges Western and Philippine academics to be cautious in their analyses of feminism in the Philippines, especially in discussions of how Filipina women have employed culturally informed notions of beauty (the quality and performance of being *maganda*) or familial kinship as feminist strategies.

30. http://www.myecdysis.com/2008/03/bi-cultural-pinay/ (accessed March 17, 2011).

31. Ibid.

32. Tadiar, "Filipinas 'Living in a Time of War,'" 374.

33. Feminist scholars have underscored similar concerns regarding readings of the blogosphere as historical archive and the dangers of celebratory narratives attached to blogs. In addition to Friedman's "On Mommyblogging," see Leow, "Reflections on Feminism," and Pierce, "Singing at the Digital Well."

Philippine and Filipina and Filipino Periodicals

Evening News Saturday Magazine (Manila)
Filipina
The Filipino People
Filipino Students' Magazine (Berkeley)
Graphic (Manila)
Herald Mid-Week Magazine (Manila)
Philippine-American
Philippine-American Advocate
The Philippine Forum
Philippines Monthly
Philippine Review
Philippines Free Press
Sunday Times Magazine (Manila)
Sunday Tribune Magazine (Manila)
This Week (Manila)
The Tribune (Manila)
Wedding Essentials
Woman's World (Manila)

Books, Articles, and Essays

Abad, Gemino H., and Edna Z. Manlapaz, eds. Man of Earth: An Anthology of Filipino Poetry and Verse from English, 1905 to the Mid-50s. Quezon City: Ateneo de Manila University Press, 1989.
Abelardo, Victoria. "Filipino Writing during the Occupation." Philippine-American 3, no. 13, 9–14.

Agoncillo, Teodoro A. *The Fateful Years: Japan's Adventure in the Philippines, 1941–1945.* 2 vols. Quezon City: University of the Philippines Press, 2001.

Aguilar, Delia D. *Toward a Nationalist Feminism: Essays.* Quezon City: Giraffe Books, 1998.

Aguilar, Delia D., and Anne E. Lacsamana, eds. *Women and Globalization.* Amherst: Humanity Books, 2004.

Agustin, Yay (Panlilio). "Letter to a War Widow." *Philippine-American* 2, no. 7 (March 1946), 7–11.

Ahmad, Dohra. "More than Romance: Genre and Geography in *Dark Princess.*" ELH 69, no. 3 (2002), 775–803.

Alegre, Edilberto N., and Doreen Fernandez, eds. *Writers and Their Milieu: An Oral History of Second Generation Writers in English.* Manila: De La Salle University Press, 1987.

Alvez, Aquilina B. "Dear Miss Filipina (an Open Letter)." *Sunday Tribune Magazine,* December 12, 1943.

Alzona, Encarnación. *Rizal's Legacy to the Filipino Woman.* Pasay City, Philippines: E. Alzona, 1956.

———. "What of the Filipino Woman?" *Philippine Review,* March 1943, 33–36.

Anderson, Benedict R. O'G. "Forms of Consciousness in *Noli Me Tangere.*" *Philippine Studies* 54, no. 4 (2003), 505–29.

———. *Imagined Communities: Reflections on the Origin and Spread of Nationalism.* London: Verso, 1991.

———. *The Spectre of Comparisons: Nationalism, Southeast Asia, and the World.* London: Verso, 1998.

An-Lim, Jaime. "The Filipino Rebel: A Fugitive Vision." *Nationalist Literature: A Centennial Forum,* ed. Elmer A. Ordoñez, 91–106. Quezon City: University of the Philippines Press and PANULAT/Philippine Writers Academy, 1996.

Anzaldúa, Gloria. *Borderlands / La Frontera: The New Mestiza.* 2nd edition. San Francisco: Aunt Lute Books, 1999.

Arcellana, Francisco. "Readers without Writers." *Herald Mid-Week Magazine,* November 1, 1939.

Arguilla, Lydia Villanueva and Maria Luna Lopez. "Our Men Writers Are Not So Hot." *Herald Mid-Week Magazine,* February 5, 1941.

Arrizón, Alicia. *Queering Mestizaje: Transculturation and Performance.* Ann Arbor: University of Michigan Press, 2006.

Balance, Christine Bacareza. "Dahil Sa Iyo: The Performative Power of Imelda's Song." *Women and Performance: A Journal of Feminist Theory* 20, no. 2 (2010), 119–40.

Balce, Nerissa. "The Filipina's Breast: Savagery, Docility, and the Erotics of the American Empire." *Social Text* 87, 24, no. 2 (2006), 89–110.

Baldoz, Richard. *The Third Asiatic Invasion: Empire and Migration in Filipino America, 1898–1946.* New York: New York University Press, 2011.

Baltasar, Silverio, et al., eds. *Philippine Literature: Past and Present*. Quezon City: Katha Publishing, 1981.

Barlow, Tani. *The Question of Women in Chinese Feminism*. Durham: Duke University Press, 2004.

Barranco, Vicente F. "The Filipino Girl—Model 1939." *Herald Mid-Week Magazine*, January 4, 1939, 8, 18.

Bascara, Victor. "The Case of the Disappearing Filipino American Houseboy: Speculations on Double Indemnity and United States Imperialism." *Kritika Kultura* 8 (2007), 35–56.

——. *Model Minority Imperialism*. Minneapolis: University of Minnesota Press, 2006.

——. "Up from Benevolent Assimilation: At Home with the Manongs of Bienvenido Santos." *MELUS: The Journal of the Society for the Study of the Multi-Ethnic Literature of the United States* 29, no. 1 (2004), 61–78.

Bautista, Maria Lourdes S., and Kingsley Bolton, eds. *Philippine English: Linguistic and Literary Perspectives*. Hong Kong: University of Hong Kong Press, 2008.

Bayani-Arcilla, Socorro. "The Development of Political Rights of Filipino Women." M.A. thesis, University of Manila, 1953.

Bayot, David Jonathan Y. "Bienvenido N. Santos: A Review of Studies and Criticism." *Reading Bienvenido N. Santos*, ed. Isagani R. Cruz and David Jonathon Y. Bayot, 1–11. Manila: De La Salle University Press, 1994.

Benavides, E. R. *The Filipino Woman's Social, Economic, and Political Status*. Manila: Cultural Foundation of the Philippines, 1958.

Benitez, Francisca Tirona. "New Education for Girls." *Philippine Review*, March 1943, 54–57.

——. "The Women's Bureau: An Agency to Promote National Welfare." *Filipina* 1, no. 2 (August 1944), 16–20.

Borstelmann, Thomas. *The Cold War and the Color Line: American Race Relations in the Global Arena*. Cambridge: Harvard University Press, 2001.

Bresnahan, Mary I. "The Politics of Language: English in the Philippines." *Journal of Communication* 29, no. 2 (Spring 1979), 64–71.

Bresnahan, Roger. *Conversations with Filipino Writers*. Quezon City: New Day, 1990.

"Bright Girls from Far Away." *Los Angeles Times*, January 31, 1909.

Brody, David. *Visualizing American Empire: Orientalism and Imperialism in the Philippines*. Chicago: University of Chicago Press, 2010.

Brown, Judith. *Glamour in Six Dimensions: Modernism and the Radiance of Form*. Ithaca: Cornell University Press, 2009.

Buaken, Manuel. *I Have Lived with the American People*. Caldwell, Idaho: Caxton Printers, 1948.

Buell, Evangeline Canonizado. *Twenty-Five Chickens and a Pig for a Bride*. San Francisco: T'boli Publishing, 2006.

Bulosan, Carlos. *America Is in the Heart*. 1946. Reprint, Seattle: University of Washington Press, 1973.

Butler, Judith. *Precarious Life: The Powers of Mourning and Violence.* London: Verso, 2003.

Byrne, David, and Fatboy Slim. *Here Lies Love.* Album. New York: Todomundo/Nonesuch Records, 2010.

Campomanes, Oscar. "Filipinos in the United States and Their Literature of Exile." *Reading the Literatures of Asian America,* ed. Shirley Lim and Amy Ling, 49–78. Philadelphia: Temple University Press, 1992.

———. "New Formations of Asian American Studies and the Question of U.S. Imperialism." *positions: east asia cultures critique* 5, no. 2 (Fall 1997), 523–50.

Campos, Pilar. "A Filipino Co-ed in America Says College Is Fun." *Philippine-American Advocate,* November 1938.

Carbó, Nick, and Eileen Tabios, eds. *Babaylan: An Anthology of Filipina and Filipina American Writers.* San Francisco: Aunt Lute Books, 2000.

Carby, Hazel. *Reconstructing Womanhood: The Emergence of the Afro-American Woman Novelist.* New York: Oxford University Press, 1987.

Casas, Lourdes. "Noli me Tangere: María Clara o la imposibilidad de constituir una nación Filipina." *INTI* 54 (2001), 121–38.

Casper, Leonard. "Greater Shouting and Greater Silences: The Novels of Bienvenido Santos." *Solidarity* 3, no. 10 (1968), 76–84.

Castrence, Pura Santillan. "The East Views the American Coed: Her Freedom Is Admirable But Isn't She Somewhat too Independent?" *Graphic,* October 22, 1936, 8, 9, 48.

———. "The Female Characters in Rizal's Novels—Maria Clara." *Philippine Magazine* 33, no. 11 (November 1936), 542, 557.

———. "The Female Characters in Rizal's Novels—Sisa." *Philippine Magazine* 33, no. 12 (December 1936), 598, 599, 632.

———. "The Period of Apprenticeship." Manuud, ed. *Brown Heritage,* 564–74.

———. "Women Characters in Rizal's Novels." *Philippine Magazine* 34, no. 11 (November 1937), 496.

———. "The Women Characters in Rizal's Novels—Doctora Doña Victorina de Los Reyes de De Espadaña." *Philippine Magazine* 34, no. 10 (October 1937), 452–53.

———. "The Women Characters in Rizal's Novels—Doña Consolacion." *Philippine Magazine* 34, no. 7 (July 1937), 310, 319–22.

———. "Women Characters of Rizal, The Tertiary Sisters, III." *Philippine Magazine* 34, no. 3 (March 1937), 124, 135–38.

———. "Yet, I Love America." *Philippine-American* 2, no. 6 (February 1946), 60–63.

Chang, Juliana. "Masquerade, Hysteria, and Neocolonial Femininity in Jessica Hagedorn's *Dogeaters.*" *Contemporary Literature* 44, no. 4 (Winter 2003), 637–63.

Chapman, Mary. "'A Revolution in Ink': Sui Sin Far and Chinese Reform Discourse." *American Quarterly* 60, no. 4 (December 2008), 975–100.

Chow, Rey. *Writing Diaspora: Tactics of Intervention in Contemporary Cultural Studies.* Bloomington: Indiana University Press, 1993.

Choy, Catherine Ceniza. *Empire of Care: Nursing and Migration in Filipino American History.* Durham: Duke University Press, 2003.

——. "A Filipino Woman in America: The Life and Work of Encarnacion Alzona." *Genre: Forms of Discourse and Culture* 39, no. 3 (Fall 2006), 127–40.

Chua, Jonathan, ed. *The Critical Villa*. Quezon City: Ateneo de Manila University Press, 2002.

Chuh, Kandice. *Imagine Otherwise: On Asian Americanist Critique*. Durham: Duke University Press, 2003.

"College Girls for Most of Them, But a Few Husbands Say 'No College Graduate for Me Again.'" *Graphic*, March 12, 1936, 4, 5, 50.

Comfort, Will Levington. "Native Tagal Women." *Washington Post*, February 4, 1900.

Conor, Liz. *The Spectacular Modern Woman: Feminine Visibility in the 1920s*. Bloomington: Indiana University Press, 2004.

Constantino, Renato. *The Philippines: A Past Revisited*. Manila: R. Constantino, 1972.

Croghan, Richard V. *The Development of Philippine Literature in English (Since 1900)*. Quezon City: Alemar-Phoenix Publishing House, 1975.

Cruz, Isagani R., ed. *The Best Philippine Short Stories of the Twentieth Century: An Anthology of Fiction in English*. Manila: Tahanan Books, 2000.

Da Costa, R. Zulueta. "Filipino Literature in English." *Herald Mid-Week Magazine*, April 24, 1940.

Dalmacio, Martin. "Filipinos and Nippongo." *Philippine Review*, March 1952, 37–41.

DeHart, Jane Sherron. "Containment at Home: Gender Sexuality and National Identity in Cold War America." *Rethinking Cold War Culture*, ed. Peter J. Kuznick and James Gilbert, 124–55. Washington: Smithsonian Institution Press, 2001.

de Jesús, Melinda L., ed. *Pinay Power: Peminist Critical Theory*. New York: Routledge, 2005.

——. "Rereading History, Rewriting Desire: Reclaiming Queerness in Carlos Bulosan's *America Is in the Heart* and Bienvenido Santos's 'Scent of Apples.'" *Journal of Asian American Studies* 5, no. 2 (June 2002), 91–111.

Delmendo, Sharon. *The Star-Entangled Banner: One Hundred Years of America in the Philippines*. New Brunswick: Rutgers University Press, 2004.

DeLoughrey, Elizabeth. *Routes and Roots: Navigating Caribbean and Pacific Island Literatures*. Honolulu: University of Hawai'i Press, 2007.

de Veyra, M. P. "The Filipino Woman." *Filipino Students' Magazine*, October 1906, 14–15.

Diaz, Vicente M. "To 'P' or Not to 'P'?: Marking the Territory between Pacific Islander and Asian American Studies." *Journal of Asian American Studies* 7, no. 3 (October 2004), 183–208.

Diaz, Vicente M., and J. Kēhaulani Kauanui. "Native Pacific Cultural Studies on the Edge." *Contemporary Pacific* 13, no. 2 (2001), 315–42.

"Discurso del Delegado Grafilo." *Constitutional Convention Record: Manila, Philippines* 4, no. 74 (October 26, 1934), 368–74.

"Discurso del Delegado José de Guzman." *Constitutional Convention Record: Manila, Philippines* 4, no. 72 (October 24, 1934), 338–42.

"Discurso del Delegado Sevilla de Bulacán." *Constitutional Convention Record: Manila, Philippines* 4, no. 77 (October 30, 1934), 489–95.

"Discurso del Sr. Abordo Contra el Sufragio Feminino." *Constitutional Convention Record: Manila, Philippines* 4, no. 74 (October 26, 1934), 381–87.

"Discurso del Sr. Bocar." *Constitutional Convention Record: Manila, Philippines* 4, no. 73 (October 25, 1934), 346–52.

"Discurso del Sr. Carin Contra el Sufragio Feminino." *Constitutional Convention Record: Manila, Philippines* 4, no.77 (October 30, 1934), 481–89.

"Discurso del Sr. Cuaderno a Favor del Sufragio Feminino." *Constitutional Convention Record: Manila, Philippines* 4, no. 79 (November 2, 1934), 565–67.

"Discurso del Sr. Joven." *Constitutional Convention Record: Manila, Philippines* 4, no. 79 (November 2, 1934), 554–57.

"Discurso del Sr. Palma." *Constitutional Convention Record: Manila, Philippines* 4, no. 76 (October 29, 1934), 432–39.

"Discurso del Señor Vinzons a Favor del Sufragio Feminino." *Constitutional Convention Record: Manila, Philippines* 4, no. 73 (October 25, 1934), 357–59.

Dizon, Alma Jill. "Felipinas Caliban: Colonialism as Marriage of Spaniard and Filipina." *Philippine Studies* 46, no. 1 (1998), 24–45.

——. "Rizal's Novels: A Divergence from Melodrama." *Philippine Studies* 44, no. 3 (1996), 412–26.

Domingo, Songalia A. *Women's Rights*. San Juan, Philippines: Atlantic Publications, 1958.

Dong, Madeline Y. "Who Is Afraid of the Chinese Modern Girl?" Weinbaum et al., eds., *The Modern Girl around the World*, 194–219.

Dower, John. *War without Mercy: Race and Power in the Pacific War*. New York: Pantheon Books, 1986.

Dudziak, Mary. *Cold War Civil Rights: Race and the Image of American Democracy*. Princeton: Princeton University Press, 2000.

Edwards, Brent Hayes. *The Practice of Diaspora: Literature, Translation, and the Rise of Black Internationalism*. Cambridge: Harvard University Press, 2003.

Edwards, Brian T. and Dilip Parameshwar Gaonkar. *Globalizing American Studies*. Chicago: University of Chicago Press, 2010.

Elliott, Emory. "Diversity in American Studies and Abroad: What Does it Mean When American Studies Is Transnational?" *American Quarterly* 59, no. 1 (March 2007), 1–22.

Encanto, Georgina Reyes. *Constructing the Filipina: A History of Women's Magazines, 1891–2002*. Quezon City: University of the Philippines Press, 2004.

Eng, David. *The Feeling of Kinship: Queer Liberalism and the Racialization of Intimacy*. Durham: Duke University Press, 2010.

Enloe, Cynthia H. *Bananas, Beaches, and Bases: Making Feminist Sense of International Politics*. Berkeley: University of California Press, 2000.

España-Maram, Linda. *Creating Masculinity in Los Angeles's Little Manila, 1920s–1950s: Working-Class Filipinos and Popular Culture*. New York: Columbia University Press, 2006.

Espiritu, Augusto Fauni. *Five Faces of Exile: The Nation and Filipino American Intellectuals*. Stanford: Stanford University Press, 2005.

———. "'To Carry Water on Both Shoulders': Carlos P. Romulo, American Empire, and the Meanings of Bandung." *Radical History Review* 95 (Spring 2006), 173–90.

Espiritu, Yen Le. *Home Bound: Filipino American Lives across Cultures, Communities, and Countries*. Berkeley: University of California Press, 2003.

Fajardo, Kale Bantigue. *Filipino Crosscurrents: Oceanographies of Seafaring, Masculinities, and Globalization*. Minneapolis: University of Minnesota Press, 2011.

———. "Transportation: Translating Filipino and Filipino American Tomboy Masculinities through Global Migration and Seafaring." *GLQ: A Journal of Lesbian and Gay Studies* 14, nos. 2–3 (2008), 403–24.

Ferens, Dominika. *Edith and Winnifred Eaton: Chinatown Missions and Japanese Romances*. Urbana: University of Illinois Press, 2002.

Field, Norma. "War and Apology: Japan, Asia, the Fiftieth, and After." *positions: east asia cultures critique* 5, no. 1 (Spring 1997), 1–49.

Firth, Stewart. "Future Directions for Pacific Studies." *Contemporary Pacific* 15, no. 1 (Summer 2003), 129–48.

Fishkin, Shelley Fisher. "Crossroads of Cultures: The Transnational Turn in American Studies." *American Quarterly* 57, no. 1 (March 2005), 17–57.

"For Mindanao's Women Guerrillas, No Recognition nor Pay." *Philippines Free Press*, July 13, 1946.

Foronda, Marcelino A., Jr. *Cultural Life in the Philippines during the Japanese Occupation, 1942–1945*. 1975. Reprint, Manila: Philippine National Historical Society, 1995.

"Four Faces of Maria Clara, The." *Wedding Essentials* 2, no. 2 (July–December 2006), 164–65.

"Four Filipino Girl Students Are Eager to Return Home to Native Food and Dress." *Washington Post*, September 16, 1906.

Friedman, May. "On Mommyblogging: Notes to a Future Feminist Historian." *Journal of Women's History* 22, no. 4 (2010), 197–208.

Fruto, Ligaya Victorio Reyes. *Yesterday and Other Stories*. Quezon City: Vibal Print, 1969.

Fusilli, Jim. "Dance Mix: Funk Meets Mrs. Marcos." Review of *Here Lies Love* by David Byrne. *Wall Street Journal*, April 19, 2010.

Gairola, Rahul K. "Deterritorialisations of Desire: 'Transgressive' Sexuality as Filipino Anti-Imperialist Resistance in Jessica Hagedorn's *Dogeaters*." *Philament* 7 (December 2005), 22–41.

Galang, Zoilo M., ed. "Ocampo, Felicidad V." *Encyclopedia of the Philippines*. Vol. 9. Manila: Philippine Education Company, 1936. 445–46.

Garner, Karen. "Global Feminism and Postwar Reconstruction: The World YWCA

Visitation to Occupied Japan, 1947." *Journal of World History* 15, no. 2 (2004), 191–227.

Gil, Baby A. "For Love of Imelda." Review of *Here Lies Love* by David Byrne. *Philippine Star*, August 30, 2010.

Gilroy, Paul. *The Black Atlantic: Modernity and Double Consciousness.* Cambridge: Harvard University Press, 1993.

Go, Julian, and Anne L. Foster, eds. *The American Colonial State in the Philippines: Global Perspectives.* Durham: Duke University Press, 2003.

Gonzales, Gabriel Jose. "*America Is in the Heart* as Colonial Immigrant Novel Engaging the Bildungsroman." *Kritika Kultura* 8 (February 2007), 99–110.

Gonzales de Estrada, Josefa. "Keeping Watch at Home." *Filipina* 1, no. 3 (September 1944), 2–3.

Gonzalez, N. V. M., and Oscar Campomanes. "Filipino American Literature." *An Interethnic Companion to Asian American Literature*, ed. King-Kok Cheung, 62–124. Cambridge: Cambridge University Press, 1997.

Gonzales, Vernadette. "Military Bases, 'Royalty Trips,' and Imperial Modernities: Gendered and Racialized Labor in the Postcolonial Philippines." *Frontiers: A Journal of Women's Studies* 28, no. 3 (2007), 28–59.

Gonzalves, Theodore S. *The Day the Dancers Stayed: Performing in the Filipino/American Diaspora.* Philadelphia: Temple University Press, 2010.

Gopinath, Gayatri. *Impossible Desires: Queer Diasporas and South Asian Public Cultures.* Durham: Duke University Press, 2005.

Goyal, Yogita. *Romance, Diaspora, and Black Atlantic Literature.* Cambridge: Cambridge University Press, 2010.

Grow, Lynn M. "The Hallowed and Hollowed Ground: An Interview with Bienvenido N. Santos." *Wichita State University Bulletin* 53, no. 4 (November 1977), 3–21.

Guterl, Matthew Pratt. *American Mediterranean: Southern Slaveholders in the Age of Emancipation.* Cambridge: Harvard University Press, 2008.

Hagedorn, Jessica. *Dogeaters.* New York: Penguin, 1990.

Halttunen, Karen. "Groundwork: American Studies in Place." *American Quarterly* 58, no. 1 (March 2006), 1–15.

Hart, Irving. "Playing with Fire." *Woman's Home Journal*, April 1932.

——. "The Boomerang." *Woman's Home Journal*, May 1932.

Hau, Caroline. *Necessary Fictions: Philippine Literature and the Nation, 1946–1980.* Quezon City: Ateneo de Manila University Press, 2001.

Hau'ofa, Epeli. *We Are the Ocean: Selected Works.* Honolulu: University of Hawai'i Press, 2008.

Hayden, Joseph. *The Philippines: A Study in National Development.* New York: Macmillan, 1942.

Hebard, Andrew. "Romantic Sovereignty: Popular Romances and the American Imperial State in the Philippines." *American Quarterly* 57, no. 3 (September 2005), 805–29.

Hicks, George. *The Comfort Women: Japan's Brutal Regime of Enforced Prostitution in the Second World War*. New York: W. W. Norton, 1995.

Hidalgo, Cristina Pantoja. *Filipino Woman Writing: Home and Exile in the Autobiographical Narratives of Ten Writers*. Manila: Ateneo de Manila University Press, 1994.

——. *A Gentle Subversion: Essays on Philippine Fiction in English*. Quezon City: University of the Philippines Press, 1998.

——. *Over a Cup of Ginger Tea: Conversations on the Literary Narratives of Filipino Women*. Quezon City: University of the Philippines Press, 2006.

Hilsdon, Anne-Marie. *Madonnas and Martyrs: Militarism and Violence in the Philippines*. Quezon City: Ateneo de Manila University Press, 1995.

Hizon, Natividad O. "A Letter to a Young Lady in Floor 18." *Woman's Home Journal*, February, 1939.

Hoganson, Kristin L. "'As Badly Off as the Filipinos': U.S. Women's Suffragists and the Imperial Issue at the Turn of the Twentieth Century." *Journal of Women's History* 13, no. 2 (Summer 2001), 9–33.

——. *Fighting for American Manhood: How Gender Politics Provoked the Spanish–American and Philippine–American Wars*. New Haven: Yale University Press, 1998.

hooks, bell. *Feminist Theory from Margin to Center*. Boston: South End Press, 2000.

Hosillos, Lucila V. *Philippine–American Literary Relations, 1898–1941*. Quezon City: University of the Philippines Press, 1969.

"The Housewife and the Emergency." *Filipina* 1, no. 3 (September 1944), 8–9.

Huang, Yunte. *Transpacific Imaginations: History, Literature, Counterpoetics*. Cambridge: Harvard University Press, 2008.

Ikehata, Setsuho and Ricardo Trota Jose, eds. *The Philippines under Japan: Occupation Policy and Reaction*. Quezon City: Ateneo University Press, 1999.

Ileto, Reynaldo. *Filipinos and Their Revolution: Event, Discourse, and Historiography*. Manila: Ateneo de Manila University Press, 1998.

——. *Pasyon and Revolution: Popular Movements in the Philippines, 1840–1910*. 1979. Reprint, Manila: Ateneo de Manila University Press, 1997.

——. "Philippine Wars and the Politics of Memory." *positions: east asia cultures critique* 13, no. 1 (2005), 215–34.

Isaac, Allan Punzalan. *American Tropics: Articulating Filipino America*. Minneapolis: University of Minnesota Press, 2006.

——. "The Byuti and Danger of Performing Transgender and Transnational Belonging in *Paper Dolls* (Bubot Niyar, Israel 2006) by Tomer Heymann." Paper presented as part of the Kritika Kultura Lecture Series. Ateneo de Manila University, Manila, July 18, 2008.

Ito, Ruri. "'The Modern Girl' Question in the Periphery of Empire: Colonial Modernity and Mobility among Okinawan Women in the 1920s and 1930s." Weinbaum et al., eds., *The Modern Girl around the World*, 240–62.

Javellana, Steven. *Without Seeing the Dawn*. Boston: Little, Brown, 1947.

J. B. R. "Guerrillas—Heroes or Bandits?" *Philippines Free Press*, August 31, 1946.

Joaquin, Nick. "The Novels of Rizal: An Appreciation." Reprinted in *La Naval de Manila and Other Essays*, 59–75. Manila: Bookmark, 1964.

Jose, F. Sionil. "Guerrilla Notes." Review of *The Crucible: An Autobiography by "Colonel Yay,"* by Yay Panlilio. *Sunday Times Magazine*, April 9, 1950.

Jose, Ricardo Trota. "The *Tribune* during the Japanese Occupation." *Philippine Studies* 38, no. 1 (1990), 45–64.

Junius II. "Brown Maiden Writes." *The Commonwealth Advocate* 1, no. 10 (October–November 1935), 59–60.

Kalaw, Maximo M. *The Case for the Filipinos*. New York: Century, 1916.

——. *The Filipino Rebel: A Romance of American Occupation in the Philippines*. Manila: Filipiniana Book Guild, 1964.

——. *Self-Government in the Philippines*. New York: Century, 1919.

Kalaw, Pura Villanueva. *Filipino Women: The Challenge They Meet*. N.p.: 1951.

——. *How the Filipina Got the Vote*. Manila, 1952.

——. "Women Can Help in the Reconstruction." *Sunday Tribune Magazine*, September 5, 1943.

Kang, Laura Hyun Yi. *Compositional Subjects: Enfiguring Asian / American Women*. Durham: Duke University Press, 2003.

Kaplan, Amy. *The Anarchy of Empire in the Making of U.S. Culture*. Cambridge: Harvard University Press, 2005.

——. " 'Left Alone with America': The Absence of Empire in the Study of American Culture." Kaplan and Pease, eds., *Cultures of United States Imperialism*, 3–21.

——. *The Social Construction of American Realism*. Chicago: University of Chicago Press, 1988.

——. "Violent Belongings and the Question of Empire Today." *American Quarterly* 56, no. 1 (March 2004), 1–18.

Kaplan, Amy, and Donald Pease, eds. *Cultures of United States Imperialism*. Durham: Duke University Press, 1993.

Kaplan, Caren, Norma Alarcón, and Minoo Moallem, eds. *Between Woman and Nation: Nationalisms, Transnational Feminisms, and the State*. Durham: Duke University Press, 1999.

Katigbak, Maria Kalaw. "May We Have Our Say?" *Philippine Review*, February 1944, 27–29.

Kauanui, J. Kēhaulani. "Native Hawaiian Decolonization and the Politics of Gender." *American Quarterly* 60, no. 2 (June 2008), 281–87.

Kim, Hyun Sook. "History and Memory: The 'Comfort Women Controversy.' " *positions: east asia cultures critique* 5, no. 1 (Spring 1997), 73–106.

Kim, Jodi. *Ends of Empire: Asian American Critique and the Cold War*. Minneapolis: University of Minnesota Press, 2010.

——. "From *Mee-gook* to Gook: The Cold War and Racialized Undocumented Capital in

Chang-rae Lee's *Native Speaker*." MELUS: *The Journal of the Society for the Study of the Multi-Ethnic Literature of the United States* 34, no. 1 (Spring 2009), 117–37.

———. "'I'm Not Here, If This Doesn't Happen': The Korean War and Cold War Epistemologies in Susan Choi's *The Foreign Student* and Heinz Insu Fenkl's *Memories of My Ghost Brother*." *Journal of Asian American Studies* 11, no. 3 (October 2008), 279–302.

Kingston, Maxine Hong. "Precarious Lives." Review of *Scent of Apples* by Bienvenido N. Santos. *New York Times Book Review*, May 4, 1980.

Kintanar, Thelma. *Women Reading: Feminist Perspectives on Philippine Literary Texts*. Quezon City: University of the Philippines Press, 1992.

Kintanar, Thelma B. et. al., eds. *Kuwentong Bayan: Noong Panahon Ng Hapon (Everyday Life in a Time of War)*. Quezon City: University of the Philippines Press, 2006.

Klein, Christina. *Cold War Orientalism: Asia in the Middlebrow Imagination, 1945–1961*. Berkeley: University of California Press, 2003.

———. "Why American Studies Needs to Think about Korean Cinema, or, Transnational Genres in the Films of Bong Joon-ho." *American Quarterly* 60, no. 4 (December 2008), 871–98.

Koikari, Mire. "Exporting Democracy: American Women, 'Feminist Reforms,' and the Politics of Imperialism in the U.S. Occupation of Japan, 1945–1952." *Frontiers* 23, no. 1 (2002), 23–45.

———. *Pedagogy of Democracy: Feminism and the Cold War in the U.S. Occupation of Japan*. Philadelphia: Temple University Press, 2008.

Koshy, Susan. "The Fiction of Asian American Literature." *Yale Journal of Criticism* 9, no. 2 (Fall 1996), 46–65.

———. *Sexual Naturalization: Asian Americans and Miscegenation*. Stanford: Stanford University Press, 2004.

Kramer, Paul. *The Blood of Government: Race, Empire, the United States, and the Philippines*. Chapel Hill: University of North Carolina Press, 2006.

Kurashige, Scott. *The Shifting Grounds of Race: Black and Japanese Americans in the Making of Multiethnic Los Angeles*. Princeton: Princeton University Press, 2010.

Laguio, Perfecto. *Our Modern Woman: A National Problem*. Manila: Philaw Book Supply, 1931.

Lanzona, Vina A. *Amazons of the Huk Rebellion: Gender, Sex, and Revolution in the Philippines*. Madison: University of Wisconsin Press, 2009.

Lardizabal, Jose. "Presumptious Literary Heirs." *Herald Mid-Week Magazine*, May 29, 1940.

"Latest Books Received." *New York Times*, October 2, 1932.

Lazam, Evangeline. "In Maria Clara's Wardrobe." *Wedding Essentials* 2, no. 2 (July–December 2006), 163.

Lee, Rachel. *The Americas of Asian American Literature: Gendered Fictions of Nation and Transnation*. Princeton: Princeton University Press, 1999.

Lee, Robert G. *Orientals: Asian Americans in Popular Culture.* Philadelphia: Temple University Press, 1999.

Leow, Rachel. "Reflections on Feminism, Blogging, and the Historical Profession." *Journal of Women's History* 22, no. 4 (2010), 235–43.

"Letter from Another Woman Writer." *Herald Mid-Week Magazine,* February 12, 1941.

Levander, Caroline F. and Robert S. Levine, eds. *Hemispheric American Studies.* New Brunswick: Rutgers University Press, 2008.

Lim, Rodrigo C. "Are All Guerrillas Heroes?" *Philippines Free Press,* July 13, 1946.

——. "Guerrillas 'Didn't Steal No Chickens for Me.'" *Philippines Free Press,* August 7, 1946.

Lim, Shirley. *A Feeling of Belonging: Asian American Women's Public Culture, 1930–1960.* New York: New York University Press, 2006.

Lim, Shirley Geok-Lin, Larry E. Smith, and Wimal Dissanayake, eds. *Transnational Asia Pacific: Gender, Culture, and the Public Sphere.* Urbana: University of Illinois Press, 1999.

Ling, Jinqi. *Narrating Nationalisms: Ideology and Form in Asian American Literature.* New York: Oxford University Press, 1998.

Linmark, R. Zamora. *Rolling the R's.* New York: Kaya, 1997.

Litonjua, Anatolio. "Is That So? The Male Writers Scout the Idea That Women Writers Will Ever Dominate Local Literary Field." *Graphic,* May 9, 1935.

Lopez, Lori Kido. "The Radical Act of 'Mommy Blogging': Redefining Motherhood through the Blogosphere." *New Media and Society* 11, no. 5 (2009), 729–47.

Lopez, Salvador P. "The Eagle's Eyrie, FilAmerican Magic." *Philippine-American* 2, no. 6 (February 1946), 64–66.

——. "Letter to GI Joe." *Philippine-American* 1, no. 1 (September 1945), 19–23.

——. "Maria Clara: Paragon or Caricature?" *Literature and Society: Essays on Life and Letters,* 37–41. Manila: University Publishing, 1940.

——. "A Word on 'Proletarian Literature.'" *The Herald Mid-Week Magazine,* July 10, 1940.

——. "Orienting the Filipino Writer." *Herald Mid-Week Magazine,* December 13, 1939.

——. "State Patronage of Letters." *Herald Mid-Week Magazine,* April 5, 1939.

Lorde, Audre. *Sister Outsider: Essays and Speeches.* 1987. Reprint. Berkeley: Crossing Press, 2007.

Lowe, Lisa. *Immigrant Acts: On Asian American Cultural Politics.* Durham: Duke University Press, 1996.

——. "The Intimacies of Four Continents." Stoler, ed., *Haunted by Empire,* 191–212.

Lumbera, Bienvenido. "The Nationalist Literary Tradition." *Nationalist Literature: A Centennial Forum,* ed. Elmer A. Ordonez, 1–16. Quezon City: University of the Philippines Press, 1996.

——. "Philippine Literature and the Filipino Personality." Manuud, ed., *Brown Heritage,* 1–15.

——. *Writing the Nation / Pag-akda ng Bansa.* Quezon City: University of the Philippines Press, 2000.

Lumbera, Bienvenido, and Cynthia Nogales Lumbera, eds. *Philippine Literature: A History and Anthology*. Manila: National Book Store, 1982.

Lye, Colleen. *America's Asia: Racial Form and American Literature, 1893–1945*. Princeton: Princeton University Press, 2004.

M. L. I. "Collaboration Begins at Home." *Sunday Tribune Magazine*, January 10, 1943.

Mabalon, Dawn, and Rico Reyes. *Filipinos in Stockton*. Charleston: Arcadia Publishing, 2008.

Manalansan, Martin. *Global Divas: Filipino Gay Men and the Diaspora*. Durham: Duke University Press, 2003.

——. "Queer Intersections: Sexuality and Gender in Migration Studies." *International Migration Review* 40, no. 1 (Spring 2006); 224–49.

Manlapaz, Edna Zapanta. "Filipino Women Writers in English." *World Englishes* 23, no. 1 (2004), 183–90.

——. *Filipino Women Writers in English: Their Story, 1905–2002*. Quezon City: Ateneo de Manila University Press, 2003.

——. "Literature in English by Filipino Women." *Feminist Studies* 26, no. 1 (2000), 187–200.

——. *Our Literary Matriarchs: Angela Manalang Gloria, Paz M. Latorena, Loreta Paras Sulit, and Paz Marquez Benitez*. Manila: Ateneo de Manila University Press, 1996.

——. *Songs of Ourselves: Writings by Filipino Women in English*. Pasig, Manila: Anvil, 1994.

Manuud, Antonio, ed. *Brown Heritage: Essays on Philippine Cultural Tradition and Literature*. Quezon City: Ateneo de Manila University Press, 1967.

Marajas, O. "Remember California Watsonville Incident." *Sunday Tribune Magazine*, July 11, 1943.

Marchetti, Gina. *Romance and the "Yellow Peril": Race, Sex, and Discursive Strategies in Hollywood Fiction*. Berkeley: University of California Press, 1993.

Marking, Yay (Panlilio). *Where a Country Begins*. 3 vols. Manila: Manila Times, 1961.

McAlister, Melanie. *Epic Encounters: Culture, Media, and U.S. Interests in the Middle East since 1945*. Revised edition. Berkeley: University of California Press, 2005.

McMahon, Jennifer. "The Malevolence of 'Benevolent Assimilation': Cultural Critique in Philippine Literature." *World Englishes* 23, no. 1 (2004), 141–53.

McReynolds, Patricia Justiniani. *Almost Americans: A Quest for Dignity*. Santa Fe: Red Crane Books, 1997.

Mendez, Paz Policarpio. *The Progress of the Filipino Woman during the Last 60 Years*. Manila: Centro Escolar University, 1965.

Mendoza, Victor Román. "Little Brown Students and the Homoerotics of 'White Love.'" *Genre: Forms of Discourse and Culture* 39, no. 4 (2006), 65–83.

——. "A Queer Nomadology of Jessica Hagedorn's *Dogeaters*." *American Literature* 77, no. 4 (December 2005), 815–45.

Mendoza-Guazon, Maria Paz. *The Development and Progress of the Filipino Woman*. Manila: Bureau of Printing, 1928.

——. *The Development and Progress of the Filipino Woman*. Revised and expanded edition. Manila: Kiko Printing Press, 1951.

——. *My Ideal Filipino Girl*. N.p., 1931.

Meyerowitz, Joanne. "Sex, Gender, and the Cold War Language of Reform." *Rethinking Cold War Culture*, ed. Peter J. Kuznick and James Gilbert, 106–123. Washington: Smithsonian Institution Press, 2001.

Michel, Sia. "Extravagance (and Shoe Love) in the Rise of a Despot." Review of "Here Lives [sic] Love [performance]," *New York Times*, February 5, 2007.

Miller, Monica. *Slaves to Fashion: Black Dandyism and the Styling of Black Diasporic Identity*. Durham: Duke University Press, 2009.

Mohanty, Chandra Talpade. *Feminism without Borders: Decolonizing Theory, Practicing Solidarity*. Durham: Duke University Press, 2003.

Mojares, Resil B. *Origins and Rise of the Filipino Novel: A Generic Study of the Novel until 1940*. Quezon City: University of the Philippines Press, 1998.

——. "Time, Memory, and the Birth of the Nation." *Waiting for Mariana Makiling: Essays in Philippine Cultural History*, 270–96. Quezon City: Ateneo de Manila University Press, 2002.

Monrayo, Angeles. *Tomorrow's Memories: a Diary, 1924–1928*. Honolulu: University of Hawai'i Press, 2003.

"Mrs. Aguinaldo's Wardrobe." *Chicago Daily Tribune*, November 18, 1899.

Mullen, Bill. *Afro-Orientalism*. Minneapolis: University of Minnesota Press, 2004.

Nakano, Satoshi. "Nation, Nationalism, and Citizenship in the Filipino World War II Veterans Equity Movement, 1945–1999." *Hitotsubashi Journal of Social Studies* 32 (December 2000), 33–53.

Nakpil, Carmen Guerrero. "Maria Clara." *Woman Enough and Other Essays*, 30–36.

——. *Woman Enough and Other Essays*. Quezon City: Ateneo de Manila University Press, 1999.

Ngai, Mae M. *Impossible Subjects: Illegal Aliens and the Making of Modern America*. Princeton: Princeton University Press, 2004.

Nguyen, Viet Thanh. *Race and Resistance: Literature and Politics in Asian America*. New York: Oxford University Press, 2002.

Ocampo, Felicidad V. *The Brown Maiden*. Boston: Meador, 1932.

——. *The Lonesome Cabin*. Boston: Meador, 1931.

——. *Portia: A Novel*. The Philippine Forum, August 1936 to April 1937.

——. "The Red Men." *The Philippine Forum* 1, no. 8 (July 1936), 71–76.

——. *The Woman Doctor*. The Philippine Forum, May–June 1937 to July 1937.

Omi, Michael, and Howard Winant. *Racial Formation in the United States: From the 1960s to the 1990s*. London: Routledge, 1994.

Ong, Aihwa. *Flexible Citizenship: The Cultural Logics of Transnationality*. Durham: Duke University Press, 1999.

Orallo, Avelina Cabanilla. "The Post War Coed." *Philippines Free Press*, March 6, 1948.

Ortuoste, Jenny. "Here Lies Myth." Review of *Here Lies Love* by David Byrne. *Manila Standard Today*, April 29, 2010.

Pacis, Vicente Albano. "Should the Women Continue Being Libertarian Tramps?" *Herald Mid-Week Magazine*, July 12, 1939, 15–16.

Palarca, Julia L. "Memo to the American People." *Philippine-American* 1, no. 3 (November 1945), 47–49.

———. "Memo: To Mother." *Filipina* 1, no. 2 (August 1944), 10, 35.

Palumbo-Liu, David. *Asian / American: Historical Crossings of a Racial Frontier*. Stanford: Stanford University Press, 1999.

Panlilio, Yay. *The Crucible: An Autobiography by "Colonel Yay," Filipina American Guerrilla*. 1950. Reprinted with an introduction and notes by Denise Cruz. New Brunswick: Rutgers University Press, 2009. Page references are to the 2009 edition.

Pareles, John. "Lyrics Lush and Gawky." Review of *Here Lies Love* by David Byrne. *New York Times*, April 8, 2010.

Park, Josephine. *Apparitions of Asia: Modernist Form and Asian American Poetics*. Oxford: Oxford University Press, 2008.

Parreñas, Rhacel Salazar. *The Force of Domesticity: Filipina Migrants and Globalization*. New York: New York University Press, 2008.

———. *Illicit Flirtations: Labor, Migration, and Sex Trafficking in Tokyo*. Stanford: Stanford University Press, 2011.

———. *Servants of Globalization: Women, Migration, and Domestic Work*. Stanford: Stanford University Press, 2001.

———. "White Trash Meets the 'Little Brown Monkeys': The Taxi Dance Hall as a Site of Interracial and Gender Alliances between White Working Class Women and Filipino Immigrant Men in the 1920s and 30s." *Amerasia Journal* 24, no. 2 (1998), 115–34.

Parry, Amie Elizabeth. *Interventions into Modernist Cultures: Poetry from beyond the Empty Screen*. Durham: Duke University Press, 2007.

Pascasio, Emy M. "The Language Situation in the Philippines from the Spanish Era to the Present." Manuud, ed., *Brown Heritage*, 225–52.

Patterson, Martha H. *The American New Woman Revisited: A Reader, 1894–1930*. New Brunswick: Rutgers University Press, 2008.

Pecson, Geronima T. *The Filipino Women in Nation Building*. Quezon City: Kayumanggi Press, 1959.

Peña, Casilda Sypresia. "The Rise of the Filipino Woman in the Social, Economic, and Political Fields since the End of the Spanish Regime up to the Present Time." M.A. thesis, University of San Carlos, 1953.

Perez, Asuncion A. "The College Girl." *Woman's World*, December 1935, 25.

Perico, A. "The Dawn of a New Era." *Sunday Tribune Magazine*, December 20, 1942, 1, 8.

Philippine Writers' League. "Direction in Our Literature." *Herald Mid-Week Magazine*, June 26, 1940.

Pierce, Tess. "Singing at the Digital Well: Blogs as Cyberfeminist Sites of Resistance." *Feminist Formations* 22, no. 3 (2010), 196–209.

Ponce, Martin Joseph. *Beyond the Nation: Diasporic Filipino Literature and Queer Reading.* New York: New York University Press, 2012.

——. "On Becoming Socially Articulate: Transnational Bulosan." *Journal of Asian American Studies* 8, no. 1 (February 2005), 49–80.

Pungol, Lady. "Largely About Our Women." *Filipina* 1, no. 2 (August 1944), 6, 7, 32.

Pratt, Mary Louise. *Imperial Eyes: Travel Writing and Transculturation.* London: Routledge, 1992.

"President Urges Women to Do Their Bit for National Sacrifice." *The Tribune,* July 9, 1944.

Quintero de Joseph, Maria Guadalupe Gutierrez. "American and Filipino Women." *The Independent,* June 22, 1905, 1412–13.

Rafael, Vicente. "Language, Identity, and Gender in Rizal's Noli." *Review of Indonesian and Malaysian Affairs* 18 (Winter 1984), 110–40.

——. *The Promise of the Foreign: Nationalism and the Technics of Translation in the Spanish Philippines.* Durham: Duke University Press, 2005.

——. *White Love and Other Events in Filipino History.* Durham: Duke University Press, 2000.

Ramamurthy, Priti. "All-Consuming Nationalism: The Indian Modern Girl in the 1920s and 1930s." Weinbaum et al., eds., *The Modern Girl around the World,* 148–73.

Raymund, Eric. "A GI Appraisal of the Filipinos." *Philippine American* 1, no. 1 (September 1945), 15–18.

"Review of *The Crucible: An Autobiography by 'Colonel Yay'* by Yay Panlilio." *New York Times,* December 29, 1949.

Reyes, Felina. *Filipino Women, Their Role in the Progress of Their Nation.* U.S. Dept. of Labor, Women's Bureau, 1951.

Reyes, Raquel A. G. *Love, Passion, and Patriotism: Sexuality and the Philippine Propaganda Movement, 1882–1892.* Singapore: NUS Press, 2008.

Reyes, Soledad S. "The Philippine Novel in English." *Bikolnon (Journal of Ateneo de Naga)* 1, no. 2 (March 1995), 117–32.

——. "The Romance Mode in Philippine Literature." *Philippine Studies* 32, no. 2 (1984), 163–80.

Rico, Victoria S. "'You Lovely People': The Texture of Alienation." *Philippine Studies* 42, no. 1 (1994), 91–104.

Rivera, Jr., Vicente. "One Woman's War." Review of *The Crucible: An Autobiography by "Colonel Yay"* by Yay Panlilio, *Evening News Saturday Magazine* (Manila), April 8, 1950.

Rizal, José. "A Letter to the Young Women of Malolos." 1889. Reprint, Manila: Bureau of Printing, 1932.

——. *Noli Me Tangere.* Translated by Soledad Lacson-Locsin. 1887. Reprint, Honolulu: University of Hawai'i Press, 1997.

——. *Noli Me Tangere.* 1887. Reprint, Caracas, Venezuela: Biblioteca Ayacucho, 1976.

Roces, Mina. "Is the Suffragist an American Colonial Construct? Defining 'the Filipino Woman' in the Colonial Philippines." *Women's Suffrage in Asia: Gender, Nationalism, and Democracy*, ed. Louise Edwards and Mina Roces, 24–58. London: Routledge Curzon, 2004.

——. "Women in Philippine Politics and Society." *Mixed Blessing: The Impact of the American Colonial Experience on Politics and Society in the Philippines*, ed. Hazel M. McFerson, 159–84. Westport, Conn.: Greenwood Press, 2002.

——. *Women, Power, and Kinship Politics: Female Power in Post-war Philippines*. Westport, Conn.: Praeger, 1998.

Rodríguez, Dylan. "'A Million Deaths?': Genocide and the 'Filipino American' Condition of Possibility." *Positively No Filipinos Allowed*, ed. Antonio T. Tiongson, Edgardo Valencia Gutierrez, Ricardo Valencia Gutierrez, 145–61. Philadelphia: Temple University Press, 2006.

——. *Suspended Apocalypse: White Supremacy, Genocide, and the Filipino Condition*. Minneapolis: University of Minnesota Press, 2009.

Rodriguez, Robyn Magalit. *Migrants for Export: How the Philippine State Brokers Labor to the World*. Minneapolis: University of Minnesota Press, 2010.

"The Role of Women in Building a Strong and Prosperous Country." *Sunday Tribune Magazine*, January 17, 1943.

Roma-Sianturi, Dinah. "'Pedagogic Invasion': The Thomasites in Occupied Philippines." *Kritika Kultura* 12 (2009), 5–26.

Romulo, Carlos P. *I Saw the Fall of the Philippines*. Garden City: Doubleday and Doran, 1942.

——. *I See the Philippines Rise*. Garden City: Doubleday, 1946.

——. *Mother America: A Living Story of Democracy*. Garden City: Doubleday and Doran, 1943.

——. *My Brother Americans*. Garden City: Doubleday and Doran, 1945.

Rosal, Fernandina Cariño. "Filipino Women Do Their Best Collaborating with Menfolk." *Sunday Tribune Magazine*, June 20, 1943.

Rotor, A. B. "Our Literary Heritage." *Herald Mid-Week Magazine*, April 10, 1940.

——. "Writers without Readers." *Herald Mid-Week Magazine*, October 25, 1939.

Rowe, John Carlos. *Literary Culture and U.S. Imperialism: From the Revolution to World War II*. New York: Oxford University Press, 2000.

Said, Edward. *Orientalism*. New York: Vintage Books, 1978.

Salas, Ramon. "Marking's Family—'Fightingest of All.'" *Philippines Free Press*, February 22, 1947.

Salman, Michael. *The Embarrassment of Slavery: Controversies over Bondage and Nationalism in the American Colonial Philippines*. Berkeley: University of California Press, 2001.

San Juan, Epifanio, Jr.. "Beyond Identity Politics: The Predicament of the Asian American Writer in Late Capitalism." *American Literary History* 3, no. 3 (Fall 1991), 542–65.

——. "Carlos Bulosan, Filipino Writer-Activist: Between a Time of Terror and the Time of Revolution." *CR: The New Centennial Review* 8, no. 1 (Spring 2008), 103–34.

———. From Exile to Diaspora: Versions of the Filipino Experience in the United States. Boulder: Westview Press, 1998.

Santos, Bienvenido N. You Lovely People. Manila: Benipayo Press, 1955.

See, Sarita. The Decolonized Eye: Filipino American Art and Performance. Minneapolis: University of Minnesota Press, 2009.

Seigel, Micol. Uneven Encounters: Making Race and Nation in Brazil and the United States. Durham: Duke University Press, 2009.

Sevilla, Salvador S. "The New Filipino Woman: She Has Shed Conservatism and Assumed New Responsibilities." Graphic, November 28, 1935.

Shah, Nayan. Contagious Divides: Epidemics and Race in San Francisco's Chinatown. Berkeley: University of California Press, 2001.

Sharpe, Jenny. Allegories of Empire: The Figure of Woman in the Colonial Text. Minneapolis: University of Minnesota Press, 1993.

Shimizu, Celine Parreñas. The Hypersexuality of Race: Performing Asian / American Women on Scene and Screen. Durham: Duke University Press, 2007.

Sinha, Mrinalini. Specters of Mother India: The Global Restructuring of an Empire. Durham: Duke University Press, 2006.

Skwiot, Christine. The Purposes of Paradise: U.S. Tourism and Empire in Cuba and Hawai'i. Philadelphia: University of Pennsylvania Press, 2010.

Slotkin, Joel. "Igorots and Indians: Racial Hierarchies and Conceptions of the Savage in Carlos Bulosan's Fiction of the Philippines." American Literature 72, no. 4 (December 2000), 843–66.

Smith, Andrea. "American Studies without America: Native Feminisms and the Nation-State." American Quarterly 60, no. 2 (June 2008), 309–15.

Sommer, Doris. Foundational Fictions: The National Romances of Latin America. Berkeley: University of California Press, 1991.

"So You're Going to the States!" Philippine-American 1, no. 4 (December 1945), 28–31.

Stephens, Michelle Ann. Black Empire: The Masculine Global Imaginary of Caribbean Intellectuals in the United States, 1914–1962. Durham: Duke University Press, 2005.

Stewart, Susan. On Longing: Narratives of the Miniature, the Gigantic, the Souvenir, the Collection. Durham: Duke University Press, 1999.

Stillman, Amy Ku'leialoha. "Pacific-ing Asian Pacific American History." Journal of Asian American Studies 7, no. 3 (October 2004), 241–70.

Stoler, Ann Laura, ed. Haunted by Empire: Geographies of Intimacy in North American History. Durham: Duke University Press, 2006.

———. "Intimidations of Empire: Predicaments of the Tactile and Unseen." Stoler, ed., Haunted by Empire, 1–22.

Stoltzfus, Brenda J. "A Woman's Place Is in the Struggle." The Philippines Reader, ed. Daniel B. Schirmer and Stephen R. Shalom, 308–12. Boston: South End Press, 1987.

Subido, Trinidad Tarrosa. The Feminist Movement in the Philippines, 1905–1955. Manila: National Federation of Women's Clubs, 1961.

Sumida, Stephen H. "Where in the World Is American Studies?" *American Quarterly* 55, no. 3 (September 2003), 333–52.

———. *And the View from the Shore: Literary Traditions of Hawaii.* Seattle: University of Washington Press, 1991.

Tadiar, Neferti Xina M. *Fantasy Production: Sexual Economies and Other Philippine Consequences for the New World Order.* Seattle: University of Washington Press, 2004.

———. "Filipinas 'Living in a Time of War.' " de Jesús, ed., *Pinay Power,* 373–385.

———. "Popular Laments: Affective Literacies of Democratization and War." *Cultural Studies* 23, no. 1 (2009), 1–26.

———. *Things Fall Away: Philippine Historical Experience and the Makings of Globalization.* Durham: Duke University Press, 2009.

Takaki, Ronald. *Strangers from a Different Shore.* Boston: Little, Brown, 1989.

Tanaka, Yuki. Introduction to *Comfort Woman: A Filipina's Story of Prostitution and Slavery under the Japanese Military,* by Maria Rose Henson. Lanham, Md.: Rowman and Littlefield, 1999.

Tate, Claudia. *Domestic Allegories of Political Desire: The Black Heroine's Text at the Turn of the Century.* New York: Oxford University Press, 1992.

Teaiwa, Teresa K. "Globalizing and Gendered Forces: The Contemporary Militarization of Pacific/Oceania." *Gender and Globalization in Asia and the Pacific: Method, Theory, Practice,* ed. Kathy E. Ferguson and Monique Mironesco, 318–32. Honolulu: University of Hawai'i Press, 2008.

"Tells of the Busy Filipino Woman." *Chicago Daily Tribune,* October 17, 1901.

Thaman, Konai Helu. "Decolonizing Pacific Studies: Indigenous Perspectives, Knowledge, and Wisdom in Higher Education." *Contemporary Pacific* 15, no. 1 (Spring 2003), 1–17.

"Those Co-eds' Resolutions: They Range from Promises to Write Regularly to the Folks Back Home to Resolves Not to Have Anything More to Do with Men." *Graphic,* January 5, 1933, 26–27.

Tolentino, Arturo M. "Filipinism Inspired by Nippon." *Philippine Review,* February 1944, 35–40.

Tolentino, Cynthia. *America's Experts: Race and the Fictions of Sociology.* Minneapolis: University of Minnesota Press, 2009.

———. " 'In the Training Center of the Skillful Servants of Mankind': Carlos Bulosan's Professional Filipinos in an Age of Benevolent Supremacy." *American Literature* 80, no. 2 (2008), 381–406.

Tolentino, Roland. "Bodies, Letters, Catalogs: Filipinas in Transnational Space." *Social Text* 48 (1996), 49–76.

———. "Macho Dancing, the Feminization of Labor, and Neoliberalism in the Philippines." *TDR: The Drama Review* 54, no. 2 (2009), 77–89.

Torre-Guzman, Paciencia. "Determination among Our Women." *Sunday Tribune Magazine,* November 4, 1943.

Trinidad, Lina Flor. "A Letter to My Daughter." Filipina 1, no. 2 (August 1944), 11.

Twelbeck, Kirsten. "Beyond a Postmodern Denial of Reference: Forms of Resistance in Jessica Hagedorn's Dogeaters." Amerikastudien / American Studies 51, no. 3 (2006), 425–37.

Ty, Leon O. "Fake Heroes." Philippines Free Press, March 23, 1946.

———. "Guerrilleras." Philippines Free Press, October 12, 1946.

Uichanco, Ursula B. "The University Lady." Woman's World, July 1935, 2.

Vergara, Benito M., Jr. Displaying Filipinos: Photography and Colonialism in Early Twentieth Century Philippines. Quezon City: University of the Philippines Press, 1995.

Viray, Manuel A. "Filipino Writing in English." This Week, August 8, 1948.

Volpp, Leti. "American Mestizo: Filipinos and Antimiscegenation Laws in California." U. C. Davis Law Review 33, no. 4 (2000), 795–835.

Von Eschen, Penny M. Race against Empire: Black Americans and Anticolonialism, 1937–1957. Ithaca: Cornell University Press, 1997.

———. Satchmo Blows Up the World: Jazz Ambassadors Play the Cold War. Cambridge: Harvard University Press, 2004.

Weinbaum, Alys Eve, Lynn M. Thomas, Priti Ramamurthy, Uta G. Poiger, Madeleine Yue Dong, and Tani E. Barlow. "The Modern Girl as Heuristic Device: Collaboration, Connective Comparison, Multidirectional Citation." Weinbaum et al., The Modern Girl around the World, 1–24.

Weinbaum, Alys Eve, et al., eds. The Modern Girl around the World: Consumption, Modernity, and Globalization. Durham: Duke University Press, 2008.

Wesling, Meg. "Colonial Education and the Politics of Knowledge in America Is in the Heart." MELUS: The Journal of the Society for the Study of the Multi-Ethnic Literature of the United States 32, no. 2 (Summer 2007), 55–77.

———. Empire's Proxy: American Literature and U.S. Imperialism in the Philippines. New York: New York University Press, 2011.

Wexler, Laura. Tender Violence: Domestic Visions in an Age of U.S. Imperialism. Chapel Hill: University of North Carolina Press, 2000.

"What Every Girl Should Know." Woman's World, January 1936.

"What Interest [sic] Them Most." Graphic, March 4, 1937.

Whitlock, Gillian. Soft Weapons: Autobiography in Transit. Chicago: University of Chicago Press, 2007.

Wilder, Marshall P. "Raising of Children is Chief Philippine Industry." Chicago Daily Tribune, June 11, 1905.

Wilson, Rob. Reimagining the American Pacific: From "South Pacific" to Bamboo Ridge and Beyond. Durham: Duke University Press, 2000.

Wolk, Douglas. "The Imelda Marcos Story—As Told by David Byrne." Review of Here Lies Love by David Byrne. Time.com, April 10, 2010.

Wong, Sau-Ling. "Denationalization Reconsidered: Asian American Cultural Criticism at a Theoretical Crossroads." Postcolonial Theory and the United States: Race,

Ethnicity, and Literature, ed. Amritjit Singh and Peter Schmidt, 122–48. Jackson: University Press of Mississippi, 2000.

Wood, Houston. "Cultural Studies for Oceania." *Contemporary Pacific* 15, no. 2 (2003), 340–74.

Worcester, Dean. *The Philippine Islands and Its People: A Record of Personal Observation and Experience, with a Short Summary of the More Important Facts in the History of the Archipelago.* New York: Macmillan, 1898.

——. *The Philippines Past and Present.* New York: Macmillan, 1921.

Wu, Ellen. "America's Chinese: Anti-Communism, Citizenship, and Cultural Diplomacy during the Cold War." *Pacific Historical Review* 77, no. 3 (2011), 391–422.

Yabes, Leopoldo Y. "Criticism and Literary Growth." *Herald Mid-Week Magazine*, July 17, 1940.

——. "The Filipino Novel in English." *Herald Mid-Week Magazine*, September 10, 1941.

——. "Filipinos Do Not Buy Books." *Herald Mid-Week Magazine*, November 27, 1940.

——. "Filipinos Write Books." *Herald Mid-Week Magazine*, October 9, 1940.

——. "A History of Filipino Literature in English." *Herald Mid-Week Magazine*, September 20, 1939.

——. "Philippine Literature in English." *Herald Mid-Week Magazine*, September 27, 1939.

——, ed. *Philippine Short Stories, 1925–1940.* Manila: University of the Philippines Press, 1999.

——, ed. *Philippine Short Stories, 1941–1955.* 2 vols. Manila: University of the Philippines Press, 1997.

——. "What Is Wrong with Our Women Writers?" *Herald Mid-Week Magazine*, January 22, 1941.

Yoneyama, Lisa. "Liberation under Siege: U.S. Military Occupation and Japanese Women's Enfranchisement." *American Quarterly* 57, no. 3 (September 2005), 885–910.

Yu, Timothy. " 'The Hand of a Chinese Master': José Garcia Villa and Modernist Orientalism." MELUS: *The Journal of the Society for the Study of the Multi-Ethnic Literature of the United States* 29, no. 1 (Spring 2004), 41–59.

Yu-Jose, Lydia, ed. *The Past, Love, Money, and Much More: Philippines–Japan Relations since the End of the Second World War.* Quezon City: Ateneo de Manila University Press, 2008.

Yu-Jose, Lydia N., and Ikehata Setsuho, eds. *Philippines–Japan Relations.* Quezon City: Ateneo de Manila University Press, 2001.

Yule, Emma Sarepta. "Filipino Feminism." *Scribner's*, June 1920, 738–46.

——. "The Woman Question in the Philippines." *The Filipino People*, February 1916.

Zafra, Jessica. "Dancing on the Grave of History." Review of *Here Lies Love* by David Byrne. *Philippine Star*, April 23, 2010.

Page numbers in *italics* indicate illustrations or photographs.

authorial practices and strategies, 8, 18, 24, 33, 112–13, 145–47, 152–53, 221, 230

awit, 116

Bagong Pinay. See *newfilipina* (*Bagong Pinay*)

Balance, Christine Bacareza, 220, 225, 226, 258n11

Balce, Nerissa, 36, 243n22

Baldoz, Richard, 134

balintawak, 102, 248n71

Bandung Conference (1955), 186

Barlow, Tani E., 71–72

Barranco, Vicente: "The Filipino Girl--Model 1939," 90–91, 93

barrio girl as icon: coed contrasted with, 70–71, 125; Guerrero Nakpil's description, 208; in Kalaw's *The Filipino Rebel*, 111, 140; Roces's analysis of, 248n76; in romance novels, 113, 124–25, 127, 129; romanticization of, 68, 72, 106, 107, 108, 230; in women's suffrage debates, 74, 99, 103–5

Bascara, Victor, 255n11

Bataan Brotherhood, 27, 165, 180, 182

benevolence, Spanish, 81–82

benevolence, U.S.: during Cold War, 217–18; critiques of, 34, 48–52, 111–12, 118, 122, 124–25, 133, 139–45, 146, 191, 194, 199, 203; exchange programs and, 188, 189–90; feminism and, 205, 211, 213; melting pot metaphor and, 169, 170–73, 180; narrative as justification for empire, 6, 11, 89, 91, 109, 181–82, 210; romanticization of, 113–15, 117; social display and, 36–47

Benitez, Francisca Tirona, 157–58, 160

blogs and bloggers, Filipina, 220–21, 222–23, 229–35

Borstelmann, Thomas, 169

Bracero program, 201

British suffragettes, 23

Brody, David, 32, 242n7

Brown Maiden, The (Ocampo), 132–47; closing lines of, 112; dedication to Sommer, 141; ending of, 112, 143–45, 181–82; interracial marriage in, 132, 135, 139–40; marketing of, 133; nationalism in, 114, 117; plot of, 111–12, 132; portrayal of Filipino male laborers in United States, 134–35, 138, 146; portrayal of indigenous peoples of the Philippines, 136–39; reception of, 112–13, 145–46; repatriation in, 143–45; skin color in, 134, 137–38

Bulletin, 156

Bulosan, Carlos: *America Is in the Heart*, 17–18, 19–20, 107, 254n2, 255n15; place in canon, 17, 18, 65, 238n24, 240n37

Bureau of Indian Affairs, 16

Bush, George W., 189

Byrne, David: *Here Lies Love*, 219–22, 223–28, 230, 231, 234, 258n11, 258n13

byways and midways, concept of, 8, 32–33, 35, 52–53, 73, 151, 187, 218, 221, 234

Carby, Hazel, 116

Carrothers, George E., 43

Castrence, Pura Santillan: "The East Views the American Coed," 97; essays on Rizal's novels, 247n33

Catt, Carrie Chapman, 21

Chicana and Chicano studies, feminist scholarship in, 17

China: early twentieth-century American attitudes, 48–49; influence in Philippines, 4; *nuxing*, 23

Chinese populations in Philippines, 33, 76, 172

Chinese women, conceptions of, 33–34, 48–49

chinita type of Filipina, 1, 2–3, 4, 5

chinos, 76

Chow, Rey, 241n53

Choy, Catherine Ceniza, 190, 212

Chuh, Kandice, 146

Clamor, Charmaine, 219

class: colonial display and, 36–47, 48; constructions in Philippines, 4, 5–6, 9–10, 16, 33, 76, 79, 103, 105–6, 125; destabilization of boundaries, 132–38, 190, 201–2; education and, 125, 127, 139–40; feminism and, 50–52, 95–98, 140–42; hierarchy, 4, 10, 14, 16, 54, 56, 73, 113, 124, 139; homosocial communities and, 199, 203–5, 254–55n9; Japanese occupation of Philippines and, 158; online access for nonelite, 233–34; tensions between Filipinos in United States, 137–39, 188, 193–97, 199; urbanidad and, 78–79; women's suffrage debates and, 105–6; writer's language and, 58–59, 65

coed as icon, 230; in 1930s, 72, 88–98, 108; in 1950s, 183–84, 188, 189–90, 191, 197–205, 210, 217–18; colonialism and, 108–9; global links, 23; Guerrero Nakpil's description, 208; Marcos linked to, 225; Maria Clara contrasted with, 90, 101–2; modern girl and, 89–98; New Order vilification of, 158, 162–63; responsibility of, 95–97; in romance novels, 113, 124–25, 139–40; scarcity of, in early twentieth-century United States, 254–55n9; sexual behavior and, 69–70, 73, 89, 91–97, 102, 125, 144, 201–3; in women's suffrage debates, 68, 69–70, 73–74, 125–26

Cold War, 185–218; feminism and, 210; imaginaries of containment and integration, 186–87, 191, 204–5; rhetoric, 155, 169, 183

colonial modernity, 71–72

Comfort, Will Levington, 38–39

Commonwealth Literary Awards, 56–57

communism: fear of, 94, 100, 155, 186–87, 188, 191; student movements and, 228

Concerned Women of the Philippines, 228

conduct manuals, 6, 68, 95–98, 107

Constantino, Renato, 246n18

Cook, Norman, 219, 258n11

corrido, 116

criollos, 76, 247n37

critical cartography, 8, 31–66, 187, 230

Cuba, 15, 243n23

Cumpas, Estrella, 219–22, 226, 231

Daly, Perla Paredes, 229

Daroy, Petronilo Bn., 244n50

dating websites, Filipina, 229–30

de Jesús, Melinda L., 211

DeLoughrey, Elizabeth: Routes and Roots, 242n4

diaspora studies, 8, 16–19, 108, 198, 247n44, 251n39, 257n3

Diaz, Trinidad, 178

Diaz, Vicente, 15

Diaz-Tutaan, Dana, 224

domesticity: barrio girl icon and, 106, 124, 127; Cold War era, 214; contemporary, 220–23, 226, 230, 233; early twentieth-century, 26–27, 39–40, 43, 47, 50; guerrilla, 168, 170, 173–78, 181–83; Japanese New Order and, 149–53, 163–64, 212; Maria Clara icon and, 99; migrant laborer's fantasy of, 196, 198, 203; nationalism and 108; white American women, 256n31

Du Bois, W. E. B., 250n23

Dudziak, Mary, 169, 187

dusky type of Filipina, 1, 2–3, 4, 5

Edwards, Brent Hayes: The Practice of Diaspora, 251n39

elite: attachment to United States, 70, 199; in commonwealth government, 70–71; destabilization of, 132–38; education and, 111–13, 114–15, 122, 127–29, 189, 191–93, 213; exceptionalism and, 115, 132–39; femininity and, 9–10, 40–41, 43, 46–47, 48–52, 68–69, 95–97, 132–45, 195–205; Filipinas during elite (cont.)

Japanese occupation, 151, 162–65; ilustrados, 78–79; insecurity of, 140, 143–
45; print culture and, 12; reimaginings
of, 221; suppression of *Noli Me Tangere*'s
satire, 88, 102; transitions between empires and, 24, 33, 36–37, 108, 117; use
of English literature for identity construction, 5–6, 9, 10–14, 16–17, 35;
women's suffrage debates and, 77,
98–106

empire: critiques of, 48–52, 127–32, 144–
45, 198–99; historiographical rewriting
of, 106, 118–24; manifestations of
sprawl of, 71–72; overlap of, 7, 8–9,
13–14, 24, 33–35, 48, 51–53, 59, 71,
88–89, 98, 100, 109, 117, 164, 188, 221–
23, 234, 247n44; U.S. exceptionalism
and, 113–14, 117, 128–29, 139–45. See
also imperialism

Eng, David, 146

Enloe, Cynthia, 198

España-Maram, Linda, 134

Espiritu, Augusto, 146, 192

essays: early twentieth-century, 12–13;
figure of Filipina in, 6, 9, 31–32, 35,
50–52, 62–66, 150–65, 186, 205–9. See
also specific authors

ethnic American studies, 16–17, 107,
115–16

exchange programs, U.S./Philippines, 11,
197, 216. See also *pensionados*

Exchange Visitor Program, 189

Fajardo, Kale Bantigue, 192–93

Fatboy Slim. See Cook, Norman

Felix, Concepcion, 20

femininity: colonial attitudes and, 36–50,
77–82, 107; conception of Asian, 31,
33–34, 36, 48–49, 152, 242n7; construction of Filipina, 24, 31–32, 34–35,
43, 46–52, 79–82, 102–6, 122–45,
205–9; domesticity and, 160–65, 212,
214, 218; Filipinas under Japanese oc-

cupation, 149–84; Filipina women
writers and, 59–66; guerrilla mother/
wife identity, 173–80; importance of, in
elites' responses, 9; the Malay woman
and, 68, 98, 102–3, 161–62, 211–12;
Maria Clara as an icon for, 1–2, 67–68,
79–88, 107, 108, 122, 136–37, 230; the
modern girl and, 22–23, 72–73, 78, 88–
98; reimagining of the Filipina during
the Cold War, 190–218; romanticization
of past, 106–7; sexuality and, 79–82, 88–
89, 101, 108, 131, 201–5, 207–8, 230–31;
single women and, 140–42, 203–5. See
also transpacific: femininities

feminism: class and, 31–32, 48–52, 95–
98, 124–30, 140–42; community partnerships with other women, 231–33;
empire and, 71–73; figure of Filipina
in, 6, 19–20, 31–32, 50–52, 111–12,
128–32, 191; Filipina coed and, 69, 72–
73, 88–98; Filipinas under Japanese
occupation, 151–53, 157–80; Filipina–
white American women alliances, 66,
127, 129–30, 133, 140–42, 178–82;
hybridity of Filipina and, 205–9, 215–
16, 256n34; the Malay woman and, 68,
98, 102–3, 161–62, 211–12; movement
in Philippines, 20–21, 209–17, 228–29;
nonnormativity of, in nationalist narratives, 17, 106, 221; Orientalist stereotypes and, 31–32, 48–50, 212–13, 222;
Philippine guerrilla resistance movement and, 150, 152, 165, 167–68, 169–
80; studies of Filipina, 209–217,
256n37, 259n29; women's club movement, 20–21, 211, 216; women's resistance and rights groups, 228–29;
women's suffrage and, 20–21, 95, 98–
99, 101, 105, 248n71

feminist analysis, 8–9, 33. See *also byways
and midways; transpacific: femininities*

Ferens, Dominika, 116

Filipina and Filipino American studies,
17–20, 146

icons, female (*cont.*)

50, 158, 163–64, 174–80, 190, 192–97, 203, 212, 214, 217–18, 222, 226; importance in nationalist narratives, 4, 16–20, 24, 91–94, 97–98, 102–3, 106, 107–8, 111–12, 130–32, 146, 198, 221; importance in women's suffrage debates, 67–71, 98–106, 248n71; mail-order bride, 220, 222–23, 229–30; Imelda Marcos, 219–22, 223–28; *newfilipina* (*Bagong Pinay*), 223, 229–31, 233–34; new woman and modern girl, 21–22, 72–73; overseas Filipina worker, 220, 222–23, 230, 257n3; in romance novels, 113, 124–32. *See also* barrio girl as icon; coed as icon; Maria Clara as icon; Malay woman as icon

Iginuhit Ng Tadhana (propaganda film), 224

Igorots, 33, 37, 38, 40, 41, 42, 78, 139, 143

Ileto, Reynaldo, 225, 246n18, 254n58, 255n11

ilustrados, 78–79, 85, 94, 101, 103, 121, 250n22

imperialism: conquests of Philippines, 4, 6–7, 118–20, 153; Filipina and Filipino involvement in anti-imperialist movement, 34; orientalism and, 48–52, 186–87, 242n7; racist attitudes and, 36–47, 159–60, 183; romanticization of benevolence, 113–15, 139–45; sexual attitudes and, 94–95; spheres of influence, 160; transitions between empires, 7, 24, 33; use of education and language, 10–12, 69, 89–98, 113–14, 122, 127–29, 154, 155–57, 213. *See also* empire; Japan; Spain; United States

Inang Bayan (Mother of the Nation), 4

independence debates: role of English and, 54–55; in United States, 134; U.S. Anti-Imperialist League and, 13; U.S. disparagement of, 44–47, 52; women's rights and, 20–21, 67–68, 69–70, 73–74, 98–99, 100–106, 108–9, 129–30, 245n1, 248n71

india type of Filipina, 2, 5, 25–26, 36, 38–39, 191, 211

indigeneity and indigenous peoples: American opinions of, 39–41, 43; American racism and, 159; elites' desire to distance themselves from, 52, 103, 106, 135–39; languages of, 13, 54; marginalization of, 10, 15–16, 72, 105–6, 211, 217; Native Americans compared with, 36–37; notions of femininity and, 6–7, 36–37, 68, 70, 72, 191, 211–12, 217; skin color and, 4–5. *See also* Igorots; *india* type of Filipina; *indios*; Malay; *morena* type of Filipina; Moros; Native Americans; Negritos

indigenous studies, feminist scholarship in, 17

indios, 16, 37, 76, 86

infieles, 16

Institute of National Language, 55

Isaac, Allan Punzalan, 14, 192–93, 225, 240n37

Jamias, Cristino, 156–57

Japan: American attitudes to, in early twentieth century, 48–49; guerrilla resistance movement against, 150, 152, 165, 167–68, 169–80, 253n49; imperialist use of education and language, 10, 53–54, 64–65, 154–55; Philippines under, 4, 7, 13–14, 24, 53–54, 64–65, 106, 149–84. *See also* New Order

Japanese language. *See* Nippongo (Nihongo)

Japanese *moga*, 23

Japanese women, conceptions of, 48–49, 161, 242n7

Japonisme, 48–49

Joaquin, Nick, 65, 75

Jones, Sharon, 219

Jose, Ricardo Trota: "The *Tribune* during the Japanese Occupation," 156, 252n18

Junius II, 112–13

Maria Clara as icon (*cont.*)

Uacterization in novel, 69, 73, 74–88, 99, 131; coed contrasted with, 90, 100–101; as epitome of Filipina femininity, 1–2, 23, 67–68, 72, 79–85, 99–100, 107, 108, 122, 132, 136–37, 230; new Maria Claras, 98–106; rebellion against, 136–37; in romance novels, 113, 124–25; story of miraculous birth, 81–82; unstable representation of, 69, 75–76, 80–86; Virgin Mary and, 85–87; *Wedding Essentials* spread, 1–5, 2–3, 9, 23, 208; in women's suffrage debates, 67, 74, 75, 98–106

Marking. *See* Agustin, Marcos V.

Marking, Yay. *See* Panlilio, Yay

Marking's Guerrillas, 167, 171–78

Marquez Benitez, Paz, 245n71

masculinity: of Filipino migrants, 135; formation of Filipino heterosexual, 185, 188, 201, 218, 254–55n9; Japanese models of, 161; of nationalist narratives, 7, 17, 82, 124; of Philippine publishing world, 61–62; U.S. empire gendered as, 115–16, 152, 182–83

McAlister, Melanie, 187

McKinley, William, 11, 213

McMahon, Jennifer: "The Malevolence of 'Benevolent Assimilation,'" 249n4

Meador (publisher), 133

Mendoza-Guazon, Maria Paz, 187, 188, 189, 191, 218; *Development and Progress of the Filipino Woman*, 186, 210–17, 245n6, 250n24; *My Ideal Filipino Girl*, 95, 97, 98–99; travel to United States, 189

Merchant, Natalie, 219

mestizaje: connection to transpacific femininities, 6; Panlilio and, 169–73

mestiza type of Filipina, 1–6, 2–3; early twentieth-century photographs of, 40, 41; Maria Clara as, 79–88, 102, 108, 132; racism and classism of, 140

mestizos: class hierarchy and, 16, 76, 172–73; position in U.S. regime, 70

Mexican Americans: Bracero program, 201; Latino and Filipino labor and, 134–37; racism and, 159

midways. *See* byways and midways

Modern Girl Around the World Research Group, 21–22, 72–73

modern girl as icon, 21–23; Filipina, 22–23, 89–98, 230–31; *ilustrados'* views of, 78; modes of dress, 94, 95–97, 242n11; New Order Filipina's rejection of, 162; sexual "aberrations" and, 93–95, 201–3

moga, 23

Mohanty, Chandra Talpade, 198

Mojares, Resil B., 58–59, 121, 238n19, 249n1

morena type of Filipina, 1, 2–3, 4, 5

Morga, Antonio de: *Sucesos de las islas Filipinas*, 78–79

Moros, 16, 33, 37, 78

multimedia projects, 220–28, 234

National Association of Colored Women, 21

National Federation of Women's Clubs, 21

nationalism, Philippine, 130–32; empire's haunting of, 71–73, 117; English literature and, 52–59; feminism and, during Japanese occupation, 151–53, 164–80; Philippine identity construction and, 76–77; "practical patriotism" concept, 153, 157–65; Rizal's *Noli Me Tangere* as foundational text, 1–3, 82–85; in romance novels, 111, 114–15, 118–32, 146–47; suffering as central to, 225; *urbanidad* and, 78–79; women's narrative exclusion, 122–24; women's symbolism in, 16–20, 24, 91–94, 97–98, 102–3, 106, 107–8, 111–12, 146, 198, 221

nation as term, 14

Native Americans: Filipinos compared with, 16, 36–37; Ocampo's observations of, 118, 135–36

Negritos, 5, 33, 37, 38, 41, 78

race: colonial display and, 36–47; constructions in Philippines, 4–5, 9–10, 16, 33, 40, 76–77, 79, 82–85, 94–95, 105–6, 172; discourses on primitive, 135–36; interracial relationships and miscegenation, 132, 135, 139–40, 142–43, 173, 202, 242n7; Japanese occupation of Philippines and, 153–54, 158, 183; Latinas contrasted with Filipinas, 243n23; melting pot metaphor and, 169, 170–73, 187; Ocampo's decoupling of from class, 137–39; passing and, 200–201; Philippine independence and, 21; prejudices in United States, 112, 114, 117, 127, 132–38, 158, 159–60, 200–201; racialized representations of motherhood, 174–76; racial uplift concept, 140, 250n23; skin color and, 3, 5, 37, 38–39, 76–77, 82, 137–38, 202

Racoma, Dine, 229

Rafael, Vicente, 16, 38, 54, 71, 85, 228

Renacimiento, El, 50–51

Repatriation Act, 134

Reyes, Raquel A. G.: Love Passion, and Patriotism, 78–79

Reyes, Soledad, 65, 116; "The Philippine Novel," 244n50; "The Romance Mode," 249n12

Rizal, José: annotated edition of Morga's Sucesos de las islas Filipinas, 78–79; "A Letter to the Young Women of Malolos," 77, 86; as nationalist figure, 67, 88, 123, 246n18; Noli Me Tangere, 1–3, 67–68, 69, 73, 74–88, 99, 105, 115, 122, 123, 130. See also Noli Me Tangere

Roces, Mina, 20, 99, 228, 248n76, 259n21, 259n29

Rodríguez, Dylan, 255n11

romance novels, 111–47; chivalric rescue narrative of, 115; destabilizing narratives in, 115–16; figure of the Filipina in, 6; as genre, 115; as means of resistance, 116. See also specific authors and titles

Romulo, Carlos, 168–69, 179, 238n24, 253nn51–52

Rosal, Fernandina Cariño, 162

Rotor, A. B.: "Our Literary Heritage," 57–58; "Writers without Readers," 11, 56

rural populations in Philippines: dalagang Filipina, 248n76; elites' disassociation from, 33, 40–41; lost voices of, 9; marginalization of, 6–7, 72. See also barrio girl as icon

Russo-Japanese War (1907), 48

Said, Edward, 186

St. Louis World's Fair (1904), 33, 37, 38, 39, 50, 52

Salman, Michael, 16

Santigold, 219

Santos, Bienvenido N., 65, 187, 188, 238n24; "Brown Coterie," 186, 190, 198–203; place in canon, 65; "Scent of Apples," 185–86, 189–90, 192, 195, 198–99, 202, 203–5, 254–55n9; "So Many Things," 186, 190, 193–97, 199, 200, 202; term "Pinoy" used by, 201–2, 232; travel to United States, 189; "Woman Afraid," 241n55; You Lovely People, 186, 191–205, 209, 214

Schwichtenberg, Laura W.: "Tells of the Busy Filipino Woman," 47

Scott, Sir Walter: Marmion, 131

Sendenbu (Japanese propaganda corps), 156

sentiment, sentimentality: during Cold War, 169, 173, 180, 185–88, 190–91, 193–96, 199, 202, 203–4, 211, 213, 216–18; of Filipino American ties during Pacific War, 180, 181–84; of Maria Clara icon, 75; in romance novels, 112–13, 116–18, 129, 137, 147

Shimizu, Celine Parreñas, 240n36

short stories, figure of Filipina in, 6, 9, 185–205. See also specific authors

Sia, 219

Sommer, Doris, 17

Vibal, Hilarion, 60
Volpp, Leti, 134, 250–51n31
Von Eschen, Penny, 169, 187

Watanna, Onoto: *A Japanese Nightingale*, 49
web designers, Filipina, 220–21, 222–23, 229–35
Wedding Essentials magazine, 1–5, 2–3, 9, 23, 208
Welch, Florence, 219
Wesling, Meg: *Empire's Proxy*, 238n15
WikiPilipinas.org, 229, 232, 233
Wilder, Marshall P.: "Raising of Children Is Chief Philippine Industry," 39–40
Women's History Month (during Japan occupation), 229
women's suffrage: Filipina categorization and, 88–89; international movement, 7, 20–21, 49–50; Kalaw's views on, 123; Philippines debates on, 7, 20–21, 67–70, 73–74, 98–99, 100–106, 107, 124, 129–30, 245n1, 248n71; Philippines independence and, 21, 108–9; Philippines legalization of, 53, 61, 67, 105; Rizal "Letter" and, 77; single women and, 95, 99
Wong, Sau-Ling: "The Fiction of Asian American Literature," 239n26

Worcester, Dean: *The Philippine Islands and Its People*, 40–41; *The Philippines Past and Present*, 40–41
working class: in Byrne's song cycle, 226; elites' attempt to control, 7; lost voices of, 9; Ocampo's portrayal of, 136, 139–41; "Pinoy" designation, 201–2, 232; Quintero de Joseph's portrayal of, 50–51; Santos's portrayal of, 193–97, 199, 201, 204
Wu, Ellen, 187

Yabes, Leopoldo: "Filipinos Do Not Buy Books," 56, 244n50; "A History of Filipino Literature in English," 238n22; "What Is Wrong with Our Women Writers?" 53–54, 60–61
Yay Regiment, 181
yellow peril, 34
Yoneyama, Lisa, 155; "Liberation under Siege," 251–52n12
Yule, Emma Sarepta: "The Woman Question in the Philippines," 31–32, 34, 48, 49–50, 123

Zafra, Jessica, 225

Denise Cruz is Assistant Professor of English and American Studies at Indiana University. She is the editor of *The Crucible: An Autobiography by "Colonel Yay,"* *Filipina American Guerrilla*, by Yay Panlilio (2009).

Library of Congress Cataloging-in-Publication Data
Cruz, Denise, 1975–
Transpacific femininities : the making of the modern
Filipina / Denise Cruz.
p. cm.
Includes bibliographical references and index.
ISBN 978-0-8223-5300-3 (cloth : alk. paper)
ISBN 978-0-8223-5316-4 (pbk. : alk. paper)
1. Philippine literature (English)—Women authors—
History and criticism. 2. Feminist literature—Philippines.
3. Women and literature—Philippines. I. Title.
PR9550.05.C78 2012
820.9′928709599—dc23   2012011607

www.ingramcontent.com/pod-product-compliance
Lightning Source LLC
Chambersburg PA
CBHW051101030726
47504CB00006B/1736